THE CINEMA OF
BASIL DEARDEN AND
MICHAEL RELPH

It is part of a director's function to see that, at each stage, the technicians who work as his associates are fired with his own enthusiasm. Since the raw material of the cinema is emotion, film people are temperamental people. A director must be able to deal with temperament in others – and must know how to exploit it himself.

(Basil Dearden 1948: 65–6)

You cannot afford to make a picture unless you are madly enthusiastic about it.

(Michael Relph, quoted in *Films and Filming*, January 1958: 5)

I believe . . . that the Cinema is genuinely a mass medium and that it has social and educative responsibilities as well as artistic ones. It has a place to fill in the national life which it cannot do unless it works within the commercial structure which can give the artist the best tools to work with and allow his work to reach the widest possible audience. I believe this the most coura-geous course to take and one which can result from time to time in films of the highest artistic merit and integrity which, nevertheless, have wide popular appeal and commercial success.

(Michael Relph 1961: 24)

The beginning, like almost everything else about me, went back to the war.

(Bill Randall, in *The Ship That Died of Shame*, 1955)

THE CINEMA OF BASIL DEARDEN AND MICHAEL RELPH

Alan Burton and Tim O'Sullivan

EDINBURGH UNIVERSITY PRESS

© Alan Burton and Tim O'Sullivan, 2009

Edinburgh University Press Ltd
22 George Square, Edinburgh

www.euppublishing.com

Typeset in 11/13 pt Monotype Bembo
by Servis Filmsetting Ltd, Stockport, Cheshire, and
printed and bound in Great Britain by
CPI Antony Rowe, Chippenham and Eastbourne

A CIP record for this book is available from the British Library

ISBN 978 0 7486 3289 3 (hardback)

Contents

Acknowledgements

Although this study will appear in public as the product of two writers, in fact, as with all scholarly endeavours, it sees the light of day at all only as a result of the support, guidance and encouragement of numerous colleagues, friends and the families of the authors, as well as those close to Basil Dearden and Michael Relph.

Among our work colleagues we would like to thank especially the following: Steve Chibnall, for making available rare documents and illustrations from his extensive collection; Robert Murphy for his typically shrewd, no-nonsense advice; Andrew Tolson, for acting as Head of Department during the latter part of 2008; Stephen Barnard, Natalie Martin and Tony Lahive for teaching cover in the same period; and for vital and impeccable assistance we are indebted to Steve Gamble and Jo Hobbs in the Faculty of Humanities, De Montfort University.

We have benefited greatly from interviews with cinematographer Douglas Slocombe and Lord Richard Attenborough, both in their time distinguished contributors to the cinema of Basil Dearden and Michael Relph. Screenwriter and executive Bryan Forbes also treated our enquiries generously. We would like to express our appreciation to them for sharing their experiences of the films of Dearden and Relph and their admiration for the filmmaking team.

Our greatest debt of gratitude is due to James Dearden and Simon Relph; for their unstinting enthusiasm for the project from the outset, generously making available invaluable recollections, family documents and photographs, and not least the remarkable collection of Final Shooting Scripts belonging to their fathers, which have afforded a unique insight into their approach to filmmaking.

The distinguished scholar of Ealing Studios, Charles Barr, offered important encouragement and guidance, and most helpfully saw us through some tricky bibliographic issues. Jeffrey Richards, Julian Petley and Mark Jancovich supported the project in its early stages, as did Max Jones, Laurie Ede, Dave Rolinson, Karen Shearsmith, Colin Sell, Andrew Spicer, Charlotte Brunsdon, Sue Harper and Vincent Porter in later moments of its development.

Half of what follows, and the research and writing time it entailed, would not have been possible without the vital support provided by the Arts and Humanities Research Council and the award of research leave to Tim O'Sullivan, which was both a relief and a challenge.

The preparation of this book has also been greatly assisted by the professionalism and patience of Sarah Edwards and Esmé Watson and their colleagues at Edinburgh University Press.

Alan Burton and Tim O'Sullivan
Pörtschach and Leicester, February 2009

Foreword

It is very satisfying that a reappraisal of the films of Basil Dearden and Michael Relph is now taking place, in my opinion (not surprisingly) one that is long overdue.

Alan Burton and Tim O'Sullivan have researched their subject with a great deal of care and a gratifying appreciation of their subject. What they are absolutely correct in establishing is the fact that the relationship was very much a partnership, every bit as much as, say, the partnership of Powell and Pressburger. Indeed, when my father was offered the job of directing the film of *Khartoum* relatively late in his career (1965), and despite the fact that there was already an American producer attached (Julian Blaustein), Michael Relph came on board as Production Supervisor, and one imagines that Michael's contribution was very much on a par with those cases when he was also the titular producer. Apart from relying on each other creatively, I think that they also offered each other a great deal of emotional support, something not to be underestimated during such a long and productive association. It is telling, I think, that I have a distinct memory of my father being extremely unhappy during the shooting of *Khartoum*, admittedly a very difficult production from the logistical point of view, but I am sure due also in no small part to being outside his 'comfort zone' in the sense that Michael was not at his side with the same authority as would have been the case when they were the producing partnership with no one else between them and the studio.

I think it is also interesting that the authors have highlighted the fact that my father's films with Michael at Ealing were not accorded the same respect both internally (from the other filmmakers at the studio) and externally (by the critics). It is ironic that they were on the whole more commercially successful and certainly generated more income for the studio in view of their much greater output. Perhaps it was a mistake on my father's part that he adopted a much less rigorous approach to his choice of assignment, preferring to keep working at all times, in a sense far more like a Hollywood director, perhaps also a reflection of the fact that he had come up 'from the ranks', cutting his teeth on Will Hay vehicles at a time when some of the other directors were still completing their degrees at Oxbridge. It is certainly telling that the Relph–Dearden partnership carried on long after the more fêted Ealing directors had ceased to make movies at all, unable to raise money or even function outside the cosy protection of Ealing. But it is also perhaps due to a lingering sense of frustration at their comparative lack of recognition that they focused on the liberal-themed 'problem' movies of what I would term their middle career. Indeed, I remember that fairly early in the Bond cycle my father was offered the opportunity to direct one of them and turned it down – to my horror, as a young boy and diehard 007 fan! When I asked him why, he said that he wasn't interested in taking on such an overtly commercial assignment, so clearly he still felt the need to protect his recent and hard-won reputation as a 'serious' filmmaker. With hindsight, and certainly from the perspective of today's marketplace, it seems an unwise career move, to say the least! The offer was certainly acknowledgement of his reputation as the consummate technician, a quality which would have gained him far greater appreciation in today's world.

★ ★ ★

I do think it was their misfortune to be a very successful part of the filmmaking establishment at a time when society was going through profound changes and throwing up its own home-grown version of the New Wave in the shape of the working-class dramas of filmmakers like Lindsay Anderson and Tony Richardson. They were there, in a sense, to be knocked down, their very 'middle-classness' a burden from which it was impossible to escape. And yet, once again, it is noteworthy that long after supposedly being consigned to history, their films remain both watchable and watched, while the great bulk of the output of those 1960s and 1970s directors who tried to replace them is both unwatched and in some cases literally unwatchable: the cinematic equivalent of flared jeans and elongated sideburns. The fact that their work survives so well is above all testament to their ability as storytellers, a never to be underestimated requirement for success as a filmmaker. What is also sometimes overlooked is that my father was extremely good with actors, due in part to his early experience in the theatre and indeed as an actor himself (though, by his own admission, not a very good one).

It is also perhaps a mistake to overemphasise their apparent lack of appreciation. *The Blue Lamp* won the award for best British picture in 1950 and *Sapphire* in 1959; the equivalent of two BAFTAs over a ten-year period – not a bad haul by any standards.

So thank you Alan, and thank you Tim, for hopefully redressing the current imbalance and positioning Basil and Michael where they belong in the canon of British filmmakers.

James Dearden

I am truly grateful to Alan Burton and Tim O'Sullivan for this reappraisal of the films that my father and Basil Dearden made together. Curiously, I was at university with Charles Barr, one of their severest critics, and at school with the younger brother of the other – Victor Perkins. Adrian Perkins, Norrie Boulting, John Boulting's son, and I ran the school Film Society. Later, I became a devotee of *Movie* magazine and its passion for Fuller, Ray and other Hollywood auteurs. I am sure that the films of Relph and Dearden represented the establishment that needed to be challenged and to some extent overturned. Before long Tony Richardson, Karel Reisz and Lindsay Anderson came along to do just that.

I joined the industry in 1961 at the very end of the studio system here, and for a brief time was an employee of the Rank Organisation. By this time my father and Basil were established independent producers who had to sell each film to their principal financier/distributors. They were in the second phase of the three careers that Alan and Tim identify in their introduction, between being employees at Ealing and finally making International films with the Hollywood studios.

I was lucky enough to see the partnership at first hand because I served as second assistant director on two films: *A Place to Go* (1963) and *The Mindbenders* (1963). I concur that there was indeed a lot of the producer in Basil and as much of the director in my father, who, as the authors suggest, made a huge creative contribution. Sadly, when they reversed roles things never worked as well.

Basil was incredibly efficient in the way that he used his time on the set, but that simply meant that he got more juice out of the orange than some of his peers who were less so. He liked adventurous set-ups and technical challenges, but above all he wanted control when he moved to the cutting room – not to be left without choice because there simply hadn't been enough time.

My father would always be there when a scene was set up and rehearsed, and between them they would agree the approach, then Basil would be left to get on with it; but in development and pre-production they were one, and equally, they worked very closely together in post-production. For two such different people they made an exceptional team and I believe had huge trust in one another.

In the Ealing days they are accused of being undiscerning in their choice of material, but the fact is that they loved to be in production and they came up with more ideas than others. Equally, I am sure there were occasions when they would have accepted a commission from Balcon that others wouldn't, simply to get him to agree to make something else dear to their hearts that he was resisting. Certainly, they were pragmatic in this way.

Both of them grew up in an industry, a manufacturing industry where the product was film and you were judged first and foremost by the audience's reaction. What is remarkable is that they started to tell stories that were way off the tried and tested. Even when they made what might seem conventional thrillers like *The Blue Lamp*, they told those stories differently, filming a great deal of them on location, which was new and unconventional. They tackled subjects like race relations and homosexuality, both under the cover of thrillers, but no one else at the time was addressing those issues in cinema and certainly not in what were intended to be popular films.

What is remarkable is that so many of their films are still being screened regularly and it is pleasing that an eminent critic like my friend and fellow 'Kingsman' Charles Barr has accepted that some of his early judgements may have been a little harsh. It is important surely to judge the films of Michael Relph and Basil Dearden not for what they weren't – the David Thomson, Victor Perkins line – but for what they were: mostly highly entertaining, often thought–provoking and sometimes original productions.

Simon Relph

Biography and Career Notes

Basil Clive Dear was born on 1 January 1911 at St Drostane, Woodfield Road, Southend, Essex (his surname was later extended to avoid confusion with his employer, the theatrical impresario Basil Dean). His father, Charles, was an electrical engineer who died tragically at sea during the First World War. This was a traumatic event for the young Basil, and the family was plunged into destitution. His mother, Dorothy, was left to raise the six children and the unfortunate Basil was placed in an orphanage, apparently on account of an uncontrollable temper. The family income derived mainly from the success of a younger brother, Peter, an extremely photogenic child actor who toured the halls and was at one point the poster boy for Pear's Soap.[1] These difficult early years clearly marked Basil, who in later life showed a great reticence to talk about his childhood.[2] In later life Basil, unusually in the film industry, showed a lack of self-esteem; apparent when, in a rare moment of candour, the director confessed his insecurities to the actress Shirley Anne Field; explaining the enforced discipline he insisted on having on the set, he revealed: 'I shout and scream because I'm afraid of everybody else. My job is to be in charge and run everything like a military operation.' Referring to his experience in the children's home, he added: 'That's the way I was brought up' (Field 1991: 120). James Dearden believes that attention to this aspect of his father's character has been overemphasised:

> I think the problem was more that he ended up overcompensating and appeared domineering, when he was in fact really a very kind and empathetic man, which not everybody got to see. Perhaps the greatest

testament to this is that in my own career I have met many studio technicians, often quite lowly, who would come up to me and tell me how much they had liked and admired my father and what a fair 'guvnor' he had been.[3]

Basil had a very patchy education and was essentially a 'self-taught man'. He first entered a London insurance company as an office boy, but eventually followed three of his siblings into the theatre. His initial stage experience had been gained during holidays in walk-on parts with the Ben Greet Company, and his theatrical career properly began when he joined the Grand Theatre, Fulham, London, as an assistant stage manager. Back with the Ben Greet troupe he combined acting and administrative roles during its Shakespearean tour of the United States. In 1932, he became production manager for the various theatrical enterprises of impresario Basil Dean. Dearden's creative energies switched to cinema in 1937 when he joined Dean at Ealing Studios, the senior man having founded Associated Talking Pictures at the West London location in 1929. However, a reference in *The Times* suggests that Dearden briefly kept some connection with the theatre, as he was credited with co-writing the thriller *Under Suspicion* with actor Leslie Harcourt (15 December 1938).

He immediately proved his versatility at Ealing, making contributions as dialogue director, writer, assistant director and associate producer. Within a year he was working with Ealing's top comedy star, George Formby, serving as assistant director on *It's in The Air* (1938) and *Come On, George* (1939). Under new studio boss Michael Balcon, Dearden contributed to the scripts and acted as associate producer on Formby's *Let George Do It!* (1940), *Spare a Copper* (1941) and *Turned Out Nice Again* (1941); while he was raised to co-director on the films of the Studio's new comedy star, Will Hay, with *The Black Sheep of Whitehall* (1942), *The Goose Steps Out* (1942) and *My Learned Friend* (1943). While routine genre films, these were crucial commercial productions for the Studio and an excellent opportunity to learn the craft of filmmaking.

Basil Dearden was the only significant creative artist from the Dean era who developed a career under the new regime of Michael Balcon at Ealing. The other young film directors were generally recruited from the editing room and had enjoyed a university education, and Dearden's natural shyness and distinctive upbringing reinforced his outsider status among his peers at the Studio.

Dearden's first solo work as director was a celebration of the wartime Auxiliary Fire Service, *The Bells Go Down* (1943). In this production he worked for the first time with art director Michael Relph, with whom he later formed a significant filmmaking team at Ealing, and the pair would become virtually inseparable throughout their career. Relph continued to supervise art direction on all of Dearden's wartime films, and with Ealing's first post-war feature, the prisoner-of-war drama *The Captive Heart* (1946), the duo's characteristic separation of responsibilities emerged: Dearden worked as director and Relph as associate producer, sometimes additionally serving as production designer, with both occasionally contributing to scripts. Their characteristic thematic concerns evolved out of Ealing Studios' commitment to promoting the 'people's war', and were encompassed within a broadly liberal outlook. Commencing with his wartime films, there emerged a consistent faith in the organic notion of society, composed of shared values, traditions and experience. In addition, the narratives favoured the virtues of public service and civic responsibility, wherein a range of collective heroes struggled tirelessly on behalf of the fire service (*The Bells Go Down*), the police (*The Blue Lamp*, 1950), the probation service (*I Believe in You*, 1952), juvenile liaison agencies (*Violent Playground*, 1957) and modern air services (*Out of the Clouds*, 1955). Dearden and Relph worked at Ealing until its closure in 1955, making the last comedy film produced at the famous studio, the unsuccessful *Who Done It!*, released in 1956. They also contributed the tragic-comedy *Davy* (1957, directed by Relph and produced by Dearden), made during the brief period when production was continued under the Ealing banner at MGM, Borehamwood.

Dearden and Relph were given responsibility for Ealing's first Technicolor film, *Saraband for Dead Lovers* (1948); however, as a team they did not undertake any of the classic comedies for which Ealing Studios became so renowned, and Dearden's association with the 'low comedy' of the Formby and Hay years unfortunately seemed to contribute to a critical downgrading of their filmmaking. Their most important work from the late 1940s to the early 1960s has generally been claimed to be a series of social problem films. These were works dealing with such issues as rapprochement with Germans (*Frieda*, 1947), law and order (*The Blue Lamp*), the criminal justice system (*I Believe in You* – Dearden's personal favourite among his films), disaffected youth (*Violent Playground*), race (*Sapphire*, 1959), homosexuality (*Victim*, 1961) and religious tolerance (*Life for Ruth*, 1962). In the event, there has been an overemphasis on this cinema of social problems and in fact only five of the Dearden and Relph films unequivocally dealt with social problems that troubled Britain in the post-war period. Such an inclusive critical view has, however, tended to obscure the commendable versatility of the partnership which also worked successfully and effectively within the genres of comedy, melodrama, contemporary drama and the noir thriller. However, Dearden and Relph's contribution to the social problem film cycle was seen as outstanding and reflected in British Film Academy awards for best picture of the year for both *The Blue*

Michael Relph and Basil Dearden: another première. (Courtesy of Simon Relph)

Lamp and *Sapphire*. In the early 1950s, Basil Dearden's standing in the industry was reflected in his election to the Council of The British Film Academy, representative of the 'senior film-makers of Great Britain' (*The Times*, 30 July 1951 and 4 February 1952).

After the continuity and security of Ealing, Dearden and Relph proved themselves as independent filmmakers, at one point helping initiate the Allied Film Makers collective for which they produced four films in the early 1960s. Dearden also directed some episodes of the television series *The Four Just Men* (1959–60), produced by former Ealing collaborator Sidney Cole, and formed with Relph a company to make TV commercials (*Kinematograph Weekly*, 15 December 1960). In the mid- and late 1960s, Dearden and Relph secured generous production finance from Hollywood companies seeking to expand into the British market. Several big-budget and elegant films emerged, but these have attracted little critical attention in contrast to those films more representative of the 'swinging' decade. As the prospects for film work began to dry up following the withdrawal of American finance, Dearden took on some of the early episodes of the prestigious TV series *The Persuaders!* (1971–72).

Their final feature film, *The Man Who Haunted Himself* (1970), was tragically prophetic in its tale of a man who dies in a road crash. On 23 March 1971, Basil Dearden suffered multiple injuries in an accident on the M4 motorway near Heathrow Airport while driving back from Pinewood Studios to Chester Square, his Belgravia home. He was declared dead at Hillingdon Hospital, Hillingdon. He was sixty years old and survived by his actress wife Melissa Stribling, who had appeared in four of his films, and their two sons, James, who later developed a career in films, and Torquil. A memorial service, held at St Paul's, Covent Garden, was attended by many former colleagues from the Ealing days, and a moving address was given by his long-time partner and friend Michael Relph.

MICHAEL RELPH

Michael Leighton George Relph was born at Riffelberg, Broadstone, Dorset, on 16 February 1915 and educated at the progressive Bembridge School on the Isle of Wight. George Relph, his father, was a distinguished stage actor and would later work with Michael at Ealing; while his mother, Deborah, was an Australian beauty of good family – her father was Attorney General of Western Australia – who had lost her heart to the handsome actor. George Relph, then enjoying considerable success in America, returned to Britain during the First World War to take a commission. At the Second Battle of Arras he was hit in the face and had to endure eighteen months of pioneering plastic surgery; sadly, George lost his matinée idol good looks and the natural confidence that went with them. Michael later recalled 'the agonies that I went through on his behalf as he struggled with the insecurities of his profession during the years between the wars'.[4]

George and Deborah divorced when Michael was seven and he was given in custody to his father. His mother remarried into the Harker family whose considerable wealth derived from the famous scene painting business in Walworth; the youngest son, Gordon, became a popular comedy actor, later starring in the West End production of *Saloon Bar*, designed by Michael, and appearing as the taxi driver in Dearden and Relph's *Out of the Clouds* (1955). The time spent at the Hampstead home of the Harkers and its legendary soirées, also later at Gordon's house in Belsize Park, and other related theatrical gatherings, introduced Michael to an attractive world of wit, humour and sophistication.

At the age of sixteen, Michael accompanied his maternal grandmother on a visit to her native Australia. The family owned three million acres of ranch at Pinjarra and the idea was for Michael to spend six months in the rough conditions of the sheep station to 'toughen him up'. On his return to England, he tried his hand at commercial art, and despite introductions arranged by his parents to influential patrons, nothing came of this venture. Michael had vaguely harboured an intention of becoming an architect, following in the footsteps of his paternal grandfather, but the period of training was long, expensive and correspondingly unattractive. Through family connections, Michael was put forward for the new apprenticeship scheme at the Gaumont-British Studios at Shepherd's Bush. As he was later to recount prosaically: 'On a blustery Spring day in 1932, I lined up with forty other young men in Lime Grove – about to begin life in the film business' (*In Search of Skyhooks*: 16).

Other than highly successful periods as a theatrical stage designer in the late 1930s and 1940s, Michael would devote himself to British cinema for over half a century as a distinguished art director and producer. The apprenticeship allowed for considerable hands-on experience and the opportunity to learn from great artists like Alfred Junge who headed the art department at Gaumont-British. In 1936, Relph joined Warner Bros'. British operations at its studio at Teddington, working prolifically on a range of low-budget 'quota quickies' and rapidly gaining experience. When the studio temporarily ceased production during the crisis that beset the film industry in 1938, Michael turned to the West End and for a number of years prospered as a stage designer. It has been claimed that at one point there were seven West End productions running simultaneously with Relph sets.[5]

Michael Relph was ineligible for war service due to a leg injury sustained in a road accident, and in 1942 was taken on at the art department at Ealing Studios. He quickly rose to head the section and establish himself as a leading art director in British film. He first worked with Basil Dearden on *The Bells Go Down* (1943), a tribute to the wartime Auxiliary Fire Service, and further collaborated on Dearden's *The Halfway House* and *They Came to a City* (both 1944); although undertaking a supervisory role for art direction across the Studio's productions, he only personally designed one film outside of his emerging partnership with Dearden, the lively tale of the Victorian music halls, *Champagne Charlie* (d. A. Cavalcanti, 1944). Perhaps his greatest achievement in this period were his designs for *Dead of Night* (1945), an acclaimed portmanteau collection of supernatural tales directed by the cream of the young directors at Ealing, including Dearden.

In 1945, Relph began a long production association with Basil Dearden, when he was promoted to associate producer on Ealing's *The Captive Heart* (1946), a popular and critical success. He produced all of Dearden's films at Ealing until its closure in 1955, and the partnership was the most prolific filmmaking team at the Studio; Relph worked only once without Dearden, as associate producer on the classic Ealing comedy *Kind Hearts and Coronets* (d. R. Hamer, 1949). Periodically, Relph also designed the productions, most notably *Saraband for Dead Lovers* (1948), a sumptuous costume drama for which he received an Academy Award nomination.

In the late 1950s, Relph turned his hand to directing, with Dearden acting as his producer on *Davy* (1957), *Rockets Galore!* (1958) and *Desert Mice* (1959). However, the experience only revealed a modest talent and he reverted to his former roles. Relph clearly played a crucial part in steering the partnership into successful independent production after the demise of Ealing. Initially, the team struck out with Rank, and in time would distribute through Allied Film Makers, Bryanston, United Artists and Paramount; marking an uninterrupted creative period of filmmaking untypical within British cinema. At the time of Dearden's tragic death, the partnership had a number of projects in the pipeline; although the early 1970s was a period of great uncertainty in the British film industry, there was no reason to believe that their reputation and experience would not have taken their careers much further.

Throughout the 1970s and 1980s, Michael Relph served diligently as an elder statesman of the British film industry. He became a governor of the British Film Institute in 1972, at the same time succeeding Michael Balcon as chairman of the Institute's Film Production Board (*The Times*, 5 July 1972); while Relph also acted as Chairman of the Film Production Association of Great Britain and later the British Film and Television Producers' Association, proving a highly vocal spokesman on the thorny issues of government support for an ailing national film industry and proper remuneration for cinema producers for films broadcast on television (*The Times*, 30 October 1973, 30 November 1973, 8 July 1981).

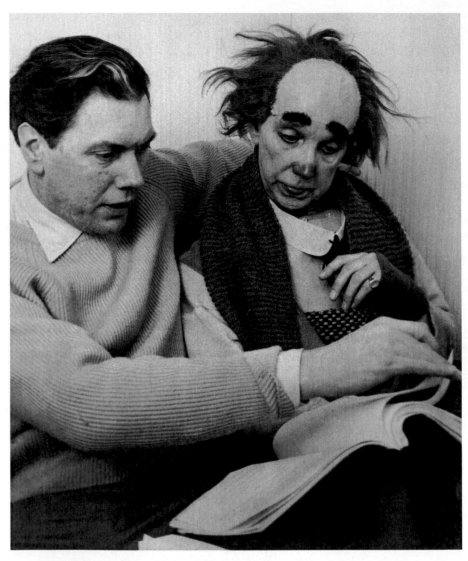

Michael Relph with his father, George, on the set of *Davy* (1957)
(Courtesy of Simon Relph)

He returned to production in the late 1970s, becoming involved with Don
Boyd's Company, Triarch Productions and Kendon Films, and such releases
as *Scum* (1979), *An Unsuitable Job for a Woman* (1982), *Heavenly Pursuits* (1985)
and *Torrents of Spring* (1989). The family name was retained in the British
film industry with the emergence of his son Simon Relph as a producer
with Skreba Films and later Greenpoint Films. Simon was the founding chief
executive of British Screen Finance and has served as chairman of the British

Academy of Film and Television Arts, as a governor of the National Film and Television School and chairman of the Screenwriters Festival. Three generations of the Relph family – George, Michael and Simon – were collectively celebrated at the Festival du Film Britannique de Dinard, France in 1992 and Michael was made an honorary DLitt by De Montfort University in 1999.

Michael Relph died in a nursing home in Selsey, Sussex, on 30 September 2004, having spent his last year there, and was survived by his son and his actress daughter, Emma.

NOTES

1. Peter played in the films *The Fruitful Vine* (1921), *The Woman Who Obeyed* and *The Royal Oak* (both 1923).
2. We would like to thank James Dearden for these insights into Basil's early life.
3. Correspondence with authors (3 February 2009).
4. Michael recounts his early life in an unpublished manuscript, *In Search of Skyhooks*, a part draft for an autobiography and kindly made available to the authors by Simon Relph. Details of his early life are largely taken from this source.
5. Relph has listed the following West End theatre productions he designed: *The Doctor's Dilemma* (with Vivien Leigh), *Up and Doing*, *Watch on the Rhine*, *The Man Who Came to Dinner* (with Robert Morley), *Frieda*, *Saloon Bar* (with Gordon Harker), *Old Acquaintance* (with Edith Evans), *Quiet Week-End*, *Heartbreak House* (with Deborah Kerr, Robert Donat and Edith Evans), *Relative Values* by Noel Coward, *A Month in the Country* by Turgenev, *The Last of Summer* (directed by John Gielgud), *Love in Idleness* by Terrence Rattigan, The *White Carnation* by R. C. Sherriff (with Ralph Richardson), *The Banbury Nose* by Peter Ustinov and *They Came to a City* by J. B. Priestley. The list appears in *In Search of Skyhooks*. In his entry for Relph in the *Dictionary of National Biography*, Brian McFarlane has also listed designs for *Nap Hand*, *The Petrified Forest* and *Quiet Wedding*.

Introduction: 'Two on a Tandem'?

Dearden and Relph: Authorship and British Cinema

[Dearden's] films are decent, empty and plodding and his association with Michael Relph is a fair representative of the British preference for bureaucratic cinema. It stands for the underlining of obvious meanings, for the showy resort to 'realism', for the middle-brow ticking off of 'serious' subjects, for the lack of cinematic sensibility, for the acceptance of all the technical shortcomings of British productions, for the complacent description of problems and the resolute refusal to adopt critical intelligence for dealing with them. (David Thomson 1980: 137)

Until we have a more detailed picture of the roles of direction within the collaborative and hierarchical interactions that constitute film production, the figure of the director, for all the critical value assigned to it, will remain something of an enigma. (Peter Hutchings 2000: 188)

The films of Basil Dearden and his producing partner Michael Relph have for too long been treated as exemplars of a safe, unimaginative and essentially dull British cinema. So, while problem pictures like *Frieda* (1947) and *Victim* (1961) have been acknowledged for their worthy liberal statements, the stifling requirements of balance and fair play, coupled with a perceived cautious cinematic treatment, are seen to deaden and defeat any effectiveness such films might offer. In the early 1960s, when a new generation of thrusting young critics set out to proclaim a cinema of auteurs, it was largely on Hollywood that they set their sights, resolutely turning their backs on their own national film industry, which was dismissed out of hand as inept and completely lacking in any artistic sensibility or merit. The scorn of the *Movie* critics was levelled in particular at Basil Dearden, the filmmaker who most 'typifies the traditional Good Director': 'in the schematic nature of his subjects; in the appalling performances he draws from good actors; and in his total lack of feeling for cinema'. The avowed polemical aim of the reviewers was to 'shout loud the names of the hacks they despise', and this was zealously pursued (Perkins [1962] 1972: 11).[1]

The following generation of writers on British cinema in the 1970s generally distanced themselves from out-and-out auteurism. Whereas previously Dearden had been placed in the spotlight – simply for critical demolition – he now receded into the background, merely the conduit for a style and narrative ideology determined by an industrial context. As such, Dearden didn't evaporate, but was reconfigured as the archetypal 'company man', an essentially colourless, almost 'robotic' technician, valued only within a discourse of professionalism. In his seminal studies of Ealing Studios, Charles Barr marked Dearden as a central member of the 'Team', considering his work as 'constituting an Ealing norm or baseline' (1977: 72); such was his snug fit with the normative values of the Studio. Similarly, for Roy Armes, Dearden 'formed the backbone of Balcon's production', the Studio's most prolific filmmaker, one who bent amenably with the prevailing winds, and as a result was ultimately lacking in any 'satisfying consistency' (Armes 1978: 182–3). Late in the decade, a retrospective season of Dearden and Relph films was held at the National Film Theatre, but even here, in an act of critical celebration and reclamation, the conventional hallmarks of 'professionalism', 'craftsmanship' and 'social awareness' were reasserted and trotted out, and their cinema presented in that most damning of critical terms: 'interesting'. Considering the entrenched disregard of film criticism for the national cinema, it was damning with faint praise to claim the films of Dearden and Relph as some of the most 'truly English pictures of the post-war period' (*NFT Programme*, February 1979: 18).

In the 1980s, critical emphasis shifted once again, and the partnership's social problem films became the focus of enquiries into ideology and representation. In their day, pictures such as *I Believe in You* (1952), *Violent Playground* (1958), *Sapphire* (1959) and *Victim* were seen as daring, even taboo-breaking; but in a climate informed by a New Leftist rejection of the liberal dream that conflict can be resolved by good sense and reason, such well-meaning sentiments were subjected to critical approbation. For John Hill, for instance, the problem pictures were 'dramas of social control', seeking only to contain the troubling excess of sex and violence that marked the post-war settlement through a 'reduction of sensation': ultimately working to fit aberrant individuals and groups into the social order (1986: 94). This was exemplified in the 'hegemonic project' of *Victim*, the film simply reproducing the 'liberal heterosexual consensus' towards homosexuality as embodied in the *Wolfenden Report* (1957) (Dyer [1977] 1993; Medhurst [1984] 1996).

The only sustained dissenting view regarding the cinema of Dearden and Relph came from the maverick critic Raymond Durgnat, who charted a highly personal and idiosyncratic course through post-war British film. In a challenging, insightful and iconoclastic article published in *Films and Filming*, Durgnat characteristically went against the critical grain when he boldly asserted that the Dearden–Relph partnership 'constitutes an auteur, in every sense as distinctive and interesting as many of the American directors currently enjoying rediscovery' (1966: 26). He proposed the filmmakers as 'moralists of the social relationship', a kind of inverted Howard Hawks, and saw no reason to deny a Dearden and Relph cult as a moral balance to the one attached to the celebrated Hollywood director. A decidedly non-polemical critic, Durgnat was at least receptive to and in tune with the achievements and potential of the national cinema. While hardly finding their films faultless – he wearied of 'the same heavy, solemn tone, and the same cautious refusal, so exasperating to many critics, to be radically more "progressive" than the middle-class public is' – he could still claim that *Sapphire*, *Victim* and *The Mind Benders*, 'loom among the best British films of the '50s [*sic*]' (26–7).

Durgnat's more sympathetic view of Dearden and Relph was developed and extended in the 1990s. Significantly, Charles Barr, adding some retrospective comments to the second edition of his *Ealing Studios*, now claimed that the partnership were 'worth foregrounding as Ealing contributors' on the same scale as writer T. E. B. Clarke, and directors Robert Hamer and Alexander Mackendrick (1993: 187). He now recognised the need to move beyond the polemic of *Movie* which posited Dearden as representative of everything that was worst about British cinema, as well as his own previously 'patronising' and 'glib' treatment of the director, and 'affirm that the pair deserve more credit than the book gives them for knowing what they are doing, at two interconnected levels, those of ideas and of cinematic form' (ibid.). Later in the decade, leading writers on British cinema were invited to review the cinema of Dearden and Relph, and the published anthology of work broke new ground in the treatment of the filmmakers: reassessing their work at Ealing; examining the comedy films of Basil Dearden and the art direction of Michael Relph; bringing a fresh view to their better-known films and introducing some of the marginal titles to critical attention; and mapping their cinema in terms of its portrayal of men and women (Burton, O'Sullivan and Wells 1997). And, more recently, Martin Hunt has challenged the established view that the documentary realism absorbed and perpetrated by Ealing ensured a 'bland', 'flat' and 'drab' visual style. On the contrary, he discerns a degree of 'formal and stylistic adventure' at Ealing, most notably in the cinema of Dearden and Relph, and finds in *Frieda* (1947), 'the beginning of an experimentation with elements of content, form and style which Dearden and production partner Michael Relph were to integrate with increasing success as the years and films progressed' (Hurt 2002: 263–4).[2]

Despite the defensible criticism that the study of British cinema is not well served by the folly of auteurism,[3] there has recently emerged a fairly robust interest in the figure of the director within what has been termed the 'New British Film History'.[4] In a series of commentaries on authorship and British cinema, Peter Hutchings has usefully set out a productive reconciliation of auteurist and industrial imperatives. He has claimed of this work:

> Ultimately, what I want to argue is that thinking about authorship and the role of the director has the potential to benefit our understanding both of British cinema and of the methods we use to make sense of it. (2001a: 30)

Hutchings rejects the past excesses of auteurism, but warns that 'ignoring or dodging round the issue of the director's role and contribution can lead to the neglect of an important level of creative agency within the British film industry'; the aim should be

> to sketch in a way of thinking about a British film director where ideas of authorship are significant but do not wholly define or limit the sorts of questions we can ask of the material and where different ideas of authorship can emerge. (2000: 180)

The view being promoted in these writings is that criticism should be sensitive to the precise industrial context within which the profession of directing is practised, and that a discussion and evaluation of a director's films needs to be matched to precisely where the filmmaker was in the industry when directing them (2001b: 20–30).

This more flexible, interactive approach to filmmakers offers a productive critical framework for this re-evaluation of the cinema of Dearden and Relph as they moved through different hierarchical, collaborative, historical and creative contexts. In contrast to a static and 'elitist' conception of authorship, an 'industry-specific' model allows us to see with greater clarity the achievements and progression of Dearden and Relph from their contributions as a director–producer team within the institutional context of Ealing, to the flexible responses demanded by independent production in the late 1950s, and finally accommodation with the new market conditions thrown up by the 1960s and the inflow of American capital into the British film industry.

Hutchings has also rightly asserted that director studies should be sensitive to the different levels of 'managerial control' possessed by filmmakers. As he points out:

> Directors can differ from each other not only on the basis of their 'creative personalities' (however one might define this) but in a more materialistic way in the range of responsibilities and activities which their jobs entail, with some directors having much more control than others over their films. (2001a: 35)

This observation is especially pertinent to Dearden and Relph, who managed an enviable degree of production control across all three phases of their career: as a stable director–producer team at Ealing; as independent producers backed by leading distributors in the British film industry; and as independent filmmakers working in Britain, financed by powerful Hollywood companies.

For some, the prospect of any real 'managerial control' for filmmakers at Ealing would seem unlikely, especially for Basil Dearden, who is usually configured as the archetypal 'company man', the director always at his happiest while working and most likely to pick up the projects avoided by more discerning filmmakers. However, with the formation of the director–producer partnership with Michael Relph on the highly successful *The Captive Heart* (1946), the team, by all accounts harmonious, mutually supportive and complementary, at least could present a united front to the executives and financiers who planned production and guided the Studio. Neither Dearden nor Relph harboured romantic notions about unfettered creative freedom for the film artist; in fact, they were essentially pragmatic in their approach to cinema and in these terms actively sought ways to reconcile the imperatives of industry and art.[5] Significantly, the dispersal of talents within the team did not fall into a simple and typical director-artist and producer-manager division: producer Michael Relph was clearly the more artistically accomplished of the two, having headed up art direction at Ealing for several years; while director Basil Dearden held a lifelong respect for the operational side of filmmaking, in the process developing an unsurpassed reputation for professionalism and budgetary reliability – ironically, qualities that eventually harmed his critical reputation.[6]

Dearden provided a clear and eloquent appreciation of the dialectic between 'economics' and 'aesthetics' in an article published in 1948, where he encapsulated the creative tension inherent to film production in the provocative if oxymoronic formulation 'organised inspiration'. He saw the film director as 'the driving force behind the industrial machine', engaged in a 'struggle between material problems and matters of taste and intuition', and was confident that 'Inspiration can be disciplined and organised'. Such thinking was the direct result of pre-planning for efficiency on *Saraband for Dead Lovers* (1948), the most expensive film produced at Ealing at that time. The aim was to 'harness inspiration to efficient production methods' through the extensive use of 'set-up sketches', where the film's action could be inexpensively rehearsed in drawings. Such a potentially restrictive procedure was embraced by Dearden, no doubt because he was secure in his relationship with his production designer and pro- ducer Michael Relph, and confident that they could work in a fully supportive and complementary manner. The director wrote in praise of 'prefabrication' and further revealed his appreciation of the commercial imperatives of cinema – *but* strictly employed without loss of 'artistic value':

> There is no doubt that more preparation which results in less shooting time on the floor will reduce costs. If a film can be made in two weeks less time, then the saving can be between twenty and thirty thousand pounds – the difference in some cases between profit and loss. Profit means further pictures in the future, loss – less pictures being made. (1948: 65–7)

This is not the kind of toadying response that seems implicit in some of the standard critiques of Dearden, but rather a more considered and experienced reaction to the overall dynamics of filmmaking. It is also an indication of the measure of 'managerial control' that Dearden and Relph exercised at Ealing, for there is little evidence that the 'system' was imposed from above, but rather embraced and developed within the team of director, producer and sketch artist-co-scriptwriter Alexander Mackendrick, an approach that was responsive both to the commercial demands of production and, at the same time, sensitive to the creative imperatives of the drama.[7]

Michael Relph also trenchantly set out his thinking on the roles and responsibilities involved in filmmaking; his comments are revealing, in terms of how he understood both the producer–director relationship with Dearden and the wider relationship of his role as associate producer with the nominal producer at Ealing, head of production Michael Balcon. He invoked a mili- tary analogy to express the overall production situation, believing that the creation of a film 'called for detailed strategic planning which yet allows scope for tactical improvisation'. In this scenario, 'The director is the tactical com- mander in control of the army in the field – the actors and technicians on the studio floor'; whereas 'The producer is the strategical commander in control of the conception as a whole. He must see that the director is serviced with the money, personnel and equipment he needs'. In the most original part of this formulation, he alludes to a role which perhaps had a particular bearing on the relationship he developed with Dearden:

> [The producer] is also, however, in strategical command of the film from an artistic viewpoint. It is easy for the director, confronted with practical difficulties of shooting, and working with the comparatively

blunt instrument formed by a hundred or so actors and technicians, to lose sight of the artistic proportions of the film as a whole.

These will have been previously determined by the producer, director and writer, and the producer must see that the director brings their joint conception to the screen. He must know the capabilities of his director, choosing a story that will exploit his talents and not expose his weaknesses. He must be constantly at hand to guide and advise, yet must avoid interference with the director's creative freedom within the strategic concept. (1954)

Within the larger framework of continuous production at Ealing, Relph equated the role of the Head of Studio to that of commander in chief, and acknowledged the 'enormous artistic contribution' they can make in addition to their primary executive function (*The Times*, 2 January 1954). Relph retained a respect for Balcon's stewardship of the Studio, but like many associate producers at Ealing, bristled at the producer credit claimed by the Head of Studio on each film. His preferred label for the function that Balcon fulfilled was 'impresario', but in later years he acknowledged that associate producers and directors were greatly protected from the boardroom battles doggedly fought by Balcon and Peter Baker with such formidable opponents as John Davis of the Rank Organisation (Relph 1990).[8]

Relph firmly believed that the associate producer performed a creative role at Ealing, and that there were opportunities to subvert the 'official' view as sanctioned by the 'front office'. He was convinced that Balcon 'was often ignorant of the machinations of the film makers in persuading him to put the studio's resources behind a particular project' and that the canny 'young creative team of film makers who cross-fertilised their ideas over a great many years', 'devised ways of getting round Balcon's prejudices or became expert in producing ideas which catered for his restrictive preferences'.[9] Of course, a central tenet of the auteur theory as it developed was the supposed creative tension that existed between the auteur and the system, the genuine auteur being in conflict with the production context and ultimately defined by a resistant transcendence of the debilitating commercial framework. However, such a simplistic polarisation of energies never reflected the real world of film production and certainly doesn't explain the careers of Dearden and Relph at Ealing. For example, Balcon always had a preference for stories about men – his favourite productions were *The Captive Heart*, *Scott of the Antarctic* and *The Cruel Sea* – and this was echoed in the team he built around him, not least Dearden and Relph. Equally, the wartime period largely witnessed the filmmakers in close accord with the direction in which Balcon was taking the Studio in response to the emergency. But even here, we argue, films like *The*

Halfway House (1944) and *They Came to a City* (1944) were highly distinctive articulations of Ealing's wartime social message. The formal experimentation that emerged in these films was developed and extended in the team's post-war cinema, and it is the series of melodramas that included *Frieda* (1947), *Saraband for Dead Lovers* and *Cage of Gold* (1950) that bear witness to the kind of subversion that Relph alludes to. The decline at Ealing in the 1950s witnessed fewer films of achievement and critical value, and probably the highest proportion of productions that Dearden and Relph took on to service the needs of the Studio. But even here, there is interest in films of modest ambition like *The Rainbow Jacket* (1954), *Out of the Clouds* (1955), *Who Done It?* (1956) and *Davy* (1957), especially in their points of intersection with the broader contours of the cinema of Dearden and Relph, such as post-war masculinity and comedy, that deserve recognition and comment.[10]

The post-Ealing period of filmmaking saw Dearden and Relph assume a much greater degree of 'managerial control' over their cinema as independent producers, although the realities of the marketplace always ensured degrees of compromise and containment.[11] There were, for example, difficulties with the distributor, Rank, over the controversial race drama *Sapphire* (1959), and a number of abandoned projects that resisted the will of the filmmakers and their potential backers. In the uncertain conditions of late 1950s British cinema, Dearden and Relph sought actively to create and preserve space for intelligent British filmmaking and were on the board of the Bryanston collective of filmmakers, linked with the distributor British Lion; while the team was central to the collaborative Allied Film Makers Group, linked to Rank, and seeking a measure of protection for artistic integrity and continuity for production.[12] As the prospects for production declined in Britain in the early1960s, Dearden and Relph were in the vanguard of filmmakers who sought deals with the major Hollywood companies. Rather than being swallowed up by American capital, the partnership secured remarkably generous and unrestrictive arrangements, whereby finance and distribution were guaranteed by United Artists and later Paramount. Dearden and Relph retained an impressive degree of 'managerial control' over these films, essentially acting as an independent production team, acquiring rights to properties, writing or contributing to scripts, and generally exercising autonomy over production as long as they remained within budget – a faculty over which they remained past masters. The degree of control exercised by Dearden and Relph over their filmmaking and their lengthy careers in British cinema allowed for a remarkable continuity of approach and the freedom, from time to time, to express long-standing interests and concerns. It also meant that the producers could engage favoured artists and technicians when available, and cinematographers Douglas Slocombe and Otto Heller, composer Philip Green, editor

John D. Guthridge and actors Mervyn Johns, Dirk Bogarde, Bernard Lee, Bill Owen and Richard Attenborough made significant contributions to their films. Regardless of the critical reception of their films, the cinema of Dearden and Relph, as it traversed the volatile and shifting contours of film production in Britain, offers the historian significant and invaluable insights into the contexts of British filmmaking in the post-war decades.

Viewed from a perspective within the British film industry, Basil Dearden eventually became a highly respected director, a thoroughly experienced professional, and daring, committed and courageous with the challenging problem pictures that he made in collaboration with Michael Relph in the 1950s and 1960s.[13] For most of his time at Ealing he seems to have been treated with snobbish disdain, dismissed as a throwback from the Basil Dean era at the Studio, with an unfashionable background in theatre and lacking an Oxbridge education.[14] Such a view was compounded by Dearden's association with low forms of comedy on the George Formby and Will Hay films he made at Ealing in the early war years, something that was simplistically absorbed into the wider critical thinking about the filmmaker.[15] Untypically, Relph also had a background in theatre and this gave him a strong affinity with the young director; it was at the urging of Cavalcanti that the two were paired as a team, the Brazilian having recognised during the production of *The Halfway House* that the designer had such a beneficial influence on his colleague.[16] In turn, Relph was impressed by Dearden's control of actors and the mechanics of scene construction; he believed the director to be 'very cinematic in this respect' and 'technically . . . far in advance of all the other directors at Ealing'.[17] However, he recognised that 'His attitude to subjects was really that of a technician as opposed to a genuinely creative artist, and anything that he could see an interesting way to treat technically he was prepared to have a go at' (1997: 243). Relph would supply the additional artistic credentials.

Cinematographer Douglas Slocombe regarded Dearden as the most 'competent' of all directors at Ealing; a filmmaker always immaculately prepared and invariably sure about how he was to proceed. Consequently, Dearden got through more set-ups per day, shot films much more quickly than other directors and always brought films in on schedule – and sometimes in advance of the deadline. The acclaimed cameraman retained great respect for the director and saw no reason why his professionalism should be equated with 'dullness' (2007).

Actor Richard Attenborough readily declared himself 'devoted' to Dearden and fully endorsed the view of the director as the complete professional: a 'really distinguished director', a filmmaker always 'meticulously prepared', an object lesson for aspiring filmmakers. Attenborough was also impressed by Dearden's handling of actors, believing he loved actors and the art of acting, although the director had little patience for unprofessionalism and performers who turned up late or forgot their lines.[18] There was never such a thing as indecision on the set, Dearden exuding a reassuring (or intimidating) authority and the sense that he would get precisely what he was after (Attenborough 2008).

William Pay, the London editor of *Motion Picture Herald*, observed Dearden at work on *The Man Who Haunted Himself* (1970) and largely confirmed the view of the director as diligent, organised, focused, if a little remote:

> Dearden brings a business-like approach to his film-making. At work on the set, he talks quietly but incisively, a man who has done his home- work and knows exactly what he wants in this shot, the next shot, the one after that. Once committed to the making of a film, he thinks of little else. Intervals in shooting find him either discussing the next scene with his actors, or prowling endlessly into the far corners of the studio.
>
> Constantly aware of precious, expensive minutes ticking by, he finds the inevitable small hold-ups in production frustrating and says so as incisively as he gives instructions to his players. Shy, reserved once off the set, Dearden is sometimes thought to be remote. That may be a matter for individual speculation, but one thing there is no doubt – his dedication. (22 October 1969)

The quality of commercial and industrial 'professionalism', and the dissipat- ing tendency of 'versatility', have been invoked by critics to beat Basil Dearden; while conversely, elsewhere, they have also been central to the praise for his contribution to national film production. These two perspectives, the critical and the industrial, have traditionally been separated and opposed; however, it is possible, as Hutchings has suggested, that a reconciliation can be achieved and a clearer appreciation of the team's filmmaking attained through atten- tion to the significant matter of the 'managerial control' that the Dearden and Relph team exerted over their filmmaking. Dearden's reliability and compe- tence meant that Michael Balcon retained considerable faith in the filmmaker, the only survivor among the directors from the pre-war Dean era. The valu- able service that Dearden performed for the Studio does not mean that he should simply be dismissed as a 'yes man work-horse'; his talents and strong personality, allied to those of his dedicated producer, ensured that theirs was a significant creative presence at Ealing and beyond, responsible for a cinema that was commercially efficient, artistically accomplished and socially aware. In light of this, the following study takes a close look at the films of Dearden and Relph, sensitive to the particular contexts of production and criticism, yet alive to the artistic, cinematic and dramatic accomplishments of many of the films. In short, it seeks to investigate the *fallout* from the historical clash of 'organisation' with 'inspiration'.

The book does not follow a simple chronological treatment of each production; rather, it groups films into discrete themes, allowing for a clearer focus on the main preoccupations and achievements in the cinema of Dearden and Relph. New attention is given to the importance of comedy in the career of Dearden, while emphasis is also placed on the art direction of Relph, providing a balance rare in the treatments of the team. Dearden and Relph first collaborated in the war years; a period that had a lasting impact on their filmmaking and during which they made a significant contribution to the developing ethos at Ealing. The war years established Dearden and Relph as important filmmakers and informed many of their responses to the post-war world in terms of masculinity and social adjustment. The wartime films are therefore crucial precursors to the mature cinema of Dearden and Relph and treated here in their formative nature. A considerable number of Dearden and Relph's post-war films concern male characters forced to confront a painful adjustment to new circumstances and social norms. One strand of these 'Dramas of Social Adjustment' observes a tragic dimension as the male characters respond to significant post-war realignments in gender and the anxieties confronted by men in changed circumstances; while a second strand constructs an alternative trope for dealing with the central issue of post-war masculine adjustment, posing narratives of men in action, with the male characters asserting (or reasserting) their masculinity through professional physical action and usually in the male group. Masculine purpose and identity is reinvigorated or rediscovered through the reconstitution of wartime experience; and the crisis is transgressive, tempting the men towards crime in an attempt to rediscover excitement, re-establish male bonding and challenge the perceived feminisation of society after the war. Similarly, the team's celebrated problem films are separated into two distinct types: five films that address *genuine* issues that were popularly accepted as contemporary social problems: race, delinquency and sexuality; and a further four films that are separated out from the social problem films by virtue of their attention to individual characters confronting acute ethical decisions rather than problems shared across society. Distinctively, they represent substantial emotional dramas concerning national identity, the politics of terrorism, religion and the abuses of modern psychology. Finally, the study brings a wholly new attention to Dearden and Relph's films of 'The International Years' of the1960s. The films of the final decade are the most unconsidered of the team's work and the study offers a valuable opportunity to assess these neglected productions. Produced for American companies, they demonstrate Dearden and Relph's standing by the 1960s as commercial filmmakers and, while often being dismissed as bloated international puddings, further confirm the filmmakers' professionalism, adaptation to new production contexts and ease with big-budget action films and international stars.

NOTES

1. Critics like Derek Hill, writing for *Tribune* and *Films and Filming*, were already deep into their crusade against British filmmakers; see Hill's demolitions of Dearden and Relph's *Out of the Clouds* (1955) and *The Ship That Died of Shame* (1955) (*Films and Filming*, April 1955 and June 1955). While the British Film Institute's *Monthly Film Bulletin* could only rarely find a good word for a Dearden film throughout the 1950s and 1960s.

2. We shall argue that this experimentation can be traced earlier to *The Halfway House* (1944) and *Dead of Night* (1945).

3. See Vincent Porter's thought-provoking review of our earlier *Liberal Directions*, where he states: 'Commercial filmmaking is not an individual activity, and critics impose criteria of personal creativity on an industrial artform at their peril' (Porter, 1999: 158).

4. Apparent in the *British Film Makers* series commissioned by Manchester University Press, which so far includes studies of Lance Comfort (1999), Jack Clayton (2000), J. Lee Thompson (2000), Launder and Gilliat (2002), Michael Reeves (2003), Terence Fisher (2001), Joseph Losey (2004), Roy Ward Baker (2004), Terence Davies (2004), Carol Reed (2005), Derek Jarman (2005), Anthony Asquith (2005), Sydney Box (2006), Karel Reisz (2007), Mike Leigh (2007) and Michael Winterbottom (2009).

5. Ealing employed a little over 400 staff, and as social democrats, Dearden and Relph felt a concern about continuity of production at the studio less as a service for capital and more in sympathy with the workforce. See the producer's comments in Relph (1990; 1997: 244) and 'Inside Ealing', reprinted in the Appendix to this volume.

6. A hopelessly romantic David Thomson sees no virtue 'in that a film was completed at 5.30 on the proper day with the due number of tea breaks. Dearden's coming in on time is replete with the obedient, leaden dullness of British studios' (1980: 137).

7. Significantly, for the argument being developed here, *Saraband* was one of the greatest artistic achievements of Dearden and Relph. Looking back on the role of the director in the production context at Ealing, Mackendrick revealingly recalled: 'We weren't paid much but we had the advantage of being very free' (quoted in Ellis 1975: 92).

8. See Relph's 'appreciation' of Balcon which appeared in *Sight and Sound* (Winter 1977/78). Here, Relph also revealingly places the Ealing operation 'under the microscope'. For an interesting impressionistic look at production at Ealing, see Tynan (1955); while scholarly accounts of the production process at Ealing and their concomitant tensions are presented in Ellis (1975), Porter (1983) and Harper and Porter (2003).

9. The views are expressed in 'Inside Ealing', reprinted in the Appendix to this volume.

10. Taking one simple example of the accord between filmmaker and Studio, Dearden seemed to relish the freedom and technical challenge of shooting on

location; while Ealing tended to promote this aspect of production due to the relative smallness of the stages at the studio. See Ellis (1975: 90).

11. Of this period of transition, Relph later recalled:

> Basil and I were lucky . . . because we did manage to go very quickly into the Rank set-up and I think we had kept a little more contact with the rest of the industry; but most of the others from Ealing were fairly ignorant of all that was going on outside. Our own policy of making a lot of films did pay off then, in a way. One was better equipped for the outside world than some of the other people who had led an excessively sheltered existence. (Brown 1981: 211)

12. The formation of AFM was reported in the following terms: 'The advantages to the members of Allied are two-fold – complete freedom in production and choice of subject members want to make (Rank has promised a no-interference policy) and, by personal distribution, a much larger slice of the profits . . . if the films are successful' (*Films and Filming*, January 1960).

13. The status of Dearden and Relph was acknowledged in two Best British Film awards from the British Film Academy, for *The Blue Lamp* (1950) and *Sapphire* (1959). The partnership was also honoured at the 1959 Versailles Film Festival where their body of work was awarded the Golden Sun Award by the French Society of Cinema and TV Writers.

14. The other young directors at Ealing were largely university-educated with backgrounds in the wholly cinematic field of editing.

15. The 'outsider' status of Dearden seems to have also been reflected in the fact that he did not participate in the lengthy drinking sessions at the Red Lion pub opposite the studio, and lighting cameraman Douglas Slocombe remembers him as a bit of a 'loner' (2007). Relph, however, was a habitual member of the drinking fraternity (see 'Inside Ealing', reprinted in the Appendix to this volume).

16. In a later interview, Relph described the circumstances thus:

> Cavalcanti was very much aware I think of what I contributed as an art director to the pictures I did with Basil Dearden. He thought that Basil had certain strengths but that there were artistic qualities that could be supplied by me. That's why he took me from being an art director and made me a producer to work with Basil. (Brown 1981: 201)

17. Relph (1990) believed that the lack of experience with actors was a problem for most of the other directors; a situation confirmed by Douglas Slocombe (2007), who found that Dearden had a confidence and ease on the studio floor far in advance of the other directors at Ealing.

18. There are some lingering accounts of Dearden being a martinet or even a bully on the set, possibly perpetrated by those who fell foul of his demanding standards. See Derek Bond's comments on filming *The Captive Heart* (1946), where he claimed the director tried to do a 'Monty' and nearly brought the extras drawn from the Black Watch regiment to mutiny (1990: 177). Shirley Anne Field also found the director intimidating; that is until in a rare moment he let his defences down and confessed his insecurity (1991: 117).

1

Apprenticeship and Beyond:
Comedy Traditions and Film Design

Dearden–Relph and the Tradition of Film Comedy

The Black Sheep of Whitehall (1941); *The Goose Steps Out* (1942); *My Learned Friend* (1943); *Who Done It?* (1956); *The Smallest Show on Earth* (1957); *Rockets Galore!* (1958) and *Desert Mice* (1959)

> The state of nations can best be judged by their ability to laugh at themselves. (Ian Johnson, *Films and Filming*, March 1963)

Dearden and Relph, both separately and together, regularly worked in a comic vein. As well as making numerous outright comedy films, the film-makers brought a measure of humour to several of their action films, thrillers and dramas, titles like *The League of Gentlemen* (1960), *Man in the Moon* (1960), *Masquerade* (1965), *Only When I Larf* (1968) and *The Assassination Bureau* (1969). This was a common commercial approach within British cinema in the period and was, moreover, a distinctive aspect of the films they made together. Michael Relph consistently praised Basil Dearden's technical skill as a filmmaker, believing that this was nowhere more evident than in his handling of humorous material; he was, according to Relph, 'very expert at directing comedy' (Relph 1997: 246). Furthermore, this was acknowledged within the film community generally, demonstrated in the case of the success-ful producer–director team of Launder and Gilliat inviting Dearden to act as mentor to the novice director Robert Day on their production of the comedy *The Green Man* (1956). It is also significant that two of the three films directed by Relph, *Rockets Galore!* and *Desert Mice*, were comedies; while his own directorial debut, the tragic melodrama *Davy* (1956), featured much comic business.

During his period of acting as assistant to Basil Dean at Associated Talking Pictures (ATP), Dearden gained his first substantial experience of film on the

George Formby comedies, acting as assistant director on *It's in the Air* (1938) and *Come On, George* (1939) (Chatten 1997: 267). At this time, Formby was the most popular British star and his films the most commercially successful productions at ATP. Like many of the comedy series produced within British cinema, the Formby films were steered by a core creative filmmaking team: writer-director Anthony Kimmins, producer Jack Kitchen, cinematographer Ronald Neame and art director Wilfrid Shingleton. This was a comedy masterclass for Dearden to cut his teeth on and was undoubtedly a significant influence on him. The *Monthly Film Bulletin* praised *Come On, George* as 'Formby fun at its best', and there was much from which Dearden could learn and absorb (6: 61/72, 1939: 200).[1] On at least one occasion, Dearden worked outside of Ealing, co-scripting the box-office success *This Man is News* (1938), produced by Anthony Havelock-Ellis at Pinewood and which aped the comedy-thriller style of MGM's popular *Thin Man* series (1934–47).

On the outbreak of war, Kimmins and Kitchens were lost to the services and the recently arrived studio boss Michael Balcon looked around to put together a new team for producing the crucial Formby films. He hired as director the highly experienced Marcel Varnel, who had worked at Gainsborough on the popular Will Hay and Crazy Gang comedies. Seeking a measure of continuity, Balcon promoted Dearden to a more creative role, allowing him to contribute to the scripts and act as associate producer on *Let George Do It!* (1940), *Spare a Copper* (1941, d. John Paddy Carstairs) and *Turned Out Nice Again* (1941), the final three films Formby made at Ealing before moving to Columbia.[2] The measure of Balcon's success can be gauged from a review appearing in *The Times*, which observed that 'The structure of Mr George Formby's films do not alter very much, and the same blue-print which has done serviceable work in the past was taken out of its drawer for the making of *Spare a Copper* (17 March 1941).

It was relatively easy to fit the Formby films into the new demands thrown up by the war: whereas George had typically had to overcome rogues and villains in his 1930s films, these were now simply replaced by spies and saboteurs. This accommodation had already been rehearsed in *It's in the Air*, which had the gormless character join the RAF in the period leading up to war. *Let George Do It!* involves the unwitting George thwarting Nazi agents in Norway; while *Spare a Copper* locates him on Merseyside as an eager war reserve policeman bringing a nest of saboteurs to book. However, audiences quickly tired of war-related stories, and *Turned Out Nice Again* reverted to the traditional formula of Formby trying to get on in an everyday world that conspired against him, this time as an overseer in a northern underwear factory, and the film is notable for its relentless extraction of the maximum innuendo offered by this subject.

In the early period of the war, the importance of humour slowly became recognised as crucial for maintaining morale and Mass Observation issued a number of reports suggesting the need to counter anxiety and depression through comic relief (Richards 1986). *Let George Do It!* was the first comedy produced at Ealing to deal directly with the war and it remains Formby's best wartime film, a pleasing blend of comedy, thrills and music, becoming the box-office hit of August 1940. The film was the object of a special Mass Observation study, which revealed many fascinating details about the critical and public response, including the view that the press, traditionally hostile to low comedy, generally found this Formby's best film to date (Richards and Sheridan 1987: 331–49). *Let George Do It!* was also a textbook example of the propaganda film that fell foul of rapidly changing circumstances, with its fantasy of the witless George dealing with Nazi spies in neutral Norway being overtaken by events as the *Wehrmacht* occupied the country with relative ease in the spring of 1940. This led some critics to view the production as tasteless and to question who would get most comfort from the film – the British or the Germans – especially as this was compounded by the notorious dream sequence that had George floating across to Germany in a balloon and administering a thrashing to that old 'windbag' Hitler (*The Times*, 15 July 1940).[3] Overall, the Formby films made at Ealing remained escapist commercial successes and attracted respectable enough notices from critics, who would never accept them as demanding entertainment. The *Monthly Film Bulletin*, for example, found *Spare a Copper* a 'good Formby film . . . with a better story than most' (7: 73/84, 1940); while *The Times* was encouraged that *Turned Out Nice Again* lessened the emphasis on slapstick to reveal a 'sound sense of straightforward comedy' (30 June 1941). It had been easy to fit the Formby persona into the requirements of wartime propaganda as the character was essentially a consensus figure, and whether it was the Great Depression or the Second World War, George could be relied on to cheer up the nation and embody the fight of the common people (Richards 1984: 191–206).

Balcon added to the studio's roster of traditional comedians when he brought Will Hay to Ealing in 1940.[4] Marcel Varnel was retained to direct *The Ghost of St Michael's* (1941), which had Hay in his familiar role as the inept schoolmaster, this time exposing a nest of traitors while serving with a school evacuated to Scotland. Dearden was once again detailed to act as associate producer. While the film got some good notices, the *Monthly Film Bulletin* judging it a 'good story, well-directed . . . and as admirable a cast as could be found' (28 February 1941), the production appears rushed and stagey, borrowing heavily from that old warhorse of comedy theatre *The Ghost Train*, which Hay and his writers had previously plundered in the classic *Oh, Mr Porter!* (1937). In a significant move, and part of a wider strategy of promotion within the ranks of the Studio's personnel, Balcon raised Dearden to director on three of the remaining Hay vehicles, *The Black Sheep of Whitehall* (1941), *The Goose Steps Out* (1942) and *My Learned Friend* (1943).[5] Hay was credited as co-director on these features, but this was a professional courtesy extended to the star and it can be assumed that Dearden took overall responsibility for dealing with the creative technicians and staging the action.[6]

The Black Sheep of Whitehall is a distinct improvement on the previous Hay film, the direction and narration being both more dynamic and cinematic.[7] The confined staging of *The Ghost of St Michael's* is replaced by a fast-moving and freewheeling comedy ranging over a large number of sets and locations as Hay confronts a Nazi plot to derail a crucial trade agreement with South America.[8] Many of the reviews commented on the admirable pace of the comedy: *Kine Weekly* declared it a 'Riotous comedy extravaganza' (20 November, 1941); while the *Monthly Film Bulletin* praised it as a 'rollicking, fast moving film, full of amusing situations and good slapstick' (30 November 1941). The writers were applauded for scripting an inventive and topical comedy, special praise being offered for the pointed satire made of government bureaucracy and the BBC; scenes in which Hay, a disreputable principal of a correspondence college, is mistaken for a distinguished professor of economics who is to oversee the treaty, and is called on to make a radio broadcast in which he reduces the complex interplay of trade between Portugal and Brazil to simply that of port and nuts – and Epsom salts.[9] For Paul Wells, this first directorial outing reveals that 'Dearden is especially drawn to the use of mistaken identity or disguise as a means of disrupting narrative orthodoxies and creating humour which has a plausible framework, yet implausible outcomes'. As such, he sees Dearden's 'special and overlooked skill' as 'his ability to stage and choreograph sequences in a way in which the premises of the plot quickly and efficiently serviced the creation of comic events' (1997: 41–2).

The Goose Steps Out similarly deploys Hay against Nazism, this time as a dissolute master of German in a minor English school, who, through his uncanny resemblance to a Nazi agent, is parachuted into the heart of enemy territory to masquerade as a trainer of spies while seeking to locate and pilfer a new bomb. While fanciful, even within the flexible terms of the genre, the film has much fun at the expense of German authoritarianism and the leadership cult of the Führer. The reviews were mixed. The *Monthly Film Bulletin* found the film 'patchy', but 'reasonably good fast fun all the same' (30 September 1942); while *Kine Weekly* was more critical, berating it for an overall lack of originality and for stooping to 'cheap and obvious' laughs. The trade paper did single out, though, the 'glorious sequence' in which Hay instructs his German pupils to give Hitler a vulgar version of the V for Victory sign (20 August 1942). *Film Report* applauded the execution of the slapstick scenes, especially

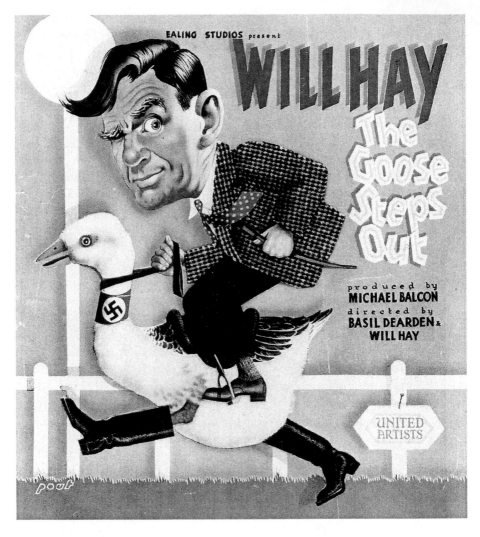

the thrilling climax aboard an aeroplane bound for England, which it found 'brilliantly handled' (21 August 1942). Clearly, though, critics were beginning to tire of comedians making easy fun of a dunderheaded enemy, an approach based on the 'threadbare and insupportable supposition that the Nazis are easily gulled'. As the reviewer concluded, 'Experience has, unhappily, proved that it takes more than an exuberant application of the ridiculous to kill Nazis' (*Kinematograph Weekly*, 20 August 1942).[10] One difficulty for the Studio was that it was problematic to mobilise the Hay persona for war work. Steven Allen has recently argued that, unlike Formby, Hay was not a figure of consensus; on the contrary, his character stood for dissension, exhibiting qualities of ineptitude, dishonesty and corruptibility. Hay's classic 1930s comedies had held up the Establishment to ridicule, and far from offering consensus, 'the films intimated a nation riddled with division, disharmony and self-interest' (2006: 255). Formby's honest ambition could be wholly embraced within the struggle for national survival; whereas Hay's 'disreputable combination of Dickensian fruitiness and Greenian seediness' (Durgnat 1970: 172) was an ill-fit, and could account for the comparative lack of critical interest in the comedian's propaganda films for Ealing.

Hay's final film for Ealing abandoned the tired formula of war propaganda for a fresh and artful comedy of murder. *My Learned Friend* went into production towards the end of 1942, but suffered some delays due to the deteriorating health of the comedian. It finally wrapped in April 1943 and proved to be the star's last film.[11] Following the trade show in July 1943, *Kine Weekly* embraced the comedy as a 'sparkling antidote to wartime worries', expressing the general sentiment that comedies should distance themselves from the day-to-day concerns of the war (15 July 1943).[12] Elsewhere, the *comédie-noire* attracted mixed reviews, and there was little sense that this film was an improvement on its predecessors. *Film Report* thought the story was 'novel', but that it lapsed into 'puerility', with the humour becoming 'feeble and laboured' (30 July 1943); while *Monthly Film Bulletin* was enthusiastic about the film's craziness and fun, praising it as 'a farce in the best and most violent tradition' (10: 109/120, 1943). In retrospect, *My Learned Friend* is the best of Hay's Ealing films, displaying a more timeless appeal against the rather forced attempts to straitjacket comedy with propaganda in the previous productions. The visual texture of the film is much denser, courtesy of art director Michael Relph, who rises above the merely functional efforts of Wilfrid Shingleton and Tom Morahan on Hay's other Ealing films.[13] There is also a more fulfilling role for Claude Hulbert, who had been used fitfully in *The Ghost of St Michael's*, but here, as usual, playing his archetypal silly-ass character, is deployed as a fitting sidekick for the mature comedian. The unusual subject of *My Learned Friend*, a comedy of serial killing, has meant that the film has attracted some subsequent critical attention. Murphy claims it the one film equal to Hay's best work at Gainsborough; while Seaton and Martin admire its 'ingeniously contrived screenplay and literary wit' (1978: 172); and for some critics it now appears a precursor to the classic Ealing comedy *Kind Hearts and Coronets* (d. R. Hamer, 1949) (Everson 2003: 333–4).[14]

Dearden had played a significant role in nurturing traditional comedy at Ealing in the early war years, and with *My Learned Friend* had graduated to directing a recognised classic of the form, a fitting *finale* for a legendary British screen comedian. Curiously, Dearden would not be involved in any further outright comedy for over a decade, and the golden age of Ealing comedies, which saw the production of such classics as *Passport to Pimlico* (d. H. Cornelius,

1949), *The Lavender Hill Mob* (d. C. Crichton, 1951) and *The Ladykillers* (d. A. Mackendrick, 1955), would pass the filmmaker by.[15] In the winter of 1954, it was announced that T. E. B. Clarke had written a film especially for comedian Benny Hill (*Kinematograph Weekly*, 16 December 1954).[16] Production commenced in August the following year on *Who Done It?* (1956), for which Dearden was assigned as director; a columnist at *To-Day's Cinema* thought it a shame that the director had 'delayed so long in once again bringing his talents to bear on comedy' (10 October 1955). It was announced in October 1955 that Ealing Studios had been sold to the BBC, which would take vacant possession in the New Year. However, *Who Done It?* would be completed at the Studio and be among the last batch of films distributed under the long-standing arrangement with the Rank Organisation (*The Times*, 20 October 1955; *Kinematograph Weekly*, 9 February 1956).

The film was released in the wake of a tremendous upsurge in popularity for British film comedy; the 1954 annual round-up of the trade paper *Kinematograph Weekly* listing *Doctor in the House*, *Trouble in Store* and *The Belles of St. Trinian's* as the biggest box-office attractions of the year and each initiated a series (16 December 1954). Sadly, the last film comedy to come out of Ealing Studios failed to repeat the success of its rivals – 'nearer run-of-the-mill Wisdom than vintage Ealing' in Durgnat's view (1966: 31). There had been considerable expectation for a comedy written by the distinguished Clarke and featuring the popular TV and variety comic Benny Hill.[17] Accordingly, *The Evening News* predicted it to be one of the comedy successes of the year (15 March 1956); while the *Manchester Guardian* believed it 'may well make a lot of money' (17 March 1956). Some reviews felt the film to be an artful exercise in the absurd, that the filmmakers had 'put on a fine demonstration of calculated chaos incorporating nearly all the traditional devices of slapstick, from banana skins onwards' (*Daily Mail*, 16 March 1956). The *Monthly Film Bulletin* bemoaned the rather 'desperate script', but still found the film 'considerably more amusing than any other recent vehicle for a new comedian', with Clarke providing some 'agreeable satire' to punctuate the slapstick (March 1956). However, for many critics, it was another irredeemable example of low comedy. 'For custard-pie-throwing addicts only', warned the *Sunday Dispatch* (18 March 1956); 'A sad bundle', mulled *The Sunday Times* (16 March 1956); and 'one of the last scrapings of the Ealing barrel before the studio was sold to the BBC', cruelly interjected the *Daily Worker* (17 March 1956).

Who Done It? has been virtually ignored by film historians and generally regarded as an unwelcome throwback to the film comedies of old. George Perry finds the film, along with several of the Studio's late comedies, a 'real embarrassment' (1985: 125); while Geoff Brown curtly dismisses it as a 'tepid farce' (1984: 17). The style of the comedy, with its emphasis on slapstick, mistaken identities, silly disguises and the centrality of the comic's performance, puts the film squarely in the former tradition of comedian comedy practised at Ealing and Gainsborough in the 1930s.[18] The casting of old stagers like

Gary Marsh and Charles Hawtrey, who had appeared in Formby and Hay films worked on by Dearden, seemed to confirm the anachronism of the film. Similarly, the plot of the film, which has Hill as a hapless private eye embroiled with foreign agents scheming to control the world by manipulating the weather, harked back to the cinema of the 1930s. Paul Wells has warned, though, that such a comedy style contextualised within the mid-1950s has a different import and meaning; noting that the traditional slapstick humour is contemporised and extended, and developed in line with a satirical treatment of new technologies and more self-conscious construction of character and performance. Such an approach to comic construction is distinguishable from the earlier style of pre-war comedy:

> The jokes need no longer reinforce an assumed consensus in the audience, but operate as mechanisms in their own right, seeking out multiple *senses* of humour. Such an approach recognises increased social fragmentation and disparateness in the postwar world; the *individual* had become a verifiable social phenomenon, while *community* was in a state of erosion. Dearden thus shows 'Englishness' in a process of change in the face of new social structures and their attendant *humours*. (1997: 50; emphases in the original)

Dearden demonstrates a sure touch in constructing the comic business, especially impressive being the culminating chase sequence, which ranges across London's streets, the National Radio Show at Earl's Court and a stock car derby, which occupies a full twenty-four minutes of screen time; however, Clarke's script lacks sparkle and originality, and Hill is unable to transfer his star power from the small to the large screen. There are some conventional digs at the new leisure rival of TV, but this is never developed into a serious satire; and one promising aspect, the physical superiority of the leading female character over the male hero (Belinda Lee, who makes her living with a strongwoman act), is totally effaced by her overwhelming desire for conventional romantic love and submission.

In the uncertain period after Ealing had left the village green studio and joined forces with MGM at Borehamwood, Dearden and Relph tentatively embarked on independent production, striking a brief relationship with the producer–director team of Frank Launder and Sidney Gilliat to work on two comedies at Shepperton Studios.[19] In an unusual arrangement, Dearden supervised former camera operator Robert Day on his first directorial assignment, *The Green Man* (1956).[20] As Frank Launder later recalled:

> Bob Day was too inexperienced to handle this type of comedy as a first effort, though he later became a capable director. So we brought in Basil

Dearden, who although he did not receive a credit either supervised or personally directed a great deal of the film. (Brown 1977: 138)[21]

Day commented on the arrangement at the time, confessing that 'it is impossible to have two directors handling every scene, so Basil is actually handling them and I contribute ideas and make suggestions'; adding, 'Basil Dearden has taught me quite a lot, particularly about floor control' (*Kinematograph Weekly*, 12 April 1956: 35, 41).

The film was a solid popular success and was immediately followed by *The Smallest Show on Earth* (1957), which began production in August 1956 with Dearden directing and Relph producing. This production had much of the feeling of Ealing about it: the script, dealing with a young couple (Bill Travers and Virginia McKenna) who inherit an ancient flea-pit cinema, was provided by studio regulars William Rose and John Eldridge; the film was shot by ace Ealing cameraman Douglas Slocombe; and the story displayed the characteristic thematic contrasts of new versus old and small versus big.[22] The film, therefore, has that curious distinction of being Dearden's 'Ealing comedy'.[23] This conundrum has tended to confound critics who respond to it as a curio, somehow out of place and out of time. For instance, James Chapman comments on *The Smallest Show on Earth* as 'insignificant, a mere trifle', lacking Dearden and Relph's 'serious themes and contemporary relevance', not seeming to 'anticipate any future developments' or reflecting 'anything which Dearden and Relph had done before'. Such a view over-attends to the cinema of social problems associated with the filmmakers and ignores their long experience working in comedy. After all, this was Dearden's third comedy in succession (including *The Green Man*), and Relph was about to embark on the tragic-comedy *Davy*, which he followed in quick succession with two more comedies. Viewed like this, *The Smallest Show on Earth* is anything but an aberration.

The reviews were mixed, *The Times* admiring the film's eccentricities, quaintness and humour (15 April 1957) and *Kine Weekly* enjoying a 'good humoured parody' on the film business (28 March 1957). But a typically sour *Monthly Film Bulletin* found the film

> a rather poor example of conventional British screen comedy, with stock characters and situations, and "straight" leads who don't quite know whether to play it straight or comic; and are as much out of their depth either way. (April 1957)

'Basil Dearden directs with a heavy touch', complained *Films and Filming*, 'No good joke (and there are one or two) is allowed to rest until it has been repeated, wrung out dry, then finally trodden underfoot', although the

Basil Dearden with the cast of *The Smallest Show on Earth* (1957) (Courtesy of Simon Relph)

reviewer was forced to admit that the film 'has a good heart' (June 1957). There was widespread praise, though, for the performances of Peter Sellers, Bernard Miles and Margaret Rutherford as the decrepit staff of the Bijou Kinema, each having the gift of 'making absurdity and pathos momentarily indistinguishable' (*Monthly Film Bulletin*, April 1957).

The Smallest Show on Earth was a considerable commercial success and is now a fondly remembered minor classic of British screen comedy, fascinatingly suggestive of the clash between nostalgia and modernity that characterised the post-war period. Dave Rolinson has recently suggested that the defining theme of 1950s British film comedies is 'consensus and its breakdown through the alienating individualism of consumerism'; and the resultant tensions are evidenced in the film's satirising of both cinema exhibition and Ealing whimsy (2003: 87). A similar inflection is offered by Wells, who stresses that 'modernity had the effect of mobilising a middle-class nostalgia for sociable humour rooted in a working-class ethos' and that Dearden's 1950s comedies were an attempt 'to look at humour in the ways in which it expressed contradiction' (1997: 45–6). Christine Geraghty has suggested that 1950s British cinema offered a problematic representation of itself, usually in ambiguous and self-deprecatory ways. She stresses the recurrent image of the unruly audience in the Bijou, and for an industry in decline this was a version of cinema that was both unsustainable and undesirable. In this sense, it is telling that when the modern young couple get their hands on the money from the sale of the Kinema to the owner of the rival Grand cinema (through highly suspect means), they leave not only the exhibition industry but also the country (2000: 18–19).[24]

The distinctive style and themes of this comedy have led critics to seek provenance for this film elsewhere than the director. It is Chapman's view that the main creative input into *The Smallest Show on Earth* came from scriptwriter William Rose, whose particular brand of cynicism informed the film and it was yet another case of Dearden proving himself a 'good director of other people's scripts' (1997: 196–9).[25] This ignores the evidence that Dearden and Relph, in films such as *Saraband for Dead Lovers* (1948), *Cage of Gold* (1950), *The Square Ring* (1953) and the forthcoming *Davy*, had produced a number of films since 1945 that promote their own cynical view of the post-war settlement.[26] Therefore, a fairer assessment of the production would acknowledge a good script (Rose), recognised as such by an able producer (Relph) and turned into a successful picture by an experienced director of film comedy (Dearden); with all working in harmony and pulling in the same direction. Like many comedies, *The Smallest Show on Earth* was heterogeneous in style; while conforming largely to the ensemble style of classic Ealing comedies and the concern to tell stories and maintain narrative coherence, it also embraced elements from the older music hall tradition, with some broad-playing, comic caricatures and slapstick sequences, and was therefore partially constructed in a comic mode more associated with Dearden than Rose.[27] Dearden and Relph's first production outside of the comfort zone of Ealing had been a marked success and the partnership could be confident about a future in independent filmmaking. Frank Launder later commented on their brief alliance on this film:

> It was our first and only film with Basil Dearden and Michael Relph as a team, and we all got on well together – with Leslie Gilliat as the go-between to smooth the path of production, as he did so well and so often on other productions. We all then went our separate ways before anything could happen to blight this serene association. (Brown 1977: 141)

Dearden and Relph's engagement with outright comedy ended in a distinctly minor key. At the end of the 1950s, Michael Relph directed two comedies that were distributed by the Rank Organisation and produced by Basil Dearden. The films now merit little more than a footnote in survey histories of British cinema, and it is surprising to find how well they were reviewed at the time. *Rockets Galore!* (1958) was a brazen attempt to emulate the success of the classic *Whisky Galore!* (1949) and can be viewed as Relph's 'Ealing comedy'.[28] The script was written by Monja Danischewsky, who had been associate producer on the earlier success, and was similarly based on a novel by Sir Compton MacKenzie. This time around, the islanders of Todday are resisting Whitehall's attempt to impose a missile base on them. *Films and Filming* thought the film 'the best comedy from the Rank Organisation for many years; indeed, the best Rank picture I've seen for a long while'. In particular, the reviewer respected the poignancy of the subject in the age of Sputnik:

> Few films could be more topical. It is to Relph and Dearden's credit that they have delivered some pretty devastating broadsides against the arms-race fanatics. The film . . . is a good film . . . good, because it is true to life. I believe it will have a very large audience. It deserves to. (November 1958)

The Times was also taken by the seriousness underpinning the mirth; enjoying the 'whimsical, ironic fun in the best Ealing Studio manner', the film's 'uproarious satire' and 'genuine indignation' (22 September 1958).[29] Writing several years later, Raymond Durgnat took a wider perspective and sensed a 'rebirth of inspiration' following what he considered the conventional dullness of the 1950s social problem films: 'for once', he applauded, 'they're identifying with the outlaws', and felt the film represented a 'withdrawal of complacency' for the filmmakers (1966: 31).

Michael Relph directing *Rockets Galore!* (1958) (Courtesy of Steve Chibnall Archive)

Desert Mice was released in December 1959, part of a cycle of service comedies that came in the wake of the hugely successful *Private's Progress* (d. J. Boulting, 1956) and *Carry on Sergeant* (d. G. Thomas, 1958).[30] A modestly budgeted picture, it seems that it was part of a production deal Dearden and Relph had with Rank which also included the more important and successful *Sapphire* (1959).[31] The film concerns an Entertainment National Service Association (ENSA) concert party sent to North Africa to entertain the troops and clearly appeals as nostalgia to a generation who had done their bit in the war or subsequently completed their National Service. ENSA had been notorious for the poor quality of shows it staged at military camps and bases, and the film mounts an affectionate tribute to the awfulness of the performers.[32] In what must rank as the most over-generous review in film history, *Films and Filming* found *Desert Mice* a 'brilliant piece of satire':

> The study of down-at-heel troupers doing their bit in wartime is done with that kind of penetrating observation that Fellini brought to his show people, notable in *I Vitelloni* and *Cabiria*. The Relph-Dearden team has been helped by a collection of near-perfect cameos from such artists as Irene Handl, Reginald Beckwith and Dora Bryan. (January 1960)

Elsewhere, reviewers found no hint of the subtleties of the continental art cinema and dismissed the film as broad farce. For once, *Monthly Film Bulletin* was nearer the mark, dismissing the 'boorish script', the 'amateurish handling' and a talented cast wasted on 'obvious *double entendres*' (January 1960). For a modern audience, lacking any 'sentimental affection' for the subject (*The Times*, 21 December 1959), *Desert Mice* comes over as the feeblest of all the Dearden–Relph productions and appears the most critically irrecoverable of all their films.[33] In an interview many years later, Michael Relph conceded that Dearden had passed up the opportunity to direct these final two comedies, a judgement that in hindsight revealed a shrewd sense of taste and discernment.

Michael Relph: Art Direction and Film Design

The Warner Years at Teddington, including *They Drive by Night* (1938); *The Bells Go Down* (1943); *My Learned Friend* (1943); *The Halfway House* (1944); *They Came to a City* (1944);*Champagne Charlie* (1944); *Dead of Night* (1945); *The Captive Heart* (1946); *Nicholas Nickleby* (1947); *Frieda* (1947); *Saraband for Dead Lovers* (1948); *Cage of Gold* (1950); *All Night Long* (1962), *The Assassination Bureau* (1969)

The entire aim of the film designer, as of all those engaged upon the film, must be to tell the story. Once a designer attempts to impose design for the sake of design and at the expense of the mood and character of the story, he becomes a liability instead of an asset. (Michael Relph 1948: 84)

Art directors should be seen but not heard. (Charles Affron and Mirella Affron 1995: 1)

Although he came from a theatrical family, there was little indication in Michael Relph's early life that he would become involved in artistic work or design, although when confronted with a need for a decision he considered architecture. It was, in fact, through a family connection that Relph joined the newly instituted apprenticeship scheme at the Gaumont-British Studios (G–B), Lime Grove in 1932; opting for the specialism of art direction. Laurie Ede has pinpointed the two significant consequences this had for Relph: first, he worked for the first time under Michael Balcon, Head of Production at G-B and later to take control at Ealing Studios; second, he served his apprenticeship under the esteemed German designer Alfred Junge at the Shepherd's Bush Studios, later becoming his assistant and who proved an important influence (1997: 249). Apprentices gained considerable practical experience and the young Relph made some unspecified contributions to significant G-B productions like *Rome Express* (d. W. Forde, 1932), *Jew Süss* (d. L. Mendes), *The Man Who Knew Too Much* (d. A. Hitchcock) and *Evergreen* (d. V. Saville – all 1934), and *Sabotage* (d. A. Hitchcock, 1935).[34]

In 1936, Relph accepted an invitation from Peter Proud to work as co-art director at the Teddington Studios operated by Warner Bros., which produced low-budget 'quota quickies' for the British market.[35] In the two years spent at the small studio, Relph art directed around thirty productions, of which *Who Killed John Savage* (d. M. Elvey, 1937), *Glamour Girl* (d. A. Woods, 1938), *Everything Happens to Me* (d. R. W. Neil, 1938), *Mr Satan* (d. A. Woods, 1938) and *They Drive by Night* (d. A. Woods, 1939) can be identified (Relph 1990). The three films directed by the promising Arthur Woods are the most significant, with *They Drive by Night* being the best known and a minor classic of the period.[36] This crime melodrama, adapted from the celebrated low-life novel by James Curtis, attracted a favourable review from Graham Greene in the *Spectator*, who compared its evocation of atmosphere and fatalism with the esteemed poetic realism of the French cinema then in vogue.[37] Shorty Edwards (Emlyn Williams), just released from prison, drops in on a former girlfriend, finds her strangled and is soon on the run for murder. The mood of the drama is quickly established through the constant presence of torrential rain as Shorty flees the scene, his anxiety marked by the succession of cramped

Michael Relph's set of the transport café for *They Drive by Night* (1938) (Courtesy of Simon Relph)

and murky spaces he occupies, the dimly lit cabs of lorries, the backstreet dens of illegal gambling clubs and the steamy transport cafés of the Great North Road. Relph, in these opening scenes, is more successful than most in creating the sordid realism of those fringe spaces populated by petty criminals, dance hall girls and transient labour. Relph demonstrates his versatility, an aspect ignored by a criticism enthralled by the earlier scenes of realism, when the story returns Shorty to London and enquiries centre on the smooth, white and streamlined art deco interiors of the Palais de Danse. A large, split-level set, Woods has the camera glide around the dance floor as the girls mingle with the patrons, playing detective and seeking clues to the murder mystery of their former colleague. Relph's most skilful and witty designs are reserved for the *finale*, played out in the mews house of the sex murderer (Ernest Thesiger), replete with discretely placed nude statuary, erotica and oriental appendages that comment tellingly on the perversion of the killer. A contemporary review in the left-wing *New Statesman* welcomed the film's 'tendency to abandon the imaginary world of mock-Tudor country houses in order to study English life in all its oddity and variety' (8 April 1939), and the production demonstrated a talent for décors of significant narrative power.[38]

Relph remembered his two years at Teddington as a 'wonderful experi-ence', with the hectic programme offering a thorough grounding in his craft and an opportunity to experiment:

> Peter used to do one and I'd do the other, and we used to do two pic-tures every fortnight. Finish two on the Friday night and start another two on the Monday morning. Sometimes they had as many as 30–40 sets in them. (Relph 1990)

During the eight years of its English operation at Teddington in the 1930s, Warner Bros. produced about 140 films for showing as second features. In the later part of the decade continuity of production was interrupted by renewed discussion on the quota legislation and a succession of changes in executives (Low 1985: 263–4). Relph seems to have been let go sometime in 1938 and, for a period of a few years, alternated bouts of theatre work, set dressing for films at Denham studios and unemployment, being kept out of the army by a leg injury.[39] He rejoined the studio system in 1942, this time through the good offices of Walter Forde, another family friend who was then directing films at Ealing. British film companies were short of experienced personnel due to wartime conscription and Balcon was happy to be reunited with the talented designer.[40] Initially, there was some unpleasantness with Tom Morahan, the irascible and bad-tempered chief of the art department, the eventual outcome of which was the promotion of Relph to head up art direction at the Studio.[41] Relph's appearance at Ealing coincided with the Studio's shift towards a more

realistic aesthetic, reflective of the grim determination of the nation to prosecute the war to its fullest. Representative films of this period were *Nine Men*
(1943) and *San Demetrio London* (1943), both with art direction by Duncan
Sutherland; while Relph designed *The Bells Go Down* (1943), a tribute to the
Auxiliary Fire Service which teamed him up with Basil Dearden for the first
time. The progress reports published in the trade press stressed the verisimili-
tude of the production. For example, the watchroom was constructed with
an 'elaborate workable and accurately represented switchboard and attendant
mechanisms, plans and charts'. To ensure authenticity, 'The officer from the
original station in Whitechapel . . . came specially to make a thorough examination of this tricky set, discovered only one error, which was quickly put
right' (*Kinematograph Weekly*, 20 August 1942).[42]

In his examination of visual design at Ealing, Laurie Ede has discerned a
shift in style, beginning in 1944 when the 'constraints of documentary' were
relaxed, set dressings were used more expressively and there was a greater
versatility in lighting.[43] This new period of 'modified realism' is attributed
both to the influence of Cavalcanti, who had arrived at the studio in 1940,
and a relaxation on the part of Balcon, who increasingly allowed his production units 'limited freedom to establish their own visual styles' (1997: 250–1).
The new approach is, in fact, discernible in Relph's second film of 1943,
My Learned Friend, a murder-comedy made once again with Basil Dearden.
The previous Will Hay comedies produced at Ealing had been rather blandly
designed by Wilfrid Shingleton and Tom Morahan, but the darker material of
My Learned Friend lent itself to a bolder treatment.[44] The extensive scenes set
in an East End drinking club, 'Jimmy's Dive', allowed Relph to reprise the
kind of work he had successfully mounted in *They Drive by Night*. In place
of the featureless interiors of Shingleton's Eldorado club in *Sailors Three*, the
subterranean nightspot was configured in depth, with a commanding staircase
descending from street level into the bowels of the dingy club, and provided
with texture in the form of bead curtains hanging at the low entrances,
potted ferns, shabby chairs and tables lining the outer walls, an enormous bar
running the length of one wall and grotesque caricatures peering down from
the stone walls. Basil Dearden, matching the drama to the space, instructed
the performers to act 'very tough' (*Kinematograph Weekly*, 4 February 1943).
In a totally different register, Relph was called upon to recreate on Stage 2
at Ealing the interior works of Big Ben. 'The art director's imagination was
allowed to run riot', reported *Kine Weekly*: 'In point of fact the workings of
Big Ben is an unexpectedly small and simple mechanism; not so the screen
counterpart, which worked and looked like some product of a collaboration
between Walt Disney and Heath Robinson' (25 February 1943).

Three forthcoming films with art direction by Michael Relph pushed the boundaries of 'modified realism' to its limits. The characters in *The Halfway House* and *They Came to a City* (both 1944) are subjected to uncanny experiences that force them to test their commitment to the war effort and the possible social changes that might follow the conflict; while *Dead of Night* (1945) is a compendium of supernatural tales bound up in a psychoanalytic dreamscape of dread and anxiety. Each of these productions reveals an increasing tendency towards expressionism, with lighting and sets passing beyond the merely functional to reflect and comment on the emotional states of the characters and the unfolding drama. Ede has suggested a subcategory within the 'modified realism' group, that of the 'dark film', where designers were most free to express themselves; films that were pessimistic about human potential and in which 'the revealing cold light of day gave way to an obscuring chilly darkness' (1999: 164–5).[45] In *The Halfway House*, Relph's expressive design is reserved for the eponymous Welsh inn. Here, the characters are transformed through their interaction with the uncanny, and Relph's sets, with their solid rustic interiors, heavily oak-beamed ceilings, bisecting twisted staircase and cramped attic corridors, offer an imaginative space in which to play out the unconventional drama. The aim was to induce a feeling of claustrophobia rather than terror in a story that had its wartime characters meet in The Halfway House, an inn that had been destroyed by bombing precisely one year earlier, and welcomed by hosts who had been killed in the enemy action. The aim was to create a homely atmosphere in the inn, a place where the characters could have their minds opened to their wartime responsibilities. The set had been designed as a 'large composite of the inn's interiors', constructed so as 'to facilitate quick and smooth "scene changing"' (*Kinematograph Weekly*, 26 August 1943).[46] A handful of surviving sketches reveals how closely Relph and Dearden collaborated on the visual design of the film. The dining room is drawn from a low angle to emphasise the oppressively beamed ceiling (with an enlarged and dominant central beam), and the effect is to elongate the room into a receding deep space. Dearden utilises this concept in constructing the scene at dinner with some fluid tracking shots along the seated guests, some telling low-angle compositions and a dramatic use of deep space imagery. Similarly, Relph conceived of some deep-focus compositions, such as the interaction between Gwyneth (Glynis Johns) and David Davies (Esmond Knight), shot from the dining room and capturing the action taking place in the kitchen in the distance, and these are faithfully executed by Dearden and lighting cameraman Wilkie Cooper.[47]

It is Ede's view that Relph's designs for film 'exhibited a strong theatrical influence', and he identifies in particular the historical films *Champagne Charlie* (1944) and *Saraband for Dead Lovers* (1948) (1999: 153). In fact, Relph produced his most theatrical set for the allegorical drama *They Came to a City*. He

Michael Relph's design for the dining room in *The Halfway House* (1944) (Courtesy of Simon Relph)

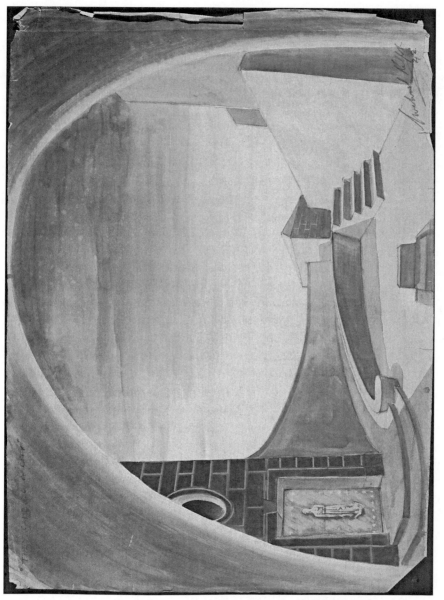

Michael Relph's stage design for *They Came to a City* (1942) (Courtesy of Simon Relph)

had designed the stage production mounted at the Globe Theatre in 1942, and surviving sketches show that there was minimal modification for the film adaptation two years later. Relph's monumental ramparts high above the utopian city borrow something of the stark grandeur of the walled cities in *Alexander Nevsky* (1938) and reflect the weight of the issues being discussed about the post-war future. While the mesmerising rectangular solid mass of the doorway to the city and the promise of the life below seem to herald the similar fascination of characters for the mysterious 'sentinel' in Stanley Kubrick's *2001: A Space Odyssey* (1968). The minimalism of the sets for *They Came to a City* and the anti-realism of its design pushed the film about as far as possible from the dominating studio aesthetic of realism. Ede does not consider *They Came to a City* one of Ealing's 'dark films'; although the general effort to bring out a certain eeriness and the film's untypically passionate outbursts and irresolvable conflicts bring it very close.

The various stories of *Dead of Night* and their differing tones demonstrate the versatility of Relph as an art director. Sets range across the simple clinical lines and solid white masses of the nursing home in the 'Hearse Driver'; the clashing period and national elements in the 'Children's Party'; the contrasting apartments in 'The Haunted Mirror': the cool, sleek and ordered modern flat of the young couple, and the fiery, brooding and vulgar bedroom of the Victorian gentleman; the whimsy of the set dressings in the comical 'Golfing Story'; and the remarkable Chez Beulah nightclub with its threatening and sexualised imagery of the Dark Continent, and prison rendered in a stark symbolist fashion in 'The Ventriloquist's Dummy', which reflect the chaotic emotions of the schizophrenic protagonist. The whole film is anchored in the central linking story, mainly set in the drawing room of Pilgrim Farm where the characters relate their experiences with the uncanny. This is an elaboration on the interiors of The Halfway House inn and is seemingly constructed as a four-walled set which intensifies the creeping claustrophobia that develops within the narrative. This unusual film in the Ealing canon, dealing with issues of sexual and psychological identity and rendered in an intangible dream-like structure, has attracted much critical attention, especially with regards to the contribution of the directors Robert Hamer and Cavalcanti.[48] Michael Relph's significant contribution is largely ignored, when in fact his sets and décor comment imaginatively on the psycho-sexual tensions and jealousies of the characters and reinforce the skulking sense of doom that overlays the film.

In 1945, Relph uniquely combined the roles of art director and associate producer on *The Captive Heart* (1946). This can be reckoned to have provided Relph with even greater authority over the design of his films and was recognised as 'an ideal which Carrick and others of the British design élite craved, but it was difficult to achieve' (Ede 1997: 252). This prisoner-of-war drama

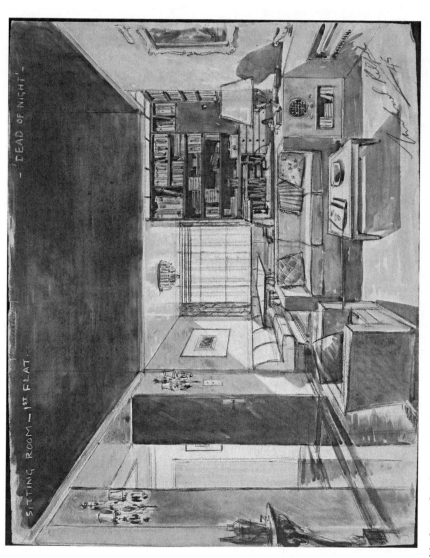

Michael Relph's design for the modern bachelor apartment in 'The Haunted Mirror' episode in *Dead of Night* (1945) (Courtesy of Simon Relph)

involved extensive location work in a former camp in north-western Germany and painstaking effort was directed at attaining realism and authenticity. Ede is wrong in supposing that all of the camp scenes were shot in Germany and that Relph's contribution was limited to 'modest sets that indicated the protagonist's backgrounds' (ibid.). In fact, only the exteriors were shot on location and Relph had to carefully match these with interiors recreated in the studio (*Kinematograph Weekly*, 1 November 1945). His guide for this work were the illustrations by John Worsley which appeared in Guy Morgan's *Only Ghosts Can Live* (1945), the source text for the production. The outcome was a faithful reproduction of the austere existence of the men and a fitting tribute to those that endured.

Michael Relph art directed or designed three costume films while at Ealing. The Studio's historical reconstructions have not fared well critically, and compared to the exuberance of the Gainsborough melodramas are seen to suffer from an 'excess of worthiness' (Ede 1997: 251). The approach to *Champagne Charlie*, a story of the Victorian music halls, and *The Life and Adventures of Nicholas Nickleby* (1947) has been assessed as stiflingly authentic. For this reason, as several critics noted, *Nicholas Nickleby*, with its privileging of 'social history over the Dickensian spirit', succeeded less well than Cineguild's *Great Expectations* (1946) in depicting 'Dickens' refracted impression of Victorian social problems' (Ede 1999: 162). The quest for probity and respectability in the historical films produced at Ealing is the reason usually given to account for their modest popularity. For Harper, Ealing's sobriety lacked the spectacle and sensual visual textures required of the costume film, and thus *Champagne Charlie* displayed the past as 'cramped' and offered 'minimal attention . . . to the aesthetics of composition' (Harper 1994: 111). She sees part of the problem lying with the director, Cavalcanti, whose primary interest was in a form of documentary realism that specialised in 'persuasion and detail' and was at odds with the demands of the genre. He carried this approach on to *Nickleby* where, as Harper has argued, every effort was made to attain consonance between script, music, décor, costume and sets. She argues that this does not serve the source text well, 'whose style is defined by the grotesque element in his social observation . . . but the Ealing version . . . eschews such resonance' (ibid.: 114). In his sympathetic study of Cavalcanti, Ian Aitken has offered a more favourable assessment of *Champagne Charlie*, admiring its 'gaudy intemperance' and celebration of pleasurable release and diversion, a quality evident in the bustling set of the Elephant and Castle pub, qualities that distinguish the film from the central Balconian moral truths of sobriety and decency. Admitting that *Nickleby* is a 'disappointment', he considers some material reflective of an authorial talent, pinpointing the scenes at a realistic Dotheboys Hall and the daringly expressionistic suicide of Ralph Nickleby as examples of 'considerable aesthetic quality' (Aitken 2000: 140–52).[49] Relph's skill is evident in the antiquarian accuracy of the sets and décor, and what strikes one most about the visual design of the film is the preponderance of dark, tight and oppressive spaces, which, with only a few exceptions, throw into unremitting relief the dingy, grubby and grasping world of 1830s England.[50]

Relph's third historical film at Ealing was much more ambitious and personal, and is now widely recognised as the art director's greatest achievement, winning for him a coveted Academy Award nomination.[51] *Saraband for Dead Lovers* was a technically ambitious production in which Relph had to contend with colour for the first time. Pre-planning was intense, with Alexander Mackendrick providing over a thousand set-up sketches of the action in collaboration with associate producer Relph and director Basil Dearden;[52] while cinematographer Douglas Slocombe was encouraged to take an unconventional approach to the lighting, developing a low-key, shadowy style which enhanced the gloomy story of power-struggles, bestial aristocrats and thwarted love, contravening the strictures of the Technicolor Corporation which preferred overall bright sets and the bold use of colour.[53] Contemporary criticism of *Saraband* tended to admire the film's daring visual design; but more recently there has emerged the feeling that this alone was not enough to rescue a 'turgid film'. Ede has even found 'problems' with the film's visual tone:

> The heavy chiaroscuro conveys a blanket Grand Guignol feeling which tramples over the more delicate character issues. For example, the affair between Sophie Dorothea (Joan Greenwood) and Königsmark (Stewart Granger) is botched partly because of the gloominess of the sets. Furthermore, the welcome escapes into fresh air (locations at Blenheim Palace and Prague) are nullified by the poor matching of exteriors to interiors. (1997: 256)

Sue Harper has also been critical of the film, believing that there was no sensitive integration of its various narrative languages and that 'the intentions of the art department went slightly askew'. This was apparently the result of two conflicting desires: the Studio's traditional wish to be 'soberly realistic' and the filmmakers' intention to be 'sumptuously symbolic' (1994: 117).

Such criticism ignores the subversive potential of visual design in *Saraband*. If we consider the opening of the film, where, through a sequence of forward movements of the camera, the viewer is brought to the deathbed of the aged Sophie-Dorothea, a prisoner in Ahlden castle for thirty-two years, we are immediately impressed with the tragedy and fatalism of the drama, and the shadowy nature of the Hanoverian court. Here, Relph extended the 'colourless emptiness' of the Ahlden marshes into the bedchamber of the dying woman, made even more stark through its contrast with the preceding

Michael Relph sketching designs for *Saraband for Dead Lovers* (1948) (Courtesy of Simon Relph)

vibrancy of the title-cards rendered in the bold style of the Italian baroque. The only concession to visual interest is the 'icy pallid violet' of Sophie-Dorothea's nightgown (Relph 1948: 79).Through the device of writing down her story for the benefit of her son, a flashback returns us to her youth and recounts the tragic events leading to her long incarceration. The young princess is called from her idyllic childhood life – all sunshine and light – to the overbearing royal court at Hanover, settings that Relph intended to mark 'the doom which is about to encompass the little princess' (ibid.: 80). Both narration and visual style draw on the contemporary interest in *noir* and this seems an entirely defensible artistic choice for a tale of ruthless ambition, repression and sexual domination that inexorably lead to the murder of Königsmark and a lifetime of enforced isolation for Sophie-Dorothea. Relph's décor and Slocombe's cinematography enhance the forbidding nature of intrigue, ambition, jealousy and emasculation and the relentless and artful pursuance by the filmmakers of this darker vision can hardly be reduced to, or discounted as, 'gloomy sets'. While the script, music and costumes, as Harper suggests, might well have conformed to Balcon's conventional demands of restraint and propriety,[54] the direction, design and cinematography actively subvert this ideal through their 'textual excess'. The incorporation of an unsettling *noir* aesthetic in the art direction and colour photography subtly eroticise the narrative and inject a pessimistic tone that is not conventionally associated with the Studio, but was becoming evident in the cinema of Dearden and Relph.[55]

Following the war, Relph increasingly devoted himself to the production of the films of Basil Dearden, and in all but a handful of cases art direction was entrusted to another party. Other than the historical films, he concentrated on melodramas, beginning with the popular success *Frieda* in 1947. The art director had designed the stage production and the film featured several large sets and location shooting at Woodstock, Oxfordshire.[56] Ede sees *Frieda* as a 'seminal text' in the *oeuvre* of Dearden and Relph, it being the first of their social problem films (1997: 253). While its story of a German war bride struggling to become assimilated into English village life can hardly be considered a 'social problem', it is reflective of the team's social awareness and concern to grapple with issues affecting post-war society. The hub of the drama is the Dawson family house in Denfield, an outwardly homely Georgian dwelling, but somehow cold and stiff. As Ede has observed, the internal design elements of the house 'indicate the unlikelihood of Frieda being able to achieve a foothold in English society'; he also comments on Relph's manipulation of his environment to reveal 'brutal human impulses' (1997: 253, 254). The centrepiece of the house is the dominating curving staircase, linking the hall with the upper floor. This immediately impresses itself on guests, including the initial welcoming of Frieda; and thus at the very heart of the drama Relph situates a vortex, a dominant motif in the film, signifying the disorientation of the German woman confronted by hatred and prejudice in the heartland of England. In some key scenes, Relph also has the background décor comment ironically or ominously on the action unfolding in the foreground, as when Frieda has fled the cinema showing newsreels of Belsen and she is posed against a large poster promoting a Hollywood movie or while at a New Year dance, a happy Frieda is talking optimistically about the future, but is mocked and reproached by a memorial for the Great War immediately behind her.

Relph's approach to the crime-melodrama *Cage of Gold* (1950) has important similarities to both *Frieda* and *Saraband for Dead Lovers*, notably in the way the home dominates the central female characters and in the use of expressionistic devices to comment on the turmoil of women subjected to differing codes of masculinity and their responsibilities.[57] *Cage of Gold* is the most thoroughly *noir* of the Dearden and Relph features and a prominent example in the cycle of expressionist crime films of the period. It has conventionally been passed over as sadly supportive of the traditional values of Balcon's Ealing, when there is a strong case, as with *Saraband*, to read against the grain and reject such ideological fixity. The superficial respectability of the household and its solid middle-class values are thoroughly undermined by its shadowy interiors and stuffy Victoriana, and contrast unfavourably with the heroine's studio apartment, all light and airy, where she had led a free and independent life of excitement. Once again staircases are a prominent feature of the sets, dark and foreboding in the family home with the camera usually set high, looking gloomily downwards, but white and cheery in the studio flat with the view craning more optimistically upwards. In innumerable ways, lighting, composition and staging comment on the restricted role of women in the post-war settlement, a factor largely unacknowledged in the criticism.[58]

In the later 1950s, Michael Relph attended to the crucial work of achieving a successful crossover for the partnership into independent production after the demise of Ealing. He also tried his hand at directing, but his three films that appeared between 1957 and 1959 were uninspired and minor achievements. He returned to designing on the tragic melodrama *All Night Long* (1962), a jazz version of *Othello*, which he also produced.[59] The drama is largely played out on a single large set, the interior of a dockland's warehouse, in which a party and continuous jazz performance take place. The brick walls, archways, metal gantries and industrial appendages are violently juxtaposed with huge canvases of modern art to provide a modish brutalism appropriate for the updated drama; while Relph characteristically introduces a wrought-iron circular staircase into the design to create a split-level set around which Ted Scaife's camera swoops and glides as the narrative focus shifts from character to character. In a manner reminiscent of *Frieda*, the elaborately embroided banner announcing the anniversary of Rex (Othello) and Delia (Desdemona) is a mocking presence in the background and comments ironically on the disintegrating relationship as Rex is driven to murderous jealousy.

Relph's final film as a designer was the historical adventure romp *The Assassination Bureau* (1969). The film won much praise for its artwork, which critics found witty and elegant. In a brief discussion of the contemporary art director, John Russell Taylor acknowledged the 'exceptionally important role played by design in the *tout ensemble*', and praised *The Assassination Bureau* as a 'designer's *tour de force*, full of little private visual jokes and a constant pleasure to look at:

> Fortunately, the story and its treatment can carry this degree of visual elaboration: it seems a legitimate extension of the film's subject-matter rather than a frantic attempt to pile on irrelevant prettiness while the basic structure cracks and crumbles. (*The Times*, 22 March 1969)

Taylor singled out for special mention the 'intricate *fin de siècle* French style of the brothel' and the 'rickety contrivance' of the pre-Great War Zeppelin. The former is the most elaborate example of a Relph staircase astride a split-level set, in this case a bifurcating stairwell joining three levels, and along and around which Dearden can execute a prolonged comic chase. While the interior workings of the dirigible are reminiscent of the fanciful clockwork mechanics of Big Ben in *My Learned Friend* from a quarter-century earlier and an equally suitable comic backdrop against which to play out the culminating struggle. Overall, Relph's approach to the film was to accentuate a sense of fun while configuring the easy elegance of an age about to lurch disastrously into industrialised warfare.

Comedy was part of the formative development of Basil Dearden as a film-maker and remained a constant, if largely unvalued, element of his film-making. As Paul Wells has acknowledged of British cultural criticism, 'His expertise in comedy is overlooked because comedy is rarely acknowledged as an *intellectual* pursuit, either in its construction or with regard to its content' (1997: 56; emphasis in original). Wells has correspondingly offered the most thorough examination and defence of Dearden's screen comedy, believing it 'facilitated his intellectual ability and practical talent' and constituted a significant part of his filmmaking (ibid.). He traces the director's development through three phases or comic modes: the *sociability* of the early working-class comedies with Formby and Hay, which offered a participatory engagement with audience expectations and which should not be undervalued; the *sentimentality* of the 1950s comedies, which marked a critical engagement with social and cultural change and reflected an evolving cynicism in the period;

and the *sensibility* of the later *Only When I Larf* (1968), a comedy of superiority and irony wherein 'Dearden shows that the commercial threat in *The Smallest Show on Earth* has become the amoral governing principle of modern culture' (ibid.: 54). As such, Wells appreciates the screen comedy of Basil Dearden as responsive to cultural change and as more sophisticated than previously allowed; a filmmaker who worked successfully and creatively in the technically demanding comedy of the music hall comedians, but was able to extend his screen practice into more ironic and self-aware forms of humour appropriate for the post-war settlement.

While not equally adept at directing film comedy, Michael Relph was a leading art director and designer in British cinema of the 1940s–1960s. As his most productive period was at Ealing, a studio widely assumed to be rather conservative and unadventurous in design, and further that he was associated mainly with Basil Dearden, the director mostly recognised with the middle course steered at the Studio, Relph has not received the acclaim and respect that is his due. In fact, as has been argued here, Dearden and Relph pursued a singularly dark and unsettling course in some aspects of their cinema, one that called for unconventional lighting, an uncharacteristic use of deep space and deep focus, and a bold approach to colour and the psychological aspects of set design. Relph was a progenitor and leading exponent of the 'modified realism' which emerged at Ealing in the later war years and typified the most visually exciting and challenging films produced at the Studio. The work of Dearden, Relph and Slocombe on *Dead of Night, Saraband for Dead Lovers* and *Cage of Gold* is evidence of a remarkable collaboration and in its own way as subversive of the Ealing norm as the celebrated comedies and melodramas of Hamer and Mackendrick.

NOTES

1. At this time, Dearden also acted as assistant director to Carol Reed on the comedy *Penny Paradise* (1938) made at ATP.
2. All of Formby's Ealing films were big box-office successes and only later at Columbia did he experience a decline in popularity.
3. Despite some exceptions, Mass Observation reported that the press found the dream sequence the funniest in the film (Richards and Sheridan 1987: 333).
4. In retrospect this would prove to be a wise move, for as the war progressed there would develop an acute shortage of comedians with strong demand coming from cinema, radio and ENSA. See *Kinematograph Weekly* (27 August 1942). Tommy Trinder was also signed by the Studio in 1940.
5. Hay also appeared in the propaganda film *The Big Blockade* (d. C. Frend, 1942) and the short *Go to Blazes* (d. W. Forde, 1942), made for the Ministry of Information.

6. Seaton and Martin do report that Hay busied himself by tinkering with the scripts (1978: 126).
7. Robert Murphy holds the opposite view, believing *The Ghost of St Michael's* a 'spirited' comedy marking a successful break from Gainsborough; but that the two subsequent films were 'tiresomely overladen with propaganda' (1989: 211). This is endorsed by Seaton and Martin (1978).
8. Locations included the grounds of Pinewood Studio and West Wycombe (Ede 1999: 156).
9. The harassed interviewer for the broadcast was the well-known BBC announcer Leslie Mitchell.
10. Apart from in a minor way in *Undercover* (1943), there would be no more carica-turing of Germans at Ealing. As Barr has reported, 'The simple displacement of all hostility on to *them* is not adequate. It is replaced by a respect for their power and resource, and a concomitant over-hauling of the structures and assumptions of our own side' (1977: 27; emphasis in original).
11. Details taken from *Kinematograph Weekly's* (5 November 1942, 21 January 1943, 11 March 1943 and 1 and 8 April 1943). Hay died after a succession of strokes in 1949.
12. Interviewed in *Kine Weekly*, scenario editor Angus McPhail described the film as 'true escapist fare – with five murders' (5 November 1942); while the film's press book informed exhibitors, 'Here's the opportunity you've been waiting for – a film that has ABSOLUTELY NOTHING to do with the war'. This was a fairly rapid turnaround of view at Ealing. At the commencement of 1942, Balcon had made a vigorous defence of films with war themes. In a general justification of the Studio's production approach for the year, he stated: 'ours would be a pretty poor Industry if it did not grab with both hands the opportunity of putting every phase of the war on the screen. Here is our chance to do what writers, poets and painters have done ever since wars began in our history . . . tell Britain's story in the most vivid medium of story-telling that has ever existed' (*Kinematograph Weekly*, 8 January 1942).
13. This was the second film designed by Relph for Dearden, following *The Bells Go Down* (1943).
14. It was Michael Relph's recollection that the film was 'not successful' at the box office, and this in conjunction with Hay's declining health could account for the decision to cease production of Hay comedies at Ealing (correspondence with authors 19 February 2004).
15. Relph was associate producer on the classic *Kind Hearts and Coronets* (1949), although he remembers being disappointed at the film's initial lack of critical regard and poor box office (1990).
16. The script was loosely based on Clarke's novel *Two and Two Make Five*.
17. Clarke later conceded that 'My authorship of *Who Done It?* is something I rarely let out of my skeleton cupboard' (Clarke 1974: 180).
18. See Sutton (2000).
19. Under pressure from Rank, Balcon had been forced to loan out directors as early

as 1954, although Dearden and Relph's actions were independently arrived at. See Harper and Porter (2003: 65).

20. At this time Relph was preparing his own directorial debut for Ealing with *Davy* (1957), and Dearden and Relph were thinking of alternating the roles of director and producer in the belief that the approach would allow for the production of a film every nine months (*Kinematograph Weekly*, 13 September 1956).

21. Day later went on to direct the popular comedies *Two Way Stretch* (1960) and *The Rebel* (1961).

22. Relph later stated that the project had been turned down by Balcon at Ealing (McFarlane 1997: 483). Rose also provided the script for Relph's next film *Davy* (1957).

23. Wells suggests that *The Smallest Show on Earth* is a parody of an Ealing comedy (1997: 50).

24. See also Vincent Porter's (2001) discussion of 1950s screen comedy, although he does not mention *The Smallest Show on Earth*.

25. This, of course, underplays any contribution co-scriptwriter John Eldridge might have made.

26. See Chapter 3.

27. Yet another, more modernist, style is also evident in the mildly self-reflexive sequences where the boundary between the screen world of the films projected in the Bijou and the experience of the venue's audience is lost. This meta-cine-matic dimension has been linked to Dearden in such films as *The Halfway House* and *They Came to a City* (both 1944), see Barr (1993: 185–6). Wells also picks up on this point when he observes that 'Dearden uses the whole repertoire of the technical failure [of the projection equipment] to heighten his own presence as the author of the comic events out of the cinematic medium itself' (1997: 52).

28. For a full discussion of *Whisky Galore!*, see McArthur (2003).

29. Typically, the *Monthly Film Bulletin* was more critical, finding 'variable invention' and 'faltering direction', although sensing a 'serious core' (25: 288/299, 1958).

30. The film reunited Relph with art director Peter Proud, both having worked at Warner Bros. Teddington Studios in the 1930s.

31. The production participation on *Desert Mice* was cross-collateralised with the profits from *Sapphire* and were accordingly lost in having to repay the loan to the National Film Finance Corporation (Relph 1990).

32. The working title for the film had been the serviceman's version of the ENSA acronym, *Every Night Something Awful*.

33. *Desert Mice* conforms to the pattern of 'social realism with a populist flavour' which characterised war comedies. However, in the sense that such films 'tunnel underneath the bedrock of the serious war films and celebrate the Englishman who triumphs over irrational authority, either by low cunning or innocent knowhow', *Desert Mice* manages a very modest contribution to the cycle (Boyd-Bowman 1984: 42).

34. These titles are listed in an unpublished manuscript, *In Search of Skyhooks*, a part-draft for an autobiography by Michael Relph and kindly made available to the

authors by Simon Relph, or mentioned in an interview published in Brown (1981).

35. Proud had also previously worked at Shepherd's Bush.

36. A keen flyer, Woods signed up for service with the RAF at the outbreak of war and was tragically killed in a crash in 1944.

37. Films such as *Pépé le Moko* (1937), *Le Quai des Brumes* (1938) and *Le Jour se Lève* (1939). 'The author of the English film has taken characters in a simple melodramatic situation and given them a chance to show with some intensity their private battlefields' (*The Spectator*, 21 April 1939).

38. Relph received no screen credit on this film.

39. The only film that has been identified on which Relph worked as a set dresser is *Dangerous Moonlight* (1941).

40. Art director Wilfrid Shingleton, for example, was lost to the fighting services in 1941.

41. The last film Tom Morahan worked on in this period at Ealing was *Went the Day Well?* (1943). He later worked on one further Dearden and Relph production, *The Rainbow Jacket* (1954), having seemingly patched up any differences. His brother Jim Morahan handled most duties in art direction at Ealing in the 1950s.

42. Other big constructions were burning warehouse and hospital sets, the appliance room and a street set built adjacent to the studio car park. See *Kinematograph Weekly*'s (17 September and 8 October 1942) and Ede (1997: 251, 1999: 153). Relph later paid tribute to the remarkable model work and process photography overseen by Roy Kellino (1990).

43. Ede has grouped the art directors at Ealing into the artisans (Wilfrid Shingleton and the Morahans) and the artists (Relph, Sutherland and William Kellner) (1999: 148–9).

44. Ede has referred to the period early in the war when Shingleton headed up art direction at Ealing as the 'White Period': 'Smooth textures were an invariable feature of the White Films. Examples included the blandly finished music shop of *Spare a Copper* (started June 1940) and the plain walls of the Eldorado club in *Sailors Three* (started April 1940). The uninspiring effect of such features was exacerbated by the characterless lighting which was another perennial ingredient of the White Films' (1999: 155).

45. Seven films are listed, *The Halfway House, Dead of Night, Pink String and Sealing Wax* (1946), *It Always Rains on Sunday* (1947), *Saraband for Dead Lovers, Kind Hearts and Coronets* (1949) and *The Man in the White Suit* (1951). One would be tempted to add *The Ladykillers* (1955), *Cage of Gold* (1950) and 'The Actor' story in *Train of Events* (1949). All of these films were directed by, or substantially involved, Dearden, Robert Hamer and Alexander Mackendrick.

46. The set was constructed at the Welwyn Studio as space was unavailable at Ealing (*Kinematograph Weekly*, 26 August 1943).

47. These scenes are discussed in more detail in Chapter 2.

48. Hamer directed 'The Haunted Mirror' sequence (see Barr 1977: 55–8); while

Cavalcanti directed 'The Ventriloquist's Dummy' sequence (see Aitken 2000: 152–61).

49. The director discusses the adaptation in Harrington (1978); see also Paroissien (1977).

50. This could have been a creative response to the relatively small stages at Ealing that did not lend themselves to the sweep and spectacle of the historical film.

51. The Oscar went to Cedric Gibbons for *Little Women* (MGM, 1948), and Relph could consider himself robbed.

52. Relph was credited as production designer on *Saraband*, while the routine work of art direction was the responsibility of Jim Morahan and William Kellner. The use of storyboards and set-up sketches was probably more common in Hollywood; the great production designer William Cameron Menzies did his own drawings, for example (Affron and Affron 1995: 14).

53. The cinematographer discusses his approach to the colour photography in *Saraband* in Slocombe (1948).

54. Relph (1948), though, claimed unity for overall design.

55. In hindsight, Relph has been hard on himself in combining the roles of designer and producer:

> I found that the more interested I was in the art direction the worse the films usually were, so that I thought I'd better give it up. *Saraband for Dead Lovers* was a perfect case because all the sets were pretty and it all looked very nice, and I thought it was turning out a good picture, but in fact it was terribly boring. So it rather destroyed one's judgement (Brown 1981: 202).

56. Art direction was handled by Jim Morahan to a design provided by Relph.

57. Again, art direction was handled by Jim Morahan to a design by Relph.

58. This perspective is further developed in Chapter 3.

59. The routine art direction was by Ray Simm.

2

The Formative Period: The War Years and the Ethos of Ealing

The Bells Go Down (1943), The Halfway House (1944),
They Came to a City (1944), Dead of Night (1945) and The
Captive Heart (1946)[1]

> The aim in making films during the war was easy enough to state but
> more difficult to achieve. It was, first and foremost, to make a good film,
> a film that people wanted to see, and at the same time to make it honest
> and truthful and to carry a message, or an example, which would be
> good propaganda for morale and the war effort. (Michael Balcon 1969:
> 148)

In his autobiography, studio chief Michael Balcon cites *San Demetrio London*
(d. C. Frend, 1943) as an 'outstanding example' of the kind of film made at
wartime Ealing: a story lifted from the news; an epic tale of human endeavour; and fine propaganda for a civilian arm of the services.[2] The Studio had
consciously moved away from the fanciful heroics and hackneyed romantic
subplots of early wartime films like *Convoy* (d. P. Tennyson, 1940) and *Ships
with Wings* (d. S. Nolbandov, 1941). In their stead, it embraced an approach to
film production that simultaneously promoted the interests of wartime propaganda, integrated a documentary approach to narrative filmmaking, constructed a populist representation of the nation as community and contributed
to an emergent sense of a genuine 'national' cinema.

Balcon had been among the vanguard of British producers aiming to place
the film industry at the disposal of the war effort, but had initially been frustrated by the obstructive attitudes of civil servants and politicians who grap-
pled with the short-term problems of putting Britain on a war footing (James
Chapman 1998a: 65–80). In the event, Balcon took the initiative and put
Ealing to producing 'films of a character which will be of national use at this
time' (quoted in Brown 1984: 29). The pressing demands of the production

schedule meant that, initially, the Studio turned out some predictable comedies with a wartime setting and, as noted above, some rather traditional war films; however, the recruitment of Alberto Cavalcanti (in 1940) and Harry Watt (in 1942) from the documentary film movement was a significant marker of the direction Balcon was leading the Studio.[3]

Balcon embraced the more expansive understanding of documentary as 'an attitude of mind toward film making'. In retrospect, he viewed the documentary movement as 'the greatest single influence on British film production', which 'more than anything else helped to establish a national style' (1969: 130). The demands of the wartime emergency led Balcon to consider more carefully the appropriate style for portraying the heroic resistance of the nation and its citizens. In 1942, he persuaded the populist writer and broadcaster J. B. Priestley to provide the story for *The Foreman Went to France*, on which Cavalcanti acted as associate producer and the first of the Ealing films to demonstrate a sense of the wartime spirit of co-operation and egalitarianism. By the following year, the studio head had mapped out his philosophy in a treatise he titled 'Realism or Tinsel?', which he delivered as a paper at the summer school of the Workers' Film Association in Brighton.[4] Here, he contrasted the artificiality of commercial films derived from stage plays and cheap romances with the 'happy marriage' achieved between progressive producers and the documentary movement, which had resulted in such accomplished films as *In Which We Serve* (d. Coward and Lean, 1942) and Ealing's own *San Demetrio London*.

The documentary influence on Ealing was evident in terms of both an aesthetic of realism and a social purposiveness of theme. The documentary films had put a new emphasis on the worker at the centre of British society, and some productions like *Housing Problems* (d. E. Anstey, 1936) had managed a degree of social criticism and were significant expressions of progressive outlook in the period leading up to the war. In a reverse trend, some documentary filmmakers had already begun to incorporate techniques and devices from the commercial narrative cinema and extend their approach into what became known as the story-documentary. Harry Watt had achieved acclaim and commercial success in 1941 with *Target for Tonight*, a dramatised account of a bombing raid over Germany using a real aircrew; and the narrative and documentary forms continued to blend and cross-fertilise in a productive manner into the war years. The conscious attention directed at ordinary working people in the documentaries of the 1930s was reconfigured in the wartime cinema as a benign populism centring on representations of community and collectivity. Such an approach won official sanction and support and was classically expressed in *Millions Like Us* (d. Launder and Gilliat, 1943), Gainsborough's treatment of the wartime recruitment of women into industrial work – a generally unpopular and potentially divisive necessity (James Chapman 1999).

In Jeffrey Richard's evocative phrase, Ealing 'found its soul in the concept of the "People's War" (1997: 14). The powerful wartime myth of unity, social levelling and community spirit, born out of the sacrifices of Dunkirk and the Blitz, and the heroism of the Battle of Britain and El Alamein, led many to assume a 'revolutionary' impact of the war on British social structure and institutions. However, criticism of the 'consensual' image of the war has emerged more recently, and in the words of Jose Harris,

> Historians have become much more sensitive to the fact that many of the 'sources' for the wartime consensus were themselves part of the consensus-creating process. Cinema, radio, war artists, Pathé News and Picture Post were not passive recording angels but active agencies for promoting a certain frame of citizen mind. (1992: 20)

Of course, Ealing Studios, with its wartime films of quiet heroism, cohesive groups and social harmony, was a central part of this 'consensus-creating process' and the 'imaginative' construction of citizenship and national identity set to support the current emergency. It has been widely assumed that Basil Dearden, more than any other filmmaker, harmonised perfectly with the new spirit at Ealing. This is explicit in the writings of both Barr (1977) and Richards (1997); and for the latter, 'Dearden seems to have conformed absolutely to both the structure and the ethos of Ealing' (16). Consequently, Dearden's wartime films at the Studio have never attracted as much interest as productions such as *Next of Kin* (1942) and *Went the Day Well?* (1943) – made by individualists like Thorold Dickinson and Cavalcanti; or been widely grouped with the classic expressions of the myth – *The Foreman Went to France*, *Nine Men* (1943) and pre-eminently *San Demetrio London*.[5] His films have tended to be passed over as mundane treatments of the mythology, lacking in directorial expression and critical interest. As will be shown, this is a far too simplistic and reductive view of a cinema that offers a distinctive handling of the wartime myths. While cheery communities and realism underpin the dramas of *The Bells Go Down* and, to an extent, *The Captive Heart*, these standard qualities are absent or undercut in *The Halfway House*, *They Came to a City* and *Dead of Night* (co-d. Cavalcanti, Hamer, Crichton). In fact, Dearden, aided by Relph, brought a healthy dose of expressionism to the filmmaking at wartime Ealing, and while never wholly subversive in the manner of Robert Hamer's and Alexander Mackendrick's later comedies, it did somewhat destabilise the predictable world of naturalism and counter the easy acceptance of myths typical at the Studio.

THE BELLS GO DOWN (1943)

> Tales of rescue and tales of tight corners abound. Many have been retold
> in the Press, many live silently in the memories of those men con-
> cerned. These and a hundred other things fade into the maze of flame
> and hot smoke, long hours and heavy equipment, noise and burning,
> much water and little sleep that goes to make up the fireman's particular
> blitzmare. (*Fire Over London*, 1941: 28)

In a bizarre coincidence, Ealing Studios was fire-bombed the very week that it
announced the production of a film commemorating the wartime fire service
(*Kinematograph Weekly*, 8 January 1942). The origins of the film lay in the
published diary of an anonymous member of London's Auxiliary Fire Service
(AFS) (*The Bells Go Down* 1942), which in fact had been written by Stephen
Black, formerly a scenic artist at Denham Studios and who had been invalided
out of the AFS in 1941 after being awarded the British Empire Medal. Black
acted as script consultant on the production and possibly assisted Michael
Relph in the art direction.[6] Later in May, it was announced that Basil Dearden
would direct the film, his first solo directorial credit, and it would feature the
Studio's rising comic star Tommy Trinder, following up his success in *The
Foreman Went to France* and once again playing the part of 'an exuberant, wise-
cracking Cockney in a dramatic story' (*Kinematograph Weekly*, 7 May 1942).

The film commenced production in early June and the technical difficulties of restaging the Blitz occupied the crew and Studio for several months.
Extensive location scenes were shot around Petticoat Lane,[7] providing much
of the background to the story: while studio recreations included an elaborate
fire station interior, a raid-battered pub and large warehouse and burning
hospital sets.[8] *The Bells Go Down* was shown to the trade in April 1943 and
received a Gala Charity première at the London Pavilion in the presence of
Herbert Morrison, Minister of Home Security, with proceeds going to the
London Fire Service Benevolent Fund.[9]

The mythologising of the Blitz was well underway as Ealing embarked
on its tribute to the volunteer firemen who rallied to London's defence. The
unprecedented scale of attack on a civilian population, the widespread organisation of civil defence and the placing of the citizenry on the 'front line' were
foundational elements of the ethos of the 'People's War'. Official publications
extolled the quiet heroism and stoical valour of the 'citizen warriors' (*Front
Line*: 7), and praised the auxiliary firemen who 'were suddenly plunged into
a savage inferno of bombardment and fire beyond the experience of even the
tried firemen of the regular brigade' (*Fire Over London*: 3). Despite the revelations about the increased incidence of crime generated through the chaos of

conflagration and initial sluggishness and uncompassionate bureaucracy on the part of the authorities, the Blitz has been comparatively resistant to the demythologisation wrought by revisionist historians. In particular, popular histories continue to construct thrilling and graphic accounts of the raids, and the extraordinary response of the people in their grim determination to resist the destruction of their cities, confront the terror and face the painful loss of life (Gaskin 2005; Mortimer 2005).

As the Blitz raged, various individuals from all walks of life sought an imaginative response to their experiences and the destruction to the urban fabric around them, which had created 'a widespread need for artistic experience, for some kind of emotional expression which would show the spiritual justification for the suffering undergone' (Hewison 1988: xiv). Interestingly, this was particularly strong among members of the AFS and probably reflects the fact that a fair number of recruits were drawn from the professional middle-class who found themselves battling in the heart of London's East End and were moved to articulate their experiences. Writers like Henry Green (*Caught* 1943) and William Sansom (*Fireman Flower* 1944) produced literature of a high quality; many others of a more limited talent and ambition kept diaries of which a number were published during the war (*The Bells Go Down*, Richardson 1941, Wassey 1941, Stedman 1943).[10] AFS men also contributed official histories: an unnamed former journalist wrote *Fire Over London* for the London County Council;[11] and William Sansom wrote *Westminster at War* (1947) for the central London borough. The diary approach conformed perfectly to the documentary impulse emerging with force throughout British culture at the time and which characterised the cinematic treatments of the AFS in both Ealing's *The Bells Go Down* and the Crown Film Unit's *Fires Were Started* (d. H. Jennings, 1943).

Ealing's production of *The Bells Go Down* departs significantly from the published diary, most notably in the shift from a first-person narrative to a more episodic structure which was becoming characteristic at the Studio and was better suited for representing the group and community. Ealing also had no use for the lewd behaviour of the East End firefighters, the ineffective and cowardly sub-officer, the fractious political disputes and occasional outbursts of violence among the men.[12] The effect is to displace the anthropological quality of the middle-class diarist observing the common people by a less detached approach that places the audience *with* the characters and the dramatic action. This is reinforced by having the middle-class recruit take up residence in the community with his bride, rather than the case of the diarist who, apart from his service, continues to reside outside the district and doggedly postpones his marriage. In contrast, the documentary film movement's *Fires Were Started* retains the Mass Observational distance of the social anthropologist, and, while rightly celebrated for its striking imagery, poetic flourishes and elegance of editing, it allows less opportunity for identification with the characters and community being portrayed.[13] As Barr comments generally about this middle-period war film at Ealing, the characters 'are offered without affectation as representative of the nation as a whole' (Barr 1977: 34); and this absence of condescension and warmth of community are powerful elements of the wartime mythology of the 'People's War' and a simple means of access to the narrative for viewer identification.

The most commented on aspect of the film is its opening narration, spoken over shots of East Enders crowding around the market in Petticoat Lane, and which eloquently suggests the organic solidarity at the heart of the film:

> Down beside the docks in the East End of London they say London isn't a town, it's a group of villages. This is the story of one of those villages, a community bounded by a few streets with its own marketplace, its church, its shops, its police station and its fire brigade.

Richards regards this sentiment as a 'specifically Ealing vision of Britain and the British', a characteristic blend of 'spirituality, community, commerce, service and authority' (1997: 18). The narration does not appear in the *Final Shooting Script* and was seemingly added in post-production.[14] In its stead is a remarkable exposition giving a vivid account of the scene, the kinetic motion of the crowds and the array of goods for sale on the stalls, the latter described as 'a visual catalogue of the lives of the people of the East End hung out without shame for all to see'. The emphasis is on what the script describes as a 'unique community', 'all of them on terms of equality and humorous intimacy with every passer-by, rich or poor, known or unknown' (*Final Shooting Script*: 1). Dearden translates this sentiment into complementary images. He begins with a shot of the peaceful August summer sky and slowly pans down and leftwards onto the general market scene and then commences a series of slow forward movements which inexorably bring the viewer into the community that is being depicted and valorised. The restless camera weaves around the district, picking out characters that will play a prominent role in the narrative: Bob (Philip Friend) and Nan (Philippa Hiatt) who nervously attend the reading of their wedding banns at the local church; Ma Turk (Beatrice Varley) who charitably dispenses cheap meals of fish and chips to the neighbourhood poor; and her wisecracking son Tommy (Trinder) who is leading his new racing dog through the local streets. Constant in the scene and often interacting with these principals are the people of the area, bustling in the frame and marking the presence of the community as a subject of the film.

The opening narration proceeds to pinpoint the focus of the story as 'the men who joined that fire brigade and how they and the people of the village stood together through the flames and destruction of the September blitz'. While several characters are retained from the original account – the middle-class recruit, here named Bob, who worries about getting married in wartime; Ted (James Mason), the professional who has to whip the raw recruits into shape; and the petty thief (Mervyn Johns), who alternates his heroism with his larceny – the film introduces new characters, notably Tommy Turk as a starring role for comic Trinder, and the figure of Brookes (William Hartnell) who had fought with the International Brigade in Spain and joined the AFS on its inception after Munich because, as he ominously declares, 'I knew what was coming'. In a preface to the script, Tommy is described as 'The complete extrovert with a flow of irrepressible humour. Tommy is congenitally incapable of taking anything seriously, however hard he tries' (*Final Shooting Script*: n. p.). For some critics the presence of a music hall comic subverted the serious nature of the picture and contrasted poorly with the 'discourse of sobriety' that underpinned the strict authenticity of the documentary *Fires Were Started*.[15] The cult of Humphrey Jennings has ensured the primacy of his tribute to the wartime fire service and unfairly deflected attention from the Ealing film with its comic turns, romantic subplots and recreation of the Blitz on the main sound stage at the studio. For Brian Winston,

> These distinctions then, impact on the most obvious set of contrasts – between firemen and actors; or between some studio sets but real external locations and a totally staged setting; or between a measure of authenticated dialogue and incident as against wholly invented melodrama and comedy. (1999: 63)

This schematic comparison overstates both the 'authenticity' of the documentary and the 'melodrama' of the narrative film. He cites the review of the Ealing film in *The Times* to demonstrate his point:

> *The Bells Go Down* is unfortunate in that it so quickly follows the documentary film *Fires Were Started*. It is by no means true that a documentary film must, by the very virtue of its office, be better . . . but here the film which was acted by men who were actually in the N.F.S. [*sic*] is superior at nearly every point. (67)[16]

This is a selective choice and by no means was *The Bells Go Down* universally felt to be inferior to the production of the Crown Film Unit. The *Monthly Film Bulletin*, to take a case in point, reviewed both films, back to back, in its issue for April 1943. The Ealing film was described as a 'semi-documentary', which succeeded in mounting an 'authentic atmosphere' and, furthermore, 'avoided the pitfalls of mock heroics' (37). Revealingly, the review of *Fires Were Started* was at pains to discern a dramatic structure to the film, what it termed a 'sure story-telling sense'. However, on this score it found the documentary ultimately wanting:

> With a more imaginative reach, however, much more could have been made of this material. This film fails to exploit the dramatic fury of acre upon acre of raging flames – an aspect which, apart from its propaganda and instructive value, has an essential place in any record of this chapter of London's victory. (ibid.)

Moreover, contemporary reviewers found the recreation of the Blitz in *The Bells Go Down* 'impressive, realistic and spectacular' (*Kinematograph Weekly*, 22 April 1943); 'a really remarkable job of producing . . . the re-enactment of London aflame, with firemen handling hoses at dizzying altitudes, walls caving in and floors collapsing to register genuine realism and thrill' (*To-Day's Cinema*, 16 April 1943). It is not inconceivable that for a popular wartime audience the blend of documentary realism, drama and comedy was more acceptable and pleasurable than an austere, humourless and naturalistic study of firemen at work.[17]

Although Ealing sanitised the account presented in the original diary, it was more confident than the official documentary to include some mildly troubling aspects of the Blitz. There was considerable rivalry, bordering at times on enmity, between the AFS and the regulars of the London Fire Brigade which undercut any cosy notions of wartime unity and comradeship, and affected morale among the volunteers. A letter signed 'An Auxiliary Fireman' was printed in *The Times* and dwelt on the 'many grounds of complaint' of the service. The spokesman believed that 'The AFS has been abominably treated by the Home Office, as far as London has been concerned by the LCC and by the press and public at large'. A particular grievance was that the volunteer firemen were entitled only to the same compensation for injury as civilians despite the greater risks they confronted (*The Times*, 9 October 1940). The regulars feared the dilution caused by voluntarism and the threat to their professional status; while the auxiliaries were angered by their lower pay and inferior working conditions. The conflict is brought out gently in the film on a number of occasions and ultimately turned to the benefit of propaganda. When, after the outbreak of war, the recruits respond to the need for men in the fire service, their patriotic enthusiasm and pride are deflated by sub-officer Ted Robbins, who sarcastically comments that 'We've got *men* in the Fire Brigade, but they seem to be taking almost anything in the AFS'.[18] His superior, District Officer MacFarlane (Finlay Currie), saunters into the scene and briskly orders Robbins to 'get this AFS nonsense finished'; and in the first instance of a recurring bit of business orders Tommy to put out his cigarette.[19]

Studio set for *The Bells Go Down* (1943) (Courtesy of Simon Relph)

The film is also prepared to reveal the basic and cramped conditions of accommodation offered the AFS in the early period, the repetition and boredom of endless training during the inactivity of the Phoney War and the humiliation dished out to them as '£3 a week Army Dodgers'. This final act of contempt occurs in a later scene, set in August 1940 as the Battle of Britain raged, when the off-duty AFS men and their women are having a quiet drink in the local pub, The Hopvine. A tipsy soldier questions their utility compared to his mate who had served at Dunkirk. This confrontation accurately reflects the accusations of dodging the fighting services that were levelled at the volunteer firemen in the period before the raids. A defensive Nan rallies to the support of the men, arguing that 'It's all right for people to laugh; it's the easiest thing in the world to do. But the war isn't over yet; not by a long way'.

The figure of Sam, the petty thief, is also used to skirt unpleasant matters like the widespread crime during wartime and the particular problem of looting in the Blitz. In the *Final Shooting Script* the character is rather darkly described as an 'enemy of the people', his expression a 'combination of truculence and cunning' (n.p.). This impression is undermined by casting the genial Ealing regular Mervyn Johns as Sam, who is involved in nothing more than lifting the odd barrel of Guinness to serve demand on the black market. As well as proving himself a hero of the community as a member of the AFS, he is further redeemed by saving from drowning the policeman who has been dogging him throughout the film.[20] This is a typical example of softening and redefining of the subject matter. Stephen Black had claimed that '*everybody loots*':

> But it is really unfair to put one fireman here and another there into jail for looting, while the rest of the Fire Brigade gets off scot free. And it's not only limited to Firemen. The A.R.P, Wardens, Demolition Men, and the rest of them – all loot. So do the Police. (*The Bells Go Down* 1942: 103; emphasis in original)

Such anti-social behaviour, so destructive to the myth, is completely effaced from the film.

While a novel like Henry Green's *Caught* was relatively free of censorship and could paint a dark and fatalistic picture of the AFS in the early days of the war, film productions were more reliant on official sanction and support and were likely to ignore the conflicts within the service (*Fires Were Started*), or tread lightly with them, using the tension dramatically to heighten the sense of release and achievement once the AFS got to grips with the raids, as was the case with Ealing's *The Bells Go Down*.[21]

After the commencement of the metropolitan raids on Saturday, 7

September 1940 the AFS was able to prove its utility and heroism to its doubters. As Neil Wallington has reported, from 8 September onwards,

> Grimy and weary crews driving homeward to their stations, found that they were constantly cheered by pedestrians. After a year of continually standing to and waiting, these moments must have been sweet for the AFS men and women. (2005: 53)

The remaining forty-five minutes of the film detail the extraordinary battle against the flames fought by the capital's fire service in this first phase of the attack on the nation's civilian population; it is a considerable technical achievement by the filmmakers. Through studio reconstruction, location work, documentary footage, process photography and models, the extended sequence creates a dramatic and believable re-enactment of the conflagration, when London was raided on fifty-seven consecutive nights, putting an enormous strain on the civil defenders. The extensive and credible firefighting sequences are leavened with examples of the famous humour of the East Enders – a tradesman delivering to the recently bombed Hopvine pub declares: 'Blimey, you had a rough night last night!' and audiences are treated to the iconic imagery of the Blitz: services in roofless churches and the anxious waiting in public shelters. The culmination of the drama is the battle to save a hospital. MacFarlane and Tommy become trapped in the building and, all hope lost, the two men share a cigarette in a final act of conciliation between the senior officer and the wilful volunteer.

The film ends with the christening of Bob and Nan's new son: in commemoration he will be called Tommy. This symbolic act of continuity and faith in the future is further captured by Dearden, who cranes upwards and back from the service in a reversal of the movement which commenced the film. In high angle, he re-surveys the scene of the busy market, now staged in battered surroundings, but vital, boisterous and defiant.

The Bells Go Down attracted many favourable reviews and certainly held its own with the critics against the official documentary *Fires Were Started*. It was generally felt to be an attractive blend of convincing detail and human drama, while the cockney humour helped relieve the potential grimness of the theme (*Film Report*, 30 April 1943). For the reviewer at the *Motion Picture Herald*, Basil Dearden's direction was dismissed as 'not very adventurous' (22 May 1943); while the opposite view was held at *Variety*, where it was considered 'praiseworthy' (12 May 1943); and looking back from the vantage point of the 1960s, Raymond Durgnat felt that the film suggested an 'intelligent talent' (1966: 28). In retrospect it can be said that Dearden achieved a creditable solo directorial debut, handling the episodic narrative with assurance and clarity, and thrillingly staging the set-piece conflagrations which won much comment and praise from critics. Of particular significance are the early indications of the director's interest in shooting on location, which would become a mark of his cinema. While Harry Watt had pioneered the approach at the studio just months earlier with his remarkable *Nine Men*, the story of a patrol cut off in the North African desert and shot on a beach in Wales, Dearden developed a characteristic method, blending studio with striking location work on the streets of London. The sequence of Bob, recently made unemployed by the war, anxiously walking round the docks, framed within massive doorways and dwarfed by the idle machinery and buildings of the riverside, is an elegant example of Dearden's skill in letting urban landscape comment on the emotions of a character.[22] It is also indicative of the director's awareness of the contribution location is to play in a drama, for this is part of the very fabric that Bob and his colleagues are going to risk their live to save in the coming months.

THE HALFWAY HOUSE (1944)

Following *The Bells Go Down*, Dearden was put to work on the final Will Hay vehicle, *My Learned Friend* (1943). This macabre comedy of murder bore at least some stylistic relation to the three further films the filmmaker made during wartime: *The Halfway House*, *They Came to a City* and *Dead of Night* being tales of the uncanny and supernatural happenings, and representing a distinct change in tone from the standard Ealing preference for documentary realism.[23] The film was an adaptation of the play *The Peaceful Inn* (1939) by Denis Ogden and concerns a cross-section of people bearing troubled consciences and their private anxieties who arrive at a remote inn, only to discover the mysterious fact that it had been destroyed exactly one year earlier. The strange experience forces the characters to confront their dilemmas and to return to the real world with renewed faith and a proper sense of their responsibilities.

The film entered production in the summer of 1943: initially, associate producer Cavalcanti was out scouting locations in Devon and South Wales; while shooting commenced in June with the final casting still in progress, and the crucial matter of finding the ideal actor for each character for what was a finely balanced ensemble piece clearly taxed the producers.[24] A modest stir was made of the casting of fourteen-year-old Sally Ann Howes, who had recently come to prominence in the Associated British production *Thursday's Child* (1942); while a far greater fuss attended the signing of the great French actress Françoise Rosay, who had recently arrived in Britain from Occupied France (*Kinematograph Weekly*, 1 July 1943).[25] The participation of such an illustrious performer necessitated substantial script revisions and the building up of the part of the French wife to a disgraced sea captain that she would play. Novice T. E. B. Clarke, who had recently been invalided out of the wartime police force and taken on at Ealing for a three-month trial, was given the job of expanding the roles (Clarke 1974: 144–7).[26] Following the shooting of the film, in what the trade press termed 'Balcon's Scoop', both Rosay and Howes were signed to contracts at the Studio (*Kinematograph Weekly*, 4 November 1943; *The Cinema*, 23 August 1944).[27]

The Halfway House was screened to the trade on 8 February 1944, but didn't gain a West End première until 14 April and was only entered into general release in August, perhaps reflective of the difficulties the Studio was experiencing with distribution at the time.[28] While reviewers were unanimous in their praise of the acting and the cleverness of the character studies – with predictable special mention of Rosay – many found the material and its presentation rather doubtful. For *Film Report*, 'The supernatural theme is not handled as impressively as it might have been, consequently the story is made still more unconvincing' (11 February 1944); a sentiment echoed at the *Monthly Film Bulletin*, which doubted if the 'realistic' medium of film could successfully render 'a combination of the material world and the ghost world' (29 February 1944). The ambivalence of the reviews was captured by *The Times*, which considered the film only 'halfway towards a true imaginative perception' (17 April 1944). *To-Day's Cinema* was more generous, praising the 'Commendably novel theme' that 'must provide food for thought for the more intelligent patron'; and, in contrast, this reviewer felt that the 'Treatment convincingly indicates eerie atmosphere at the inn' and that the unusual theme was 'lucidly propounded' (11 February 1944).[29]

The drama concerns the moral and spiritual regeneration of the guests vacationing at the ghostly inn. An opening sequence of exposition introduces the characters, relates their current unease and brings all together at the Halfway House. Classical musician David Davies (Esmond Knight) appears conducting a performance in Cardiff. He is visibly exhausted and his doctor urges him to cancel his tour for the British Council, or risk dying from the strain. His dresser suggests that he spend some time at the Halfway House for quiet reflection, but the doctor interjects that the inn has been fire-bombed. Davies agrees that he will find somewhere peaceful to consider his decision.[30]

Squadron Leader French and his wife Jill (Richard Bird and Valerie White) are about to divorce, but their teenage daughter Joanna (Sally Ann Howes) conspires to bring them together at the Halfway House for a reconciliation. Captain Fortescue (Guy Middleton) has been gaoled for the embezzlement of regimental funds and on his release is urged by the prison governor to swallow his pride and rejoin the army as a private. However, he prefers to take up with black marketeer Oakley (Alfred Drayton), whom he meets on the road to the Halfway House. Captain and Mrs Meadows (Tom Walls and Françoise Rosay) are acutely distressed by the loss of their son in wartime action, while the captain also bears the shame of disgrace, having too hastily abandoned his merchant ship during action at sea. And finally, an engaged couple, Margaret (Philippa Hiatt) and her Irish fiancé Terence (Pat McGrath), are threatened in their relationship by his strict adherence to neutrality and intention to accept a post at the Irish legation in Berlin.

Upon arrival at the Halfway House, Fortescue is welcomed by the revenant host Rhys (Mervyn Johns) and is surprised to be told that he was expected. The theme of the film is encapsulated in the announcement by Rhys that 'Quite a lot of people who don't know where they're going arrive here'. The unusual nature of the drama had confused commentators while the film was in production, it being variously described as a 'drama of human problems' (*Kinematograph Weekly*, 6 May 1943), a 'psychological thriller' (*Kinematograph Weekly*, 24 June 1943) and an 'interesting experiment in the supernatural' (*The Cinema*, 2 February 1944).[31] This generic and dramatic uncertainty stems from the renouncement of the Studio's established and venerated realism for an excursion into the uncanny. What is crucial, though, is that *The Halfway House* does not abandon Ealing's wartime patriotic project through an invocation of the uncanny as a threatening Otherness. While Peter Hutchings (2004) has shown that British film and television has repeatedly constructed the national landscape as alienating and disturbing, mainly in fantasy-based genres like horror and science fiction, *The Halfway House* presents its landscapes picturesquely, configuring them as soothing and regenerative spaces.[32] In this sense, its use of the Welsh landscape as redemptive – offered most thoroughly in the sequences of the guests travelling to and arriving at the inn – is akin to the presentation of Kent in Michael Powell's contemporaneous *A Canterbury Tale* (1944), wherein the modern-day pilgrims are 'blessed' through their 'uncanny' encounters with the English countryside and its traditions.[33]

Through staying at the inn and the gradual realisation of their true circumstances, the guests assume a clearer appreciation of their predicaments and troubles. This is achieved mainly through the interaction of the visitors with Rhys and his daughter Gwyneth (Glynis Johns), whose calm presence and lucid reasoning bring the guests to a proper sense of their responsibilities. The source play had a pre-war setting and its metaphysical concerns were more melodramatic: at its heart was a revenge-murder which led to the destruction of the inn by fire. Into this scenario come some unsuspecting guests: a vicar who rediscovers his faith;[34] a father who finds the bravery and purpose that had deserted him at the accident that had killed his child and consequently reclaims the respect of his wife; a gossip columnist who is given proof that she actually helps and guides people; and a socialite who finds purpose after a barren and indulgent life. The film reworks this material for a wartime agenda and the characters are led to a fuller awareness of their roles and responsibilities in the conflict.[35] Davies decides to continue with his tour of neutral Spain and Portugal; Squadron Leader and Mrs French patch up their differences for the sake of the family; Captain Meadows decides to return to sea and his wife Alice accepts that sacrifice is a duty of mothers in war; Terence learns that a sense of humanity is more important than a narrow nationalism and refuses the post in Germany; and the rogues Oakley and Fortescue find their 'citizens conscience';[36] the former, consumed by guilt, handing himself over to the law as an act of atonement, and the latter joining the ranks to re-engage in the fight.

While *The Halfway House* conforms to Ealing's wartime norm of community, sacrifice and social responsibility, it comes to these values from the opposite direction. In *The Bells Go Down* the community simply girds its loins and confronts the challenge in a defiant expression of unity. In contrast, *The Halfway House* focuses on those characters that are notably absent from the earlier film: the big-time criminal, the traumatised, the disgraced and others out of sorts with wartime harmony. While the petty thief Sam is easily absorbed into the defence of the community in *The Bells Go Down*, a more dramatic intervention is required to bring the malcontents of *The Halfway House* back into the fold of the national family and the war effort.

The Halfway House has long been ignored as an insignificant wartime production at Ealing. Durgnat, suggests that, although

> the film is meant as an interrogation of individual conscience, its values are so conformist that it's all but an attack on individuality in the name of morality; for none of the characters decide to do anything that isn't in the book of moral-rules-of-thumb.

However, he acknowledged 'in its sense of an *esprit de corps* involving everyone' a certain 'urgency and poetry' (1966: 28). Charles Barr set the critical tone in his classic studies of the Studio in the 1970s, where he was harshly dismissive of this film and the subsequent *They Came to a City*, rejecting both as 'arid, abstract, statuesquely posed and declaimed' (Barr 1977: 52). Since those landmark studies a minor revolution has occurred in the critical handling of the film. In the second edition of his book, Barr no longer sees *The Halfway House* as a 'dismal experience' (ibid.), but rather as 'bold, eloquent and powerful'. He is particularly impressed by the 'metacinematic dimension' of the film, its complex handling of time and the way it neatly reproduces the experience of cinema (Barr 1993: 185–6). In a similar vein, Winston Wheeler Dixon sees the film's style as thoroughly 'modern':

> The cinematic technique on display in *The Halfway House* is ener-
> getic and forward-looking, engagingly plastic and kinetic, both in its
> *Citizen Kane*/William Cameron Menzies-styled framing, and in its con-
> comitant editorial and syntactic strategies, which at times seem almost
> Eisensteinian in their freshness and intensity. (1997: 108)[37]

While the subjective and self-reflexive qualities of *The Halfway House* make
it an intriguing film within the realist tradition at Ealing, the material is not
constructed in a particularly artful way. Slapstick humour, as in the case of
Oakley's and Fortescue's brakeless decent to the inn on bicycle, is an unwelcome intrusion and clumsily handled with obvious use of stand-ins and poor
process work. And the big set-piece of Joanna's rescue from the cascading
river at the weir – an act of 'mortal peril' staged to reunite her parents – is less
a case of a 'frenzy of montage that recalls the Russian formalists' (Dixon 1997:
113) and more a *mélange* of unconvincing studio recreations, back-projection,
model-work and location inserts. The film also lacks an internal logic. While
the audience is asked to accept the existence of the ghostly Rhys and his
daughter, the séance staged by Alice Meadows in her desperation to make
contact with her son is debunked and ridiculed – something of a contradiction.[38] On balance, then, the merits of the film lie somewhere between the
two extremes indicated above.

One tendency of the new criticism is to over-praise the contribution of
associate producer Cavalcanti. It has long been recognised that Cavalcanti was
a central creative figure at Ealing and a crucial influence on the largely inexperienced directors that Balcon raised to office in the war period. However,
Ian Aitken surely goes too far in attributing all that has merit in the film to
the Brazilian. Aitken sees the film as an uneven mixture of the theatrical and
the cinematic, with Cavalcanti responsible for the latter virtues. He maintains
that

> His influence in *The Halfway House* can be found in particular stylistic
> effects, the treatment of acting performances, and the use of sound and
> image relationships, particularly during the séance scene . . . [Cavalcanti]
> managed to inject a degree of dark ambiguity into what would otherwise
> have been a rather stage-bound film. (Aitken 2000: 110)

Cavalcanti's significant contribution is acknowledged in the unusual case of
a shared title-card for associate producer and director, but it is best to see the
film as exemplary of that community of endeavour that reigned at Ealing
in the 1940s. Dearden and his producer clearly discussed the production
intimately, and key technicians like Wilkie Cooper the lighting cameraman
and art director Michael Relph also made significant contributions to the

creative process. However, it is most unlikely that Dearden stood aside while Cavalcanti shaped whole scenes, moulded individual performances or selected particular shots in the manner described by Aitken.[39]

While the film incorporates some beautifully picturesque shots of the countryside, which were much admired by contemporary critics, Dearden's most accomplished work was reserved for the interiors. Here, he was ably abetted by Michael Relph's solidly convincing and atmospheric recreation of a Welsh inn, whose space is used to reinforce dramatically the emotional turns of the characters. A good example is the short sequence after the evening meal. Rhys is clearing the table and Captain Meadows is consoling himself with a bottle of whisky. The scene begins with a high-angle wide-shot of the cluttered table with Meadows alone at the far end. Rhys comes into the shot and begins to clear the table, slowly moving up to the near end where he remains in unhurried conversation, trying to make Meadows see sense; the image is in deep focus, emphasising the isolation of the disgraced mariner. Dearden uses two shots to cut towards the figure of the desolate captain, culminating in a striking composition caught in deep space: the whisky bottle looms large in the foreground; Meadows hunched over in a brooding manner in the near middle ground; and Rhys who has moved into the background. It is an effective visual representation of the twin forces vying for the captain's soul.

This is followed by another impressive scene. Davies has accompanied Gwyneth into the kitchen to wash the dishes. In the most extreme example of deep focus in the film, Rhys is momentarily in the foreground and the other two characters are isolated in the far distance, partly obscured by solid masses of dark oak beams and other kitchen artefacts to announce their intention for intimacy. As Rhys exits the shot, Dearden cuts to Davies and Gwyneth at the sink. In a calm and comforting manner, she reveals to the musician that she knows of his illness and reassures him not to be afraid. She advises him to continue with his work on behalf of the war effort and he ends the conversation confidently asserting, 'Come on, let's get on with the job'. Cinematographer Wilkie Cooper lights the scene in a modestly expressionistic fashion, just enough to intimate at the otherworldly nature of the interaction, but not too much to overburden it with a sense of Gothic horror.[40]

The Halfway House was part of that tendency, emerging mid-war at Ealing, to reveal fissures in the edifice of national solidarity and unity. *Next of Kin* and *Went the Day Well?* had featured traitors in league with the enemy who had to be ruthlessly suppressed; *The Halfway House* a broader cross-section of characters who were actively against the national interest (criminals), were unwittingly harming the social fabric (warring families), or were simply absenting themselves from the fight (neutrals, ailing artists, bereaved parents). *The Halfway House* also introduced the newly fashionable expressionist style to

Ealing and this would become something of a feature of the work of Dearden and Relph at the Studio in the coming years. Their next film maintained the momentum as a drama of uncanny experiences, constructed in a stark experimental style and an even more ruthless treatment of wartime citizenship and its responsibilities.

THEY CAME TO A CITY (1944)

> I dream'd in a dream I saw a city: Invincible to the attacks of the whole of the rest of the earth. I dream'd that was the new city of friends. (Walt Whitman, 1860)

This adaptation of J. B. Priestley's successful play about the varied responses of a group of disparate characters to the prospect of a utopian socialist city is usually passed over as a worthy if dull production, compromised by over-theatrical treatment. In that sense, it is exemplary of the standard critical attitude towards the cinema of Dearden and Relph. Priestley wrote the two-act play in 1942, and it was first performed as the inaugural production of the People's Entertainment Society, a radical theatrical organisation which had been established by the Co-operative Movement to provide the public with 'a voice in ownership and control' in the commercial theatre (*The Co-operative News*, 31 January 1942). The play enjoyed a long provincial tour and later a successful run at the Globe Theatre, London, quickly establishing itself as a favourite of repertory theatre.[41] In his introduction to the published play, Priestley explained his reason for writing the drama:

> During the war I was impressed by the very different attitudes of mind that people had to any Post-War changes, which were then being widely discussed. It seemed to me there was a play in this . . . The unknown city gave me exactly what I wanted. (Priestley 1950: xi)

Given the 'mild revolution' that was taking place at Ealing it is unsurprising that the Studio should be attracted to this successful progressive drama. Priestley, through numerous radio broadcasts, a series of novels and some plays, was the individual most associated with the wartime mood of social reconstruction and transformation. His greatest impact had been achieved through his hugely popular *Postscripts*, broadcast on BBC Radio on Sunday nights after the news, in which he had forcefully expressed his characteristic theme of betterment through collectivity and commonwealth, and inaugurated a popular demand for social change (Nicholas 1995). He had worked at Ealing as early as 1934 in the days of Studio chief Basil Dean, co-scripting the popular musical-comedy *Sing As We Go*, which centred on unemployment and the Depression. More recently, new head Michael Balcon had invited Priestley to provide the story for *The Foreman Went to France* (1942). *They Came to a City* was scripted by Dearden in collaboration with Sidney Cole, the most notable Leftist at Ealing, an activist in the Association of Cine-Technicians and participant in the union's film work in the Spanish Civil War.[42] Cole had seen the play and, believing that it 'captured the mood of the moment', suggested to Balcon that Ealing make it into a film (McFarlane 1997: 137).[43] Of the scripting process, he recalls that he and Dearden went to see Priestley, who wasn't precious about his play and generously accepted the minor changes suggested by the screenwriters (Cole 1997: 263).[44]

Production commenced on *They Came to a City* in the first week of January 1944 and was completed only six weeks later (*The Cinema*, 12 January and 9 February 1944). With a small number of sets and the same cast who had played in the theatrical success, it was by all accounts a straightforward and untroubled production. The film was first screened to the film trade in August 1944 and released into provincial cinemas in September (*To-Day's Cinema*, 12 September 1944). It attracted generally favourable reviews. *To-Day's Cinema* considered it 'praiseworthy' and 'enthralling entertainment', but, potentially damaging for a popular film, felt its appeal to be restricted to the 'more thoughtful patronage' (18 August 1944). Similarly, the British edition of the *Motion Picture Herald* thought the film one for the discriminating exhibitor who 'will know how to put it over with his audience' (9 September 1944). *Film Report* took the same line, believing that the drama's timely message 'may not be apparent to the average cinemagoer' (25 August 1944). *The Times* considered the drama 'more impressive on the screen than it was on the stage' (31 January 1945); while *Monthly Film Bulletin* judged that the 'Direction, acting and photography are all excellent', but felt that overall the film was 'not true cinema as it is practically all talk and no action'. In what would become a common line in the film's critical reception, the *Bulletin* praised the worthiness of the production while deriding its hopeless utopianism and lack of cinematic style (September 1944).

By most accounts *They Came to a City* was not a commercial success and its box-office performance fell far short of what the play had achieved on the stage.[45] Balcon could not have been too surprised at this, as the production was comparatively experimental and potentially controversial. The film was shrewdly produced on a modest budget of around £24,000 and so was not a disaster for the small Studio. As the critics had predicted the film's success among discerning audiences, its commercial prospects were no doubt harmed by the delay of its release into the West End until February 1945.[46]

The film was a faithful adaptation of the play, losing some of the repetitive dialogue and 'opening up' the action of the stage version in only two

respects: the 'uncanny' deliverance of the characters onto the ramparts of the
city, which is retrospectively explained by the characters through dialogue in
the play, is visualised in the film;[47] and the addition of three short sequences:
a prologue; an insert between the two acts; and an epilogue, all featuring
Priestley telling the story related in the film to a young couple. Priestley has
been specific about the point of his drama, claiming that 'what is important in
the play is not the city but the respective attitudes of the characters towards
it' (Priestley 1950: xi).[48] An examination of these characters and their aspirations and prejudices provides a clear outline of the social reformist ideology of the drama and its conceptions regarding social morality and urban
reconstruction.

The prologue commences with a young couple (Ralph Michael and Brenda
Bruce) in service dress on a hillside above an industrial town. They are arguing
about the prospect for change after the war: the man is sceptical and the girl
idealistic.[49] Into the frame walks Priestley and the girl asks him his opinion. He
replies that some people will insist on change and others won't, and elaborates
on this observation in the form of a tale. The prologue then segues to the main
title and credits, and further onto the narrative proper, commencing with a
short sequence introducing each of the main characters and their 'uncanny'
transportation to the ramparts of the unnamed city.

The group is made up of a feisty waitress (Alice Foster – Googie Withers),
a 'bolshie' ship's hand, (Joe Dinmore – John Clements), a mother and daughter of the gentry class (Lady and Philippa Loxfield – Mabel Terry Lewis and
Frances Rowe), a white-collar employee of the West Midland Bank and
his wife (Malcolm and Dorothy Stritton – Raymond Huntley and Renée
Gadd), a charwoman (Mrs Batley), an aristocrat (Sir George Gedney – A. E.
Matthews) and a businessman (Cudworth – Norman Shelley). Some characters are demarcated along obvious class lines: Alice, Joe and Mrs Batley of the
working class on one side, and Sir George and Lady Loxfield of the upper
class on the other. The latter are sympathetically joined by the self-serving
Mr Cudworth and the snobbish Mrs Stritton; while Mr Stritton shows greater
natural empathy with the former group. Although Philippa Loxfield is dominated by her mother, she slowly comes under the spell of the city below and
what it might represent.[50]

Eventually, the group becomes aware of a closed doorway and their expectations are raised regarding access to the city below. Philippa and Alice are
convinced that something wonderful awaits them there; while Cudworth is
keen to exploit this opportunity for personal gain. In a forceful confrontation,
Joe accuses Cudworth of being a 'typical specimen of the boss class. Grab,
grab, grab – that's all they care about'. Meanwhile, Joe himself is undergoing
something of a crisis of faith and declares himself a 'revolutionary who can't

believe in the revolution', and, fearful of yet another disappointment, is wary about the promise of the city.[51] In a surprising revelation to Joe, Malcolm Stritton accuses the West Midland Bank of being 'completely out of date and an obstacle to true economic progress'.

As the first Act ends and the characters descend through the doorway to experience the city below, the scene returns to the hillside with Priestley and the service couple. The girl has grasped the significance of the fable and is vainly trying to explain to the man that the issue is not about 'bricks and mortar', but about how people organise themselves socially. Priestley confirms this, stating, 'It's a question of how people would react towards something that represented a new way of life'. In a key articulation of the ideals embodied in the drama, Priestley explains of his characters:

> They've had the privilege, we'll say, of seeing a city entirely owned and run by people who live in it, a place where men and women don't work for machines and money, but machines and money work for men and women, where everybody has a reasonable chance but no special privileges.[52]

As the man begins to grasp the significance of the events and the issues at stake, the scene returns to the open doorway on the ramparts. After a day in the city, the characters begin to emerge from the entrance and reveal their experiences in the city and their taste for community living. Cudworth, Sir George Gedney, Lady Loxfield and Mrs Stritton have had a wretched time and are desperate to return to their safe and ordered life. In contrast, Alice, Joe, Philippa, Mrs Batley and Mr Stritton are rhapsodic about their experience. In such a mood, Alice witnesses Mrs Stritton's hateful outburst and, indicative of the passions involved, claims she could 'kill her'. Joe is overwhelmed by his encounter with a 'really civilised city' and turns on the quartet of misanthropes and individualists, accusing them of failing to accept the need for social justice.

For the first time in her life Philippa is moved to defy her mother and, unwilling to return to a 'living death' in the genteel hotels of Bournemouth, decides to stay in the city. Lady Loxfield, failing in her appeal to her daughter's duty, is unable to overcome her distaste of social levelling and, after watching a jubilant Philippa descend to her new life, slowly ambles after Sir George and Cudworth and the certainties of a privileged life.

Mrs Stritton is equally drawn to the emotional blackmail of her husband, but unlike Lady Loxfield is successful. Malcolm is spellbound by the happy and decent people he has met and wishes to join and help them. However, he remains protective of his hysterical wife and reluctantly agrees to accompany her to their former dull life.

The most complex response to the ideal city comes from Joe and Alice. She wants to begin a new life with Joe in the wonderful city, but he sees the need to return to their former lives and preach the virtues of the city far and wide, in particular, to counter the negative impression that Cudworth and the others are bound to voice. He calms Alice's fear that 'It'll seem worse than ever when we get back', displaying a typically Priestleyan faith in 'the people' and their 'eternal desire and vision and hope of making this world a better place to live in':

> Not every man, nor every woman, wants to cry out for it, to work for it, to live for it, and if necessary die for it – but there's one here, one there, a few down this street, some more down that street – until you begin to see there are millions of us – yes armies and armies of us – enough to build ten thousand new cities.

Joe leads a tearful yet determined Alice away from the city and the scene dissolves back to Priestley and the young couple on the hillside. The man is now transformed by the vision and has clearly gained a sense of what he is fighting for in this war.[53] Priestley, his work done, rises and walks off towards the horizon. Overlaying this final image Joe speaks Whitman's famous lines: 'I dream'd in a dream I saw a city: Invincible to the attacks of the whole of the rest of the earth. I dream'd that was the new city of friends.'[54]

As a play and film, *They Came to a City* offered Priestley and Ealing a platform for their established (Priestley) and emergent (Ealing) radicalism. For the former, it was the vehicle to express what John Baxendale has called his 'overlap between the two force-fields of radical dissent and modernist planning' (2001: 89). For the latter, it was the most explicit expression of the Studio's wartime 'mild revolution'. In a thoroughgoing examination of Priestley's ideology, Baxendale sees the writer's distinctive vision in terms of 'the perfection of urban civilization' (ibid.: 89). As Priestley expressed it in *English Journey* (1934): 'Our business now was not to sentimentalise the Middle Ages, but to take the whole roaring machine-ridden world as it is and make a civilised job of it' (quoted in ibid.: 94).

In an important sense, the drama's vision of a utopian urban future was in tune with the aspirant idealism associated with the radical planning of Britain's blitzed cities (Hasegawa 1999).[55] Priestley loathed those corrupted and corrupting industrial towns that blighted the British landscape he had encountered in numbers on his *English Journey*. In 1942, he had a character in his novel *Blackout in Gretley* despair of the 'whole cynical industrial game':

> They were run up as cheaply as possible as money-making machines to provide people who never came near the places, with country mansions,

grouse moors, deer forests, yachts and winters in Cannes and Monte Carlo. In most other countries people simply wouldn't live in a town that offered them so little of what a town can offer. But the British can take it. I hoped they'd go on taking it until the day Hitler screamed for the last time, and that then they'd pull these damn places down and throw the bricks at the greedy old fakers who'd pop up to tell them they were now all poor again. (quoted in Henthorne 2004: 160)

It is in this vein that Priestley is determined not to let Cudworth, Gedney and Loxfield into the utopian city to pollute and corrupt it.

For Ealing, *They Came to a City* was its most radical wartime statement and it has not been appreciated how distinctive this production was for the Studio. Ealing's classic wartime films promoting a 'People's War' ethos – *The Foreman Went to France, Nine Men, San Demetrio London* – work by bringing together a disparate group of individuals and forging them into a team. Through the mythic promotion of consensus, solidarity and shared endeavour, class and regional boundaries are dissolved and national unity achieved. Significantly, *They Came to a City* resolutely refused to perform the act of harmonisation that had been central to these dramas as well as the propaganda of *The Halfway House*. The contrasting individuals fail to unite as a whole, largely remain divided by class and outlook, and include characters – a financier, elite types and a snobbish and spiteful bourgeois woman – who refuse to participate in a commonwealth.

Distinctively, *They Came to a City* conforms to the later viewpoint of revisionist historians who perceive a more divided wartime Britain, wherein self-interest and privilege are not swept aside for the duration and class relations remain antagonistic and inflexible (Rose 2003). While previous films such as *The Foreman Went to France, Next of Kin* and *Went the Day Well?* had featured isolated and individual cases of traitors among the upper classes; no other film approached the matter so schematically, with a host of characters from the middle class, the gentry and the aristocracy articulating their structural contempt for a socialist commonwealth. In the grasping plutocrat and the propertied classes Priestley had his stock characters of scorn, derided in numerous wartime broadcasts, speeches and publications as obstacles to victory and freedom.

However, the drama was founded on no simple Us (lower orders) and Them (upper classes) divide, and Priestley was perceptive enough to have a member of both the middle class (Mr Stritton) and the privileged class (Philippa Loxfield) wanting to stay in the city and embrace its communal values. These two characters, roughly in their thirties, were precisely the types radicalised in wartime Britain, who, like Balcon and his colleagues, voted Labour for the first time in 1945.[56]

Unsurprisingly, the greatest critical champion of the film was *The Daily Worker*, which found the production 'one of the most enterprising efforts ever made in the British cinema' and praised it as a 'very definite reminder that the new Britain must be fought for and won despite all the obstacles and discouragement' (quoted in Richards 1997: 24–5). This uncommonly generous view of the film has been recently reasserted by Tony Williams, who believes its vision to be 'one of the most outstanding achievements in British cinema' (2000: 85). Indeed, it is the film's radical theme and historicity that mark its lasting interest. The modest budget ensured that the production would be theatrical in approach and declamatory in style. However, despite these drawbacks, reviewers were generally complimentary of Dearden's direction and Relph's design, which were felt to have brought the best out of the actors and captured the distinctive mood of the drama. Moreover, in an abrupt reversal of his original critical attitude to the film, Charles Barr no longer sees the theatrical stylisation of the film as a 'problem', that in fact Dearden was both 'bold' and 'artful' in foregrounding the mechanics of the original stage drama through having Priestley in the film 'summoning up' a cast to play out his themes (1993: 186).

DEAD OF NIGHT (1945)

We appear to attribute an 'uncanny' quality to impressions that seek to confirm the omnipotence of thought and the animistic mode of thinking in general, after we have reached a stage at which, in our judgement, we have abandoned such beliefs. (Sigmund Freud, *Totem and Taboo*, 1913)

'This is ghost-story telling with a vengeance!' (Ivan Butler 1967: 78)

Producers and distributors had been steered away from horror films during the war when their macabre themes had been unwelcome. Ealing's *Dead of Night*, which went into production early in 1945, was the first film to take advantage of the relaxation in attitudes and has since been recognised as British cinema's 'first significant entry into the sphere of the supernatural' (Butler 1967: 73); the 'first important recognisably British horror film' (Hutchings 1993: 24). The Studio was looking for new directions and the idea of an anthology of ghost stories would display the all-round talents of the creative teams that had been built up at the Studio (Balcon 1969: 157).[57] The intention had been to dramatise a number of the well-known tales by M. R. James, but on reflection these seemed to lack a requisite visual quality and the film combined new with original dramas. It was announced that the film was to be directed by an 'ace team' of directors and would 'boast one of the strongest casts ever assembled for a British film' (*Kinematograph Weekly*, 25 January 1945).[58]

Cavalcanti was responsible for 'The Ventriloquist's Dummy' and 'Children's Party' episodes; Robert Hamer directed 'The Haunted Mirror' sequence; Charles Crichton the comic 'Golfing Story'; and Dearden handled the 'Hearse Driver' and linking story. The film gathered generally excellent reviews and there was widespread praise for the writing, direction, music and acting. For the *Observer*, it was a film you 'must see'; a '*tour de force*', 'so obviously the result of harmonious team work' (9 September 1945). According to the *Daily Sketch*, 'This is a British film that deserves a success – for it has originality and distinction, and it does what its sets out to do: it makes the flesh creep' (7 September 1945). *Monthly Film Bulletin* described it as the 'smoothest film yet to come from an English studio' (30 September 1945) – a singular compliment given the inherently disjointed nature of the project. The film was a considerable commercial success.

Many reviewers singled out 'The Ventriloquist's Dummy' for special praise, with honourable mention for the 'The Haunted Mirror' and the welcome light relief of the 'Golfing Story'. Few critics picked out Dearden's 'Hearse Driver', while the linking story attracted mixed views. More recently, the whimsy of H. G. Wells' 'Golfing Story' (originally published as *The Story of the Inexperienced Ghost*, 1902) has been decidedly rejected, and following the influential readings by Pirie (1973: 23–4) and Barr (1977: 55–8), critical favour has centred on 'The Haunted Mirror', with its story of repression and intense sexual jealousy making it a distinctive text in the Ealing canon. More recently, Aitken has redirected critical emphasis onto Cavalcanti's 'The Ventriloquist's Dummy', and in the modern manner of seeking out transgressive potential, argues that 'its emphasis on mental illness, self-obsession, and implicit sado–masochism and homosexuality, is deeply subversive of Balconian mores' (Aitken 2000: 158). It is common to see these two episodes as the most powerful in a film that 'lifts the lid on the forces of sex, violence and fantasy which Ealing's wartime project had kept almost out of sight' (Barr 1986: 18).

Dearden's 'Hearse Driver' sequence, the briefest of the tales, offered the director little scope for the kind of imaginative treatment and thematic complexity of either 'The Haunted Mirror' or 'The Ventriloquist's Dummy'; while the linking story has been unduly ignored, with the consequent failure to recognise the brilliant execution of this sequence and its centrality to the larger drama.[59] Associate producer Sidney Cole recalls that the film was essentially shot by two parallel teams working in friendly rivalry: Dearden and Crichton on one side and Cavalcanti and Hamer on the other. Aitken has predictably concluded that 'Friendly rivalry there may have been, but, given the superiority of talent in the latter team, this was a contest which could only ever have had one winner' (2000: 152). This rigid demarcation ignores the centrality of Dearden's linking story and its interaction with each of the individual episodes in turn and characteristically avoids any critical focus on this significant sequence.

The framing narrative, loosely derived from E. F. Benson's *The Room in the Tower* (1912), sets the scene perfectly for the presentation of a series of supernatural tales. An architect, Walter Craig (Mervyn Johns), visiting Pilgrim's Farm in Kent, announces to the guests assembled in the sitting room that he has experienced all of these events previously in a recurring dream. Dr van Straaten (Frederick Valk), a continental psychoanalyst, offers a perfectly rational explanation derived from Freudian first principles, and is then challenged by each of the guests in turn with a strange and inexplicable occurrence. The ensuing serial conflict between Freudian psychoanalysis and the uncanny manifestation of the paranormal is superbly rich in interpretative potential with its dramatic fabric of dread, anxiety, foreknowledge, repression and oneiric metaphor.

First to come to Craig's defence is Hugh Grainger (Anthony Baird), who relates the story of the 'Hearse Driver'. The purpose of this tale is to provide some credibility for Craig through the recounting of a further case of premonition and therefore serves a fairly utilitarian function. It was based on E. F. Benson's short story *The Bus-Conductor* (1906), about a confident man-about-town who is sceptical of the supernatural, but has to concede to a friend a decidedly uncanny experience he has had. This is transposed in the film to the recounting of the story by Grainger to the psychoanalyst, with the significant addition that the act of premonition follows a near-death crash while motor racing. We first encounter Grainger delirious in a clinic, and this fact, coupled with first-person narration, flashback structure and some explicit point-of view camerawork, marks a high degree of subjectivity. One evening, at 9.45 pm, when Grainger is settling to go to sleep, he becomes aware of a sudden stillness and silence. Inexplicably, his clock reads 4.15 am; he approaches his window and drawing back the curtains is amazed to discover a bright, sunlit day and ominously located below him, a hearse. The driver looks up at him and announces: 'Just room for one inside, Sir.' Grainger backs into his hospital room in some distress, and seated on his bed glances at the clock which now reads 9.50 pm, while the sounds of the evening slowly build on the soundtrack.[60] His doctor explains away the affair as the 'psychological crisis' resulting from the crash; that is, the resurfacing of Grainger's expectation of death at the time of the accident. Within a week a much recovered Grainger is released from the clinic and, about to board a bus, he recognises the conductor as the driver of the hearse. He freezes at the comment: 'Just room for one inside, Sir.' He is then witness to the bus veering off the road and crashing down a steep embankment.

Van Straaten, echoing the diagnosis of the previous doctor, explains the experience as an obsession arising from the crash, and given the construction of the sequence one wouldn't argue with him. The whole is strongly overlaid with subjectivity and simply could be the imaginings of the delirious patient; or, on the evening in question, Grainger has fallen into a half-sleep, precisely that time when the unconscious mind is likely to rise to dominance. Importantly, for the unfolding drama at Pilgrim Farm, it is not a resounding victory for the supernatural and further challenges are necessary to be put to the rational 'man of science'.

Dearden turns in an efficient translation of this slight story and manages to get enough out of a somewhat colourless performer, although one writer on the horror film singled out this episode for particular praise and felt that the 'sense of eeriness is most beautifully caught in this little cameo' (Butler 1967: 75). The possibilities of the linking narrative are altogether a much more appetising challenge for the director and he makes full use of them. In a further rare defence of Dearden, Butler makes the prescient observation that 'The linking story is handled with a skill apt to be overshadowed by the more flamboyant episodes' (1967: 77). As the weight of evidence for the paranormal accumulates and Craig becomes increasingly anxious, the claustrophobia of the sitting room is intensified; the heavy oak-beamed ceiling becomes more dominant in the compositions; and expressionistic shadows are cast around the room by a fire, now the principal light source in the scene. Dearden keeps the characters in constant motion in the tight set, persistently reframing as the narrative line moves from one to another, thus relieving the potential boredom of static compositions and marking the rising anxiety in the scene.[61]

After van Straaten has recounted the case-history of dual personality in 'The Ventriloquist's Dummy', the drama is set for its dénouement. All of Craig's predictions have been realised and he fatalistically submits to an irresistible force driving him towards 'unspeakable evil'. The expressionism is heightened as Craig enacts his compulsion of murdering van Straaten; the scene then segues into an intensely subjective sequence of Craig's madness, a phantasmagoria of unbalanced angles, chiaroscuro lighting and rapid camera movements, as he feverishly interacts with each of the supernatural dramas that have been previously related. The sequence culminates with Craig being strangled by the ventriloquist's dummy in a prison cell, and the rapid pulling back of the camera dissolves into the seeming present of Craig awaking from a nightmare. The celebrated twist of the story is that the architect is about to re-experience the events of the drama as he accepts an invitation to visit Pilgrim's Farm.[62]

The uncertain ground between objectivity and subjectivity in the film allows for virtually endless speculation and interpretative possibility. The (only partly sarcastic) comment of one of the characters – 'We none of us exist at

all. We're nothing but characters in Mr Craig's dream' – alludes to the tenta-
tive materiality on display, and there is no firm reason to believe that things
are otherwise and that we ever leave the confines of a dream. Aitken is surely
right when he states: '*Dead of Night* undermines the rule of reason itself, and
remains fundamentally inexplicable' (2000: 160). As with *The Halfway House*
and *They Came to a City*, *Dead of Night* has a pronounced self-reflexive quality,
marked, for example, by the comment following one of van Straaten's refuta-
tions of the paranormal: 'Well, I must say, it's very disappointing – not to be
one of the leading characters in a sort of supernatural drama, after all.' This
dimension has been most thoroughly explored by Hutchings, who unravels
a complex arrangement of looking/seeing and vision in *Dead of Night*. This
concern is tellingly present in the detail of van Straaten obsessively taking off
and putting on his spectacles; the smashing of these glasses making possible the
'victory' of the forces of the supernatural through rendering the psychiatrist
impotent and defenceless.

The really novel and exciting aspect of the film is the integration of the
traditional British ghost story – classically realised in the form of the telling
of supernatural tales – with the contemporary interest in psychoanalysis. The
prominence of the psychoanalytic dimension in *Dead of Night* has never been
thoroughly explored, and unfortunately there is not sufficient space here to
offer a developed discussion. However, what is crucial to recognise is the centrality of the linking story to this dimension of the narrative and how it invites
Freudian interpretation of both the individual stories and the wider film.[63]
The Final Shooting Script had foregrounded the Freudian element even more
prominently and included a decidedly knowing confrontation between Craig
and van Straaten, wherein the former, with irony, apologises that his nightmare 'sounds awfully childish'; while van Straaten asserts: 'The operations of
the unconscious mind are childish. Infantile, in fact' (7). Unfortunately, this
allusion to Freudian dogma didn't make it to the release print and the film
makes no direct attempt to explore the possibility of repressed incestuous
desire.[64] However, the very nature of a nightmare vision, precognitive experiences, *déjà vecu* (the sensation that the present moment has been lived through
before) and multiple personality disorder classically leading to murder are
open invitations to psychoanalytic interpretations of the text.[65] The characterisations and the drama within the linking story structure this potential, and
Dearden and Relph's brilliance in constructing this crucial sequence should be
acknowledged and applauded.

Hutchings has argued that the wider social meaning of the film is bound up
with male trauma and neurosis resulting from wartime experience: 'Seen in
this way, the film is a complex imagining of a gender crisis, one which focuses
in particular on fears, anxieties and uncertainties about the role of the male in

a postwar British society' (1993: 33–4). Thus, Grainger, the man of action, is emasculated and immobilised, dependent on the care of his nurse, with whom he will marry and settle down. In a wider sense, the structuring narrative of Craig's nightmare could be conceived as deriving from a wartime trauma, the result of intense bombing or injury in combat.[66] Furthermore, the almost complete restriction of the narrative to domestic spaces dominated by several strong females further emphasises the problems for masculinity and sexuality suggested by the film. These are concerns that Dearden will take forward in an aspect of his cinema of the post-war decade, where a partial shift occurs, away from the public sphere and social focus of the wartime films towards a more private and interior realm where repression and anxiety can registered in the confrontation with social change.

THE CAPTIVE HEART (1946)

Memory deals with peaks, not plains. We remember the days when the mail came better than the days when it didn't. Thus we will remember the comradeship, the freedom of mind, the rare moments of community spirit; we will forget the wet days, the wet weeks, the days when it was an effort to do anything, the days when it was an effort to do nothing and our bunks seemed the only escape. (Guy Morgan, Prisoner of War, 1944–45, 1945: 132)

Although put into production after the conflict in Europe was over, *The Captive Heart* stands as a monument to the wartime ethos of community and sacrifice portrayed so markedly at Ealing. It is also a measure of how far Dearden had come as a filmmaker at the Studio in the period: from contributing to scripts on George Formby comedies he was now heading the creative team on a prestige production with an extensive cast. This was also the first film for which Relph was raised to associate producer, while additionally serving as art director. The idea for a film commemorating the endurance of prisoners of war had been suggested to Balcon by his wife, Aileen, who served in the British Red Cross and had listened to the stories of returning POWs (Balcon 1969: 144). A 'reconnaissance party' was assembled and sent out to Germany in July 1945; it consisted of Dearden, Cavalcanti, Relph, cinematographer Douglas Slocombe, chief engineer Eric Williams and Hal Mason the studio manager.[67] It was reported in the trade press that, 'The object of the expedition is to find an actual prisoner-of-war camp where the life of the British prisoners can be reconstructed authentically' (*Daily Film Renter*, 5 July 1945). The party was hosted by No. 21 Army Group and travelled some 2,000 miles searching for locations, eventually settling on the former

Studio set for *The Captive Heart* (1946) (Courtesy of Simon Relph)

POW camp at Westertimke as the main base of operations.[68] After some understandable logistical problems, the main film unit arrived from England and was expertly put into order by Hal Mason. Officers of the 51st Highland Division performed as background players, while German prisoners acted as casual labour. The crew worked for two months in extremely testing conditions and Dearden testified to the 'great spirit of co-operation that existed in the unit' (1946: 7).

Following a court action over the disputed use of the title *Lovers' Meeting*, the film was eventually released as *The Captive Heart* in April 1946 (*Kinematograph Weekly*'s, 18 October and 20 December 1945). It received its première at the Odeon, Leicester Square in the presence of the Princess Royal and in aid of the Victory Ex-Services Club Fund (*The Times*, 14 March 1946). There was high regard for the scenes of men in captivity and the 'impressive and deeply moving picture of this comradeship under duress'. As the *Monthly Film Bulletin* continued, it was 'a moving, sincere and often beautifully directed picture and should take its place among our more exceptional war films' (April 1946). C. A. Lejeune, felt it had been presented 'quietly, factually, and without hate. It strives for truth rather than sensation; it is content to rely on the sympathies, and not the passions, of the spectator . . . I can imagine no one in this country who will not be deeply moved by its many incidents' (Lejeune 1947: 178). However, there was not unqualified praise for the film. Many reviewers were hostile to the 'artificial stories' imposed on the realistic drama of captivity, namely the scenes presented in flashback of the men's memories and longings of home, which tended to 'disintegrate the whole into episodic and unconvincing pieces' (*The Times*, 29 March 1946). In a nutshell: 'Where *The Captive Heart* fails is in its effort to compromise between fiction and fact' (Lejeune 1947: 178).[69]

The melodramatic fabrications of the film were unfavourably compared with the truthful realism of prisoner life which seemed to inform the memoirs that were published soon after the war's end; and it was felt that it was 'too much to expect that the commercial cinema can penetrate into the subtleties which made J. R. Ackerley's *Prisoners of War* a neglected masterpiece' (*The Times*, 29 March 1946). In fact, considerable effort was directed at making all elements in *The Captive Heart* realistic. Guy Morgan, a former journalist and POW, co-authored the script with Angus MacPhail (adapted from a story by Patrick Kirwan), and his own memoir of captivity published in 1945, *Only Ghosts Can Live*, demonstrates the authenticity of most of the events depicted in the film. Furthermore, the military adviser on the film, Major Guy Adams DSO, had been a prisoner in Germany for four years, eighteen months of that served at the very camp at Westertimke used as the location in the film; and Dearden praised him as 'a pillar of strength to us throughout the Ealing Campaign' (Dearden 1946: 3).[70]

Despite the misgivings of the critics regarding the accuracy of the representation in the film, it is the quality of honesty and truthfulness in *The Captive Heart* that so forcibly strikes the modern viewer schooled in the *Boy's Own* excess of later prisoner-of-war films, like *The Colditz Story* (d. G. Hamilton, 1955) and *Danger Within* (d. D. Chaffey, 1959), with their dominating narratives of escape.[71] Indeed, escaping became central to the mythology of British POWs held in Nazi Germany, with its attendant understated heroism and absurd sense of humour, when in fact 'Privation, boredom, uncertainty, occasional danger, and much else besides made POW life for most men resemble an endurance test rather than a light-hearted game' (MacKenzie 2004: 2). It is these latter, more mundane qualities that are foregrounded in *The Captive Heart* and while many of these elements were acclaimed by the critics, those that were dismissed as contrived were in fact part of the emotional and psychological reality of captivity for British servicemen.[72]

The opening credit sequence is played over shots of men of the defeated British Expeditionary Force on their forced march into captivity in June 1940. Something of the notorious pain and brutality of 'The March', as it became known, is captured in the imagery and performances. The narrator informs the viewer:

> This film is dedicated to prisoners of war. Their unbroken spirit is the symbol of a moral victory for which no bells have pealed . . . It was a war in which no decorations could be given, but to have come out of it with a whole spirit is its highest honour.

Douglas Slocombe captures the scenes with a deliberately low camera, suggesting the dejection of the men and introducing a main motif of the film, the big sky that is to hang over the captives for five long years, dominating a restricted visual horizon. Such introductory scenes of capture, interrogation, transit and processing would be largely ignored in the later 'mythical' treatments of POWs, yet the experience 'ranked for many prisoners as one of the most testing of their entire time in enemy hands' (MacKenzie 2004: 64). The sequence is punctuated by the memories of some of the soldiers who naturally let their minds wander back to their families and loved ones in England; such digressions spoilt the purity of the realistic depiction of the men under duress for many critics.

Many of the scenes of camp life and daily routine depicted in the film are already present in Morgan's earlier memoir, testified to in numerous other published accounts and confirmed in authoritative histories.[73] The attention to detail in *The Captive Heart* is impressive and the investment in the long and difficult demands of location was clearly rewarded. Lejeune details the scenes which critics generally accepted as veridical and pertinent:

> Whenever it deals with ordinary people, people we know and under-
> stand and can believe in, like the Cockney corporal (Jack Warner), with
> his little house in Hammersmith, the Welsh private (Mervyn Johns),
> tending his vegetables and his rabbits, or the wholly human major (Basil
> Radford), who keeps his men in good heart without losing one inch in
> stature; whenever it shows British soldiers reacting to foreign conditions
> in their own peculiarly racial way, the picture is strong and true and
> moving. (Lejeune 1947: 178)[74]

What were valued in these scenes were the qualities of restraint, understate-
ment and humour, believed to be so typical of the wartime national spirit and
character. As we have seen, though, there was a tendency to divide the picture
sharply into two halves, 'one original and very good, the other conventional
and silly' (Hammond n.d.: 56). Exemplary of this so-called bogus material
infiltrating an 'honest story' was the

> completely phony story about a Czech refugee who has taken the name
> and identity of a dead British captain. The device compels him to carry
> on a correspondence with the captain's wife, to fall in love with her
> photograph, and in the end to go back to England and presumably marry
> her. (Lejeune 1947: 178)[75]

Much of the criticism centred on the scenes involving the family and loved
ones of the men, usually introduced through the mechanism of receiving and
sending letters. The effect was dismissed as melodramatic and irritating and
'makes us long to get back to the prisoners, back to real people' (Noble 1946:
10). However, all those POWs who recorded their experience testified to the
crucial importance of mail from and contact with home. According to Guy
Morgan:

> If food was the first topic of conversation, mail (or lack of it) was the
> second, followed in a debatable order by the Second Front, post-war
> plans, 'Old So and So', service reminiscence, and, a bad last, sex. (1945:
> 122)[76]

Letters provided news for men starved of information; but more important
emotionally, they offered direct contact to a life at home, confirming its materiality and continuance, and dampened despair and hopelessness. Robert Kee
captured the essence of this when he wrote:

> Letters were fantastic tricks of the imagination, tangible messages
> received from the world of day dreams. As with all good day dreams you
> were confident that one day this world would materialise and yet at the
> same time it seemed as unattainable as another planet. So letters were

unearthly and invaluable, even if they only came from Barclays Bank.
([1947] 1990: 70)

While the critics did not deny the importance of mail *per se*, they were ungenerous in not allowing for an emotional response from the captives, who in all likelihood were going to use some of their abundant time to reflect on their loved ones, worry about their safety and fidelity, and long to rejoin them and the comforts of home life.[77] It was entirely pertinent of the producers to evoke the mechanism of correspondence as the thread binding camp with home and the motivation for the men to dwell on their other lives.

It was generally felt that Dearden had caught exactly the right mood and effect in the camp scenes: the gentle humour, quiet fortitude and unconquerable spirit of the men; the essential Britishness of the characterisations; the proper measure of emotional display, presented with tact and restraint, and carefully guarded from degenerating into hysterical outbursts. Special mention was made of the handling of the scene of the first arrival of the Red Cross parcels, the dreadful news broken to Private Matthews (Gordon Jackson) that he has been permanently blinded, the gentle montage sequences of the men rehearsing for drama productions, playing cricket and tending their cottage gardens scraped from the unpromising earth, of Evans quietly listening to the news of his wife's death in childbirth while he strokes the ears of an Angora rabbit, the tense scene of helping the Czech Hasek to escape among some repatriated men, and the subdued but moving reunion of Corporal Horsfall with his wife on the front step of their small house.

With *The Captive Heart*, Dearden was judged to have fulfilled his earlier promise and had 'emerged as a leading film-maker with his direction of one of Ealing's most successful pictures to date' (Newnham 1946: 40). The film was a considerable popular success and the sixth Bernstein questionnaire, issued in December 1946, placed *The Captive Heart* third in popularity in a poll of Granada cinema patrons: 56 per cent considered the film 'outstanding'; 35 per cent judged it as 'good'; and only 1 per cent dismissed it as 'bad' (digested in Miller 1948: 217–19).

Basil Dearden and Michael Relph proved themselves considerable talents at Ealing in the wartime period. As head of the Art Department, Relph had raised design at the Studio to new heights, while his individual work on such productions as *Champagne Charlie* (1944) and *Dead of Night* brought him recognition as a leading art director in British film. Dearden also began to attract some critical recognition; having graduated from 'working to a formula' on the Hay comedies, he was now demonstrating himself 'possessed of a sure touch and a personality of his own'. Critic John K. Newnham was impressed by the director's engagement in a 'series of widely and different experimental subjects such as *The Halfway House, They Came to a City*, the hearse sequence in *Dead of Night*, and then *The Captive Heart*'. From such pictures 'it can be seen that he has shown himself, so far, to excel in subjects rather than personalities, but the human touches in *The Captive Heart* gave a strong hint that he is developing into a director who can handle pictures possessing great emotional appeal' (1946: 40–1). It was unusual to find someone even partly differentiating Basil Dearden from the 'norm' or 'baseline' of production at Ealing, and it hasn't been sufficiently recognised that the director worked up a distinctive approach within the conventional demands of production practised at the Studio. While *The Bells Go Down* and *The Captive Heart* conformed perfectly to the 'surface naturalism and empirical behaviour' of the wartime propaganda films, *The Halfway House* and *They Came to a City* did not unproblematically fit that 'ideal world where men and women of all classes lived and worked harmoniously together, untroubled by the economic and class differences which existed in the real world'. Moreover, Dearden's fundamental contribution of the linking story to *Dead of Night*, with its prominent Freudian elements and anxious interiority, makes nonsense of the bald claim that 'The only Ealing films where the worlds of the subconscious and reality interact are the comedies' (Porter 1983: 206). Dearden and Relph were clearly established as a team on *The Captive Heart* and they would continue to complement each other in their Ealing films of the post-war period, wherein the darker vision that had surfaced in their wartime cinema would continue to play its part. The strains and anxieties that are articulated in *Dead of Night*, regarding, in particular, the role of the male in post-war society, would continue to figure in the cinema of Dearden and Relph in a series of dramas of masculine adjustment continuing through to the demise of Ealing in the mid-1950s and beyond.

NOTES

1. As well as the five feature films treated here, Dearden, as writer and director, contributed to the programme of propaganda shorts undertaken by the Studio and under the eventual stewardship of Cavalcanti (*The Times*, 10 February 1940; *Kinematograph Weekly*'s, 8 January 1942 and 18 February 1943).
2. Barr similarly identifies *San Demetrio London* as exemplary of Ealing's wartime project (Charles Barr 1974a: 99–103).
3. See Relph's comments on the influence of Cavalcanti on the direction Ealing took during the war (1990).
4. The lecture was published as a pamphlet by the Workers' Film Association in 1943.
5. Untypically, Andrew Higson (1984) includes *The Bells Go Down* among the five films he uses for discussing wartime cinema, but in an exploratory paper it receives little attention.

6. Details taken from '*The Bells Go Down' Exhibitors' Campaign Sheet* and *Kinematograph Weekly* (8 January 1942). The script was written by Roger MacDougall, who was intermittently used by Ealing in the 1940s.

7. *Kine Weekly* reported the popular Petticoat Lane traders, who appeared in the Sunday market scenes: Joe Assenheim (ice cream), J. Levy (gowns), Syd Zargel (shoes), Mike Stern (bed linen), Arnold's china and J. Harris (watches) (30 July 1942).

8. Details taken from *Kinematograph Weekly*'s (4 June, 25 June, 30 July, 20 August, 17 September and 8 October 1942).

9. Details taken from *The Times* (14 April 1943), *The Cinema* (21 April 1943), *Kinematograph Weekly* (22 April 1943).

10. As one hard-pressed diarist expressed it: 'Not much sense saving it up in note-books for a future novel. Better get it down quick' (quoted in Hewison 1988: 42).

11. Details given in *The Times* (23 September 1941).

12. A production report in *Kine Weekly* stated that the adaptation 'has necessarily been toned down considerably from its original ruthless candour' (30 July 1942).

13. This film also used an AFS diarist, M. L. Richardson, as script consultant. The celebrated director Humphrey Jennings had been a founder of Mass Observation in the 1930s.

14. The script is dated April 1942.

15. The phrase originates with Bill Nichols and is invoked by Brian Winston (1999: 61).

16. The main body of the review deals with what it clearly considers the embarrassing presence of Trinder. *The Times* (15 April 1943).

17. The standard critical view even overcame Relph, who later claimed *Fires Were Started* to be a far more important film (1990). It was also his recollection that the film was 'not successful' at the box office (correspondence with authors 19 February 2004).

18. The *Final Shooting Script* is explicit on how this scene must be played: '[Ted's] attitude towards the AFS, though apparently scathing, is based on competitive rivalry which extends even into conversation. When Ted, therefore, cracks at them, it must not be forgotten that he is wise-cracking' (17).

19. The *Final Shooting Script* includes a scene where the AFS men confront MacFarlane and request equal treatment. The District Officer declares this a 'mutiny' and dismisses the volunteers as 'a bunch of lazy good-for-nothing shirkers' (103–4). The confrontation is defused when Ted bursts in with the news that Hitler has invaded Norway. This material was presumably thought too strong to include in the release print.

20. The *Final Shooting Script* includes two shots of Sam's criminal accomplice imprisoned in a cell on the evening of 7 September 1940 and reacting in 'uncontrolled terror' to the commencement of the Blitz, while other shots in the sequence show the fortitude of the local citizens who come out to protect their community. This

was cut from the release print along with some shots of nervous shelterers, of enemy planes disgorging bombs and a wounded fireman (112–14).

21. Green's 'psychopathologies of sex' did face some difficulties with the printer, who requested various bowdlerisations, fearing action from the Ministry of Labour which controlled paper supplies. See Jeremy Treglown's 'Introduction' to the edition published by Harvill (1991).

22. Dearden would make even greater use of these locations in *Pool of London* (1951).

23. It had been announced in the production schedule for 1943 that Dearden's next film for Ealing after *My Learned Friend* would be *Blackthorn Winter*, a story of British agriculture between the wars written by Roger MacDougall. The production never materialised and the director was switched to *The Halfway House* (*Kinematograph Weekly*, 14 January 1943).

24. Details taken from *Kinematograph Weekly*'s (6 May, 13 May and 24 June 1943).

25. Rosay had appeared in such distinguished French films as *La Kermesse héroïque* (1935) and *Un carnet de bal* (1937).

26. The screenplay was by Angus Macphail and Diana Morgan. Clarke and Roland Pertwee were provided with the credit 'Script Contribution'.

27. The acclaimed actress featured heavily in the marketing of the film; see the one-page promotion Ealing took out in *Kinematograph Weekly* (4 November 1943). An entirely different version of the events involving Rosay is presented by Aitken (2000: 109). Drawing on a study of Cavalcanti published in Italy, he reports that Rosay approached the Brazilian for a role and he generously worked her into the script, but that ultimately she was disappointed with her part and contributed a laboured performance. All this is contradicted by Clarke, who recalls that Rosay was extremely grateful for the opportunity and generously supported the inexperienced writer, and ignores the fact that her performance was widely praised at the time.

28. Details taken from *The Cinema* (2 February and 5 April 1944), *To-Day's Cinema* (15 August 1944).

29. According to Michael Relph, the film was a popular success (correspondence with authors, 19 February 2004). See also the list of attendances for specific cinemas published in *To-Day's Cinema* (15 August 1944).

30. Viewers are made aware of the apparitional nature of the inn and its hosts well in advance of the characters.

31. See the four pages of promotion in *To-Day's Cinema* where the film is announced as 'The Problem Film of 1944' (8 February 1944). Michael Balcon's comment, made in 1946, that the film was one of the British wartime 'non-propagandist escapist film comedies' is curiously wide of the mark (Balcon 1971: 71).

32. The original play had been set on a more sinister Dartmoor; while The Halfway House is located at the reassuringly sounding Cwm Bach (Dear Valley).

33. The following year Powell made *I Know Where I'm Going* (1945), a title resonant of Rhys's announcement, wherein a strident young woman only comes to realise her true desires through an encounter with the Celtic landscape and its traditions.

34. The vicar was played by Esmond Knight, the only actor to appear in both play and film.
35. The credits state that *The Halfway House* was 'suggested' by *The Peaceful Inn*, reflecting the significant shift in material and emphasis. The adaptation is more thoroughly explored by Colin Sell (2006). The play was also adapted for BBC radio in the 1940s.
36. The phrase is used in the publicity material presented in *To-Day's Cinema* (8 February 1944).
37. These views come in the wake of the critical reappraisal of Michael Powell and such astonishingly self-reflexive films as *A Matter of Life and Death* (1946).
38. Spiritualism was a highly topical issue and there had recently occurred the sensational conviction of Helen Duncan under The Witchcraft Act 1735. See Collins (1945).
39. The sense of teamwork is what comes through in Clarke's account of the production. Dearden's copy of the *Final Shooting Script* is characteristically annotated in minute detail – detailing shot set-ups, blocking of actors etc. – and confirms the director's intimate involvement with planning the scenes.
40. These two scenes, and the later scene of the séance, with their prominent low ceilings, deep focus compositions, extreme camera angles and expressionism, reveal the clear influence of *Citizen Kane* (d. Welles, 1941).
41. A rather cautious review of the London production can be found in *The Times* (22 April 1943).
42. Cole worked on *Spanish ABC* (1938) and *Behind Spanish Lines* (1938).
43. Cole also acted as associate producer on *They Came to a City*.
44. The screen credits listing Priestley as a contributor to the screenplay are probably a courtesy. Durgnat is way off beam when he suggests that *They Came to a City* was a 'repudiation of the Welfare State, although Priestley, in view of his political opinions, presumably meant only to repudiate its colourless uniformity' (1966: 28).
45. It is Relph's recollection that the film was 'quite successful'; however, it is possible that he is confusing it with the stage production (correspondence with authors, 19 February 2004).
46. The film had a troubled time in distribution, with Kemp (1998) arguing that the film was denied access to the major circuits because of its radical content and that this ultimately led to Ealing's partial absorption into the Rank empire. For a less sensational reassessment of the circumstances, see Burton (2009).
47. The filmmakers use the device of an unexpected 'blackout', familiar from wartime experience.
48. Many reviewers missed this point and saw it as a fault that the film didn't give a glimpse of the utopian city.
49. The hillside above a town was *the* characteristic location for such discussions in British wartime films, as, for example, with the deliberations about the future between Charlie Forbes (Eric Portman) and Jennifer Knowles (Anne Crawford) in *Millions Like Us*.
50. The anticipatory Philippa is the first to see the city below as it comes into view following the parting of clouds.

51. Philip Kemp perceptively suggests that Joe might have fought in Spain (1998: 46).
52. In the play, this speech is given to Joe just before he concludes the drama with his recitation of Walt Whitman.
53. In the *Final Shooting Script*, the man is described as serving in the Eighth Army – harbinger of victory at El Alamein – and the girl in the Women's Auxiliary Air Force, and both are clearly representatives of the citizen army fighting this war. Casting greatly reinforces this notion as the man is played by Ralph Michael, Ealing's Everyman of the wartime period. See Barr (1977: 52–5).
54. The brief epilogue does not appear in the *Final Shooting Script* and seemingly was an afterthought. In the script the film ends with Joe and Alice walking into the distance where they are eventually swallowed up in a mist. Suddenly, the mist clears to reveal a 'grimy, soot-blackened industrial town' and over this image Joe begins his recital of the American poet. The image is then replaced and concludes with that of the doorway to the utopian city.
55. The contextual issues are investigated more thoroughly in Burton (2009).
56. Balcon's and Ealing's radicalism was not quite exhausted with *They Came to City*. Shortly after the release of the film it was announced that the Studio was planning a film biopic of the socialist activist and historian Beatrice Webb, for which Sydney Webb granted consent and Left historian Margaret Cole was hired to advise. However, the production didn't materialise and Ealing was never again engaged on an explicitly progressive film (*The Co-operative News*, 28 October 1944).
57. See the comments announcing Ealing's production programme for 1945 and the uncertainty regarding audience taste with the coming of peace (*Kinematograph Weekly*, 11 January 1945).
58. The script was written by Angus Macphail and John Baines, with additional dialogue by T. E. B. Clarke. Baines wrote the two original stories, 'The Haunted Mirror' and 'The Ventriloquist's Dummy'. Sidney Cole recalls a slightly different genesis of the film, claiming that he and Charles Frend had originally thought of the concept of a collection of ghost stories, about which Balcon was initially unenthusiastic (Relph 1990).
59. Briefly in the1960s, the 'Hearse Driver' episode was championed by Ivan Butler, who thought it 'one of the best' (1967: 75), and Raymond Durgnat, who found it a 'short, sharp, brilliant little episode' (Durgnat 1966: 28).
60. The song *Always*, a prominent part of the soundtrack, ironically comments on the disruption of the time continuum in the sequence.
61. Dearden's copy of the *Final Shooting Script* is heavily annotated for these scenes, with his notes and plans for blocking the performers and camera placements, showing the care and foresight he brought to the linking story. The sequence was photographed by Douglas Slocombe, the first of many occasions he worked with Dearden.
62. One of the few critics to pay any attention to the linking story is Ivan Butler, who finds it 'as strange and ingenious as any of the others' (1967: 73).
63. Barr (1977) began this critical work with his reading of sexual repression in *The Haunted Mirror*.

64. For the classic study of this nature, see Jones (1951). This work had first appeared in 1910.
65. Interesting near-contemporary psychoanalytic enquiries are offered in Hadfield ([1954] 1967).
66. For a contemporary psychoanalytic discussion of war neuroses, see Sperling (1950).
67. All subsequent details of the production are taken from Dearden (1946). Cavalcanti served as a kind of 'supervising producer' to the inexperienced Relph, but quickly absented himself from the production (Relph 1990).
68. Two adjacent camps had been operated at the site: Marlag and Milag Nord, for navy and merchant navy captives respectively.
69. The complex critical issues surrounding the film are thoroughly explored in Burton (1997).
70. The *Final Shooting Script* is prefaced with several pages of notes and observations by both Morgan and Adams to ensure accuracy and authenticity of detail. The filmmakers were also able to draw on the advice of actors Derek Bond and Sam Kydd who had served as POWs. See Bond (1990) and Kydd (1973).
71. For a brief review of this important sub-genre of the war film, see Murphy (2000: 212–16).
72. In the commemorative brochure published for the première, Guy Morgan details the care devoted to obtaining an 'authentic background 'and confirms that the 'psychological stages have been accurately mapped by medical men who were prisoners themselves'. The authenticity of the physical and emotional behaviour of the characters is also attested to by a sociologist who worked with POWs (Lunden 1949).
73. The business of Horsfall (Jack Warner) having to sacrifice his lovingly crafted model ship for a final brew-up as fuel ran out, of Evans (Mervyn Johns) learning of his becoming a father while in captivity, the attack by a guard dog on a prisoner caught in the compound after curfew, the overwhelming joy and relief at the arrival of Red Cross parcels, the captives jeering at the blatant propaganda broadcast in the compound and the tense process of repatriation are all dealt with in Morgan's original account. See also the corroboration in Rolf (1988), MacKenzie (2004) and Nichol and Rennell (2003).
74. The film, of course, employs artistic licence in mixing the officers and other ranks in a single camp.
75. Even this derived from an incident recounted by Morgan involving a mysterious continental with an uncertain background sharing the rooming block (1945: 76–80).
76. Interestingly, lack of sex was much more of a problem for Latin POWs (French, Italian) than for Anglo-Saxon ones (British, German) (Lunden 1949: 731–2).
77. Such matters are constants in the memoirs and recollections.

3

Dramas of Masculine Adjustment I: Tragic Melodramas

Saraband for Dead Lovers (1948); *Train of Events (co-dir. Cole and Crichton,* 1949); *Cage of Gold* (1950); *Pool of London* (1951); *The Square Ring* (1953); *The Rainbow Jacket* (1954); *Davy* (1957); *The Secret Partner* (1961); *All Night Long* (1962); *A Place to Go* (1963); *The Man Who Haunted Himself* (1970).

A consistent theme in Dearden and Relph's post-war films concerns male characters forced to confront painful adjustment to new circumstances and changing social norms and expectations; indeed, it is a preoccupation which informed the work of a number of other British filmmakers of the time. Within this broad classification, this chapter sets out to examine those films which observe a tragic dimension, whereby the narratives result either in the death of the main male protagonist or a significant subsidiary character, or in his imprisonment, or in some such seriously diminished ambition or circumstance. In these tragic melodramas, the films do not address recognised and accepted social problems, Dearden and Relph foreground and deal with these elsewhere (see Chapter 5). The films do, however, attend to significant post-war realignments in gender and the consequent anxieties and contradictions confronted by men in making their way in worlds of changed and changing social circumstances.[1]

In exploring these issues, Dearden and Relph worked across a variety of genres and settings, including: the historical costume drama, the contemporary melodrama, the sports film, the crime film and the psychological thriller, demonstrating both their maturing flexibility as a filmmaking partnership and the centrality and consistency of the theme to their work together.

In her discussion of melodramas of the post-war era and the 1950s, Marcia Landy has suggested:

> During the war years, tragic melodramas were set in the context of combat or of the home front and generally in the context of family. Like

the films of empire before them, war films were geared towards affirming male competence, stoic endurance, sacrifice and camaraderie . . .
After the war, the representation of males was to become increasingly
darker and more problematic, the possibility of overcoming social and
personal obstacles more difficult. (1991: 259)

This chapter closely attends to eleven films in which Dearden and Relph
reflect on the anxieties of men struggling to manage their traditional aspirations
in the face of newly imposed obligations and responsibilities.

SARABAND FOR DEAD LOVERS (1948)

We all remember the historical film of the past with its puppets in
period costume; it's *zounds*, its *prithees* and its *od's bodikins*. We have
tried in *Saraband for Dead Lovers* not only to achieve historical accuracy
(which is easy enough) but also to present the characters as the human
beings they were (which is much more difficult). (Michael Balcon
1948: 11)[2]

Based on the historical novel by Helen Simpson, first published in 1935, *Saraband
for Dead Lovers* was Ealing's first colour film. It was perhaps a sign of Dearden
and Relph's growing reputation for reliability that Balcon entrusted them with
what was reputedly 'his pet project' (Harper 1994: 117).[3] It represented Ealing's
recognition of, and response to, the box-office success of the historical costume
melodrama, especially those associated with Gainsborough Studios, and it was,
as a consequence, part of a general boom in costume pictures made in Britain
in the later 1940s. Murphy, for instance, argues that at least seventy were made
in Britain in 1946–50 (1989: 134). In the event, and in spite of its big-budget,
star cast, innovative design and use of colour, it was a curious project, caught
between several contradictory tensions and generally remembered as 'a big disappointment', as Michael Relph was to put it in a later interview (Relph 1990).

The screenplay for *Saraband for Dead Lovers* was developed from the original
novel by John Dighton and Alexander Mackendrick. Dighton had adapted
Nicholas Nickleby (1947), an Ealing precursor of the historical melodrama in
this period; a film directed by Cavalcanti, with art design by Michael Relph.[4]
Mackendrick had studied at Glasgow School of Art, worked in advertising and
served in propaganda and psychological warfare capacities during the war. He
had gained an introduction to Ealing through his cousin Roger MacDougall,
the scriptwriter. His role in the film's production combined the function of
co-writer and sketch artist, working alongside Dearden and Relph on the 'set-
up' illustrations (what would now be referred to as the storyboards), which
were to guide the detail of the eventual filming (Dearden 1948: 65–8, 73).[5]

Mackendrick, who would soon become a leading director at Ealing, later recalled his experience on the film:

> I had a marvellous training as a director. I stood at the elbow of Basil Dearden; and he, on a set-plan, said, 'I want a shot from here,' and I'd say, 'Well, if you want it like that, this will be in the background; do you want it like this?' And he'd say, 'No, bigger,' or, 'Farther away,' or, 'I want it to pan over here' – and I did this very, very rapidly in little sketches, then went away a did about a thousand drawings. (quoted in Kemp 1991: 18)

The adaptation of the original novel flattens it out in a number of ways, re-sequences it and refines a number of its moments of licentiousness and sexuality.[6]

'As befitted Ealing's adherence to realism, the film was based on real historical events,' reports Murphy in his discussion (1989: 133) – or at least the film presents a version of these events. Against the background of the vicious political intrigue and corruption of the seventeenth-century Hanoverian court, the film relates the little-known, tragic love story of Princess Sophie-Dorothea (Joan Greenwood), who at an early age is forced into a marriage of convenience to her cousin, the brutal and dissolute George-Louis (Peter Bull), who was later to succeed to the English throne as George I. The marriage is loveless, although Sophie-Dorothea gives birth to two children in the years that follow, one of whom would eventually become George II of England. Life for Sophie-Dorothea at court is miserable and lonely, and she is despised and manipulated by her mother-in-law, the austere and snobbish Electress Sophia (Françoise Rosay),[7] grand-daughter of James I, niece of Charles I, and the scheming Countess Platen (Flora Robson),[8] the Elector's mistress. Both are self-seeking and ambitious, preoccupied with securing the succession to the English throne, which is achieved at the expense of Sophie-Dorothea. The plot which leads to this – and to the downfall of the innocent Sophie-Dorothea – hinges on the figure of the Swedish Count Philip Königsmark (Stewart Granger), who arrives at the court as a soldier of fortune. Initially, he is drawn into an affair with the ageing Countess Platen, but rejects her advances when he meets and falls in love with Sophie-Dorothea during the annual carnival. Countess Platen learns of this liaison and of their clandestine plans to escape together. As a result, their future is tragically thwarted; Königsmark is brutally assassinated by Durer (Anthony Quayle) in a scene that sees Countess Platen stamp with her heel on his dying lips as he pleads for the innocence of Sophie-Dorothea. The Princess's brief, doomed and tragic tryst with Königsmark, however, is enough to see her brought before the Elector and George-Louis, her despised husband, to sign a warrant which results in her formal separation from him, the loss of her children and her imprisonment for life in the Castle of Ahlden, ironically part of her dowry when she was married against her will. And it is here that the film both starts and ends, having related the tragic events leading to her lonely death, some thirty years later.

Dearden and Relph's shooting scripts are dated June 1947, and they give a detailed breakdown of the extensive range of sets and locations used in making the film. As well as the additional costs incurred by filming in Technicolor, the budget for the film was expanded to allow not only expensively designed and constructed studio sets, but also costly locations at Blenheim Palace and in Prague.[9] The shooting scripts are heavily annotated and contain many retyped new pages indicating extensive work amending dialogue, scene organisation and sequence.

The film is visually arresting, and the boldness of Relph's production design, with its rich, dark and atmospheric use of reds and browns, is striking. Most reviews of the time commented on this aspect of the film. *The Daily Herald*, for instance, felt that 'No compliments are too high for the director and designer, Basil Dearden and Michael Relph. Their rococo court and spectacular outdoor scenes, often crowded, are a triumph of Technicolor artistry and imagination' (16 September 1948). For many reviewers, however, the gorgeous splendour of the spectacle did not compensate for the lack of melodramatic romance perceived in the story. While reviewers commented favourably on the performances of Peter Bull and Flora Robson, it was felt that Stewart Granger and Joan Greenwood were not allowed to give free rein to their talents. Perhaps, as Dilys Powell, writing in *The Sunday Times*, noted: 'The very magnificence of the background defeats its own object; amidst so much splendour the destiny of the human figure seems confused and, sometimes, lost' (12 September 1948). Other reviewers were not as kind or as diplomatic; 'a great, big, beautiful bore' was how *The Sunday Graphic* summed up the film for its readers (10 September 1948). And from a later vantage point, Alexander Mackendrick looked back on *Saraband* as a film full of

> Talk meant to be listened to, rather than urgently acted upon . . . What I hated about *Saraband* was a tone which I cannot blame wholly on Basil or Michael or Johnny [Dighton], the Victorian relish for a grand manner. The archness and the loftiness and the swish of silk. (quoted in Kemp 1991: 19)

Subsequent commentaries have sought to explain how this expensive experiment in seventeenth-century costume drama became Ealing's costliest failure at the box office. A number have taken their lead from Michael Relph's comments when interviewed by Brian McFarlane:

Michael Relph's design for the Library in the Old Palace in *Saraband for Dead Lovers* (1948) (Courtesy of Simon Relph)

It was a magnificent-looking film, but it wasn't a success at the time. We were trying to get away from the Gainsborough-type romantic costume picture which was totally unreal, and to do a serious historical epic. The public probably wasn't ready for it and it also ended up being a bit heavy. (1997: 482)[10]

In its attempt to rework the conventions of the historical costume film, *Saraband for Dead Lovers* tried to introduce a dose of Ealing realism and didacticism into the visual flamboyance and romantic melodrama associated with Gainsborough and found the two to be incompatible. As Harper notes, the film was 'caught between two conflicting desires: to be soberly realistic, or sumptuously symbolic' (1994: 117). For Spicer, the film was an 'ambitious mis-fire; its reworking of generic conventions was too pronounced; audiences wanted Granger to be dynamic and athletic not restrained' (2001: 65–6). Harper also suggests that there are a number of other factors to be taken into account. First, she argues that the film was a failure at the box office, 'probably because of its idiosyncratic choice of historical period; it is difficult to see how the corrupt Hanoverian genealogy of the British Royal Family could be of interest to the audiences of 1948'. Second, in her view, the film failed to offer an attractive set of alternatives to the female audience (she attributes this partly to Balcon's influence), where the women in the film are of two types, either 'pretty, vapid celibates like Sophie-Dorothea, or rapacious, ugly harridans like Countess Platen'. Finally, she suggests that audiences for film in the later 1940s had far outgrown any reverence they might have once had for the factual basis or supposed authenticity of the historical stories they chose to watch on the screen (1994: 116–17).

In one of Relph's obituaries, the film was referred to as a 'florid period piece' (*The Daily Telegraph*, 1 October 2004), and a number of commentators have remarked on the style and direction of the film. For Durgnat, for instance:

The images, dominated by harsh flickering firelight reds and black shadow-locked spaces, by low, heavy ceilings and hard walls, evoke a stifling oppressiveness, all-too-briefly disrupted by outbursts of frantic cutting (the drunken carnival, the fireworks ironically celebrating a bestial honeymoon). If the task of maintaining a rigid, formal, encasing style without dampening emotional intensity remains difficult, the film hits on some admirable compositions – sometimes in passing, on the way to yet another regulation mid-shot, as if R–D didn't quite dare trust the public to respond to their stiff, hard, melancholy, and poignant long-shots. (1970: 179–80)

In a similar vein, Murphy notes that Dearden, 'the most showy and melodramatic of the Ealing directors . . . never quite manages to impose order and coherence over this ambitious, sprawling melodrama' (1989: 133–4).

Richards has attempted a more positive reassessment of the film, suggesting that it is a 'unique and extraordinary film to find in the Ealing canon'. From this point of view, its difference from the standard Gainsborough fare is significant and worthy of praise in terms of the ethos of Ealing it embodies:

> Despite the presence of Gainsborough icon, Stewart Granger, *Saraband for Dead Lovers* is far removed from the Gainsborough ethic and its celebration of conspicuous consumption, flamboyance, sensuality and self-indulgence. In fact, it is quite the opposite. It is a profoundly moral, sternly disapproving, bleak, dark, pessimistic film – the antidote to Gainsborough. (1997: 28)

His key point is that the film presents a critique of the misuse of power for its own sake and that as a result, it encapsulates the studio ethos: 'In the Ealing universe, power exists only for service and for the greatest good of the greatest number' (ibid.). The tragic dimension of the film, he notes, lies in the way in which the brief romantic idyll between Königsmark and Sophie-Dorothea was unrequited and ultimately worthless.

Critical assessments of *Saraband* have thus ranged over the unwise application of Ealing realism and restraint to a genre conventionally marked by flamboyance and excess, the corresponding lack of pleasures and identification the film afforded its female audience, and the failure of the filmmakers to find an appropriate style for this austere costume melodrama. William K. Everson unexpectedly includes *Saraband* in his discussion of the British *film noir* and this seems a perceptive way to account for the picture's unusually dark and repressive nature (1987: 343). The opening scene of an elderly Sophie-Dorothea expiring in her bed at Ahlden Castle and the flashback to her happier, younger self are narratively and visually reminiscent of that proto-type *noir Citizen Kane* (d. Orson Welles, 1941).[11] The severe fatalism of the story, the emasculation of the protagonists in the face of the merciless dominance of state authority, and the presence of a powerful, sexualised and ruthless *femme fatale* in the guise of Countess Platen, all give credence to this reading.[12] These subversive and destabilising traits are distinctive and troubling within the normative framework of Ealing cinema. As Tony Williams has acknowledged: '*Saraband* significantly expresses features that later Ealing comedies conceal, deny, and depend on – a community world of sexual and social repression' (2000: 160). That is, the film makes explicit what other Ealing melodramas and comedies only address implicitly and subtextually. While history and a faithful script furnished a tale already endowed with tragic

qualities, Dearden, Relph and key collaborators like Douglas Slocombe, the
lighting cameraman, deployed a narrative and visual style that accentuated
the pessimism of the story and enhanced the fatalistic mood. The filmmakers
would continue in this vein of generic experimentation and combination, and
expressionistic design as their cinema further explored the tragic dimensions
of social existence in post-war Britain. In this sense, it is wrong to see *Saraband*
as an aberration, some kind of honourable failure, as it marks a path Dearden
and Relph would continue to traverse in the years to come. The figure of
Königsmark is also significant, for with him Dearden and Relph present their
first male character trapped in tragic circumstances. A warrior, he is entangled
in the domestic confinements and intrigues of the court, his potency sapped
by the scheming of the sexualised Countess Platen who, in her desperate
infatuation, is prepared to see him die rather than lose him. Forthcoming films
from the partnership of Dearden and Relph would feature a series of men
returned from war, adrift in an environment they no longer appreciate, social
relations with women they no longer recognise and lives lacking in purpose
and excitement.

TRAIN OF EVENTS (1949)

> Dearden seems to have conformed absolutely to both the structure and
> ethos of Ealing. He was a team player, contributing happily to those
> 'portmanteau' pictures on which several Ealing directors collaborated.
> (Richards 1997: 16)

As Perry (1985: 143) and others have noted, *Train of Events* was an attempt to
harness several members of the Ealing team in just such a 'portmanteau' film,
a formula that had worked to some success and critical acclaim with *Dead
of Night* four years earlier. 'Portmanteau' films (also referred to as 'omnibus'
or 'compendium' films), consist of a series of often interwoven but separate
stories and plotlines, which may be connected by a unifying theme, a setting
or in some cases simply the reputation of the author.[13] In the case of *Train
of Events*, and *Dead of Night* before it, however, these films regularly utilised
several genres, writers and directors, each responsible for one of the narrative
segments. However, the film seeks to minimise its inherent episodic nature,
and the various story events are more interspersed and integrated than in the
preceding *Dead of Night*.[14]

In *Train of Events*, the unifying story of 'The Engine Driver' was directed
by Sidney Cole; Dearden directed two of the three contained stories, 'The
Prisoner of War' and 'The Actor'; while Charles Crichton was given charge
of the episode 'The Composer'. There were four writers on the film: Ronald

Millar, who had written *Frieda* (1947), records that he wrote the comedy of manners, 'The Composer' (1993: 141); while it is likely that Dearden, with his background in theatre, provided the tale of 'The Actor', which he also directed; leaving Angus McPhail the episode of the 'POW' and T. E. B. Clarke, the linking tale of 'The Engine Driver'. Michael Relph acted as associate producer.

In the case of *Train of Events*, the unifying narrative location and occupational milieu is established as the immediate post-war railway system and the people who work there. The epicentre is London's Euston Station, and courtesy of Sidney Cole's direction, the film is laced liberally with documentary-style shots of trains at speed, marshalling yards and the period steam locomotive atmosphere of the station itself.[15] The film begins as the 3.45 London-to-Liverpool train starts its journey. In separate, apparently randomly chosen compartments of the train, the film foregrounds two couples and one man and then cuts forward in time to a sequence further north on the same journey, when Jim Hardcastle (Jack Warner) the engine-driver, is unable to avert disaster as the train ploughs into a fuel tanker on a level crossing. Forewarned by this early revelation of the ultimately doomed fate of the train, the viewer is left to speculate on the significance of this for the events which now unfold, a suspense which is motivated by the device of a flashback, to 'London: Three Days Earlier . . .'. From this point, the film works through a patchwork of interwoven segments or episodes and tells the four principal stories, and as Perry has noted: 'the mood of each segment was deliberately contrasted' (1981: 143).

Dearden's two cameo pieces are clear distillations of the director's thematic and stylistic preoccupations at this time, and it is telling that these are the only stories in the film that end tragically. 'The Prisoner of War' is a dark and desperate tragic melodrama focusing on the plight of a pair of young lovers on the run. A poster with the slogan 'Emigrate to Canada' is the device used to introduce Ella (Joan Dowling), one of the couples on the train detailed in the initial sequences of the film. She is evading the police, flitting through dingy backstreets to an impoverished bedsit where Richard (Laurence Payne) is revealed as an escaped German prisoner of war on the run from the police and deportation. Ella is an orphan 'blitz-kid', both are in love and desperate to escape. Ella brings an identity card for Richard and a ring to make them look respectable. The fag-smoking landlady, however, wants them out. As she goes for change for the meter, Ella, in desperation, steals money from the landlady's cashbox. Dearden was influenced by the Italian neo-realists in this sequence, with his fatalistic attention to the drab, rain-swept streets and derelict bombsites of austerity London, the suffocating space of the attic perched atop the decrepit boarding house, and the friendless and frightened young couple.[16] With this short sequence, and in contrast to the characteristically flat visual style of the new Italian cinema, Dearden continues his experiments in deep-staging: crowding his principal characters – or significant objects like the cashbox – into the near foreground of the image; having one player within the shot moving slowly into the deep background; or, alternatively, staging a dramatic displacement of attention onto a new character or development deep within the shot. This technique neatly captures the contradictory qualities of isolation and claustrophobia felt by the couple.[17]

As it transpires in the next episode of their story, the stolen money is only enough to buy one ticket to Canada. Their paranoia results in a short chase sequence, from Trafalgar Square to the Strand Tube station, shot almost entirely on location. As it turns out on this occasion, their fear of surveillance is unfounded, but it drives them to another dismal rented room, 'a rat-hole' in Camden Town. Here, Richard rails against their plight, always hiding and afraid. Ella in her innocence asks if they could not make a home in Germany. Looking out of the dingy room over railway sidings, Richard voices his bitterness at his particular situation. There are telling, veiled and explicit references to the recent experience of war in three of the four stories that constitute the film. But Richard is constructed to represent the German point of view at this juncture in the story.[18] In a direct reference to Hitler, he admits to a terminal sense of disillusion and the impossibility of them ever returning to his homeland: 'He was going to make us the greatest nation on earth, he failed in everything. He destroyed Germany . . .' His mounting desperation to get away drives the altruistic Ella to return to the travel agency, where she books a ticket for him. The next, almost final encounter with Ella and Richard takes place at the ticket barrier as they join the train for Liverpool.

The second story directed by Dearden, 'The Actor', is equally stylised, but in a totally different register. A tragic crime melodrama, it is constructed in a hyperbolic expressionist manner and anticipates the noirish *Cage of Gold*, which resulted from the Dearden–Relph partnership the following year. The story is concerned with Philip Mason (Peter Finch),[19] a young actor working in repertory with The Macauley Shakespearean Company, and the cast and company are to travel to Liverpool on the Friday train to join a ship.[20] Mason is first encountered in a rehearsal of *Richard II*, where he is cast as Sir Pierce of Exton, and there is an amusing nod towards austerity privations as the actors go through their paces wearing overcoats and scarves in the unheated theatre.[21] The film follows Philip from the theatre to his digs, where he is taken aback to find his estranged wife, the cigarette-smoking and gin-drinking Louise (Mary Morris) listening to 'These Foolish Things' on the gramophone. In the dark and shadowy subsequent interchanges, Dearden condenses many of the characteristic elements of his cinema of tragic melodrama. She greets

Philip with the admonition, 'Don't look like that. I never could bear your tragic look'. Louise has been serially unfaithful to Philip for a long time. Their bitter recriminations come round to the war, and his absence due to six years in the army. Here, the sequence invokes the motif of war service and masculine anxieties centred on female infidelity during male absence. 'You were away a long time', she says. 'So were a lot of men,' he counters. Louise is the archetype of the 'spider-woman', manipulative, self-serving and sexualised. She taunts him as weak, soft and sentimental, 'a fine soldier you must have been'; but the tables are turned, 'six years of war toughened me', and, mis-reading the signs, she is excited by her newly assertive husband. As she responds to what she thinks are his caresses, Philip strangles her. Is this a case of justifiable revenge? The story now shifts mode as Philip hides her body in his travelling theatrical basket and tries to live with what he has done. After a nerve-wracking encounter with his landlady's husband, who concludes that Philip has been drinking, this sequence ends with the chimes of Big Ben. The sequence is a compendium of contemporary *noir* motifs, of expressionistic shadows, polished night for night photography, narrow staircases, unbalanced angles and deep-focus compositions. The crucial dramatic moment of Philip's decision to murder Louise is captured by Dearden in a telling composition. In close-up, the man occupies the near-right foreground of the image, while the woman in full figure is seated in the right background of the frame. As she taunts Philip and indicates that she is leaving for good and never wants to see him again, the realisation is registered on Philip's face and he informs her sardonically that she won't, 'after tonight'.

On the following day, on stage during full dress rehearsal, Philip is paralysed with fear at the sight of a travelling basket at the edge of the stage. He is unable to perform his lines and runs back to his lodgings to check his basket.[22] As the basket is being removed, he is further haunted by the appearance of the police (Michael Hordern) following up enquiries about his wife. The police leave, but not until the basket has fallen down the staircase, en route to its, and Philip's, destination on the train. Dearden encourages Finch to play these scenes in an astonishingly neurotic fashion, a man clearly incapable of containing his 'guilt of conscience'.

The threads of the four stories and their respective characters and predicaments are drawn together and resolved in the final stages and climax of the film. Richard and Ella board the train, while Philip sees the theatre basket containing his murdered wife safely loaded and joins other members of the cast in their compartment. The train pulls out of the station and the final journey begins.

Two plainclothes policemen (led by Michael Hordern) begin to walk through the train looking for Philip. Their presence also serves to alarm

Richard and Ella. Philip is on the point of being apprehended when the sequence from the beginning of the film is replayed, and as we knew it would, the train crashes. In the immediate aftermath of the wreck, a dazed Philip is helped from the train but then dies, crushed on top of his theatrical basket by falling wreckage. Ella, the innocent, tragically dies from her injuries and Richard, with Hitler's voice ringing in his ears, is forced to flee the scene, leaving his ticket to Canada blowing among the debris.

The Charles Barr, in his brief summary of the film, notes that this was the last portmanteau-style production at Ealing: 'Henceforth, though other companies continue to use the format, Ealing will do so only indirectly, presenting the individual's story as part of a more meaningful social continuum than this, and sticking to one director at a time' (1977: 189).

The film was not a critical or box-office success and has received scant attention subsequently. Contemporary reviews tended to opt for their favourite story or actor and commented on the omnibus format, suggesting, however, a 'contrived ending'. In some cases, Dearden was singled out as the director in the group with a discernible style, but even then it was implicitly dismissed as modish and flashy: 'There are three directors, stiff, bloodless, highly conscientious, their styles indistinguishable except for Dearden's pronounced use of melodramatic angles' (*Monthly Film Bulletin*, September 1949).

In spite of the positive verdict of one reviewer ('Thrilling stuff, photographed with imagination' (*Sunday Despatch*, 21 August 1949), there is some truth in Durgnat's later assessment that 'such films as *Train of Events* (1949) and *Dance Hall* (1950) evoke the drab fatigue of austerity's shortages' (1970: 51), and there are a number of points worthy of note. First, the film provides continuing evidence of Dearden and Relph's abilities to work as leading, flexible members of the team at Ealing, even if the films they worked on were not always of their own creative choice (see Harper and Porter 2003: 68). The two segments that Dearden directed conform to tragic melodramas and there is evidence of a maturing and distinctive style of thematic and cinematic representation. The director further reveals his keen awareness and appreciation of contemporary film practice, here in terms of the stark realism he brings to the tale of the POW; and contrastingly, his invocation of the emergent *noir* style in the story of the murder of the unfaithful wife. In common with many of their other films, *Train of Events* brings together a number of apparently randomly chosen individuals, revealing and tracing their stories, their destinies, fallibilities and flaws. In the moral universe of the film, characters act as agents or 'bearers' of particular values and dilemmas. Significantly, both Dearden stories deal with the tragic legacy of war-time experience for men in their lives after the conflict; most obviously Philip, but also Richard, the German escaped POW, conform to what Spicer in these terms has labelled 'damaged men' (2001: 163).

CAGE OF GOLD (1950)

Even the lads of that *haut école*, Ealing Studios have a shot at murky melodrama. (Jympson Harman, *Evening Standard*, 21 September 1950)

Cage of Gold is an unpredictable, roller-coaster melodrama from Ealing under the direction of Dearden, with Relph acting as associate producer and designer. Harper and Porter indicate that the filmmakers ('with bilious resentment') were forced by Balcon to take the project on at very short notice (2003: 68); although the partnership were linked to the film in the annual statement of production plans issued by the studio in December 1949, fully two months before the commencement of shooting (*Kinematograph Weekly*, 15 December 1949). The copiously annotated and amended shooting script (with many pink, late substitute sheets indicating revisions) attests to some adjustment and accommodation.[23] Unlike many of Dearden and Relph's films, *Cage of Gold* has attracted a degree of critical interest and a number of informed and insightful discussions are presented in Barr (1977), Perry (1985), Hill (1986), Landy (1991), Murphy (1997) and Geraghty (2000).[24] The film's narrative action oscillates between London and Paris, and the relationships between two men and two women.

At the epicentre of the bustling crowds in the Tube, and indeed for the rest of the film's narrative, is Judith (Judy) Moray (Jean Simmons). A young artist, on her way to a date in Chelsea, she is hailed by Bill Glennon (David Farrar), who breaks off his rather furtive interchange with a nameless acquaintance to pursue her onto the train, and it transpires that Bill and Judy were once very close. During the war, when Bill was serving in the RAF as a Wing Commander, he was her first serious boy friend. Despite Judy's apparent coolness, Bill seems eager to recapture their relationship and accompanies her to The Palette Club in Chelsea. Here, they meet her date, Alan Kearn (James Donald), a doctor whom she perfunctorily introduces to Bill, and then she and Alan leave for their meal. Not to be put off, however, Bill follows them into the restaurant, sitting at a table opposite (in a striking composition he intervenes between them) and he insists on buying them a bottle of the best champagne. Judy refuses this and leaves with Alan, who is understandably mystified by events. As they walk along the Embankment, she tries to explain just who Bill, the 'Champagne Merchant', was to her. From this, the film cuts to Alan's home, introducing his father (Harcourt Williams), an elderly doctor in general practice, and hints at another dilemma that confronts Alan's future: whether to join a wealthy private practice in the West End or follow in his father's footsteps in the family National Health Service practice in Battersea.

On the next day, the persistent Bill arrives at Judy's studio flat, greeting her housekeeper Waddy (Gladys Henson) like a long-lost friend. Judy begins to paint his portrait, in his RAF uniform, as he was, when they knew each other during the war. In spite of Judy's warning to him that 'it's been a long time and other things have happened', Bill refuses to acknowledge that anything may have changed between them. He sweeps Judy off her feet and takes her out that evening. This is followed by a montage whirl of shots of them together: at a fairground, dancing, at an ice-hockey game, an air show, a boxing match. At some point following this, Alan arrives at Judy's flat, and in front of the now completed portrait of Bill – an image which again intervenes between them – asks Judy to marry him. He also confirms that he has joined the lucrative private practice in Mayfair with Dr Saville.[25] Judy's noncommittal response sees Alan leave, encountering Bill as he goes. Judy confesses to Bill that she hates the way she has treated Alan, but Bill recognises that there is more to this than meets the eye, and realising that Judy is going to have his baby he proposes marriage immediately. When Judy tells Waddy of this development, she is instantly guarded, suspicious of Bill's real motives. 'Does he know that you haven't any money?' she asks ominously.

Bill and Judy are married in a soulless Registry Office. The film does not show their wedding but sees them acting as witnesses to the couple ahead of them. This device is used to underscore the true significance of marriage. After they leave the Registry Office, Bill and Judy encounter a friend of Bill's who asks after Bill's 'racket', and subsequently Bill tells Judy that since the war he has been involved in black market currency smuggling. Later that evening, Bill discovers that Judy is in fact penniless and that her family fortune no longer exists. On the morning after their wedding, Judy awakes to find Bill gone, taking with him the jewelled watch he gave her as a wedding gift. In a note that subsequently arrives with a bouquet of flowers, Bill explains that he is 'flat broke' and that he is leaving her forever.

The film's location and narrative now shift to Paris, to the exotic 'Cage of Gold' nightclub of the film's title. Here we enter Bill's 'other world', where he is welcomed with open arms by the glamorous singer Marie (Madeleine Lebeau). This encounter also introduces the shadowy Rahman (Herbert Lom), clearly less than delighted to see Bill again. Marie takes Bill to task about his absence and the whereabouts of her money. In return, he gives her the watch that he gave Judy as her wedding present. Switching back to London, the film sees Judy, in desperation, visit Alan's wealthy practice where she confesses her pregnancy, her marriage to Bill and his subsequent desertion. In response, Alan replies that he 'won't do what you came here to ask' – he will not terminate her pregnancy. In Paris, Bill is reduced to working behind the bar at the 'Cage of Gold' under the surveillance of Marie; but he encounters Antoinette (Maria

Mauban), a beautiful, wealthy banker's daughter. Rahman negotiates with Bill to use his passport for a 'mule' smuggling contraband diamonds to New York. For the infatuated Marie, this keeps Bill in Paris; but it does not prevent him from making a play for Antoinette, motivated by her wealth and fortune.

In London, Alan decides to follow in his father's footsteps, rejecting Harley Street for the honest, nationalised toil of Battersea. He attends when his father delivers Judy's baby, Nicholas, who is 'like Bill'; and not long after this, Alan gives Judy a newspaper which reports on its front page the apparent death of Bill in a mid-Atlantic air crash. In a neat exchange, Bill learns of Judy's baby through a chance encounter with a society magazine in Paris. Undaunted by this he proposes marriage to Antoinette and they plan to elope. He goes to see her father, the banker, and tries unsuccessfully to extort money in return for his leaving Paris and Antoinette. Following this abortive blackmail attempt, Bill returns to the nightclub and departs with a false passport, abandoning Marie, apparently trapped in the 'Cage of Gold'.

The film returns across the Channel to a Christmas party scene some years later, with Alan now married to Judy, preparing for Nicholas's birthday party.[26] When Alan leaves to collect young party guests, Bill arrives out of the blue. Shocked, Judy is distraught and despatches the menacing and over-familiar Bill before Alan returns. During the subsequent Punch and Judy show for the children, however, she faints in the turmoil of this turn of events. Her attempts to keep the truth from Alan are ultimately undone, as Bill confronts Alan in his surgery. Bill hints at a monetary means of resolution, but is rebuffed by Alan. He then contacts Judy and arranges for her to meet him at his flat. She agrees and goes through the fog, carrying with her a pistol taken from Alan's father's room. At Bill's flat, his blackmail ploy becomes more apparent and he dismisses as paltry her offer of £265. After Bill telephones Alan – 'I have your wife here; quite like old times' – Judy pulls the gun on him, the crisis signalled by a close-up of the violently boiling kettle.

Alan finds Judy wandering in the fog, but leaves her to confront Bill. After breaking into his flat, he finds Bill dead from gunshot wounds, and as he feverishly attempts to remove fingerprints, a police constable enters to find him holding the gun. At this stage, Inspector Grey (Bernard Lee) appears to be investigating two prime suspects: Alan, who has confessed to the crime, and Judy who also claims that she pulled the trigger. This apparent impasse is resolved when the film cuts to Marie, who, it transpires, has followed Bill to London with murderous intent and committed *un amour fou*. She leaps to her death from the boat train. This extraordinary and tragic turn of events allows the film's resolution to see Judy's return to the family home, to Alan, Nicholas, Waddy and the old man upstairs, still trying to find an alternative to 'crooners and comics' on the radio.

Contemporary reviews of the film tended to find it highly contrived, and several haughtily dismissed it as a lightweight, trashy 'novelette'. For other reviewers, such as C. A. Lejeune, the film was perceived to transgress the Ealing tradition and it was condemned as 'a regrettable incident in the honourable career of Ealing Studios and a waste of everybody's talent and the audience's time' (*Observer*, 24 September 1950). While Michael Relph later remembered that *Cage of Gold* was 'not successful',[27] figures cited in Harper and Porter suggest the opposite, with earnings of £192,000 being relatively successful for an Ealing production of the period (2003: 285).

Subsequent critical commentaries have been kinder and have found the film to be of interest in a number of ways. First, as Barr has noted: '*Cage of Gold* is virtually the last Ealing film to give a decent part to a woman (old ladies aside) – and there are 35 films to come' (1977: 150); and Geraghty has developed this aspect in her analysis. What is striking about the film, she suggests, is that it foregrounds the woman's – Judy's – point of view. It is distinctive, in that it has a woman as the central character and narrative viewpoint: 'The audience follows the story from their point of view and is given access to their thoughts and feelings . . . we know why they do what they do' (2000: 83). And it is in these terms that the narrative structure of the film, characteristic of melodrama, works in the tensions between a highly polarised set of oppositions and choices: between individual ambition and social obligation, respectable integrity and disciplined duty against personal agency, excitement and desire. Most obviously the stark choices that Judy faces are condensed in the values embodied in Bill and Alan. Whereas Alan – after his initial temptation by the world of private practice – is quickly redeemed by his return to family ethics and nationalised service, and represents a steady, if unglamorous choice, Bill stands for everything Alan is not. In a bald statement made moments before his death, Bill expresses his dilemma: in his own peculiar way he had loved Judy, she had everything he wanted – except money – whereas Marie only had money. As Murphy has noted, he represents an interesting composite villain, combining aspects of the spiv in his illegal dealings; but he 'also owes something to an older type, the upper-class bounder who cheats at cards and seduces his friends' sisters' (1997: 157). In the context of the film, however, Bill fuses these types and their characteristics with those of his status as a decorated wartime hero, perhaps unable to come to terms with changed post-war circumstances; one of a cadre of 'ex-servicemen who turn up like bad pennies to blight the lives of those who knew them during the war' (ibid.: 158).[28] There is persistent commentary on Bill's wartime service in the RAF: immediately after their marriage Bill cynically confesses to Judy that: 'To live you have to have money. If your only trade is shooting down aeroplanes you have to make it the best way you can'. Judy, just prior to her desertion, still shows confidence in Bill, pleading, 'If you could do what you did in the war, you would be good for anything'. In these terms, Bill's activities and his motivations can be seen as a betrayal of his wartime service and heroism, as Richards suggests (1997: 30); or, to counter this, it may be the case that his wartime reputation was gained precisely as a result of his self-seeking, manipulative charm and disregard for others.[29] The film does not really allow resolution of this issue and on this hangs the degree to which he can ultimately be seen as a tragic figure, as opposed to a 'dyed-in-the-wool', self-serving villain and cad, who finally gets his just desserts.[30]

For Hill, *Cage of Gold* is a hybrid '*noir* melodrama', in that its domestic focus is realised through a *noir* structure and style (1986: 71–4). As he notes, however, the film structurally displaces the conventional female *noir* universe of Madonna/whore onto the male characters; with Alan as the 'puritan' and Bill the 'playboy'. Spicer in these terms neatly classifies Bill as a '*homme fatale*' (2001: 174).

If *Cage of Gold* was simply just another 'job', handed to them by the Studio, then Dearden, as director, and Relph, as designer and producer, managed to invest the film with much ingenuity, flair and interest. It certainly allowed them to develop and extend the expressionistic approach they had employed in *Train of Events* the previous year, a characteristic element of their cinema from *The Halfway House* (1944) through *Dead of Night* (1945), *Frieda* (1947) and *Saraband for Dead Lovers* (1948). In terms of British cinema, Dearden is rarely placed among those 'talented and capable individuals with the sensibility and style to do *film noir* . . . Carol Reed, John Boulting, Anthony Kimmins, Terence Fisher and David Lean' (Miller 1994: 160), when, in fact, he was superior to all of these filmmakers except Reed considered solely in terms of achievements in *noir* melodrama.

In a moment of self-reflexivity, the film signals its generic leanings, when it has Bill, sitting for Judy to start his portrait, ingratiating himself back into her life and inviting her to dinner with the words, 'I'll ring twice, like the postman always does'. The story draws on the classic *noir* trope of a troubling event or character that resurfaces from 'out of the past', to revisit the dread and anguish of former times.[31] Director, designer and cinematographer Douglas Slocombe combine to create some stunning *noir* set-pieces and flourishes: there are repeated triangulated compositions, first of Alan, Judy and Bill; and later Bill, Marie and Rahman; the persistent appearance of mirrors and reflective surfaces as characters question themselves, their desires and motives (Judy), or, alternatively, signal their duplicity to the viewer (Bill); and a nimble and fluid camera allied with a telling use of deep focus, never emphatic or over-obvious, but dramatically sensitive to character interaction and psychological interplay. The culminating sequence of Bill's return from the grave – his attempt to blackmail Judy and Alan, his murder and the subsequent police investigation – is a prime example of Dearden's cinematic artistry, daring visual sense and technical ability. It occupies a full thirty minutes of screen time and its relentless drive towards the tragic dénouement is a tribute to the director's sureness with narrative and genre cinema. The action occupies a succession of dimly lit rooms and the camera assumes a perceptively lower level to register the fearful and dejected state of the intimidated characters. So, in two scenes, when Bill drops in unexpectedly at Alan's surgery, and during the police interrogations of Judy and Alan, the set is lit by a single lamp, shot from below and prominently configured in the composition. The film's most striking images occur during the fog-shrouded journeys to Bill's bedsit. The starkly backlit characters straddling huge expanses of diffused light border on the abstract, and comment powerfully on the swirling and unfocused mental states of the protagonists.[32] The final confrontation between Judy and Bill culminates in one of those 'impossible' shots beloved of cinéastes. The heroine has pulled a gun on the reprehensible first husband and a rapid montage of close-up faces, the pistol and a boiling-over kettle is brought to a conclusion as the camera tracks towards the gun and into the blackness of the barrel. A match–cut brings us to an extreme close-up of a button and a compensating track out reveals the finger of Alan anxiously sounding the horn of his car, stuck in the fog en route to Bill's.

The *Monthly Film Bulletin*, which took the film to task for its script and narrative, had the following to say about Dearden's direction:

> Basil Dearden has realised this abortive subject with his usual adroitness, creating at moments at least the illusion of tension; too often, though, he carries his partiality for the shock cut, the vivid effect, into the region of self-caricature. (October 1950)

The director's propensity for the 'shock-cut' is nowhere more evident than in the sequence outlined above, when Marie leaps from the train, the effect is doubled. However, it is a perfectly acceptable technique for a crime melodrama observing the twin demands of narrative pace and emotional excess, and is probably something the ciné-literate Dearden absorbed from Alfred Hitchcock.

The choice that confronts Judy, between Alan and Bill, is also echoed in the opposition drawn between the locations of the Kearn family household and the Cage of Gold nightclub in Paris. Ultimately, and perhaps inevitably, the film ends with Judy restored to her place in the home, redeemed from her earlier hedonistic encounters with Bill and all that he represented. The degree to which she in fact had any real choice is an intriguing question, as Richards argues:

The film makes it clear that the true life is the Ealing life-service, sacrifice, settled affection. (*Sacrifice* was the working title of the film.) The
false life is the life of materialism, hedonism and sensuality, symbolised
by The Cage of Gold. Judy, torn between the two, settles for the true
path. (1997: 29)

There is, however, also a sense that the house itself is also a type of cage and
that the apparent happy ending is a compromised and lacklustre settlement.
This is evident in the composition of the image of Judy's return to the house.
She enters, crosses the hallway and is framed within a solid archway formed
by the upper floor. Strong verticals created by the lighting and reinforced by
the mise-en-scène of the banister rails on the staircase produce an obvious
visual echo of the stage set of the Cage of Gold nightclub. For Hill (1986) and
Geraghty (2000), the film is ultimately conformist, and Judy's early exciting
relationship with Bill and her subsequent restoration to home and marriage
with Alan, act as a sobering metaphor for women to accept and return to
their traditional domestic roles and to settle back into the less than glamorous
realities of post-war society. There are, however, sufficiently troubling aspects
of narrative and mise-en-scène to be wary of a too literal reading of the film.
For instance, the brief interchange between Judy and Alan, moments before
Nicholas's party, signals her uncertainty about her domestic role when Alan,
almost pathetically, reminds her that there is 'no champagne in Battersea'.
Without conviction Judy suggests that she hated that life, whispering ominously, 'Bill's ghost again'. This acts as a prophetic statement, conjuring up
the spectre of Bill once again from deep within her subconscious and the
promise of fulfilment and excitement that she fails – and will fail to find in her
marriage to Alan. Judy finally returns to a home characterised in its architecture by restraint and confinement, and the ambivalent reunion of the family
at the conclusion prefigures the 'unhappy, happy endings' of the more critical
Hollywood melodramas of the 1950s.

POOL OF LONDON (1951)

If only one film could be preserved for posterity, to illustrate the essence
of Ealing before decadence set in, this would be a good choice, with its
clear-cut embodiment of Ealing attitudes to women, violence, social
responsibility and cinematic form. (Charles Barr 1977: 190)

Pool of London is a film that resists easy generic classification. For some writers
(for instance, Hill 1986, and Landy 1991), it is straightforwardly identified as
a 'social problem' film as a result of its address to race and prejudice in early
post-war Britain. From this point of view, the film anticipates and sows the

Judy and Bill in *Cage of Gold* (1950) Courtesy of Steve Chibnall Archive)

seeds of a theme which was to resurface in Dearden and Relph's post-Ealing work, notably in *Sapphire* (1959). For others, however, the film is a hybrid episodic mix, drawing on the formula of *The Blue Lamp* (1950), interweaving documentary realism, crime thriller and *noir* melodrama, and the soap opera with a sidelong exploration of the race issue (Perry 1985; Higson 1997). The shooting script is dated late July 1950 and filming commenced in August, with seven weeks of location shooting required to capture life on the Thames, 'the Pool' of the title, its adjacent docks and settings for the stories.[33] Research for the film was initially undertaken by T. E. B. Clarke, but script development was switched to Jack Whittingham and John Eldridge when Balcon was taken by the possibilities of Clarke's idea for what emerged as *The Lavender Hill Mob* (1951).[34]

The film opens with the cargo ship *MV Dunbar* inbound from Holland, making its regular passage up the Thames, under Tower Bridge to dock in the Pool of London. This is shot in documentary, almost travelogue style, and as customs officers come on board, the film moves into the all-male world of the ship and introduces the crew and its central characters. They are preparing for a weekend ashore and the film narrative is structured by action taking place on the Friday afternoon and evening, through Saturday and Sunday, to its conclusion in the early hours of Monday. Among the crew, the film foregrounds Dan MacDonald (Bonar Colleano),[35] a wise-cracking, good-natured but spivish Canadian, introduced preparing to smuggle a few cigarettes and nylons ashore, and his young, black Jamaican pal Johnny (Earl Cameron), who, in comparison to Dan, seems innocent and naïve.[36] The film introduces Sally (Renée Asherson), a clerk in the nearby shipping office, waiting for Harry (Leslie Phillips), another member of the crew. Dan enlists Johnny's help in smuggling a couple of packets of cigarettes ashore past Customs and in the nearby public house, Johnny discovers that these were not ordinary cigarettes,[37] but after a drink he accompanies Dan to the Queen's Theatre to 'deliver the goods'. Here, while waiting for Dan, Johnny encounters the commissionaire, a racist bigot.[38] Pat (Susan Shaw), in the box office, witnesses this and sympathises with Johnny. Meanwhile, Dan is introduced to Vernon (Max Adrian), 'The Gentleman Acrobat', by his criminal contact, Mike (Christopher Hewitt). Vernon wants Dan to smuggle something to Holland when the ship sails. From this point, the film interweaves three principal plot-lines: the relationship between Johnny and Pat, which develops as they meet later that evening; Dan's story, as he meets Maisie (Moira Lister), his girlfriend; and the unfolding robbery, involving Vernon and his criminal gang. Friday evening ends with Johnny walking back to the ship.

Saturday sees Dan at the shipping office where he meets Sally. Returning to the ship, Mike tells him to meet Vernon at the theatre. However, having returned to the ship, his attempt to go ashore carrying a few pairs of contraband nylon stockings is detected by the sharp-eyed customs officer Andrews (Michael Golden). As punishment, he is ordered to stand watch until 5 o'clock. When Johnny takes a message to Vernon explaining Dan's delay, he meets Pat and they arrange to meet in the evening. After his enforced deck watch, Dan meets a jittery Vernon in his dressing room at the theatre and he agrees to smuggle a parcel to Rotterdam for £100. After this, Dan, Johnny and Pat all go to The Palais dance hall to meet Maisie, who walks out on Dan when she discovers the loss of her promised nylons, and she makes a spiteful, racist remark to Pat about Johnny.[39] Pat follows Johnny and they walk together onto Tower Bridge. She sympathises with his hurt feelings and he recalls that Dan once got into a fight because of a similar racist incident. He also talks about returning to Jamaica and how he intends to quit the sea soon. Pat undertakes to show him some of the sights of London on the following day and Johnny returns to the ship in a much happier frame of mind. Dan meets Sally and after they get drunk on pink gins they go back to her basement lodgings. In a seedy café, meanwhile, Mike, Vernon and the gang members, make their final plans for the robbery.

Sunday is ushered in by church bells echoing around the Pool of London, and against this backdrop the film interweaves the story of the robbery with Johnny and Pat's excursion around London. Initially, Dan asks Johnny to bring a parcel on board for him later in the day, and unaware of what he is dealing with, Johnny agrees to help his friend. The robbery begins with the theft of a getaway car and Vernon, using his acrobatic skills, scales the rooftops to jump across to the building where the safe is located. When he enters, he brutally coshes the elderly caretaker before letting the gang in to blow the safe. The object of the raid is revealed as a cache of valuable diamonds, and as the gang make their getaway, Vernon escapes over the roof, but not before he has pushed the old caretaker down the stairs, leaving him fatally injured. The police, alerted by an observant constable, arrive at the scene and a full-scale car chase begins, culminating with the gang dumping their vehicle in the river and escaping on foot. Vernon arrives at his rendezvous with Dan in a church and hands him the package to be smuggled on board the ship.

In parallel with these developments, the film follows Johnny and Pat as they climb to the top of St. Paul's Cathedral (where Pat momentarily catches sight of Vernon on the roof). The film follows them as they take a river trip to the Maritime Museum and Royal Observatory at Greenwich; and here on the site of the zero degree line of longitude, Johnny muses with Pat about the nature of the black and white world they inhabit. In response to Pat's assertion that colour 'doesn't matter', Johnny counters that 'it does, you know . . . maybe one day . . .', implying the possibility of a better future, if more white people were like Pat. On the tram on the way back, Johnny almost declares his love for Pat, but can see no future in their relationship. Instead, they part as friends.

When Dan goes to see Maisie, she opens the packet to reveal the diamonds and as soon as she sees them she realises where they are from, telling Dan that she heard on the radio news of the jewel robbery and the death of the watchman. Dan panics, but Maisie calms him down and hides the diamonds in a tin of brilliantine. Dan is now anxious not to involve Johnny with the diamonds, but Maisie persuades him against his better judgement. Their conversation has, however, been overheard by Maisie's younger sister, and after a fight between the two women, the police learn that the diamonds are in possession of a sailor on the *Dunbar* and police and Customs arrive on board to prevent the ship from sailing. Dan nervously meets Johnny in a pub and passes him the tin containing the diamonds. Returning to the ship, Johnny finds out that the departure of the *Dunbar* has been delayed and he immediately sets off for the Camberwell Palace, where he knows Pat is meeting friends. However, when he arrives and sees her with a crowd of her white friends, he feels alienated and unable to join her, turns on his heel and disconsolately leaves, intending to return to the ship.

The police now have Dan's name and are looking for him. When he returns to the ship to discover that Johnny isn't there, he goes in search of him. He first tries the pub, where the police arrive looking for him. When he goes to Maisie's house, she tells him that he is wanted for murder and reveals her true colours by refusing to help him and threatening to call the police. With nowhere else to go, he flees to Sally's lodgings. At first she too wants him to go, but relents when he tells her of his desperate circumstances and how he has involved the hapless Johnny. Her advice – that he should tell the police everything – is accompanied by her reassurance that she will stand by him. Charged with a new sense of moral purpose, Dan leaves, resolved to find Johnny, retrieve the jewels and to turn himself in to the police. However, he is picked up at gun point by the gang and Vernon, who have also been looking for him and their loot. They speed off with him in a car, but are spotted and a police chase ensues. As they race through the Rotherhithe Tunnel, Dan struggles and the car crashes. He escapes onto the roof, pursued by Mike and Vernon, and is shot and wounded and falls into the river below. The police overpower Mike and then give chase to Vernon as he makes a suitably acrobatic bid to escape by jumping across a ventilator shaft high above the tunnel. This time, however, his leap fails and he falls to his death.

In parallel with this dramatic sequence, the film follows Johnny as he makes his way from one pub to another, and in a drinking club he is fleeced of all his money (but not the diamonds) by another drunk. When he discovers this

Dan, Johnny and the diamonds in *Pool of London* (1951) (Courtesy of Steve Chibnall Archive)

and goes berserk he is thrown out of the club. '*They're* all the same' says the barman as Johnny is thrown into the gutter. He staggers to his feet and lurches his way back towards the ship. Hidden aboard an old sailing barge, Dan wakes to find it under sail and moving down the Thames. With this possibility of escape beckoning, he grapples with his conscience and, with Sally's voice exhorting him to redeem himself and Johnny's involvement, he leaves the barge and returns to the London docks to find his pal. The police and customs officers now believe that Dan and Johnny were in the plot together. Johnny awakes early to find himself in the bombed-out ruins of an old church near the river. He rushes through the streets to the ship and as he nears the docks Dan intercepts him and reclaims the diamonds. Johnny is concerned for Dan and realises that something is not right. Dan, however, intentionally rebuffs his friend and taunts him: 'What's wrong, that skin of yours so thick you don't know when you're not wanted?' Apparently rejected by Dan, Johnny turns away and goes aboard. The film closes with the *Dunbar* casting off from the Pool of London. On the dockside, Dan gives himself and the diamonds up to the police and waves to Johnny as the ship sails. Sally learns of his surrender in her office overlooking the Pool. The *Dunbar* sails under the raised Tower Bridge and disappears into the fog of the river.

On release in February 1951, the film attracted extensive but mixed attention from contemporary reviewers. *Kine Weekly* trumpeted it as an

> Outstanding semi-documentary romantic crime melodrama, centring upon the mighty, bizarre and forbidding Pool of London. Definitely another highly successful Ealing attempt to put our vast city on the box-office map, it's easily the equal of 'The Blue Lamp'. (22 February 1951)

However, this tone of approval was largely reserved for the film's documentary quality and cinematography. A more qualified assessment was offered by the renowned documentary filmmaker Paul Rotha, who also felt that the film was better than its predecessor *The Blue Lamp*, suggesting that the film represented a significant movement:

> Ealing Studios are trying very sincerely, I believe, to build up a school of authentic British cinema and are certainly in the attempt taking their cameras out and about, that fact in itself is welcome. (*Public Opinion*, 2 March 1951)

But Rotha, like many other critics of the time, was less than appreciative of the relationship between the documentary backgrounds of the film and the multiple, episodic narratives superimposed upon them. From his point of view these did not organically grow out of the situations: 'Perhaps there are too many characters and too much incident? . . . Perhaps the makers tried to pack in too much?' (ibid.). Other voices from the Left praised the authentic London docks atmosphere and the film's willingness to tackle the race theme. However, for Thomas Spencer of the *Daily Worker* it was yet another regrettable example of true, native settings being sacrificed to Hollywood conventions, unnecessary 'cops and robbers' business and 'unattractive American personalities' (quoted in Stead 1989: 164), a theme taken up in many other critical commentaries: 'I wish the incidents could have been as stirring as the pictures, which are symphonic in their beauty. This is however a stale and sordid little drama' (*Daily Express*, 22 February 1951).

In the same vein, *The Times* lauded the 'beautiful photography', but lamented that the film 'has to dabble in a threadbare, artificial story of crime', ending with the 'inevitable' chase (26 February 1951); and true to form, the *Monthly Film Bulletin* grudgingly damned with faint praise:

> Dearden handles the scenes of violence in a craftsmanlike if rather contrived and artificial manner, but tenderness and feeling escape him. *Pool of London* has the elements of an average melodrama, but they are never satisfactorily brought together, and the result is a diffuse film, lacking shape and control. (March 1951)

The tension in the film between documentary authenticity and melodramatic excess probably resulted from the two very different writers of the screenplay. John Eldridge was schooled in wartime documentary and *Pool of London* was his first studio writing assignment, whereas Jack Whittingham had a strong commercial background in genre cinema and had written the crime melodrama *Cage of Gold* the previous year.[40] Contemporary British film criticism demonstrated a clear preference for social realism and readily rejected the polluting influence of 'tinsel', as had been previously demonstrated in the critical response to *The Captive Heart* (1946).

The theme of racism and the relationship the film draws between Johnny and Pat was widely commented upon. However, while most reviewers applauded the film's address to the issue, Cameron's performance and his embodiment of the experience of prejudice, many followed the *Express*:

> This wet-foot drama has its best moments in the scenes between Earl Cameron, a sympathetic negro and Susan Shaw, as a London girl who likes him. But the film dodges the implications of the situation it has created. (22 February 1951)

The film appears to have been only a modest commercial success. Michael Relph recalled it as 'not really successful',[41] while figures cited in Harper and Porter state earnings as £130,000 (2003: 285).

Subsequent critical discussions of the film, especially those which classify it as a social problem film, have been somewhat ambivalent. Landy notes that 'the film focuses on working class characters but introduces the race issue, a rare concern in British cinema of the era' (1991: 470). However, she argues that the relationship between Pat and Johnny is highly problematic and awkwardly handled, citing Hill:

> As with so many liberal films the concern to represent blacks positively had led to an over-compensation. Johnny (Earl Cameron) represents the model 'coon' – polite, deferential and reflective, trusting to a point where he becomes unwittingly involved in crime. As such, Johnny represents no 'threat' and this is underlined by the film's treatment of sexuality. Johnny pursues a rather antiseptic relationship with 'nice girl' Pat (Susan Shaw) before decently deciding it won't work because of the colour bar. (1986: 83)

Hill goes on to note that the narrative structure of later Dearden and Relph films – including *Sapphire* (1959) – allow for a more complex exploration of race and black sexuality. In this instance, however, Durgnat took a more qualified and perhaps historically sympathetic stance:

> It's to the credit of Relph and Dearden that, while the English were con-gratulating themselves on their infinite fair-mindedness, they showed, in *Pool of London* (1951), a coloured seaman (Earl Cameron) who feels victim of race prejudice. (1970: 105)

Perhaps, as Higson in his careful analysis has suggested, within the clash of conventions in the multi-generic nature of the film and its consequent lack of unity, the issue could only be placed on the agenda, not fully explored or developed. This, he argues, is the result of the way in which 'the story of Johnny and his relations with others is both extraneous to the central crime thriller involving Dan, and imposed upon the locale, in that Johnny has been imported into this authentic place' (1997: 167).

The cross-generic nature of *Pool of London*, and indeed much of Dearden's cinema, invites a complexity of reading extending beyond the normative Ealing film. As well as the contentious issue of miscegenation, critics have dis-cerned other disturbingly un-Ealing traits like homosexuality in the film. There have been claims for a homoerotic bonding between Dan and Johnny, visu-ally expressed through the interplay of looks in bare-chested or partially robed scenes. This subconscious 'gay imagery' is made explicit in the 'unmistakable gay overtones' of Vernon, who, as an accomplice mentions, 'wants to meet a nice obliging sailor' (Williams 2000: 184). Moreover, the documentary realism is subverted through the unsettling resort to *noir* photography, signifying the 'connections between the dark worlds of racism and homosexuality, which further disrupt wartime consensus ideology and rigid heterosexual boundaries' (ibid.: 185). One has to be careful not to read backwards from *Sapphire* (1959) and *Victim* (1961) and impress later and subsequent themes onto the earlier cinema of Dearden and Relph. But it should be noted that the tensions generated through clashing a realist aesthetic with *noir* stylisation and the introduction of controversial themes like racism tend to attract a criticism that seeks fissures in the body politic of Ealing and sense a harsher cinema that anticipates 'features that would erupt in British society during the 1950s – the Notting Hill racial riots and the Wolfenden Report on Homosexuality' (ibid.).

THE SQUARE RING (1953)

> [Boxing] is the most tragic of all sports because more than any other human activity it consumes the very excellence it displays – its drama is this very consumption. (Joyce Carol Oates 1987: 13)

> It is dark, and the rooftops' silhouette is obscure. Suddenly, an electric sign is switched on. The sign is made from electric-light bulbs set in an iron frame. The sign spells out the word B O X I N G, one letter at a time. (*Final Shooting Script*, 1953)

This stark device was to be used to open *The Square Ring,* and the film was to end with the lights in the sign going off, one by one. In the event, these opening and closing moments of the film were discarded and the film begins with the deserted square ring of the title suddenly floodlit and with lights fading out at the end. In the intervening 83 minutes of action, the film chronicles the events taking place in an evening's series of bouts, set in a dark, urban location, following the fortunes of six professional fighters and their respective stories. The film was based closely on the successful stage play by the Australian dramatist Ralph W. Peterson, which had run to some acclaim at the Lyric Theatre, Hammersmith in late 1952.[42] Its transfer from theatre to screen involved a number of the actors from the stage production, notably Bill Owen and George Rose.[43] Robert Westerby developed the screenplay, with additional dialogue by Peter Myers and Alec Graham, and the film was released in late June 1953. As Barr has suggested:

> One can see why Ealing snapped up the rights to this play, and why it was Dearden who filmed it: it offers a neat cross-section of boxers, from starry-eyed novice to punch-drunk veteran, and an unflattering picture of commercial exploitation. (1977: 191)[44]

The film betrays its theatrical origins in a number of ways, but most obviously in its dependence on interior sets and minimal use of external locations.[45]

The action switches between interiors, the twin 'hubs' of the changing room and the ring, and the surrounding environs of the hall, the crowd, the promoter's office, the bar and the nearby café. The film also follows the predictable schedule of the evening's programme, including the mid-point intermission. It creates a claustrophobic atmosphere, and as a result its narrative is heavily character-driven, focused primarily on the masculine worlds of the men who fight in the evening's billing and the melodramatic relationships that both lead them to, and follow them from, the ring. Elements of documentary realism are tempered by a moderate *noir* aesthetic, most apparent in the filming of the action in the ring, in the close observation of the brutal encounters intercut with the associated reactions of the crowd.

As the lights come up on the boxing ring and the deserted hall comes to life in readiness for the evening bouts, the film follows Danny Felton (Jack Warner) as he makes his way to the changing room. This is his domain, where he prepares the promoter's fighters on the evening's bill, seeing them into the ring and dealing with them when they return. Warner is well cast in this role, combining his established paternalism with experience and clear-cut morality. He runs through the list for the night with his chirpy assistant Frank (Alfie Bass). The first fighter to arrive is the nervous novice, Eddie Lloyd (Ronald Lewis – in his first film role), a Welsh boy from Cardiff, and here for his first professional bout. His naïveté is evident and Danny and Frank try, good-naturedly, to reassure him. By contrast, the next fighter to arrive is brash and cocksure. Happy Burns (Bill Owen) arrives in a smart convertible with horns blaring, accompanied by three attractive young women (including Joan Sims). He greets Danny like a long-lost friend; 'seventeen fights in six months and not a mark on my beautiful kisser' he brags as he prepares for the evening ahead. Rick Martell (Maxwell Reed) is the next boxer to arrive, with his manager Warren (Michael Golden) and the glamorous Frankie (Joan Collins) in tow.[46] The film constructs him as a much less straightforward character, confirmed as the camera follows his manager, to tip off a contact that 'he'll go in the fourth'. Despite Frankie's adoring support, here is the first hint that all may not be 'square' in the ring, something reinforced by Rick's sullen cynicism towards the young Eddie, when he enters the changing room: 'What a bill', he complains, 'kids and has-beens'.

The unkempt, shambling figure of Rowdy Rawlings (Bill Travers) arrives next, an archetypal gentle, child-like giant, whose life outside the ring seems to be dominated by the science fiction books he reads incessantly, to some comic effect, as the film develops. Following on his heels is Whitey Johnson (George Rose), an older fighter, whose lengthy time in the ring has left him punch-drunk, with poor eyesight and slurred, repetitive speech. On his way in, Whitey encounters Adams (Sid James), the owner and promoter, oozing seediness and insincerity, even when he encounters three officials from the Boxing Board, in attendance for the evening.

As Whitey enters the dressing room, the young Welshman, Eddie, confesses to Happy that he wants to do well that night because his parents have come to watch him. His innocent suggestion that 'it's always been a bit of sport before' is met by another mocking rejoinder from Martell, the hardened professional: 'Sport? You'll learn.' At this point, Martell is taken to one side by his manager, who reminds him that he had better go down in the fourth round and make a better job than he did the previous month. Martell bridles at this, asserting that this will be the last time he throws a fight, but he is nevertheless revealed as a corrupt and embittered character.

The final fighter to arrive, Jim 'Kid' Curtis (Robert Beatty), the former British and Empire light-heavyweight champion, first calls into the Stadium Café, where he is not welcomed by the proprietor, the father of Peg (Bernadette O'Farrell), his estranged wife. Boxing came between them and caused their break-up some years earlier. Peg hated him fighting and although she wishes him good luck in the fight tonight, she insists that they will never have a future together as long as he continues to fight. He leaves and makes his way through the crowds in the hall where his arrival provokes some excitement and he encounters Lou Lewis (Eddie Byrne) and his wife, Eve (Kay Kendall). Lewis is a successful manager who currently manages Happy Burns, and in the interchange between them, it is clear that Curtis and Eve have known each other in the past. 'He'll manage you, if you win tonight,' she promises.

Adams is warned by the official from the Boxing Board that he expects to see a better standard of fighting and refereeing than the week before and he passes this on to the boxers. Curtis arrives in the dressing room just after Whitey goes up for the first fight of the night, betting with Martell that he'll win before the sixth round.

Having introduced the boxers and sketched a little of their respective characters, the film follows them as they go to fight in the ring and then return to the dressing room. With the exception of Curtis, who fights last, there is little or – in the case of Whitey Johnson and Rowdy Rawlings – no actual film of their fights. The roars of the crowd heard from the dressing room give a flavour of their respective fortunes in the ring and their stories are relayed as they return.

Whitey Johnson, who nobody really expected to win, returns with old scars bleeding around his eyes having knocked out his opponent in the fourth round. After he has been patched up, however, he is called to the promoter's office to be told by the doctor that he must never fight again and that his licence to box is withdrawn on grounds of his health: 'You're too old', says the doctor. Unable to understand how winning his fight warranted such a reward, he shambles off into an uncertain future with the sounds of the crowd echoing in his ears.

The young novice, Eddie Lloyd, is next in the ring and some of this fight is shown. Initially, he appears to be doing well against an older and more experienced opponent. The camera cuts from his action in the ring to the hopeful faces of his parents and friends cheering him on. Just as he appears to be getting the upper hand, however, his opponent rubs resin from the floor onto his glove and hits Eddie in the eye with it. He then uses dirty tactics to subdue Eddie and gives him a brutal beating. With his shocked parents looking on, Eddie is carried back to the dressing room, beaten and disillusioned, his Corinthian ideals shattered by his underhand treatment. After he recovers, in spite of Danny and the other fighters' assurances that it was just bad luck, he leaves, resolved never to fight again; 'It wasn't fair, that's all' are his parting words.

Rowdy Rawlings, meanwhile, is prised from his science fiction comic and its fantastic tales of the 'Uranium Lady' long enough to go up to the ring for his fight. He returns having knocked out his opponent, 'because he hit me'. Rick Martell is next, and when he learns that there are officials from the Boxing Board in attendance, he confronts his corrupt manager, refusing to throw the fight as planned. Warren threatens that Frankie will suffer if Martell doesn't stick to the arrangement on which bets have already been placed, and Frankie confirms that she has been threatened with razor slashing when she sees Martell. He enters the ring having indicated to Warren that he will after all comply with their agreement. Ironically, he is outmanoeuvred by a more crooked opponent who goes down in the second round. Martell returns to the dressing room as a laughing-stock and leaves hurriedly to protect Frankie from harm. She panics in the crowd during the intermission, but he finds her in time to knock out a man who appears to be about to attack her. They make their way to the exit, where he reassures her that they are quitting the boxing game for good.

The final two fights of the evening begin with Happy Burns being called into the ring. He plays to the crowd, and while he is fighting, Danny talks with the troubled 'Kid' Curtis about Peg and their lack of any future together as long as he remains a boxer. Unknown to Curtis, Danny has seen Peg to try to reconcile them, but Curtis is clearly worried about his future and asks Danny if he thinks he has a year left in him in the ring. Danny assures him he does, if he takes care of himself. At this moment, loud cheers herald the return of the victorious Happy; however, his win has been achieved at some cost. To his great indignity he reveals his nose which is swollen and bleeding, although it later proves not to be broken.

In the final event of the evening, Curtis enters the ring to fight a younger and stronger fighter and, initially, his experience enables him to dominate his opponent. In the dressing room, Danny confides to Frank that he hopes that Curtis doesn't win, explaining that he is worried by his future prospects and health if he does. In the ring, Curtis's stamina and technique falter as the younger opponent begins to assert his strength. After Curtis has been knocked down twice, Lewis and Eve and others in the crowd leave, sensing a foregone conclusion. On the ropes in the tenth round and taking a beating, Curtis does not see Peg arrive, as he is knocked down again. But he hangs on and in desperation lands a final combination of punches that puts his opponent down to be counted out. Peg and Danny are appalled by what they have seen. Curtis slumps in his corner and the doctor is called. He is carried back to the dressing room where he is pronounced dead. Danny sees Peg out of the Hall and then also leaves, encountering Happy Burns and his raucous entourage as they spill out of the pub. The film ends with the lights fading out on the now deserted square ring.

The film was generally well reviewed: 'Here at least is the determination to be different', wrote Roger Manvell;[47] and against the grain of its usual grudging approach to their work, the *Monthly Film Bulletin* commented: 'This slick and unpretentious entertainment picture is perhaps the most satisfactory film that Basil Dearden has yet directed . . . Sets the level of what the superior British entertainment film should be, but not very often is' (August 1953).[48]

The Times found it 'both a good boxing film and a good film in itself' (6 July 1953); while *Kine Weekly* considered it to be 'a near masterpiece, although we can hardly see it breaking down the average woman's antipathy to "leatherpusher's" fare . . . Grand man's film, but ticklish family and better class hall proposition'; and this concern continued: 'brilliant mosaic that it is, contains more brawn than heart', with the suggestion that it might be wise to bill it with the 'support of a romantically inclined "second"' (2 July 1953).

Most contemporary reviewers recognised that the film presented a stark critique of the boxing world and the brutality and corruption that rendered the ring anything but 'square'; it was 'a bold and uncompromising attack on boxing', argued *The Sunday Times* (12 July 1953); and this theme has been developed in subsequent attempts to 'place' the film in the Ealing post-war universe and Dearden and Relph's *oeuvre*. For a number of commentators and historians, the film articulates a 'distaste for post-war Britain', presenting a critique of the corrupt, inhuman commercialism associated with professional boxing, indicative of the values driving the emergent 'mass' consumer culture characteristic of the time (Richards 1997: 30).[49] The film manages to portray all the boxers as characters deserving sympathy, partly because they seem

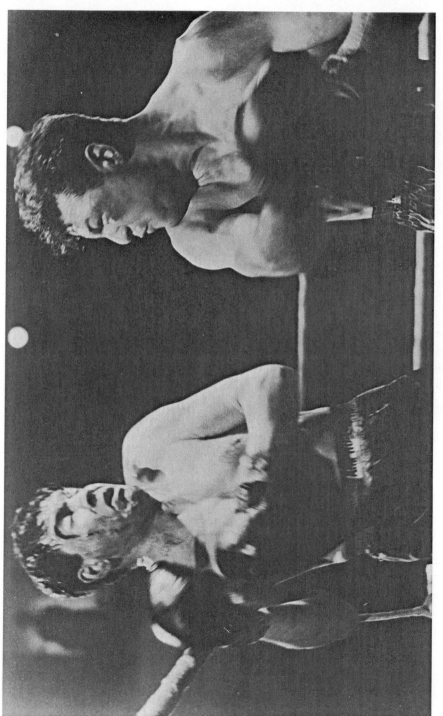

Kid Curtis receives the fatal blow in *The Square Ring* (1953) (Courtesy of Steve Chibnall Archive)

trapped in an unforgiving world whose prime motivation is their exploitation. With one or two exceptions, the crowd is also represented as uncaring,
brutalised and obsessed by sensation and gain,[50] in contrast with the stadium
crowd in *The Blue Lamp* (1950), where the racegoers converge on Riley as the
community renders up the delinquent to law and order. Here, the fight fans
are constructed as threatening, a baying mob terrifying Frankie, who is unable
to distinguish friend from foe. Only Danny, and to a lesser extent Peg, are able
to stand outside of the values of this world and represent a deeper truth and
commitment to tradition.[51]

In this way, the film is emblematic of the tragic melodrama characteristic
of this strand of Dearden and Relph's work together, in part derived from
the conventions of a genre that was experiencing renewed popularity in
1940s–1950s Hollywood. The popular and critical successes of *Body and
Soul* (1947) and *The Champion* (1949), in which the tragic trajectory of
'the hero's rise from the gutter of ghetto life to the dizzying heights of a
penthouse overlooking the city, followed by an equally dramatic fall', was
'pure formula' by the time of *The Square Ring* (Stanfield 2005: 66).[52] The
British film was far more parochial in outlook, but similarly deployed an
attenuated version of the 'American success story', especially in respect of
Kid Curtis and Happy Burns. Many Hollywood boxing films were produced by Leftists as vehicles for broader social commentary, and even if
this was not a first choice project for Dearden and Relph, then this aspect
could have appealed to them in terms of the exploitation of the working-
class fighters.[53]

Structurally, *The Square Ring* adopts the characteristic interweaving of
what Durgnat refers to as 'little stories', episodes in the lives of an apparently
random cross-section of men, brought together by chance and circumstance,
in this case, for an evening in the ring (1970: 51). In this instance, the film
steadfastly refuses any reference to the war. Three of the fighters end as tragic
figures, most obviously Curtis, whose dreams of a comeback and the resurrec-
tion of his marriage to Peg are fatally undone.[54] To a lesser extent, and perhaps
as a metaphor for the unforgiving nature of either end of the boxing career,
there are tragic elements in the film's resolution of both Whitey's and Lewis's
respective evenings in the ring. There is also the indication that life will not
always be so happy for Burns and his confident claims: his career is on the up,
he aims for the title, he'll defend it three times, then quit while at the top.
A cynical Curtis, speaking from experience, tells him straight 'You'll never
get out, not when you're on top you won't.' The penultimate image of the
film has the party-loving Happy Burns with his hangers-on roaring off into
the night, shouting his name, 'The next lightweight champion of the world',
unaware of the fate of Curtis.[55]

The style of the film is austere; for example, there is no music other than the march, which plays over the title and end credits. However, like many other Dearden films, it is distinguished by its photography and narrative construction. Despite the story's confinement to cramped interior spaces, the visual interest of the film never flags and the forward momentum of the action is maintained throughout. A fluid and mobile camera supports the relentless march of the drama, tracking figures along curving corridors, constantly reframing as characters disperse and regroup, and effectively switching dramatic focus. Otto Heller provides some gently noirish imagery: the outdoor location scenes are shot night for night, with glistening pavements, street lights and vibrant neon; the camera adopts a marginally lower level than the norm, enhancing the physicality of the fighters and bringing into shot the cheap lights of the stadium and dressing rooms with their naked bulbs; and some unobtrusive, deep-focus compositions as characters confront their emotional problems standing in the archways leading to the arena with the ring ominously in shot in the far distance.[56]

Heller's best work, though, is reserved for the action in the ring. Dearden intelligently builds to these obvious climaxes; the first bout, featuring Whitey Johnson, is covered from low level down at ringside and the viewer sees only the legs of the fighters as they give and gain ground. The next fight, involving the novice Lloyd, though receiving more direct coverage, is still partial, interspersed with other events as attention is deflected backstage to the dramas involving the other fighters. Martell's bout is only glimpsed as attention is given to the background drama of fixing and whether he will take a dive. Dearden's skill in decentring the narrative from the ostensible principal events serves the wider picture as the various sub-themes and other dramatic elements are not rendered subservient to the simple display of raw combat. The only fight to be provided with extensive coverage is the main event featuring Curtis. Heller captures this in glossy high-contrast images, with the ring and the fighters bathed in a luminescent white light and backgrounds receding into velvety blackness and some stark, low-angle shots looking up at the bloodied and solitary figure of Curtis, isolated in the image, posed against the glare of the stadium lights, patently with nowhere to go. The choreography of camera with fighters is well planned and thoughtful, and results in an exciting and authentic display of professional boxing that matches the very best of Hollywood's efforts.

In one of the few cutaways from the ring during the culminating fight, Danny explains the tragedy of Curtis to Burns. 'He has to fight,' he says. 'And he *must* end up a loser.' A shock-cut returns the viewer to the ring as Curtis takes a vicious blow to the head. The older man is beginning to take a pounding and the tragic dénouement unfurls, as predicted by the old pro.[57]

THE RAINBOW JACKET (1954)

Racing lends itself easily to plot-making and paves the way for sudden changes of fortune; there is, besides, the excitement of the race itself, although here it is the student of film conventions rather than of form who will spot the winner. (*The Times*, 6 July 1953)

Following on from the success of *The Square Ring*, Dearden and Relph's next venture was another film with a sporting theme. *The Rainbow Jacket* goes behind the scenes of the horse racing world. Dearden's final shooting script is dated October 1953, but it is clear from the location sheets in the script that filming actually began much earlier on a film that had the working title *Newmarket Heath*. In fact, very soon after the release of *The Square Ring*, shooting began from early July and through August in order to capture the documentary backgrounds and action from the actual race meetings at Newmarket, Sandown Park, Lingfield, Epsom and Doncaster.[58] Some of this simply consisted of background inserts, but also involved key members of the cast performing significant segments of the eventual narrative.[59] Logistically, this must have been quite a challenge, not only for Dearden and Relph, but also for Hal Mason (general manager and production supervisor), Jack Rix (production manager) and Harry Kratz (location manager). Three assistant directors were employed in the production of the film which was shot in Technicolor by Otto Heller.

The screenplay for *The Rainbow Jacket* was an original piece of work by T. E. B. Clarke, which had allowed him to indulge his passion for horse racing.[60] It was the first time he had collaborated with Dearden and Relph since *The Blue Lamp* (1950). The film tells the story of an older jockey, Sam Lilley (Bill Owen), and his young protégé, Georgie Crain (Fella Edmonds), a working-class boy from Battersea, who dreams of becoming a jockey. Sam was once a star jockey, but he has been disgraced and lost his licence for 'pulling a horse at Ascot'. He lives now on the margins of the horse racing world, banned from the race courses, making a living by means of small bets and tips that contacts with his old life can afford. The opening scenes of the film at Lingfield Park see the irrepressible Sam trading tips with Harry (Sid James), the lugubrious and dissatisfied owner of a mobile snack-bar. Denied legitimate access to the race meeting, Sam is reduced to breaking in by means of a loose fence panel, and it is here that he first meets Georgie. Taken by Georgie's intuitive knowledge and sense of horses and jockeys, Sam accompanies the lad back to his home, where they meet his mother, Barbara (Kay Walsh), narrowly evading the headmaster seeking an explanation for young Georgie's absence from school. Sam introduces himself to the mother and, in spite of her reservations that 'it was racing that ruined his father' (now deceased), she is won over by his vision of a 'once in a million' future for her son as a top jockey, and Sam resolves to find him a start as an apprentice jockey in a racing stable.[61]

After initial, fruitless enquiries with old contacts, a chance encounter at Sandown Park with a horse that has lost its rider proves to be the key. Sam and Georgie rein in the runaway horse and Sam lets Georgie ride it back to the enclosure. As a result, Georgie gets his chance to become an apprentice at the Newmarket Stables patronised by Lord Logan (Robert Morley), owned by the trainer, Mr Tyler (Edward Underdown) and his wife, Monica (Honor Blackman). He settles into the routines of the stables under the kindly eye of Mr Voss (Charles Victor), and his precocious promise as a jockey is soon recognised when he is given the chance to ride The Duke of Agincourt in an apprentice's race.[62] His letters home are read eagerly by his mother and Sam, and this news leads Sam to borrow and bet £100 on his protégé. The film follows Georgie through the preparatory rituals for the race. In the event, following a photo-finish, he comes an unexpectedly close second to the favourite, but he has made his mark. From a distance Sam watches the race with pride. However, his lost bet has put him in debt to the crooked bookmaker Tod Fenwick (Bernard Lee)[63] and his spivish henchmen, including Bernie Rudd (Ronald Ward), who loses no time in using the debt as a lever to get inside information about Georgie's next race. Sam is adamant that he will not involve Georgie in any shady dealings. However, his debt remains unpaid and Barbara witnesses a strong-arm incident as the pressure on Sam to 'pay up' escalates. Their relationship is now clearly developing beyond simple friendship. Unaware of these circumstances, Georgie gives his mother an inside 'tip' for Black Pirate, a horse at the stables running at Epsom the following day. Barbara sees this as a means to clear Sam's debt and she steals £50 from the safe where she works as a stake for the bet.

On the day of the race she places the stolen money on Black Pirate, but Georgie has unexpectedly been given the chance to ride an outsider, Gretna Green, in the same race. When Sam hears of this, he switches the small stake he has borrowed from Harry, who wants to sell his snack-bar, to back Georgie. In a close finish, Georgie is barged into the railings in the final furlongs by the favourite; and following an objection, Georgie is declared the winner. As a result, Georgie's performance wins Sam £100, but loses his mother the stolen £50 she placed on the favourite. Sam pays off his debt immediately, but then learns of Barbara's predicament. He resolves to help her repay the money before it is missed, and goes 'cap in hand' to Fenwick to borrow the £50. In his opulent surroundings, Fenwick is constructed as a doting father, but not without an edge of malevolence. The scene also confirms his involvement in Sam's professional disgrace and furthermore that any money advanced will be conditional on Sam being able to persuade Georgie not to win his next race on the much fancied Duke of Agincourt. As a result, Sam goes to visit Georgie, partly confessing his situation and, when Georgie refuses to 'pull the race', Sam tells him how to disable the horse by manipulating feed and water. Georgie begs Sam not to force him to do it, torn between loyalty to his friend and his sense of what is right (and wrong).

In the event, Georgie almost succumbs to the proposed plan but opts for a different course of action; while leading the race, he intentionally falls from his mount and is injured and Sam's concern for the boy is noticed by Lord Logan. However, Sam collects his reward from Fenwick and is able to give Barbara the money in time for her to place it in the safe and conceal her crime. As a result of the events in the race, however, Georgie is called to face an official inquiry. In front of the Board, when pressed about his friendship with Sam Lilley, Georgie defends his friend and is exonerated. His career proceeds apace and with win after win he becomes a racing celebrity,[64] and as he does, Sam's fortunes prosper. With this newfound wealth, Sam proposes marriage to Barbara in his new, luxurious flat. She is, however, wary, preferring a solid, regular job to the ups and downs of the betting life. This temporary rift is overcome, however, when Sam receives a letter confirming that his licence to race has been restored. Georgie is overjoyed at this news, but is then given more reason to celebrate when he is asked to ride one of the favourite horses, Fair Noon, in the forthcoming St Leger. His joy is however cut short by the visit of Bernie, the fixer for crooked bookmaker Fenwick, who tries to blackmail him to lose the race with the cheque that was used to pay Sam off, threatening to disclose it to the stewards. Despite his refusal to co-operate, Georgie is distraught and caught in an unenviable double-bind. He can either 'throw' the race against his youthful principles or betray Sam, his friend and mentor, to whom he owes everything. Sam, it transpires, is also to ride in the race.

Against this tense back-drop, the day of the St Leger dawns and, with Raymond Glendenning providing the commentary,[65] the tension builds as Sam realises that all is not well with Georgie. 'You are riding to win, aren't you?' he asks before the race, but Georgie's response provides him with scant reassurance. Inevitably, the race sees the older jockey Sam and his novice protégé fighting for the lead in the closing stages. In an act of great selflessness, Sam whips Georgie's horse through to victory, thus countering Georgie's attempt to lose the race. Georgie wins, and Sam returns to the enclosure to face again the public ignominy and disgrace of an inquiry, which suspends him, this time for life. Just before Georgie goes out to his next race (in fact replacing Sam), they meet in the changing room and Sam discovers the truth behind Georgie's actions.

The film ends with background commentary as Georgie wins this next

Neck-and-neck, Georgie and Sam in *The Rainbow Jacket* (1954) (Courtesy of Steve Chibnall Archive)

race, and Sam and Barbara are united and walk together into their new future. Sam is bowed but not beaten, and the final scenes of the film convey a sense of his qualified, but honourable compromise. He settles for a steady job close to the race-courses he loves; he has just enough money to 'buy the little old snack-bar' from Harry. Barr suggests that this conclusion to the film is 'a characteristic Dearden climax of atonement', and indeed he makes much of the purchase of the snack-bar (*little* and *old*) and what it represented in terms of the Ealing at the time, towards petrification, conformism and middle-aged complacency (1977: 157–8). Unlike *Mandy* (d. A. Mackendrick, 1952), he argues that *The Rainbow Jacket* 'is overwhelmingly with the adults and the way they resolve things', and that the youthful promise of the boy is suffocated by the deference-ridden institutional system of the racing world. In a similar vein, Harper and Porter have argued that the film is characteristic of 'Phase Two' films at Ealing, preoccupied with repetition, whereby 'only minor tinkering is possible with the determinism of time' (2003: 65).[66] While this may be the case, the film succeeded in giving a flavour of the life of the horse racing world at the time and of the types who inhabited it; and in articulating albeit an oblique critique of the criminal aspects of the betting culture associated with it.[67] This was how some of the contemporary reviews saw it:

> Thrill packed, amusing and deeply moving racing comedy melodrama, superbly photographed in Technicolor . . . The gallery of types is amazingly complete and together with the many exciting encounters on the turf and sharp digs at the low-down street corner bookmaking fraternity, smoothly rounds off one of the greatest screen sporting prints ever. (*Kinematograph Weekly*, 3 June 1954)

Other reviewers took a slightly more qualified stance. The *Monthly Film Bulletin* found it to be

> a capably fashioned entertainment picture, stamped with the Ealing Studios' brand of realism which, at best, has gone much further than this . . . Only in the last third of the picture do the limitations of a dramatised journalistic approach make themselves felt . . . Basil Dearden's direction, as in *The Square Ring*, is more sober and more genuinely incisive than in his earlier films, and maintains an admirable competence. (July 1954)

The film enjoyed a promising opening in the West End, but then failed to replicate this on general release.

As a sporting melodrama, the film is much softer, more light-hearted and undoubtedly less hard-hitting than *The Square Ring*. The tragic dimension is less clear-cut and is restricted to the figure of Sam, who clearly sacrifices his own future in favour of Georgie, his protégé and generational surrogate. His altruism permanently ends any possibility of his return to the racing he loves. However, in this act, he also redeems his own tarnished past and secures a future, as Richards notes: 'losing a career as a jockey but gaining a family and a small business – the Ealing ideal' (1997: 31). Furthermore, this is a future that Sam appears to embrace wholeheartedly and it does not seem to represent either a temporary compromise or unsatisfactory way forward.

DAVY (1957)

I'm more than pleased to hear that Michael Relph plans to enter the directorial field, since I feel he really has something to offer.
'Now what I would really like to do', he said, 'is to make a CinemaScope film in black and white. Some people say that the widescreen is not so intimate. They argue that the shape is all wrong. I disagree. I believe that the CinemaScope screen is very intimate because it draws you right into the picture.' (*To-Day's Cinema*, 10 October 1955)

Davy was the last comedy to be made under the Ealing banner, but outside of the studios at Ealing. It was also the last script written for Ealing by William Rose before he returned to America. It marked Michael Relph's formal directorial debut; Dearden acted as producer on the film in a role-reversal that Relph had hinted at in an interview two years earlier (ibid.). The film was made as part of a rather unsuccessful six-film deal that Balcon had nego-tiated with MGM, following the announcement of the BBC's purchase of Ealing Studios in late 1955.[68] Harper and Porter give an insightful account of Balcon's rather ineffectual strategies in this uneasy period, as the snarling MGM Lion replaced the resonant Rank Gong at the opening of the films.[69] Many years later, in an interview with Sidney Cole, Michael Relph remem-bered this, his first experience of directing a film, with some regret, indicating that the production was made when Ealing had begun to fold: 'the steam had gone out of the whole operation by that time', he commented. In particular, he recalled the sense of a new and changed 'pecking order': *Davy* was 'made in a pre-fab, on a back lot at Elstree, where we were very much the poor relations' (Relph 1990).

Relph and Dearden's shooting scripts are dated January 1957. They confirm that the facilities of the Royal Opera House, Covent Garden, includ-ing orchestra and chorus, were used in several of the scenes, when Davy auditions. It is tempting to suggest that rather like the earlier *Who Done It?* (1956), a vehicle for the emerging popularity of Benny Hill, *Davy* was cast to capitalise on the rapidly growing public reputation of its star, Harry Secombe. The Welshman had performed a number of small parts in films prior to *Davy* and by the mid–1950s he was getting regular work and recognition in the new medium of television.[70] However, his principal claim to fame was in radio, as one of the members of 'The Goons'.[71] His performance in the film combines comic slapstick elements from his Goon personae with his operatic abilities.

The cast also included George Relph, Michael's father, and this may have had an additional bearing on Relph's involvement as director.[72] The film was shot by Douglas Slocombe in Technicolor and the widescreen Technirama process. Late in 1954, it had been announced that all future Rank and Ealing films would be shot in VistaVision, with the view to making the films more saleable in the United States (*Kinematograph Weekly*, 16 December 1954). This never came about, but Ealing employed the similar system of Technirama on *Davy*, the first time the process was used on a British film.[73]

The film has as its central focus a comedy variety act, The Mad Morgans, introduced as they are about to go on stage at Collins, a popular but second-rate music hall in London. As they arrive in their backstage changing room to prepare for their matinée performance, the film introduces Gwen Morgan (Susan Shaw), her husband, George (Ron Randell), their young son, Tim (Peter Frampton), Uncle Pat (George Relph), Davy (Harry Secombe) and their friend Eric (Bill Owen). This is a close-knit family group of performers, in an equally close backstage world of friends and fellow artistes, and Davy is introduced as the most popular of them all, joking and helping everyone with wit and generosity. On this occasion, George brings news that their act has been spotted by an agent of the famous impresario Val Parnell, and that they may have prospects for real fame and fortune: 'Finsbury Park Empire – TV – maybe even The Palladium'. Tensions are immediately made apparent between George and Eric, as George plans to change their act; and tellingly, Uncle Pat asks if it is not just Davy who has been spotted. Just as they are about to go on stage, they are disconcerted to learn that Davy is going to an audition at The Royal Opera House, after the matinée show. Having introduced the principal characters and hinted at their respective issues, the film cuts to The Mad Morgans on stage, beginning with a bravura performance from Davy, playing the crowd with his singing and comedy, watched from above the stage with great amusement by young Tim. Davy is clearly the centre of attraction. His extraordinary singing voice and slapstick comic timing holds the whole show together, making an ordinary act exceptional. Even the theatre manager, watching from the wings, joins in with the laughter, remembering the days when Davy's father was part of the act.

To great applause, the act finishes and they leave the stage and return to the dingy dressing-room where Davy's audition continues to dominate the discussion. In the face of mounting pressure from Uncle Pat, Gwen and George, who are clearly worried about their futures if he were to leave, Davy asks for

The Mad Morgans in *Davy* (1957) (Courtesy of Steve Chibnall Archive)

this one chance to prove himself. Eric is the only one who supports him, and with Uncle Pat's admonishments about not deserting a family act ringing in his ears, Davy leaves for his audition, taking young Tim with him, to save the boy from any further bickering and upset.

The film now cuts to a series of sequences shot on location in the splendour of a full chorus rehearsal on the stage of The Royal Opera House. Davy waits nervously in a café and there are signs that his normal ebullience is deserting him in these unfamiliar surroundings. He is momentarily buoyed up by banter with the waitresses (Gladys Henson and Joan Sims) and is befriended by Joanna Reeves (Adele Leigh), also nervously awaiting an audition. They are called into the auditorium and, into the presence of the great operatic impresario Sir Giles Manning (Alexander Knox), who first hears Joanna sing. She performs Mozart delightfully and it is then Davy's turn. His nervousness by now is palpable, and he is overawed when he takes to the stage. After a false start, however, he sings 'Nessun Dorma' as he has never sung before, with great power and emotion. However, as he reaches the final climax, Tim, who has climbed up onto a gantry above the stage, accidentally sends a set crashing to the ground. Davy rushes to save the boy and in a combination of embarrassment and anxiety, he flees the scene. 'I'm a comic, not a singer', he confides to the boy as they make their way back, 'I bet they're all laughing their heads off.'

Back at the theatre they encounter a scene of some disarray; Uncle Pat, dressed as a clown, is drunk and maudlin, Gwen and George are on the verge of separation, while Eric tries to hold them all together. When Davy arrives they want to know what happened at the audition and when he replies that nothing happened, George taunts Davy, insinuating that he 'flopped'. Just as they are about to come to blows, a commotion heralds the arrival of Sir Giles and Joanna. Davy apologises to Sir Giles for his abrupt departure from The Royal Opera House, and with some embarrassment invites them into the backstage dressing room. Eric realises that Davy's audition must have impressed Sir Giles and as they wait outside, he rounds on the other members of the act, confronting them with their selfishness. In the dressing room, Sir Giles confirms that, in his opinion, Davy can sing and has great potential, and he invites Davy to join the opera company. Davy explains that he cannot leave the family act and outlines the dilemma that he finds himself in: that his leaving would spell disaster for his family and friend. Sir Giles, although somewhat taken aback by this response, leaves, respecting Davy for his decision. Davy bids farewell to Joanna, accepting that any romance between them would now be impossible. He returns to a much chastened family team, who believe that he has accepted Sir Giles' offer. It is left to the young boy to voice the question 'Did you say yes?', and when he replies to the contrary, Tim asks why Davy has chosen to stay. Davy replies that 'I think we should all stick together – all families should', and with this reassurance, normal, raucous life is suddenly restored. In a burst of frenzied activity, the film ends with The Mad Morgans taking to the stage for their next performance.

Reviews of the film were decidedly mixed, most commenting on Secombe's performance and the 'slightness' of the script. Jympson Harman, writing in *The Evening News*, found it to be 'probably the most "corny", unsophisticated picture ever to slip through Sir Michael Balcon's academic sieve' (2 January 1958). Several reviews compared *Davy* with *The Naked Truth*, which had been released about the same time, pitting the two Goons, Secombe and Sellers, against each other, and Sellers was adjudged to be much the more successful. Anthony Carthew for instance, went so far as to suggest that such a comparison was 'unfair to Secombe' and that his appearance in the film had caused 'reputation harm' (*Daily Herald*, 3 January 1958; see also *The Times*, 6 January 1958). During the production there had been speculation as to whether Secombe would make the grade as a screen comedian. 'I think so', commented Michael Relph:

> In the past we have made the mistake of trying to take a comedian's stage personality and build a story around it. This time we have based our story line on the comedian's own natural personality. (*Kinematograph Weekly*, 28 February 1957)[74]

Other reviews tried to put a brave face on the film. *Kine Weekly*, in particular, assessed it as an 'Excellent British Star booking . . . the picture straddles the music hall and the opera house and brings to the screen the best of the two extremes in entertainment' (28 November 1957). But on this occasion, the general critical tenor was well summed up by the *Monthly Film Bulletin*: 'An uneasy combination of broad farce and crude backstage melodrama, this rather sad production further suffers from a most clumsy and disjointed script' (January 1957).

The brief and limited subsequent commentaries on the film by Barr (1977) and Perry (1981) concur with these contemporary assessments, finding it to be an embarrassing failure, unhappily characteristic of Ealing's last gasp. As an awkward attempt at a tragic-comic melodrama, the underlying message of the film appears to be 'know one's place' and that individual talent and ambition – including the promise of romance – must be unquestioningly disciplined by loyalties and obligations to the family. In the clash of cultures between the known, familiar world of the Music Hall and the élite, rarefied atmosphere of The Royal Opera House, Davy inevitably opts for the 'old' and rejects the 'new', for the status quo, rather than change. While such a sentiment might have held sway during the heyday of Ealing, it had now become outmoded and mawkish, at odds and out of touch with changing more assertive times. It was certainly not a theme which survived in Relph and Dearden's partnership together.[75] *Davy* stands as a resonant metaphor for the predicament that Ealing found itself in during 1956–58, a time of disintegration and fragmentation when old loyalties could count for much.

While competent, Michael Relph's direction of the film is unadventurous and lacks the boldness that he brought to his production design.[76] *Films and Filming* felt that the director had set a too leisurely pace and that the story seemed to 'drag' (January 1958). Relph had been drawn to the project through an interest in staging an intimate drama in widescreen, but had been forced to abandon his wish to work in black and white due to Ealing's decision to use the Technirama process. Overcoming this imposition, the drab, muted greens and browns of the backstage areas are pleasingly contrasted with the bright saturated colours of The Mad Morgans and Davy in performance; and the family melodrama, which observes the unity of time, rarely leaves the cramped spaces of the dressing rooms and corridors behind the stage. Relph constructs the story largely in sequence-shots, playing out scenes with the minimum of editing, and only dollying and reframing where required and relying on the widescreen image to cover the characters in dynamic interaction. There are few close-ups and little attempt at individuation, other than with Davy's solo performances. Though further intensifying the theatricality of the film, the approach tends to mark the cohesiveness of the family troupe and stylistically underpins the dominant theme of the drama.

Lighting cameraman Douglas Slocombe likened the Technirama camera to 'a block of flats' and the bulky apparatus must have limited the filmmakers in their construction of the scenes, restricting camera movement and mobility in the confined spaces. Visually, the most impressive scenes are those staged in the auditorium of the Opera House. These include the principals and chorus in a rehearsal of Wagner's *The Mastersingers of Nuremburg*, and Joanna and Davy auditioning for the company, dwarfed by the cavernous interior and its weight of tradition.[77]

As a tragic-comedy, *Davy* is insufficient in both tragedy and comedy. The anachronistic stage routines draw few laughs from all but the diegetic theatre audience, while Rose's script and Relph's treatment fail to register the pain of Davy's twin sacrifices as he denies himself both artistic fulfilment and love for a rather nebulous loyalty to a family that persistently bickers and argues. The device of directing and playing the melodramatic tensions and revelations at and through the child further weakens the emotional impact. After Davy has turned down the opportunity to sing opera, the boy hopefully asks Davy if 'Everything will be the same' the comic, without bitterness or resignation, answers in the affirmative. There is no sense of the stultifying entrapment or cruelty that some Hollywood family melodramas were perpetrating at this time, and it is without irony that Davy and The Mad Morgans troop happily into their performance at the dismal music hall at the conclusion of the film. Relph stages these final confrontations in an entirely British manner; avoiding embarrassment and too much emotion, the characters make their reconciliations through the medium of Davy's dressing room mirror. Unfortunately, this refraction of reserved feeling is all too apparent in a film that refuses to display the passion demanded by the drama.

THE SECRET PARTNER (1961)

Shoe-horned in between their work on their Allied Film Makers projects,[78] Dearden and Relph took on *The Secret Partner* for MGM. The film was released in Britain in January 1961 and there is scant information about the production context of the film, but it was possibly part of an ongoing relationship that Relph had engineered with MGM post-*Davy* and Ealing. They had worked with the film's stars – Stewart Granger, Bernard Lee, Norman Bird – and others in the cast before; Melissa Stribling was Dearden's wife. Haya Harareet was an Israeli actress, who had played Esther in the successful epic *Ben Hur* (1959) and it is likely that her casting was part of the package from MGM. The script was based on an original screenplay by David Pursall and Jack Seddon.[79]

The film is a curious and convoluted crime mystery melodrama, shot in black and white by Harry Waxman, with *noir* overtones, in places accentuated by the *Peter Gunn*-style jazz score, courtesy of Philip Green. It is also fitted up with a Saul Bass-type graphically heavy title-sequence. There are echoes of *Pool of London* in some of the location shots of dockside settings, and the film has a B-movie feel and style although it runs for 91 minutes.

The film opens with John Brent (Stewart Granger) arriving at the Martlet Shipping Company offices, where he holds an executive position. His superior colleague, Charles Standish (Hugh Burden), checks that arrangements for the company party that Brent is hosting at his home are all in order. The party will be attended by Mr Strakarios (Peter Illing), the company president, whose maxim is 'happy at home – happy at work'. Brent, however, has just learned that his wife Nicole (Haya Harareet) has left him because she suspects him of infidelity. He confides this news to Standish and after work they meet and are joined by Helen, Standish's wife (Melissa Stribling).

The film cuts to the party, a cosmopolitan affair in Brent's stylish home. The party is in full swing with Strakarios and other friends, including Clive Lang (John Lee) an interior designer and Dr Alan Richford (Conrad Phillips). The sudden appearance of Nicole, expecting to find Brent's 'other woman', interrupts the party. She creates a scene and then leaves, with Brent denying the existence of another relationship to Richford and others. After the party, Brent receives another visitor in the form of Ralph Beldon (Norman Bird), his dentist, a drunk and his long-term blackmailer. Quite what the basis is for the extortion is not revealed, as Brent throws Beldon out. The film then follows Beldon lurching back to his rooms, where in turn he receives a mystery visitor, a masked gunman with a hoarse voice, who outlines a plan to make money, promising Beldon a 'fool-proof £15,000' if he will carry out certain instructions during his next dental appointment with Brent. Under duress, but attracted by the promise of easy money, Beldon agrees to drug Brent and to extract information from him to enable a robbery. The masked man leaves the surgery and is driven away by Nicole.

Brent, meanwhile, is showing signs of stress at work, but he goes to his dental appointment at Beldon's. Under the guise of extracting a tooth, Beldon uses gas to put Brent out, takes impressions of Brent's keys and then injects him with the 'truth drug' Pentothal. Under the influence of the drug, Brent admits that his real name is John Wilson and, in response to Beldon's questioning, he also gives the combination of the safe at the shipping office where he works. When he comes round, Brent complains of a taste of garlic, which Beldon explains as a possible side-effect of the gas. Brent pays Beldon his 'normal instalment' and leaves. Beldon has a phone conversation with the masked man, and as a result the robbery is carried out that night. The masked man enters the company offices, drugs the night watchman, opens the safe and leaves with its contents, £135,000. Detective Superintendent Hanbury (Bernard Lee), chain-smoking his way to imminent retirement, is assigned to the case and his younger colleague, Detective Inspector Henderson (Lee Montague), is quick to point out the obvious, that it must have been an inside job. Standish is the first suspect, but he has an alibi. The only other person who had the keys and who knew the combination to the safe is Brent, who has just left for a sailing holiday. After he is apprehended off the coast of France, the detectives take Brent to his home where they discover the tools needed to make copies of keys. As the apparent case against him gathers force, Brent gives the police the slip and goes on the run.

At this stage of the narrative, Brent is positioned as the victim of a strange conspiracy, who needs somehow to prove his innocence. He takes a room in a sleazy hotel (with Willoughby Goddard in a cameo appearance as the desk clerk) and sets out to track down a mysterious woman named Sandra, to whom he thinks he may have given the details of the safe, while drowning his sorrows following his separation from Nicole. At one point in this venture, he finds himself in front of a television shop, where his image on the screens in the window underline his fugitive status. Meanwhile, Hanbury

Stewart Granger confronts his dentist/blackmailer in *The Secret Partner* (1961) (Courtesy of Steve Chibnall Archive)

questions Lang, Richford and Standish, and discovers that Brent was soon to be promoted over Standish. Brent clandestinely visits Standish at the dockside, sees Lang and when it starts to dawn on him that his time under gas at the dentist's surgery might hold the key to the whole affair, he goes to Richford's house to ask for his medical advice. Richford is pistol shooting in his basement and, after a tense exchange, where Richford confirms that Brent might have been given Pentothal and hence revealed the safe's combination, Brent takes Richford's gun and forces him to accompany him to Beldon's house. Once there, he phones Hanbury who arrives to hear Beldon's confession and the enigma of the masked man. Richford leaves and goes to see Nicole, confirming that Brent is now free. She returns to her flat, only to encounter the masked man, who reveals himself as Brent. He confirms that he alone was responsible for the complicated plot to rid himself of Beldon's blackmailing attentions. Beldon knew that Brent had at an earlier stage in his career served time in prison, and had used this to extort money by threatening to compromise Brent's position at work. The robbery has also generated sufficient funds for Brent and Nicole to start a new life. However, Nicole feels used, and it is she who walks out on Brent, to start a new life with Richford, who has declared his love for her. Brent is left with the money and nothing else.

The final scenes of the film see Brent called into the police station, where Hanbury is about to be presented with his retirement clock. He has also been sent a parcel containing all the money from the robbery. Hanbury clearly understands what has happened and that Brent is no innocent, but is unable to prove it. As Hanbury goes in to accept his retirement present, to the applause of his colleagues, a disconsolate Brent walks off over Tower Bridge into an uncertain future, a plaintive saxophone sounding in the background. As a result of his complicated plotting, he is free of his blackmailer, but he has lost his wife, job and the money which motivated the robbery.

Reviews of the film were decidedly mixed, some commenting that it was a crime-suspense mystery which followed in the footsteps of Hitchcock. Penelope Gilliatt characterised it as the 'Best British thriller for some time' (*Observer*, 28 May 1961) and Isabel Quigley, writing in *The Spectator*, commented that it was 'A British thriller with individuality, pace and surprises' (2 June 1961), while Ernest Betts noted that the 'Thames-side scenes are pictorially fascinating as well as dramatic' (*The People*, 28 May 1961). There was also a surprisingly favourable account of *The Secret Partner* in *Films and Filming*, which found a 'relentless driving force' and 'many unlooked for originalities' in a novel thriller. It also welcomed a freshness of characterisation and a pleasing contrast between 'realistic' and 'bizarre' sets, the latter distinguished by the dentist's seedy surgery, 'a riot of English un-hygiene' (June 1961).[80] Other reviewers were less generous and took issue with the improbability of the plot. Patrick Gibb, for instance, writing in *The Daily Telegraph*, punned that the film suffered from a 'Weak Filling':

> If you were being blackmailed by your dentist, would you still go to him for treatment, allowing him to give you gas and extract a tooth? *The Secret Partner*, directed by Basil Dearden, absolutely founders on the improbability of the situation, on which the plot turns . . . Much ingenuity but little reality, in fact, in this rigmarole. (27 May 1961)

The Secret Partner is a minor work by Dearden and Relph; it has none of the gravity or stylistic exuberance of *Saraband for Dead Lovers*, their previous film with Granger, nor the thematic complexity of *Cage of Gold*, their earlier *noir* melodrama. At this time MGM British was largely serving up double-feature fare consisting of thrillers and comedies, the most successful of which were the adaptations of Agatha Christie starring Margaret Rutherford as Miss Marple. And even a sympathetic historian of the studio can conjure up no more enthusiasm for *The Secret Partner* than to pass it off as 'Another respectable if unsensational programmer from the British studio' (Eames 1979: 302). The film has a jaded feel about it, as though none of the key participants could muster any more enthusiasm than was necessary, it simply being a work opportunity in between the more important and interesting productions for AFM. The routine quality of the production was sensed by the reviewer at the *Monthly Film Bulletin* who noted that Basil Dearden's

> efforts to create tension have a contrived and pedantic air; the jazz score has a canned sound, strident and intrusive; and the supporting performances, particularly Haya Haraeet's Nicole, are for the most part stiff. (July 1961)

It is a difficult production to place within the *oeuvre* of Dearden and Relph and the film's historical importance probably lies in its being a precursor to the later films the partnership would make for American companies, beginning with *Woman of Straw* in 1964. However, *The Secret Partner* was a far more parochial affair and was hardly produced with the international market in mind, at best achieving little more than the status of a superior B-film thriller. The film has a weaker sense of tragedy than other pictures assessed in this chapter. The modest *noir* stylisation tilts it in the direction of tragic melodrama, but even here Dearden is uncharacteristically perfunctory and the imagery and underlying jazz do little more than state the thriller genre.[81] Such tragedy as there is here lies in the character of Brent, his vaunting ambition and calculating plan. It is, however, difficult to recuperate him as a tragic hero in this crime melodrama. He has not been 'damaged' by the war, and there are few redeeming characteristics about him – other than that he is being blackmailed and has an unfortunate past and superficial charm. His tragedy is that all he has schemed and worked for, which he brings to brilliant fruition, is ultimately worthless. At the moment of his triumph, his wife and partner in crime, having discerned his true character and ruthless ambition, loses her respect for him – and herself.

ALL NIGHT LONG (1962)

Sizzling miscegenation melodrama. (*Kinematograph Weekly*, 25 January 1962)

Whenever a film appears with jazz as either its main subject or its background, if you listen carefully you can hear a scampering sound. It is me running for my life, because the dismal truth is that most films involving jazz are made by people with no sympathy or knowledge of the subject they are treating. (Benny Green 1962, sleeve notes to *All Night Long* LP, Epic LA 16032)

Hard on the heels of their critically acclaimed work on *Victim* (1961), Dearden and Relph's next project was *All Night Long*, made for Rank. Production commenced in the summer of 1961, with Dearden directing and Relph producing and designing. Its British release came in February 1962.[82] Made in black and white, the film is an interesting experimental adaptation, transposing *Othello* to the London jazz scene of the early 1960s,[83] and one of the attractions of the film was undoubtedly the way in which it showcased internationally famous jazz luminaries and virtuosos, including Dave Brubeck, Charlie Mingus, Johnny Dankworth, Tubby Hayes and many others.[84] Little information survives concerning the circumstances under which the film came to be made, and Dearden and Relph, with the exception of Richard Attenborough, were working with a new cast and group of technicians. Ted Scaife was director of photography, and would later work with Dearden on the epic *Khartoum* (1966). The screenplay was an original development from *Othello*, by Nel King and Peter Achilles. Achilles was the pseudonym of Paul Jarrico, who had been blacklisted in America during the McCarthy era; and executive producer Bob Roberts gained his first production credit since the early 1950s after being similarly blacklisted in Hollywood.[85] Roberts held the rights to the script and, impressed by *Sapphire*, which had shown that 'a good enough film with a racial theme could be successful', approached Dearden and Relph to head up the production.

Instead of a street in Venice, this modern version of The Moor opens outside an opulent address in Mayfair and following The Honourable Rodney Hamilton (Richard Attenborough) in his Rolls Royce, driving through a thunderstorm to an old dockside warehouse in Rotherhithe.[86] He enters this building, which he has had converted into a large performing studio with a luxury apartment upstairs, to find Charlie Mingus playing the bass on stage. Preparations are under way for a surprise party that Rod, a wealthy and titled jazz aficionado, has organised for the first wedding anniversary of Aurelius Rex (Paul Harris), a famous black jazz pianist and bandleader, and Delia (Marti Stevens), his white wife, a former jazz singer. Other friends arrive and drift into this affluent, bohemian setting. These include Cass Michaels (Keith Michell) a saxophonist in Rex's band, his girlfriend Benny (Maria Velasco), Johnny Cousin (Patrick McGoohan), Rex's drummer, and his wife, Emily (Betsy Blair).[87] Johnny Dankworth, Tubby Hayes, Dave Brubeck and other musicians arrive as themselves, and the jazz begins to swing. The mounting anticipation culminates in the arrival of Rex and Delia, and the party, and the music begins in earnest.

The film follows this evening of celebration through to the early hours, interspersed with diegetic jazz solo sets as performers combine, extemporise and change places; and against this background, the story unfolds. In this adaptation, the Cousin/Iago character, played with great malevolence by McGoohan,[88] is jealous of Rex/Othello and poisons his relationship with Delia/Desdemona by suggesting that she has been unfaithful with Cass/ Cassio. His motives partly concern his wish to establish his own band with Delia as the singer; and it is revealed that he has a recording contract with Lou Berger/Lodovico (Bernard Braden), a powerful agent, who attends the party, but only on the proviso that Delia, who after marriage to Rex has given up performing, is part of the act. Driven by jealous ambition, Cousin is revealed as the two-faced, malignant force in the drama, luring Cass back to his addictive ways with reefer cigarettes, finally publicly branded an immoral, pathological liar by his suffering wife.

His schemes wreck the party. First, he orchestrates the suspicion in Rex's distrustful imagination, and then by means of editing a tape-recording of Cass and Delia (in place of the handkerchief), he purports to provide tangible evidence of their affair. Taken in by these ploys, Rex is consumed by jealousy and tries to strangle Delia in blind rage. When Cass tries to intervene, he knocks him over the railing onto the studio floor below. For a brief moment it appears that Cousin has triumphed and that his twisted ambition will be realised. However, the film pulls back from the full force of the original tragedy, when Delia and Cass survive Rex's attacks and Emily and Cass publicly denounce Cousins' plotting in front of the assembled crowd. When it dawns on Rex that he has been duped, it is only Delia's intervention that prevents him from killing Cousin. He returns to a somewhat subdued party to make his peace with Cass. There is also an ambiguous hint of his possible

'If Cassio do remain': *All Night Long* (1962) (Courtesy of Steve Chibnall Archive)

reconciliation with Delia, as she follows him out into the damp, early morning streets to leave the party, which is breaking up. In the now deserted studio space, Johnny Cousin is left alone with Emily. He scorns her love, asserting his hatred and inability to love – not only her, but even himself. She leaves, followed by Rod, and the film closes with a manic and frenzied drum solo, as Cousin plays alone, shunned and outcast.

Ever since Verdi's *Othello*, Shakespeare's play has invited musical expression (Howard 2000: 304). Many reviewers commented on the novel transposition of the play to the jazz world, enjoyed the music, but felt let down by the film and its Shakespearian pretensions: '[A]t best clumsy, at worst unbelievably awful' was one verdict (*Financial Times*, 2 February 1962). Tom Pocock felt that 'the acting is not as smooth as the jazz but this is an enjoyable film' (*Evening Standard*, 1 February 1962); while *Kine Weekly*, in characteristically robust style, thought the film strong in feminine appeal and could 'hardly fail at the popular box-office . . . it answers the astute showman's prayers' (25 January 1962). 'Anything Shakespeare can do they can do better, has been the illusion of more than one director in the past. The illusion is evidently shared by the Relph–Dearden partnership' was the damning verdict of *Time and Tide* (8 February 1962); and the rewritten ending to the Bard's work was taken up with great gusto by several other commentators. David Lewin, for example, could not believe the 'absurd happy ending' (*Daily Express*, 2 February 1962) and Julian Holland berated the altered ending, arguing that it had turned Shakespeare's most human tragedy into 'a soap opera' (*Evening News*, 1 February 1962). Against this, Paul Dehn, somewhat wishfully, offered the view that: 'The film's best feature is that it may tempt teenagers into reading or re-reading the play' (*Daily Herald*, 3 February 1962). As with many adaptations of Shakespeare, though, critical judgements tended to be harsh. The film:

> Never for one moment succeeds in achieving anything like the power and persuasion of the original. Its characters move excitedly about, exchange flip dialogue, conspire, connive, love, loathe; but for all their agitated activity, they remain dramatic dwarfs, stunted shadows, puppets whose strings are not jerked by any logical sequence of events, but rather only in a direct imitation of a previous work. (*Films and Filming*, March 1962)

Many years later, when the film was reviewed as a DVD release, Geoffrey MacNab found Dearden's 'kitsch but enjoyable foray into the world of jazz' to be 'an intriguing historical document' (*Sight and Sound*, 4 April 2004). Part of this intrigue must reside in its depiction of race, and in particular the relationship the film draws between Rex/Othello and Delia/Desdemona.

One reviewer at the time, for instance, confessed himself to be irritated by the film's 'pretence of being daring with a shot of white fingers exploring black skin – but never permitting a full lovers' kiss between the Negro and his wife' (*Daily Express*, 2 February 1962). On the other hand, the apparently natural construction of a racially diverse – albeit jazz – sub-culture in the film was singled out for telling, if dated comment: 'the white and coloured types intermingle smoothly and fraternisation creates deep emotional pangs, rather than embarrassment' (*Kinematograph Weekly*, 25 January 1962). And indeed, subsequent critical commentaries have tended to remember the film principally in these terms. For Murphy (1992), it is a 'stylised and allegorical film', not the true successor to Dearden and Relph's more realistic *Sapphire* (1959) in terms of its 'return to the race theme' (Murphy 1992: 40). Ray Durgnat – inevitably – took a slightly different and typically wry view:

> After *Sapphire*, their *All Night Long* (1962) tries to show us how the coloured outsider feels. This jazz world transposition of *Othello* is probably reassuring for the white Englishman, in showing that not all coloured men are unstoppable big black bucks, and have psychosexual frailties too. Yet one can't help wishing for the story in 'negative', since sexual paranoia seems more characteristic of the British. Hence some spectators felt that the coloured man's role as victim dodged the crunch and wished upon the blacks a white insanity, *as well*. (1970: 105)

Those reviewers who had anything to say about the direction or 'look' of the production found it excessively 'mechanical' and condemned Dearden's style as 'crass and head-on' (*Films and Filming*, March 1962). The *Monthly Film Bulletin* suggested that viewers would be 'distracted by the excessive use of crane and tracking shots' (March 1962), a criticism perhaps over-sensitive to the film's dynamic style and the swooping, probing camera which prowls around Relph's split-level warehouse set, entirely consistent with the dramatic confrontations taking place and revealing the highly charged emotional energies at stake. Scaife's high-contrast jazz–*noir* photography is the perfect choice to mark out the distinction between surface and substance at the heart of the drama and, moreover, assumes some admirable abstract compositions to minimise the potential dullness posed by the limited number of interior sets. In particular, the repeated placement of the camera on stage with the musicians, with deep-space compositions revealing the intrigue and subterfuge taking place in the darkened, background areas of the set, effectively presents the unfolding melodrama and successfully integrates the jazz milieu and its performers into the shifting allegiances and surging emotions of the characters attending the party.

A PLACE TO GO (1963)

> The film is very much concerned with the wind of change which is blowing through the East End of London, a wind which is sweeping away the close-packed streets of drab little houses and bringing new, shining modern flats in their place. The trouble is that this wind blows too fast for the old but not fast enough for the young. (*Daily Cinema*, 25 July 1963)

> The view we have formed and tested more or less daily for three years is that very few people wish to leave the East End. They are attached to Mum and Dad, to the markets, to the pubs and settlements, to Club Row and the London Hospital. There are, of course, exceptions. (Michael Young and Peter Willmott 1962: 186)

Made entirely on location and shot in black and white in the East End of London, *A Place to Go* was based on the novel *Bethnal Green* (1961) by Michael Fisher, which had been published two years earlier and this was the working title for the film in its development stages. It was made for distribution by British Lion/Bryanston, which had been formed in 1959, absorbing a number of former Ealing personnel, and was 'determined to tackle the kind of unusual subject that the timid circuit-dominated studios so often neglect' (*Films and Filming*, June 1959). Its first chairman was Michael Balcon and for a while Dearden and Relph were linked with the company, although until *A Place to Go*, their main energies were behind the AFM initiative.

As well as producing the film, Michael Relph was responsible for adapting the script from the novel, with additional dialogue supplied by Clive Exton.[89] Following the novel, the film taps into several contemporary social issues, most prominently, the changing traditional urban working-class communities, the emergence of youth culture and crime. The film therefore echoes themes broached in earlier work – in *I Believe in You* (1952) and *Violent Playground* (1958), for instance – but updates and revisits them in the early 1960s, just as the Beatles and the full-blown pop era was taking off.

The young stars of the film are Mike Sarne and Rita Tushingham. Sarne had recorded a number one hit in June 1962[90] and Tushingham, having made her debut film appearance the year before in *A Taste of Honey* (d. Tony Richardson), was at the beginning of a distinguished career. The film opens on Christmas Eve, in a smoky local pub in Bethnal Green, with Ricky Flint (Mike Sarne) singing the title song. The film follows him through backstreets to his terraced home and introduces his family: Lil (Doris Hare) his mother, his heavily pregnant sister Betsy (Barbara Ferris), her husband Jim (David Andrews) and his father Matt (Bernard Lee), a big, strong docker. When

Cat and Ricky in *A Place to Go* (1963) (Courtesy of Steve Chibnall Archive)

Ricky arrives, his sister is watching the television and asks Jim: 'When are we going to get a place of our own?'[91] As they prepare for Christmas, there is a hint that Matt's work is not secure, due to unspecified 'union troubles', and Ricky is depicted as someone who wants to escape from home and Bethnal Green and see the world. On Christmas Day, amidst raucous family celebrations, Betsy's baby arrives.

From this opening sequence, the film develops by means of three inter-woven stories: the criminal, the romantic and the domestic melodrama. The first of these concerns Ricky's involvement in the planning and execution of a robbery at his workplace, the local 'Coolstream' cigarette factory. His motives are not made explicit, but it is presumably to make money to allow him to travel and find 'a place to go'. The robbery is the idea of a local crook, Jack Immelman (John Slater), aided and abetted by Charlie Batey (William Marlowe) and 'Pug' (Michael Wynne), both small-time villains. The film introduces them at Haringey dog track, and hints at a longstanding enmity between Jack and Matt Flint (later in the film Jack confides to Ricky that it started when they were young and competed for Lil's affections). Matt despises Jack and his easy money and ill-gotten wealth, and he insults Jack at every opportunity. The robbery involves Ricky – with his inside access – disabling the alarm system in the factory. It also involves Jim, his brother-in-law, who initially agrees to drive his lorry to transport the stolen goods. However, at the last minute Jim tells Ricky that he can't jeopardise his wife and new baby's future in the venture and pulls out. In this event, Ricky drives the lorry himself and the robbery takes place. At first all goes well, the gang break into the factory, and Ricky is left on watch with a length of lead pipe and instructions to use it necessary. However, when a police constable appears, Ricky is unable to hit him. Charlie, however, has no such qualms and knocks the constable unconscious. In a panic, Ricky drives off in the empty lorry and the gang flee via the fire escape. The outcome of this bungled affair is that, in revenge for Ricky's lack of 'bottle', Charlie and Pug set fire to the lorry and in his attempt to put the fire out, Ricky is badly burned when the fuel tank explodes. As a result he has to spend a long time in hospital, and when he finally is discharged, he is set on his own revenge against Charlie.

The romantic narrative involves the relationship between Ricky and Catherine ('Cat') Donovan (Rita Tushingham). Ricky first meets her at the dog track, in the company of Charlie and Pug. She is a tough and independent-minded, distinctive in her looks and fiery attitude. Ricky is attracted to her and they strike up a relationship. They visit the pictures (he wants to go the Essoldo, whereas she chooses the Odeon – and she gets her way) and he takes her to his hideout, a cellar in a demolished house, where they make love. However, this is no steady, predictable relationship and, as a later scene in the communal washhouse shows, Cat is able to hold her own against Ricky and regards herself as no man's property. When Ricky is bandaged up like the 'Invisible Man' in hospital, she visits him, but is noncommittal about their future together. Furthermore, she admits that she has been seeing Charlie, before she kisses him and leaves. This competition for Cat adds another dimension to Ricky's vendetta against Charlie.

These two narrative strands criss-cross the domestic melodrama which acts as the background to the film. The film attempts to realise the close-knit milieu and culture of the Bethnal Green community of the time, with its shots of pubs, markets,[92] dockside streets and associated locations, and to embody these in the Flint family and their fortunes. Like a series of celebrated studies of neighbourhood life in the East End of London in this period,[93] it also seeks to chart the major changes taking place as slum clearance and urban relocation programmes, coupled with the decline of traditional industries, take their toll. Three stories concerning the family are employed as metaphors. First, the fate of Matt Flint, the ageing, but unbowed docker, who quits his job in as a result of 'union troubles'. Matt has been the traditional head of the household – the breadwinner – but loses his place at the head of the table when he confesses to Lil that he has given up his job. To earn money, he resorts to an escapology act, busking in front of cinema and theatre queues in the West End; and in the scenes when Lil watches him struggling to break out of his chains and straitjacket, he cuts a pathetic and undignified figure. It is after this that he returns to the house to find Jack Immelman (discussing the robbery) with Ricky, and as he warns Jack to keep away, he suffers a fatal stroke. The second story concerns Lil on her own, dealing with an eviction notice and moving to a new and alien environment in a high-rise flat away from Bethnal Green. There is poignancy in her final, unspoken farewell to the old terrace house that she and Matt moved into in the year of the General Strike and in the photograph she finds just before she leaves, showing her, with a uniformed Matt, outside the house, bedecked in bunting for VE Day. Her old world is irrevocably behind her and when she leaves a gang of kids immediately stone the house, smashing the windows. When Ricky leaves hospital, his first port of call is his mother's new flat in the high-rise block. 'It's not the same, Ricky, it's the people, they're not proper Bethnal Green people.' He also sees Betsy, his sister, who, with the assistance of the insurance money from the burning of Jim's lorry and his new job in the factory, has finally been able to move into a 'place of our own'. But her story, a compressed final aside in the family trilogy, is not one of unqualified success and realised dreams. In fact, she relates a similar tale to her mother, one of social isolation and loneliness, unfriendly people, none of the old networks and, above all, the use of the 'telly' as a means of passing the time.

In the final stages of the film, Ricky goes to find Charlie, intent on revenge. He finds him in a pub with Cat, and they fight. In the general free-for-all that ensues, Charlie pulls a flick-knife. As the police arrive to break up the fracas, Ricky is arrested with the knife in his hand.[94] He is taken to the police station and charged with possession of the knife and his involvement in the general affray. Lil arrives to stand his bail and he appears in court alongside Charlie on the following morning. Witnesses confirm that the knife was Charlie's and the magistrate questions Ricky about his relationship with Cat, the girl they were fighting over. He claims that they are engaged. Cat is called to the witness box and perjures herself by backing Ricky's account – and his claim. The magistrate, as a result of this, exercises leniency and binds Ricky over for a year. He and Cat leave the court and walk by the river where he proposes to her and she accepts. In the closing scene, they find themselves near the cellar where they used to meet; like much of their old Bethnal Green, however, it is being bulldozed to make way for the new world.[95]

The film was not a success in box-office or critical terms and it may be that the delay in its release partly contributed to this. Completed by the end of April 1963, it did not go on release until a year later.[96] Walker refers to the film as one of a number of 'martyred movies' that suffered from a delayed release of up to a year (1974: 249–50).[97] This resulted from the compromising position that British Lion found itself in with regard to the cinema circuits. With a few exceptions (*The Leather Boys*, 1963 and *The Caretaker*, 1964) Walker argues that the films were of dubious quality, 'films that had got left behind as trends changed':

> They were what is called 'programmers', films made to fill a bill and now, in 1963 , seeming little different from the plays that were weekly attractions on both the BBC TV and ITV networks, except that there the themes and treatments were often more adventurous and radical. (1974: 251)

Contemporary reviews of the film were divided between rather wishful attempts to promote it – 'Here is an unpretentious slice of Cockney life with some songs, some sentiment, some humour and some excitement. Reliable home-grown product' (*Kinematograph Weekly*, 2 April 1964) – and those that sought to distance themselves from its perceived tone and tenor:

> Relph and Dearden and 'new realism'. Everything is there, from child-birth at a Christmas party and teenage violence, to union troubles and slum clearance evictions, all glued together with a patronising brand of sentimentality, and punctuated from time to time by those dear old shots of urban chimney-stacks. (*Monthly Film Bulletin*, June 1964)

For Murphy, the film marks something of a watershed in Dearden and Relph's partnership, in that after this production they 'abandoned realism and social problems in favour of a glossy cosmopolitanism' (1992: 43). Like Murphy, Hill sees *A Place to Go* as a 'fitting epitaph to the social problem films of Basil Dearden' (1986: 95). However, this overstates the nature of any social problems in a film that is best understood as a crime melodrama. The attitudes and behaviour of Ricky, Cat and the other young people in the film are not configured as a social problem in the way, for instance, that Johnny is a threat to the family and community in *Violent Playground*. Characters like Charlie and Spud are professional criminals, long a constituent element of London's East End and not a new form of social deviancy. Similarly, the break-up of traditional working-class communities can hardly be considered a social problem – it was offered as social advance – and it is dealt with here as impacting on the domestic sphere and hence part of the film's melodramatic framework.

A Place to Go neatly interweaves its crime and family drama through the implicit question hanging over Ricky's paternity. In the home, the emergent oedipal conflicts are resolved by Lil when she seats Ricky at the head of the family table after Matt loses his job. Meanwhile, the parallel crime drama brings Ricky under the closer supervision of Jack Immelman, a former suitor of Lil, and from his kind tolerance of Ricky and interest in his well-being (he musses the young man's hair), and Matt's blind hatred of his rival, it is inferred that the gangster could be the young man's father.

The film was a late and undistinguished entry in the cycle of 'kitchen sink' films which stormed British cinema in the period 1958–63.[98] Unfortunately, the style had become stale, Walker dismissing the film as an

> anthology of every British 'new wave' back-street cliché, including pub sing-songs, flick-knife fights, loneliness in the new tenement, eviction from the old street, Dad forever on the dole and Mum just as eternally laying the table for high-tea. (1974: 250)[99]

Dearden and Relph don't appear entirely comfortable in this milieu and although the extensive location shooting produces some stunning back-grounds and the communal washroom in the basement of Cat's tenement stands out, Dearden and his cameraman Reg Wyer fail to shake off entirely their traditional studio backgrounds and approaches to match the invention and spontaneity that Tony Richardson and Walter Lassally brought to *A Taste of Honey* the previous year.[100]

The tragic qualities of the drama are dispersed among the Flint family, most obviously with Matt, who through his rigid independence loses his job and refuses all assistance from the mobster Immelman. His emasculation is marked by his loss of status in the family and community, reduced to a pathetic display of his power and masculinity busking to crowds.[101] After his death, Lil is left to confront the loss of her home and new, unfamiliar and friendless surroundings alone. The film is also ambivalent about the future of Ricky and Cat. In an ending reminiscent of *Saturday Night and Sunday Morning* (1960), the young couple, wander over wasteground towards an imposing skyline dominated by high-rise flats. This can hardly be judged optimistic considering the film's condemnation of this lifestyle.

THE MAN WHO HAUNTED HIMSELF (1970)

> The Schizophrenic is more commonly approached as a person who took himself off to a fantasy world because he was inadequately loved in this one. The difficulties of persuading him to abandon self-love for object-love and to accept the harsher realities of life are most likely attributed to the fact that he is having too wonderful a time as king of his fantasy world to leave it (Hyman Spotnitz 1961/1962: 40)

> A quasi-science fiction melodrama provided Roger Moore with a moustache and a *doppelganger*. (Alexander Walker 1974: 431)

The final film considered in this chapter was also the last film that Dearden and Relph made together. Within a year of the release of *The Man Who Haunted Himself*, while driving from Pinewood Studios to his home in London, Dearden died tragically in a car accident on the M4 near Heathrow Airport. A number of press reports noted the bitter parallel between his death and the events which befall Harold Pelham (Roger Moore) in the film (*The Daily Telegraph*, 25 March 1971). The film was based on a short story by Anthony Armstrong, *The Strange Case of Mr Pelham*,[102] which was adapted for the screen by Dearden and Relph, with additional, unaccredited dialogue work by Bryan Forbes.[103] The film was one of the first three to be produced by EMI/ABP at Elstree, during Forbes' uneasy and short-lived reign as head of production, when he was under pressure to get things moving at the studio and to show results.[104] Production commenced late in August 1969 on a film that Dearden and Relph considered 'the most unusual that they have ever attempted' (*Kinematograph Weekly*, 30 August 1969). It was filmed in Technicolor and starred Roger Moore as Pelham. Moore had built up a significant reputation and celebrity image by this time, largely based on his television work, especially as the character Simon Templar in the ATV series *The Saint*.[105] For Forbes, the combination of Moore, the script and Dearden and Relph's reputation represented at the time 'a big plus for my programme of films'.[106] With a budget of under £300,000, the film was shot at Elstree, on sets constructed in a warehouse by the Thames, and to keep costs down, wherever possible real locations were used; the scenes in the snooker hall, for instance, were filmed in the RAC Club.[107]

The film starts with the bowler-hatted, outwardly conservative business-man, Mr Harold Pelham (Roger Moore), leaving his office in the City to return home. In his car, a large solid Rover, he puts on his seat belt and drives carefully through the traffic past Big Ben and out onto the West Way. As he reaches the motorway section, however, he suddenly and mysteri-ously appears to change; unbuckling his seat belt, and driving at great speed, weaving his way dangerously through the traffic. As his speed increases, the car also appears to undergo a transformation, from staid, respectable Rover, to a sleek Italian Maserati. At high speed, the car skids, spins out of control and crashes.

In hospital, following the accident, Pelham undergoes emergency surgery. On the operating table, he dies momentarily, but is resuscitated, and curiously for a moment, the ECG machine registers two heartbeats. After this bizarre beginning, the film cuts forward to the present, when Pelham, apparently recuperated from the accident, leaves his home, his wife Eve (Hildegard Neil) and his sons, to drive a new Rover, on his return to work. He arrives for a board meeting of his company, a marine engineering concern, which is considering an offer from a rival conglomerate to buy it out. Pelham speaks against the offer, seeing it as little more than a takeover, inspired by a new marine automation system that they have developed. At the end of the meeting, however, Pelham is disconcerted by a colleague who claims he ignored him a few days ago when he was abroad on leave, recuperating. After work he goes for a swim with his colleague Alex (Anton Rodgers) and at the pool he encounters the glamorous photographer, Julie (Olga Georges-Picot). When he arrives home, he is perplexed to find another friend, the bumptious Bellamy (Thorley Walters) waiting for him with Eve. Apparently, Pelham asked Bellamy round for drinks when he met him at the club, playing snooker, the week before. Pelham is mystified as he knows that he wasn't in the country when this invitation was allegedly issued. As he drives to a late meeting with Alex, however, he passes the silver blue Maserati parked outside his house. When he returns, he has a brief row with Eve, and it appears that all is not well with their relationship as she wants another baby, but is married to 'an overworked executive who doesn't make love to his wife', she says. And from the window, she sees the Maserati drive off.

A succession of other episodes seems to suggest that Pelham is experienc-ing some kind of mental breakdown, linked to his bizarre accident. When he visits his club he is greeted by acquaintances who insist on settling bets with him over a brilliant game he reportedly played against Bellamy the week before. On a visit to the firm's research laboratory, they are convinced that he was there ten days before. When he takes Eve to the Casino, he discovers that he was apparently there the night before, and when they encounter Julie there, she remarks enigmatically 'you didn't tell me that you were married'. On the following day, his barber insists that he cut his hair the day before. At the club, he discovers that he was there only an hour ago. When he visits Julie at her Chelsea flat he discovers that he is supposed to have been there before; she is undressed and familiar, 'his' record is playing, and it is clear that she is convinced that they have been having a relationship since they met at the pool. The strains of these events begin to tell on his marriage, and Eve leaves with the children, convinced that he is deceiving her.

At work, it also appears that Pelham has a strange double, who has become involved in the merger, undertaking surreptitious meetings with the rival company representative Ashton (John Carson) at the Monument, The Planetarium and The Serpentine.[108] As a result of this, his unknowing intervention, the deal goes through at a much improved price. Under intense pressure, Pelham rings home to find that he is supposedly already there. He races home to find that 'he' has just left. Alex advises him to see a psychiatrist, Dr Harris (Freddie Jones), who diagnoses a 'double psychosis'. Pelham is reluctant to accept this explanation at first, insisting that there must be a rational explanation for the events that have overtaken him. In search of this, he again goes to see Julie, arriving just after 'he' has apparently left in the Maserati. This convinces him that he needs medical help and he returns to Dr Harris, who administers drug treatment to resolve his problems. While Pelham is under treatment, his doppelgänger in the Maserati apparently arrives home to be greeted by Eve. 'He' also attends the board meeting where the merger is under investigation and is able to convince the board that he has acted in their best interests.

Following his therapy, the psychiatrist concludes that Pelham's condition has resulted from a sort of schizophrenic strain between his dominant orderly self and his repressed, pleasure-seeking, unconventional self. He advises Pelham to release his other side and to enjoy, without guilt, 'all the pleasures of life'. And so Pelham apparently does, dancing with his wife at a club, driving their 'new toy', a Maserati, home where he goes to bed with his wife. However, at this stage it is not clear which Mr Pelham this is, as the other Pelham is seen on the following morning leaving the clinic, dressed in a more relaxed stylish suit and tie, one who when he arrives at work is shocked to find that he dictated a letter accepting the terms of the merger the day before. This Pelham has no knowledge of these events and when he rings home, he speaks to his other self on the phone, one who seems in charge of his home and personality. He returns home to confront his other self, and such is his deranged state of mind

Pelham meets Pelham: *The Man Who Haunted Himself* (1970) (Courtesy of Steve
Chibnall Archive)

that he is disowned by his family and Alex as an 'impersonator'; his surrogate
now appears the more convincing Mr Pelham, and it is he who tells the old
Pelham that when he died on the operating table, he was liberated as a result.
In a thunderstorm, the old Pelham flees the house, driving away in his old

Rover pursued by his double in the Maserati (their simultaneous appearance confounds Dr Harris who suddenly appears on the pavement). A chase ensues through the driving rain and in the final scenes of the film, haunted by images of his other self in the rear view mirror, the Rover crashes through the parapet of a bridge and plunges Pelham to his death. His double, watching from the bridge, clutches at his heart, for a minute experiencing a twin heartbeat, which then finally settles into a singular, normal rhythm.[109]

Alexander Walker, commenting on the film as one of the first three made under Forbes' newly appointed period of executive command at EMI/ABP, indicates wryly that they appeared 'dismayingly "square", but safe in their audience appeal. "Square" they were: safe they were not' (1974: 431), he concludes. And so it appeared in terms of the box-office record and critical reception of the film. Forbes was later to lament that he had 'no control over the exhibition of my films' and how the promotion and advertising for these films were 'very poor'. And while he remembered this film in particular as one which was supposed to show Roger Moore to be a more versatile actor than had been generally acknowledged, it emerged as 'an interesting film full of nuances – badly sold – thrown away out of petty spite'.[110] But such disclaimers did not hold any water for many contemporary reviewers. Where *The Sunday Telegraph* found it to be 'an ingenious thriller' (26 July 1970) and *Kinematograph Weekly* recommended it as a 'Good, general attraction' (4 July 1970), the general tenor of the reviews was to find the film symptomatic of a kind of moribund lack of finesse and adventure that was perceived to be afflicting British cinema at this crucial, make-or-break time. Stanley Price, writing in the *Observer*, did not hold back:

> [T]he third of Bryan Forbes's new programme at Associated British Productions. It can only add to the general dismay at the current activities of our only fully active production company . . . It is an unmitigated piece of hokum that looks and sounds more like Pinewood 1948 than Elstree 1970. (26 July 1970)

Nor did the *Monthly Film Bulletin*:

> *The Man Who Haunted Himself* is one of the first productions in a programme designed to give new life blood to the British cinema; on this evidence the patient seems unlikely to survive . . . As it is Basil Dearden plays by all the tired conventions of the British Fifties psychological thriller, and the result is deadly dull and more than a little ridiculous when colourful minor characters like Freddie Jones' twitching, pill-swallowing Scottish psychiatrist are given their head. The dialogue is consistent only in its banality, the colour processing and special effects

are abominable, and stylistically the film might well have been made in the Fifties since Dearden has not yet progressed beyond that tedious old scene-changing device of the visual hyphen. (August 1970)

Subsequent critiques of the film have been kinder, especially in their evaluation of Moore's performance and the story, Wiseman, for instance, suggesting that the film 'is a tense psychological thriller that is without doubt Roger Moore's finest appearance on film' (*Cinema Retro*, May 2005). Conrich has provided an insightful account of the film's production and reception contexts and the (Freudian) significance of the conflict which develops in the film between the 'two' Pelhams. In his view, the film 'had rejected the values of an increasingly unconstrained contemporary British cinema, and had bravely attempted to maintain a conventional approach to film production' (1997: 229). In his conclusion, he points neatly to the ironic parallel in that 'the Pelham who is the genuine and established is, like Dearden, eclipsed by the Pelham who is new and unreserved' (ibid.).

Dearden and Relph's prisoner-of-war melodrama, *The Captive Heart* (1946), marked the moment of transition referred to by one contemporary as 'that twilight period between the darkness of war and the clear daylight of established peace' (Dill 1944: 111). At the culmination of the film, the POWs are repatriated and face an uncertain future of adjustment and rehabilitation; and this dilemma, of male anxiety, doubt and unease, becomes a significant element, sublimated very often within genre frameworks, of the post-war cinema of the filmmaking team. Eleven of their films, varying in the intensity with which they play out the theme, are configured as tragic melodramas. It is not an anxiety wholly restricted to men, as the experience of 'tragedy' is visited on some female characters, notably the enforced isolation of Sophie-Dorothea in *Saraband*, the domestic entrapment of Judy in *Cage of Gold* and the unhappy uprooting of Lil Flint in *A Place to Go*; but in each film, a significant male character has to confront an unwelcome choice: face a loss of agency or potency, remain bound by social and domestic restrictions, or have ambitions thwarted. Several of the characters in these films are servicemen who had enjoyed 'a good war' – or at least found a structure for male assertion and achievement. The final film in the cycle, *The Man Who Haunted Himself*, represents a significant culminating point in this tendency, a male narcissistic fantasy fuelled by excessive images of masculine potency and hedonism generated in the 1950s and 1960s. In it, the domesticated model of manhood is crushed and destroyed by its nemesis, the 'Playboy' ideal. The casting of Moore was highly prescient as his immediate characterisations following the film – Lord Brett Sinclair in *The Persuaders!* and James Bond – confirmed the new potency of unreconstructed masculinity. Psychoanalysts have located the development of schizophrenia in the corrosive accumulation of 'frustration-aggression', which for the male could arise from the unsatisfactory discharge of impulses due to unfavourable environmental pressures (Spotnitz 1961/1962). It is tempting to see this unfortunate outcome as the logical culmination of the period of 'masculinity in crisis' since the war. After ten films treating the tragic outcomes of post-war men, Dearden and Relph let their 'narcissistic defences' down and set walking this earth the rampant alter ego of the socially desirable, community-minded male who had populated the wartime cinema of Ealing and who had manfully tried to make his peace with the post-war settlement.[111] *The Man Who Haunted Himself*, in its rejection of passivity, bears some relation to a separate, smaller group of films produced in the post-war period, in which Dearden and Relph explore an alternative response by men to the post-war settlement, stories in which former servicemen actively seek to re-establish the comforting framework of comradeship, homosocial society and male purpose. These films are the subject of the next chapter.

NOTES

1. A theme which is addressed substantially in the work of Spicer (2001) and Geraghty (2000).
2. The saraband in the title is a stately baroque dance, Spanish colonial in origin with a distinctive rhythm. The music was composed and directed by Alan Rawsthorne.
3. Other accounts call this into question. Richards, for instance, suggests that it was a project 'reluctantly embraced by Balcon in a bid to secure international sales' (1997: 27). Perry notes that it was an unlikely subject for Ealing to tackle, but 'was an attempt, at Mr Rank's urging, to go after the prestige market' (1981: 105). Murphy concurs: 'The Studio, now under the Rank aegis, was encouraged to embark on a more lavish costume drama' (1988: 133). Stewart Granger was a Rank contract artist made available to star in the production.
4. Other historical pictures produced at Ealing in this period include *Champagne Charlie* (1944), *Pink String and Sealing Wax* (1945) and *The Loves of Joanna Godden* (1947).
5. Stewart Granger recalls that actress Françoise Rosay refused to comply with the strictures of the pre-planning and won the approval and support of the cast. Granger paints Relph as the villain of the piece, 'a very supercilious gentleman', and the drawings and producer disappeared (Granger 1982: 113). Granger's version is unlikely on several counts and none of its elaborate intrigue is remembered by cinematographer Douglas Slocombe (2007).
6. The novel is structured into three principal parts, each corresponding with the key female protagonists: Duchess Sophia, Princess Sophie-Dorothea and Countess Clara Von Platen. The film elides this structuring device, opting for

a chronological sequence. Unlike the book, the film begins and ends at Ahlden with the dying Sophie-Dorothea. The film, to borrow Harper's term, 'purifies' the dissolute past of Königsmark and aspects of his relationship with Countess Platen (1994: 207). In contrast, the final imprisonment of Sophie-Dorothea is presented in the film much more severely than it is in the book.

7. Douglas Slocombe indicates that there was some tension between the great French actress and Basil Dearden, in part occasioned by linguistic difficulties. Slocombe relates how his fluent French led him to try to mediate rather unsuccessfully in the relationship between the two as the production progressed (2007). Dearden had directed Rosay previously, seemingly without incident, in *The Halfway House* (1944).

8. Michael Relph records that initial approaches for this role were made to Marlene Dietrich, but that there was confusion over whether she was being asked to perform the part of the younger Princess Sophie-Dorothea. When it was confirmed that she was being asked to take on the role of the older Countess Platen, she turned down the role (1990).

9. Technical staff on the 'Saraband' Unit to Prague consisted of over 30 people. This was a time of intense international production at Ealing, which at one point in 1947 had units in Antarctica and Norway (*Scott of the Antarctic*, 1948), Belgium (*Against the Wind*, 1948), Australia (*Eureka Stockade*, 1949), as well as Czechoslovakia. The only film shooting in the home studio was *It Always Rains on Sunday* (1947) (*Kinematograph Weekly*, 17 April 1947).

10. A similar attempt by Cineguild to produce an 'intelligent' costume drama with *Blanche Fury* (1948) also ended in financial disappointment.

11. Douglas Slocombe has indicated how much Dearden admired *Citizen Kane* (Slocombe 2007). The initial influence of this film is apparent in the deep-focus shots and oppressive ceilings of *The Halfway House*; it is also evident in these bracketing scenes of *Saraband*, which detail a lone lighted window in a castle, a forward movement to the interior space of a room where is found the dying protagonist and the flashback to investigate their story.

12. The following year, Hollywood attempted two 'off-genre' costume *noirs* with Anthony Mann's *Reign of Terror* and Gregory Ratoff's *Black Magic*. Neither was a major studio production, and while Mann's film (shot by John Alton) was visually arresting, neither was as accomplished or as substantial as *Saraband*.

13. Perhaps the best example being the series of films which adapted selected short stories of Somerset Maugham: *Quartet* (1948), *Trio* (1950), and *Encore* (1951).

14. In 1933, Michael Balcon oversaw the production of *Friday the Thirteenth* (d. V. Saville) while at Gainsborough Studios. In this film, several people are involved in a London bus crash and the film turns the clock back to trace their respective stories up to the crash and its aftermath and to weigh up their destinies. There are striking structural similarities between this earlier film and the portmanteau of *Train of Events*.

15. The film acknowledges the support of the London Midland Region of British

Railways and Dearden's shooting script, dated 11 January 1949, indicates a range of locations, including Euston Station, Willesden Junction and Camden locomotive yards.

16. The approach would be further developed in *Pool of London* (1951).

17. It is on this more experimental level of the Continental art cinema that the episode differs from the realism of Cole's 'Engine Driver' sequence, which conforms to the more homely strictures of the indigenous documentary film movement.

18. Again, a preoccupation to reveal and explore the voice of the 'Other', in this case the German, reflecting on their wartime experience, a theme which was substantially addressed by Dearden and Relph in *Frieda*.

19. While the opening credits announce 'Introducing Peter Finch . . .' it was not his debut – he had played small parts since 1938.

20. Dearden, of course, had trod the boards with a Shakespearean company early in his career.

21. The cast are working on the concluding scene, wherein Exton has just struck down the King, for which Bolingbroke bestows on him the 'guilt of conscience'; and with the words 'With Cain go wander through the shades of night, And never show thy head by day nor light', motivates the stylistic shift into *noir* expressionism that characterises the following scenes.

22. The cast are rehearsing the same concluding scene of *Richard II* and some new lines are introduced to the original play to make a more pointed parallel with Philip's predicament. When Exton informs Bolingbroke that he has killed the King, the following dialogue is given to Bolingbroke: 'though I did wish him dead, I hate the murderer, and love him murdered', delivered with a pointed finger of accusation.

23. *Final Shooting Script*, dated 6 February 1950. Paris and London locations detailed pp. 1–3. The script also indicates some major cuts and amendments, for example: concerning the birth of Nicholas (p. 56); Alan consulting with woman patient in private practice (p. 43); and scene in Selfridges (p. 73). It contains many detailed adjustments throughout – to dialogue, correcting French, and camera directions. In the shooting script and in some reviews there is confusion over the names Glennon/Brennon, Kearn/Burne.

24. Barr (1977) juxtaposes *Cage of Gold* with *Mandy* (d. A. Mackendrick, 1952); Geraghty (2000) assesses the film alongside *It Always Rains on Sunday* (d. R. Hamer, 1947) and *Dance Hall* (d. C. Crichton, 1950).

25. Barr comments insightfully on the Ealing in-joke references in the film to Victor Saville and Alexander Mackendrick (1977: 10).

26. Given the appearance of the child, some years have elapsed here. In this and some other points in the narrative (for example, Judy's pregnancy) time is compressed considerably, Murphy notes that the film in this respect has 'an awkward time structure' (1997: 155).

27. Correspondence with authors (19 February 2004).

28. As Murphy notes, there are parallels here with the characters Jack Havoc in

Tiger in the Smoke (1956) and George Hoskins in Dearden and Relph's own *The Ship That Died of Shame* (1955). Richards also makes this point (1997: 30).

29. As in the later case of Silas in Dearden's *Only When I Larf* (1968).

30. In a pre-production announcement, Ealing gave a characteristically explicit interpretation of these narrative events. The project was then intriguingly called *Sacrifice* (who's?) and described as 'the story of a Battle of Britain hero who is unable to adjust himself to post-war conditions. His rake's progress leads him into blackmail and to his own eventual murder after his wife has remarried, believing him to be dead' (*Kinematograph Weekly*, 15 December 1949). The film, more satisfyingly, is less certain on the character of its villain.

31. *Cage of Gold* has the distinction of having its antagonist reappear *twice*.

32. Both of these devices, the prominent placement of single lamps as the available light source in a tense scene and the dramatic diffusion of light through fog, were part of the celebrated visual arrangement of the later Hollywood *noir The Big Combo* (1953), photographed by John Alton.

33. Filming took place on location, in sets at Ealing and in an old converted warehouse in Bermondsey, to allow for the intervention of poor weather. Communication between Ealing and the location units was maintained by radio-telephony. As well as considerable co-operation from the Port of London Authority, Scotland Yard and Customs & Excise, the Gdynia-America Line made their vessel *M/S Czech* available for the scenes filmed on and around the ship (*Pool of London*, Exploitation Folder, dated 1 February 1951).

34. See Balcon's comments on Clarke's 'insubordination' while preparing for *Pool of London* (1969: 160–1).

35. Bonar Colleano's casting in this central role may have been part of a deliberate attempt to address and reach out to American audiences (Higson 1997: 163).

36. Cameron recounts how he arrived in Britain from the West Indies as a merchant seaman in October 1939. After some time working as an actor in stage productions a chance contact with Ealing came about: '[T]hey had seen my picture in *Spotlight*, and wanted me to see the director Basil Dearden, who was looking for a black actor to play Johnny, the merchant seaman in *Pool of London*. A meeting was arranged and I got on well with Dearden. He sent me the script and I was thrilled . . . I got to know the director, Basil Dearden, very well. He was a very nice man. He did *Pool of London* with his partner, (producer) Michael Relph, but at that time Michael Balcon, who ran Ealing Studios, was not happy about including the racial theme. But Dearden and Relph insisted and, I suppose, this started them on the road to making the so-called "social problem" pictures, including *Sapphire*' (Bourne 2001: 107–8).

37. 'You're taking a risk aren't you peddling that stuff?' he says to Dan. The implication is clearly that the cigarettes contain dope.

38. 'We've got enough of *your sort* paying for seats in there . . .'

39. 'You must be hard up to go with *him* to get them.' Johnny reacts defensively to this slur and leaves.

40. Whittingham would later work with Dearden and Relph on *I Believe in You*

(1952), while Eldridge would work on *Out of the Clouds* (1955) and *The Smallest Show on Earth* (1957).

41. Correspondence with authors (19 February 2004).
42. See Peterson (1954). The play was reviewed in *The Times* (22 October 1952).
43. *The West London Observer* (16 January 1953) notes that Owen, Rose, Lewis and Travers were all in the stage play, and indicates in an aside that John Mills may have been considered for the film.
44. Although it is worth noting that Relph, in a later letter to Michael Balcon, indicated that this was not a project they chose to undertake voluntarily or embraced wholeheartedly, in fact, it was one 'that they had to do, although we knew that boxing subjects were doubtful box-office' (Harper and Porter 2003: 68). This was Ealing's second foray into the world of boxing, the first being *There Ain't No Justice* (d. Penrose Tennyson, 1939).
45. Only one location is nominated in the shooting script: 'Ext. Stadium St. Pub and Box-office'. The script contains many detailed annotations indicating shot set-ups, camera angles, etc. and minor dialogue alterations. Soundtrack directions for crowd scenes especially off-camera in the changing room are also noted in detail.
46. Reed was Collins' first husband.
47. Recorded in the film's microfiche at the BFI Library.
48. The reviewer, however, noted that the film was marred by a 'lifeless performance by Bernadette O'Farrell'.
49. See Barr (1977: 146–7) and Harper and Porter's account (2003: 62, 73).
50. Note the running dialogue between the two 'wiseacres' in the crowd and the incident of the collection box, revealed towards the end of the film, broken into and robbed of its money.
51. It has been argued that American boxing films often present a critique of the myths of opportunity and self-improvement embedded in the ideology of the American Dream: The films 'constantly unmask the trappings of fairness and express the liability of difference. Everywhere the fix is on, the fighter is cornered, the game is rigged' (Grindon 1996: 55). In the different environment encasing the British boxing film of the time, this critique confronts post-war affluence, American-style entertainment and the notion of 'easy money'.
52. The demise of the ruthless protagonist at the end of his fight in *The Champion* was also chosen as the fate for the driven, but hardly ruthless, Kid Curtis in *The Square Ring*.
53. Bob Roberts, who produced *Body and Soul* in Hollywood, would later work with Dearden and Relph as executive producer on *All Night Long* (1962).
54. Curtis is the archetypal *noir* protagonist in the film, torn between his love for the Madonna figure of Peg and the temptations of the whorish and unsubtly named Eve, ultimately destroyed by the dilemma. His character also conforms to the conventions of the fight film: 'A dominant theme of the boxing genre is how the fighter deals with his waning physical powers: can he overcome the deterioration of the body by cultivating his soul?' (Grindon 1996: 55).

55. One review of the play had appreciated Burns predicament, 'whose future is so bright and so dark' (*The Times*, 22 October 1952).

56. The film inaugurated Dearden and Relph's relationship with Czech-born lighting cameraman Otto Heller. He would shoot a total of seven films for the partnership.

57. *The Square Ring* was restaged in June 1959 as an ITV 'Play of the Week' with a cast including Alan Bates and Sean Connery.

58. This was the designated 'location period' and some filming was entrusted to the 'documentary unit'.

59. This would have included background filming for a number of the close-up race sequences, which employed matte shots. In his later commentary, Perry finds this device unsatisfactory: 'the most disappointing sequences in the film were the races, in which static riders on mechanical mounts were combined with such ragged back projection that the illusion was destroyed' (1981: 163).

60. Clarke gives an interesting account of the film and its production in his biography, which includes the following: 'Michael Relph and I knew enough about racing to make a lot of research work not strictly necessary; but unfortunately it was all new to Basil, which meant we had to spend many weeks showing him the ropes. As always he was fully conversant with his subject by the time he began his work as director. For our equine cast the Studios bought a dozen racehorses which had disappointed their owners and were acquired for little more than £100 apiece' (1974: 173). After the film had been completed, Clarke bought one of these horses and eventually saw it win at 10-1, at Folkestone.

61. As the film progresses, Sam becomes the new father for Georgie and husband for Barbara.

62. One of the stable lads was David Hemmings in his first (unaccredited) screen appearance, later to work with Dearden and Relph again on *Only When I Larf*.

63. Bernard Lee is not nominated in the cast list of the shooting script and may have been a late appointment to the film.

64. Riding against Sir Gordon Richards, the celebrated jockey who won the 1953 Derby, and who makes two appearances in this section of the film.

65. Glendenning was the broadcasting 'voice' of horse racing in this period.

66. Their discussion also refers to Relph's conflict with Balcon: 'we were not a party to the original decision to make a racing subject, being handed a complete script' (2003: 68); although this is somewhat at odds with the account given in Clarke's biography (1974: 172-9).

67. Relph recalled that the film was commercially 'quite successful' (correspondence with authors, 19 February 2004).

68. See, for instance, 'Ealing: "the right thing" – Balcon', *Today's Cinema* (21 October 1955). The other films made at MGM Borehamwood were *Man in the Sky* (1957), *The Shiralee* (1957), *Barnacle Bill* (1957), *Dunkirk* (1958) and *Nowhere to Go* (1958). The first two of these were largely shot on location, reducing the urgency for new studio space.

69. They suggest that MGM exploited Balcon's naïveté and that *Davy*, for instance, benefited from NFFC money to the tune of £29,849. With an overall budget of £198,997, the film made a significant loss on investment, and was the least successful of the films made by Ealing at MGM (2003: 68–71, 287).

70. Including *Helter Skelter* (1949), *Penny Points to Paradise* (1951), *Forces Sweetheart* (1953) and *Svengali* (1954).

71. 'The Goon Show', BBC Radio, 250 episodes, ten series, 1951–60.

72. George Relph was an accomplished stage actor for many years. He also had roles in a number of films of this period, including Dearden and Relph's *I Believe in You* (1952). He had appeared in *Nicholas Nickleby* (1947), *The Final Test* (1953) and *The Titfield Thunderbolt* (1953), and was nominated for a Tony award on Broadway in 1958 for his performance in John Osborne's *The Entertainer*, which echoes some of the themes in *Davy*. He died in 1960.

73. Technical details on Technirama are given in Carr and Hayes (1988).

74. It was even suggested in the publicity that *Davy* was based closely on the life of Secombe (*Kinematograph Weekly*, 24 January 1957).

75. It had been announced that Relph would follow this directorial debut with an adaptation of H. E. Bates' *The Jacaranda Tree*, but the project was turned down by Balcon. In the event, Ealing's reprise was short-lived and Dearden and Relph would enter the world of independent production (*Films and Filming*, January 1957: 28; Harper and Porter 2003: 70).

76. Slocombe remembered Relph as an outstanding art director and producer, but that on this, his first film as director, his 'lack of floor experience showed markedly' (Slocombe 2007).

77. Slocombe described the Covent Garden sequences as his biggest lighting assignment to date (*Kinematograph Weekly*, 28 February 1957).

78. *The League of Gentlemen* (1960), *Man in the Moon* (1960), *Victim* (1961) and *Life for Ruth* (1962). Two other films were made under the aegis of AFM – *Whistle Down the Wind* (1961) and *Séance on a Wet Afternoon* (1964) – but these did not involve Dearden and Relph in direction or production.

79. Their credits include work on Agatha Christie film and TV adaptations, *The Blue Max* (1966), *Carry On England* (1976) and television work, including *The Liver Birds* (BBC, 1972).

80. Durgnat later wrote favourably of the film in *Films and Filming*, similarly noting the 'lyrical seediness' of the sets, 'some incisive little cameos of nasty people' and the whole evoking the 'festering evil of Grahame [*sic*] Greenland' (1966: 32). Art direction was by Elliot Scott.

81. The cinematographer was Harry Waxman who had shot such *noir* melodramas as *Brighton Rock* (1947) and *The Long Memory* (1952), and had previously worked successfully with Dearden on *Sapphire* and *Man in the Moon*.

82. With a midnight première at the Odeon, Leicester Square featured in *Kine Weekly* (8 February 1962).

83. Following in the footsteps of other film adaptations of Shakespeare to a modern

setting: *Joe Macbeth* (1955), *Kiss Me Kate* (1953), *Forbidden Planet* (1956), *West Side Story* (1961), etc.

84. Johnny Scott, Kenny Napper, Allan Ganley, Keith Christie, Bert Courtley, Ray Dempsey and Colin Purbrook and Barry Morgan. Mingus and Brubeck were touring Europe and were opportunistically signed for the film. The musical director, Philip Green, was a favourite composer of Dearden and Relph, and scored ten of their films in all. He discussed his work in *Films and Filming* (June 1957).

85. In 1950, while working on his script for the Howard Hughes film *The White Tower*, Jarrico was reported to the House of Un-American Activities Committee. Although blacklisted as a result, he produced the radical *Salt of the Earth* (d. H. Biberman, 1954). In 1958, he moved to Europe where he worked in film and television for over twenty years, often writing under the pseudonym Peter Achilles. Roberts had been in partnership with the Leftist actor John Garfield and produced the classics *Body and Soul* (1947) and *Force of Evil* (1948) before fleeing to England in the early 1950s. Both men were no doubt attracted to a tragedy centred on poisonous whispers, rumourmongering and hateful deceits.

86. Attenborough's recollections of the film were dominated by the devastating news that he received during shooting, concerning the tragic death of his mother in a car accident.

87. The parallels with Shakespeare are signposted in the 'brightest neon' notes Michael Brooke in his discussion of the film (BFI Screenonline); Rex is *Othello*, Rod *Roderigo*, Johnny Cousin *Iago*, Cass *Cassio*, Delia *Desdemona*, Emily *Emilia*, Benny *Bianca*, Lou *Lodovico*, etc.

88. At the time of filming, McGoohan was beginning his interesting and distinctive rise to (cult) stardom. He had worked in television and film from the mid-1950s, for instance, in *Hell Drivers* (1957), gradually gaining recognition. From this point on it was television work that would propel especially his career – first as John Drake in *Danger Man* (1960–67) and then as the hero of *The Prisoner* (1967–68). He appeared briefly in *League of Gentlemen* (1960) and Dearden and Relph soon worked with him again on *Life for Ruth* (1962). In 1973, McGoohan directed *Catch My Soul*, a film version of Jack Good's rock opera *Othello*.

89. This was one of Exton's first film engagements. His distinguished career, principally in television scriptwriting, included working on scripts for *Bonanza*, *Gunsmoke*, *Mission Impossible*, *Starsky & Hutch*, *Rosemary & Thyme* and many others.

90. *Come Outside*, with Wendy Richard. His later career involved work in music, criticism, television and film, including co-scripting and directing *Myra Breckinridge* (1970).

91. She asks this a number of times to the point that it echoes the film's title.

92. George Sewell appears as a market trader in one scene which acts as a metaphor; Ricky buys a canary in a cage which he gives to Cat. She releases the bird and

despite the attentions of a passing cat, it just, briefly, survives. They too are trapped but also unable to live outside the cage.

93. Most obviously the classic study by Young and Willmott (1957). See also Mogey (1955).

94. The film was crudely cut at this point, probably in response to British Board of Censors intervention. The flick-knife is never shown, although the click as Charlie opens it results in a reaction shot of Ricky's face, and it then seems 'magically' to appear in Ricky's possession when the police arrive.

95. In this ending, the film considerably truncates that outlined in the shooting script. Here, Ricky confronts Immelman at his wharf-side workshop and is given a savage beating by Charlie and Pug. They let him go after this, and he and Cat are last seen drifting into the fog of the river in an old boat, together but facing an unknown future.

96. *Kinematograph Weekly* published a production feature with location photographs of Dearden and the cast (28 March 1963). However, its later review of the film (2 April 1964) confirms the release date as 19 April 1964.

97. The complete list of these 'martyred' films, together with the delays in their releases (some never were), is itemised in Kelly, Norton and Perry (1966: 35).

98. Chibnall (1999) has shown how the British crime film adopted the New Wave realism of the early 1960s, but does not discuss *A Place to Go*.

99. Of course, the novelty of *A Place to Go* was its London setting, as the other New Wave films were set in the Industrial North.

100. Durgnat sensed the unease of Dearden and Relph in Woodfall territory, 'as if the class barrier had turned out to be wider than R–D had anticipated'. With this film, he believed that 'The British cinema's decreased respect towards paternalistic authority, and its abandonment of paternalism towards the proletariat, seem to have brought R–D to a temporary impasse' (1966: 33).

101. In one of many examples in the film there is an obvious symbolism in Matt's escapology; as one character puts it: 'You've got nothing to lose but your chains.'

102. George Anthony Armstrong Willis was a novelist and playwright with an extensive career in publishing which started in the early 1920s. He wrote crime and fantasy novels and short stories. *The Strange Case of Mr Pelham* was first published in 1957. An earlier version of the story had been made in 1955 as part of the 'Alfred Hitchcock Presents' TV series in America. A 'tie-in' version of the book by Ralph Martin was published by Tandem Books (1970).

103. This is confirmed by Forbes on the commentary that accompanies the Studio Canal DVD CC030032. He indicates that this work was done 'under the counter', as a result of his position as the Head of Production at EMI.

104. Bernard Delfont appointed Forbes to the post at EMI in April 1969 and he took up his post from 1 May. By 24 May it was also announced that John Hargeaves (who had worked with Forbes at Allied Film Makers), would act as Forbes' production assistant. In August, a 'Programme of fifteen major features' to be produced by ABP, Delfont and Forbes was announced, within the next

two years (details taken from *Kinematograph Weekly*'s, 12 April, 24 May 1969 and 16 August 1969). Walker provides an insightful summary of Forbes' time there – he resigned the post after a stormy relationship with the EMI board in March 1971 (1974: 426–40). The other two films produced and released 'back to back' with *The Man Who Haunted Himself* were *And Soon the Darkness* (d. R. Fuest) and *Hoffmann* (A. Rakoff). As Walker notes, their release unfortunately 'coincided with the World Cup football play-offs, a heat wave and a general election' (1974: 431). See also Forbes (1974).

105. *The Saint* was a popular television series based on the Leslie Charteris novels. It ran for 118 episodes (1962–69). Moore had also appeared in earlier TV series including *Ivanhoe* (1958), *The Alaskans* (1959) and *Maverick* (1957–62), as well as in other film and theatre roles. After his work on this film, he appeared in *The Persuaders!* (1971) and succeeded Sean Connery as James Bond, in seven films (1973–85).

106. Bryan Forbes, audio commentary DVD.

107. The scripts indicate that the film was made by Relph-Dearden Productions Ltd, but the credits indicate Excalibur Films Ltd (the company that was responsible for *A Place to Go*). Forbes on the DVD commentary suggests that this company was probably a front for tax purposes.

108. *Kine Weekly* carried a short feature on the challenges faced by Tony Spratling, the lighting cameraman for the film, when shooting the scenes in the low-light conditions of The Planetarium (8 November 1969).

109. It is interesting to note that this ending truncates the final scenes itemised in the shooting script. Here, these events are followed by a shot of the Ferrari (*sic*) driving at speed along a tree-lined road in France, en route to Cannes. In the car, the surviving Pelham is accompanied by a heavily pregnant and radiant Eve. The film was to end with a cut to a reaction shot of Pelham's face as she tells him that the consultant that examined her thinks that she might be having twins. 'The camera then tracks above the Ferrari, pulls up and away as it streaks like a silver arrow towards the South' (*Final Shooting Script*: 124).

110. Bryan Forbes, DVD Audio commentary. Elspeth Grant, writing in the *Tatler*, thought that the film gave Moore 'the best chance he has had so far to prove he can shed the old TV image of The Saint and really act' (quoted in *Kinematograph Weekly*, 6 June 1970). Moore himself is indebted to Dearden, a 'marvellous director, technically and dramatically', believing that for the first time he was invited to 'act' (Moore 2008: 153–4).

111. The deployment of Freud's 'wall of narcissism' into the concept of 'narcissistic defence' is developed in Spotnitz (1961/62).

4

Dramas of Masculine Adjustment II: Men in Action

Out of the Clouds (1955); The Ship that Died of Shame (1955); The League of Gentlemen (1960) and Man in the Moon (1960)

> Dearden's men are often at their happiest in action, dressed appropriately, and it is through the loss of action that their anxiety or distress is suggested – the most poignantly felt lack is that of an appropriate arena of action, and this is the major narrative premise of several films. (Pat Kirkham and Janet Thumim 1997: 100)

> What sort of men were we, that the war had been so good to us and the peace so rotten? (Nicholas Monsarrat 1961)

If Dearden and Relph's films after the war often exploited the form of the tragic melodrama to explore masculine adjustment and responses to the changing social circumstances of the post-war world, in a small number of films they also constructed an alternative trope for exploring this central issue: narratives of men after action – seeking action. These films are sometimes marked by a tragic dimension, but the films are more substantially determined by their exploration of stories of men asserting – or reasserting – their masculinity through professional, physical action; usually in an all-male group. Masculine purpose and identity are temporarily rediscovered and reinvigorated through a reconstitution of wartime experience; and the crisis is often transgressive, most obviously in tempting the men towards crime in an attempt to rediscover excitement, regain a sense of purpose, re-establish male bonding and challenge the perceived feminisation of society after the war.

These four films stand in comparison with the popular cycle of war films that commenced in the 1950s, productions such as *The Dambusters*

(d. M. Anderson, 1954) and *The Colditz Story* (d. G. Hamilton, 1954), conventionally understood as nostalgic evocations of wartime masculine achievement and purpose (Rattigan 1991; Chapman 1998b; Murphy 2000). However, they avoid the simple transference back to a happier time to show men confronting loss of agency, attempting to reconstitute the protective and reassuring comradeship of conflict, but in the time after war.

While usually harking back to military or forces experiences of the war, the final film in this group, *Man in the Moon*, peers forward and configures interestingly the dilemmas of the modern man in the confrontation of new technologies and the unexplored boundaries of outer space. In its satiric vision, the film poses the timeless question of whether the man of action – Britain's pioneer astronaut, a perfect specimen of manhood – can conquer the challenge of new frontiers if entangled in the snares of femininity and the de-individualising regimes of a technocratic society.

OUT OF THE CLOUDS (1955)

> It has grown from little more than an open field with a few tents on it to become the magnificently equipped international terminal of today . . . now it is the greatest airport in the world, the springboard from which huge machines leap across oceans and continents to the far places of the earth. (John Fores 1956: 8)

> Yet another of Ealing's attempts at a behind-the-scenes approach – this time an anatomy of London Airport, a much smaller community in the mid-Fifties than now . . . As is usual in such Ealing pictures, and in this one more than most, the background and setting are more interesting than the fore-grounded characters, and Paul Beeson's Eastmancolor photography provides a fascinating record of how Heathrow looked in its early days. (Perry 1985: 164)

Based very loosely on the novel *The Springboard* by John Fores,[1] the film was adapted by Rex Reinits, and Michael Relph and John Eldridge wrote the screenplay. Eldridge had worked with Dearden and Relph several years earlier on *Pool of London* (1951) and was originally appointed to direct *Out of the Clouds*, however, his ill-health resulted in the project being reassigned to Dearden and Relph.[2] Harper and Porter note that Dearden and Relph 'were made to do *Out of the Clouds* (1955) instead of another film withdrawn at short notice' (2003: 68). The shooting scripts date from early June 1954 and contain detailed notes on the London Airport location that provides the background to the film. A temporary production office was established at the airport, together with related facilities for crew, cast and personnel for the duration of the shoot.[3] At the same time, the film employed an Aerial Unit[4] and made use of one of Ealing's largest-ever sets to create the interior of the terminal building (Perry 1985: 164). The film acknowledges co-operation from the Ministry of Transport and Civil Aviation and technical assistance and facilities provided by BOAC, BEA and Pan American, whose logos are prominently figured as a result in many sequences in the film. In its locations and narrative, the film unwittingly captures that period of post-war aviation development, when flying was a glamorous and romantic adventure, exemplified by the planes of the pre-jet era themselves – the Constellations, the Stratocruisers and Viscounts – but also by the deportment, status and style of their pilots and air hostesses.[5] The film thus offers the modern viewer an historical insight into aviation culture as it was in the mid-1950s. In this vein, as Richards suggests, the film bears the Ealing hallmark of a commitment to service and is in part a celebration of the values associated with the new post-war public transport systems – of the air (1997: 17).

Three main stories are interwoven into the compendium which makes up the film. The airport provides the narrative hub and background for the events which unfold, and as in a number of their other films, Dearden and Relph combine a documentary behind-the-scenes approach for several 'life-stories'; the dramas of apparently randomly selected, ordinary people as they move and intersect across this stage. Barr, however, was later to note:

> The Relph/Dearden 'omnibus' formula progressively seizes up, the little human dramas becoming more schematic and the containing authority structure more rigid, as in this drama of airline pilots and passengers, their work, love-life and peccadilloes. (1977: 193)

While the formula had admittedly become stale, Dearden threw himself into the technical challenge of interweaving the multiple lines of narrative development; relishing the opportunities offered in the large interior set of the terminal concourse where the camera tracks and glides along with the character of the busy duty officer and the narrative line is continually passed around staff and passengers.

The film begins with Leah Roche (Margo Lorenz), a passenger on board a BEA Viscount flying into London from Frankfurt, on her way to America. At virtually the same time, but arriving from New York on a Pan-Am Stratocruiser, is Bill Steiner (David Knight), en route for Israel. In the uniform of a BOAC captain, Gus Randall (Anthony Steel) – 'an attractive, typical ex-RAF type' (*Shooting Script*: 4) – is dropped off in the airport car park by Eleanor (Jill Harcourt), who reminds him that he will have 'something' for her when he returns from his flight to Karachi via Rome and Cairo. On this slightly mysterious note, they part company and on his way into the terminal, he encounters Nick Millbourne (Robert Beatty),[6] gazing with undisguised envy at a large plane taking off. In their subsequent interchange, in which Gus characteristically draws on the self-deprecating wartime lingo of the RAF, where planes are 'crates' or 'kites' that travel on 'bus routes', it transpires that Nick is the BOAC duty officer, in charge of managing operations on the ground, but that he is also a former pilot who desperately wants to return to flying and has an important medical examination later that day which may allow him to do so. Inside the busy terminal building they begin their respective preparations for their working day – Gus, for his flight to Cairo and Karachi; Nick, in dealing with the many demands of passengers, planes and crews. In these early sequences, the film establishes the multiple possibilities of romance, of criminality and of male ambition. This latter dimension is given a further twist when it appears that Nick and Gus are rivals for the affections of Penny (Eunice Gayson), an attractive air hostess on Gus's flight to Cairo.

Amidst the bustle of the airport, the film includes a number of comic asides dealing with the unfamiliarity of flying for some passengers and the unpredictable and quirky comings and goings that flow through its daily operations. Nick appears a model of sympathetic efficiency, respected by the staff he works with and troubleshooting with good humoured professionalism. Gus and his crew are checked for their flight by Stevens, the customs officer (Bernard Lee),[7] but not without a joking but uneasy interchange between them about smuggling. After this the crew depart, and as she leaves, Penny tries to convince Nick that his job is vital to the airport, a view which he bitterly refuses to accept; but he is soon called away to deal with other matters. As Gus and Penny's flight takes off, leaving an envious/impotent Nick by the runway, he is called to deal with a mechanical problem on one of the planes. Captain Brent (James Robertson-Justice, in typical ebullient form) is less than happy with the state of his engines, despite all reassurances to the contrary.

Leah and Bill meet in the transit lounge and immediately seem drawn to each other. At first she is apprehensive, thinking that they have been isolated because they are both Jewish, and not without cause – as she explains to Bill, her parents died in Auschwitz. They exchange their stories of destination – Bill, to Israel to work as a hydrologist; Leah, to America to be married to an older, wealthy man whom she met in Germany after the war. Leah's flight is called, interrupting their time together. Bill is clearly smitten as he watches her leave to board the plane to New York. However, the plane is the one piloted by Captain Brent and although it takes off into worsening foggy conditions, mechanical difficulties force them to return to the airport, landing by 'Talk-Down' with full emergency drill. As a result, they are reunited, and Bill is so overjoyed at this turn of events that he promptly embraces and kisses her.

With all flights postponed for twelve hours, Bill insists that they are taken to the same hotel.

As they leave, Nick ponders his own situation with the motherly senior ground stewardess, Mrs Malcolm (Isabel Dean), confessing that he is due for his medical that day. She responds that she can't understand why he wants to get back in the air: 'It wouldn't hurt some people I know to come down out of the clouds'; in return he admits that he has been flying all of his life and that he just can't live without it. Just as he is called away, she indicates that he will find what he wants 'on the ground' – and so will Penny. This mention of Penny cues a cut to the Constellation, piloted by Gus flying over the Pyramids into Cairo. In the hotel, Gus encounters the curious, ingratiating Hafadi (Harold Kasket), Eleanor's contact, sent to arrange some kind of contraband deal. Gus remains noncommittal about this and when Hafadi leaves, he is joined by Penny. During their evening together, Gus becomes an inversion of Nick, confessing to her that he finds the so-called 'glamour' of the modern, international pilot's life superficial and empty, and with this, he proposes to her. She turns him down as 'just not the marrying kind', but in response to his question, refuses to confirm that she is in love with Nick. In a linked aside, back at the airport in London, Nick is in discussion with Stevens, the Customs man, who has suspicions about Gus. The suggestion here leaves the relationship between Nick and Penny – and Gus's possible criminal future – suspended and open.

In contrast to the exotic locations of Egypt, Bill takes Leah on a tour of fog-bound London. In an ancient taxi, with a driver (Gordon Harker) who has a rather morbid interest in tombs, they 'see' – through thick fog – the sights: Big Ben, St Paul's and the Tower, before they are taken to an old waterfront pub in the East End. While the friendly landlady (Megs Jenkins) prepares their meal, they embrace overlooking the Thames and when they return to the hotel, Bill tells Leah he loves her and proposes that they marry and go to Israel together. Clearly attracted by this prospect which throws her future plans and relationship into turmoil, Leah, however, insists that she cannot accompany him and that she must continue on her original course, and they part, seemingly forever.

At the airport, Nick undergoes his medical examination. Despite admitting to only the odd pipe after work and a gin before dinner, the doctor refuses to pass him for flying duties. He confirms that Nick is in pretty good shape for his age, but is troubled by the possible effects of his wartime experience – 'three days and four nights in the sea during mid-winter' – and on this basis he advises him to carry on with his existing, essential job on the ground. Bitterly disappointed, Nick leaves, apparently unconvinced by this advice. In Cairo, Gus has awoken to the news that he and his crew must fly an incoming plane back to London, and in an interchange with the crooked Hafadi, it appears that he accepts £500 to smuggle a packet back to London. As he goes through Egyptian customs for the flight, he jokes that he has only 'diamonds, hashish and gold' to declare.

In the final stages of the film, the threads of the three stories criss-cross and are finally resolved, in typical circular fashion, back at the airport. This involves aerial, as well as emotional geography, as a downcast Bill leaves London on a flight for Rome and Israel; while Leah awakes to find her flight to New York delayed and sends a telegram to New York confessing that she can no longer honour her promised marriage arrangement. Unaware of this, in Rome, Bill on impulse changes flights to return to follow Leah, and joins the Constellation piloted by Gus and his crew returning from Cairo.

Back in London, the flight to New York duly takes off, before the incoming flight piloted by Gus lands carrying an anxious Bill. Unexpectedly, however, Bill is reunited with Leah and the whirlwind romance seems secure. Gus, on the other hand, returning through Customs from the Cairo flight, is pulled up by Stevens, searched and given 'the full treatment'. However, against expectations, he is found to be carrying nothing illegal. He subsequently confronts Eleanor, as his 'deadly nightshade', and warns her off, confirming that Hafadi is by now in a Cairo jail for the drugs he was supposed to carry for her.

The film ends with Nick tracked by a fluid camera though the crowded, multilingual babble of the concourse to meet Gus and then Penny, and in response to their questions, he tells them of his failure in the medical. However, he seems now reconciled to the doctor's advice concerning the importance of his job on the ground and that it outweighs his ambitions to return to flying. Gus too seems transformed, departing with the maternal Mrs Malcolm, seeking her advice on 'how to settle down'. And Penny leaves with Nick, confirming that she could never have married a pilot; with the clear implication is that they will now marry. With these matters resolved, the final shot of the film captures a BEA Viscount flying overhead – presumably carrying Bill and Leah – en route to their 'Promised Land'.

In each of the three principal stories there are elements of conversion. Bill and Leah find true romance together and thus she is saved from a life of loveless obligation. Gus comes to realise that there is more to life than the supposed glamour of international flying and, although tempted, turns his back on the possibilities offered by criminal activity. Nick, finally, comes to appreciate that his dreams and ambition can no longer be defined by his wartime and subsequent life as a pilot, and that his service on the ground, doing a job he is good at, offers him a more secure and rewarding future; one that also brings him romantic fulfilment in the shape of marriage to Penny.

Reviews of the film were almost universally poor, condemning it as a real disappointment and with predictable recourse to the language of flying. For

EUNICE GAYSON, ANTHONY STEEL
and ROBERT BEATTY
in a scene from

OUT OF THE CLOUDS
IN EASTMAN COLOUR
G.F.D. DISTRIBUTION   Cert "U"

Uniforms: *Out of the Clouds* (1955) (Courtesy of Steve Chibnall Archive)

Leonard Mosley, it was a 'Nose Dive' (*Daily Express*, 11 February 1955); F. Majdeburg noted that 'On both levels – aeronautical and passionate – the film seems an awful long way short of breaking through any sound barrier' (*Daily Mail*, 11 February 1955); while *The Spectator* noted: 'Michael Relph and Basil Dearden, the co-directors [*sic*], usually so skilled and imaginative, seem to have become temporarily grounded' (11 February 1955). *The Financial Times* labelled the film 'a rare crash-landing from the well-intentioned studios of Ealing' (14 February 1955); and *The Daily Sketch* critic found it to be a 'cliché ridden account of love and life at London Airport' and continued: 'I never thought Ealing Studios could turn out a really bad picture; they have done so this time' (11 February 1955). For *The New Statesman* the film seemed 'more novelette than life' (19 February 1955); and Dilys Powell, writing in *The Sunday Times*, found it to contain 'Good background detail but the film as a whole is weakly conventional in structure and incident' (13 February 1955). Even *Kine Weekly* found it difficult to rescue the film. Despite noting the 'exhilarating flying sequences' which should 'please all classes', it concluded that 'the film is barely strong enough to make a successful solo flight', and recommended that 'wise exhibitors will see that it is accompanied by a good second' (3 February 1955). For the *Monthly Film Bulletin*, the film followed a predictable pattern, was superficial and lacked conviction: 'continually deserting the centre for the periphery', and as a result 'never looks like adding up to a satisfactory whole' (March 1955). Derek Hill, writing in *Films and Filming*, thought the film 'a comprehensive guide to the most blatant faults of British films . . . The script and direction are so unimaginative that the film plods along with almost unbearable tedium', and he ended by berating 'the colourless footage of this tired, stale production' (April 1955).

Despite this widespread criticism, *Out of the Clouds* was seemingly a popular hit; Michael Relph recalling that it was 'quite successful' at the box office.[8] This probably had more to do with the novel background of London Airport, the stylish attraction of air travel and the star power of Anthony Steel than the somewhat routine drama.

With *Out of the Clouds*, Ealing had just about exhausted the formula of its 'behind-the-scenes' dramas coupling together various lines of narrative. Dearden manages his usual efficiency in keeping all the plates spinning, but the diverting asides to comic cameos become tiresome, the central romance is hopelessly underpowered and the authentic backgrounds are insufficient in themselves to overcome the conventional drama and two-dimensional characterisations. The real interest of the film lies in its variation on the theme of 'Men in Action'; in particular, the accommodation that Nick and Gus make in terms of sacrificing their desire for glamour, speed and movement with the mundane certainties of domesticity. Both men exhibit a lust for thrills and glamorous travel, and this is effectively linked back to their wartime experience as pilots. Throughout the film, the men are continually brought back to earth through the countervailing feminine common-sense desire for domesticity: Mrs Malcolm tells Nick that she is entirely happy with holidays in Shoreham and has plans for a 'place of our own', where she can settle down and look after her family; while Penny, on a night out with a contemplative Gus in Cairo, applauds the signs of him 'growing up' at last. In a rare confession, he admits that flying has always been an 'escape' for him, but he is now tired of just 'flapping around, chasing the bright spots' and hints at settling down. Caught in an inverse dynamic, Nick reconciles himself to his confirmed status of being permanently 'grounded', content with an 'ordinary job'; and by the end of the film he has jettisoned his past, including his wartime experience, and looks forward to a new and settled future. In contrast to *The Ship That Died of Shame* and *The League of Gentlemen*, films that hardly admit the feminine in order to allow the men uninterrupted access to action, Nick and Gus are continually confronted with the influence of women and drawn towards the realm of the domestic. A decade after the war, it is now time for men of action to confront the necessity of choice.

THE SHIP THAT DIED OF SHAME (1955)

The Ship that Died of Shame had its origin in a post-war encounter in a small naval 'get-together' club in London. The principal function of this shoddy establishment was to serve as a meeting place for ex-naval types who needed an excuse for getting boozy, who couldn't find jobs, and who hoped meanwhile to sell each other life-insurance. Among these forlorn step-children of war I met a man who had served in the same corvette with me in 1940 or 1941. He offered me a job, smuggling brandy and watches across from France in a converted gun-boat. I decided to become a civil servant instead. But the memory of that curious post-war crossroads remained, and I wrote the story in Johannesburg about six years later. My friend subsequently went to jail. (Nicholas Monsarrat 1961: 202) [9]

Monsarrat's fictionalised account of his wartime experiences on Atlantic convoys in the Navy had formed the basis for the highly successful Ealing production *The Cruel Sea* (d. L. Norman, 1953), and it can be assumed that this was an influential factor which led Relph, Dearden and John Whiting to work on the screenplay for *The Ship That Died of Shame* a year or so later.[10] Gordon Dines, who had been the lighting cameraman on *The Cruel Sea*, was appointed to work with Dearden on this new project. The final shooting scripts are dated September 1954 and the film was released in April 1955. In the case of *The Cruel Sea*, the narrative was based on a relatively straightforward set of clear-cut, wartime oppositions set out in the opening narration: 'The men are the heroes. The heroines are the ships. The only villain is the sea – the cruel sea.' In *The Ship That Died of Shame*, however, this narrative is subtly warped; the men *were* heroes, and while the ship *remains* the heroine, the enemy now appears more social than marine; rooted in the post-war masculine malaise of moral corrosion, greed and a rudderless inability to adjust appropriately to peacetime circumstance.

Perry, in his later assessment of the film, found this frustrating, in that it 'began in a promising Ealing vein as if it was going to be a war film, but developed into a story highlighting the problems of servicemen trying to adjust to the difficulties of civilian life'. Furthermore, he continued: 'By 1955 such a theme had become dated and irrelevant – another case of Ealing failing to take into account the shift in attitudes' (1981: 165). This easy dismissal fails to take account of the ways in which the themes of what Spicer refers to as 'Damaged Men' (2001: 161) resonated and mutated in other British films throughout the 1950s and beyond (see also Murphy 2000: 186–202); nor indeed the ways in which this had been a developing preoccupation in the cinema of Dearden and Relph since the war.

The film, in large part, remains true to the narrative established in Monsarrat's short story, although the ending is radically revised;[11] and the original text does not include the 'Birdie' Dick (Bill Owen) character. The narrative, rather like a moral fable, is organised into three main segments. The first introduces the wartime past experiences of the three main characters; the second features their post-war reunion and the beginnings of their collective fall from grace; and the third deals with their resultant final dishonour, death or suitably qualified survival. Throughout the film, the only true and reliable moral compass emerges as 'The Ship', the talismanic motor gunboat *1087*;[12] although Bill Randall (George Baker),[13] its wartime commander, has his qualms and moments, motivated in part by the memory of his dead wife Helen (Virginia McKenna) and by the remembered moral certitudes of war service. And the film begins with Randall's memories as he muses: 'The beginning, like almost everything else about me, went back to the war'.

The opening scenes, initially narrated by Randall, and then switching to a conventional objective narration, establish the speed and the thrills of his war as the commander of *1087* in the Royal Navy Coastal Forces, the 'beat-up boys', dicing with death in the English Channel on missions against the enemy.[14] As Jim Cook has argued: 'It is difficult not to describe the opening scenes . . . in terms of dreamlike picaresque' (1986: 362), and this quality is used in a number of telling scenes throughout the film. These initial shots of the boat in action on a cross-Channel raid, scything through the sea under Randall's command, are also used to introduce the two other principal characters – George Hoskins (Richard Attenborough), the second-in-command, and 'Birdie' the coxswain – and to emphasise their close, battle-hardened camaraderie and unity. The narrative 'past' is therefore established in nostalgic, masculine mode, and as the film develops, only two issues are allowed to contradict this harmony of remembered, 'flashback' action and purpose. The first concerns Hoskins, whose eagerness to claim unproven 'kills' on the painted score he keeps on the side of the boat's bridge indicates a degree of brash self-promotion and a disregard for honour, which is to become responsible for driving the narrative as it enters the second and final phases of the film. At this stage, however, he is subordinate to Randall's class and naval authority and disciplined in the interests of the service. The second involves an element of tragic melodrama and is focused on Randall's relationship with his very recently married wife, Helen, the only female in the film – apart from *1087*, which is referred to as she/her throughout. Helen meets Randall and the boat as they return from this first raid, and in a short sequence following this, they stay together in a borrowed, idyllic cottage and are shown to be very much in love.[15] For Randall, Helen adds a vital personal imperative to the moral cause of the war: 'Since I've known you, there's seemed to be a purpose in things – even in this damned war'; and in return, with heavy foreboding, she makes him promise never 'to do anything silly with that ship of yours'. The harmony between Randall and Helen and the promise of their future life together prove tragically short-lived, for when he returns from his next mission he learns that she has been killed, the victim of a random German air attack. Bereft of her humanising influence, Randall is left with only the ship and the war as outlets for his embittered wish to avenge Helen's death.[16] But the film compresses time, as the end of the war is signalled in an almost newsreel-style sequence, which sees the decommissioning of *1087* and her crew. Randall is thus left with no ship, wife, crew or war to guide him.

The second narrative segment of the film shifts into the 'now' of post-war Britain and initially condenses around Randall, as his attempt to establish his own boatyard fails and he is then further humbled when his cap-in-hand attempt to regain his pre-war job meets patronising rejection. In debt, disillusioned and demoralised, by chance he attends a reunion at the Coastal Forces Club. This seems a desultory affair, serving only to deepen his depression, but the sudden arrival of Hoskins, brash and breezy, with the manners and money of a spiv – from 'doing this and that' – jolts Randall out of his malaise. Before long, he agrees to help Hoskins in his proposal for a 'side-line': smuggling – 'nylons, a spot of wine, brandy perhaps' – across the Channel 'to lighten up the post-war darkness', a commitment which is cemented when Hoskins

The 'Old Firm' reunited under new colours; Birdie, Hoskins and Randall on 1087 in *The Ship that Died of Shame* (1955) (Courtesy of Steve Chibnall Archive)

knowingly holds out the possibility of using old *1087* as their vessel in the enterprise. Hoskins has located their old ship and they go to rescue her from ignominy, neglected on a nameless mud-flat. Randall spots her first, identifying the palimpsest of 'kills' inscribed by Hoskins during the war. Inspired by the challenge of restoring her to her former glory, Randall regains his sense of purpose and esteem and is aided by the chance appearance of Birdie, who begs to rejoin the 'old firm'. After some initial reluctance, Randall agrees and the refurbished *1087* begins her new life of profitable contraband runs across the Channel. For a while it appears that the boat and the crew are rejuvenated and have recaptured the spirit of unity and purpose that inspired them during the war. Returning from one of these early forays, however, they are intercepted by Customs; an older, experienced officer, Brewster (Bernard Lee), played with northern bluffness, and his inexperienced junior (Harold Goodwin). Brewster reminisces about his time in the war when he owed his survival to a little ship like *1087* and he instantly mistrusts the smooth-talking, 'La-di-dah' Hoskins. On this occasion, by means of a ruse, they escape detection, but this encounter is enough for them to adopt a more legitimate front for their enterprise and this segment of the film ends with them operating tourist excursions by day as a cover for their smuggling activities by night.

The final segment of the film sees their rediscovered unity torn apart by tensions which escalate as Hoskins, in pursuit of money, gradually takes command. While he leaves the running of the boat to Randall and Birdie, it is he who now deals with the increasingly 'sordid details' of their activities, driving them into more dangerous and reprehensible activities. This is first signalled when they repulse an armed hijack at sea, returning one night from a cross-Channel run; and in this action, the film introduces the shadowy villain Fordyce (Roland Culver), an ex-major, who Hoskins tracks down to a seedy garage. Fordyce is another embittered ex-service man who has turned to organised crime: 'I found things had changed a bit when I got out of the army – got a bit tired of working for the plebs after fighting for them' is his off-hand justification. Hoskins and he agree to a partnership, although Hoskins laughingly refuses a drink with Fordyce to seal his proffered 'gentleman's agreement, old boy'.

If the earlier part of the film and the depiction of their smuggling is based on a sense of the illicit but nonetheless acceptable import of 'a few luxuries people are short of', as Randall puts it, the new relationship with Fordyce heralds a shift in their activities, which, by degrees, moves them into much less acceptable, more nefarious work. And this is responsible for cranking up the tensions and antagonism between Randall and Hoskins. In spite of his qualms, the naïve Randall continues in the enterprise as they carry cargoes first of forged currency – ironically printed by the Nazis during the war – and then of contraband guns. In both cases, as if to underscore the moral depths to which they are sinking, the engines of *1087*, normally so dependable and well-tuned, begin, at crucial moments, to misfire. It appears that the heart and conscience of the boat is both marking and refusing to co-operate with their moral descent. [17]

The climax of the film results from a final run across the Channel, starting with a rendezvous on the British coast, where they take on board a nondescript, hunted little man (John Chandos). After collecting him and escaping into the fog towards the French coast, the engines signal their unease by failing again – 'she's losing heart', realises Randall. Pursued by French coastal patrols, Hoskins callously pushes the anonymous 'passenger' over the side and they return to port. Here, Randall finally turns on Hoskins, telling him that he wants no more to do with him and the work they have been doing. He hits out when Hoskins attempts to blackmail him into continuing, and taunts him about his 'softness' and his moral scruples, and refers to Helen. The film uses the device of newspaper headlines to confirm that their human cargo of the night before was an escaped child killer, and Randall again confronts Hoskins, who protests his ignorance. Unconvinced, Randall is forced by Hoskins – who uses Birdie's involvement as a lever – into agreeing to a final escape run. The police and Customs hunt for the boat involves Brewster, who recalls the encounter with the 'La-di-dah' Hoskins whom he runs to ground at the garage, where the Customs man is shot by the murderous Fordyce, also cornered and desperate. Birdie witnesses this and returns the boat to tell Randall just as Hoskins and Fordyce appear. At gunpoint they force Randall and Birdie to set out into stormy seas to escape to Portugal. In the ensuing maelstrom, Fordyce shoots and wounds Birdie and is then shot by Randall. When Randall goes to turn the boat back, he and Hoskins fight and, although at the last moment, Randall tries to save him, Hoskins is killed by the boat's propellers as he is swept over the stern.[18] Randall and the wounded Birdie are left alone on the boat in the final scenes, and as the engines falter and cut out, Birdie says, 'She won't do it, she's got her pride – you can't blame her.' Without power they are swept towards the coast and Randall recalls Helen's warning 'not to do anything silly with that ship of yours'. As if in response, he confesses to Birdie, 'we did do something silly; useless, futile and pathetic'. When the boat smashes onto the rocks, Randall manages to save himself and Birdie, and together they witness the final and ignominious wreck of *1087* as she sinks. The film ends with Randall's voice-over: 'And so she died – she gave up and died – in anger and in shame. Yes, she had her pride.' Just before the final credits, a sudden dissolve flashback to *1087* as she really was ends the film: at full speed, under honourable wartime command, in stark counterpoint to her salutary, subsequent fate.

The film opened to mixed reviews,[19] many of which predictably found it wanting by comparison with *The Cruel Sea*, although they were often intrigued by the story and generally lauded Attenborough's performance in particular. 'British film stars may not be the best in the world, but they are certainly the most waterproof,' commented *Films and Filming* in the wake of a spate of nautical films. Derek Hill continued in sterner, characteristic terms, part of his developing crusade against British films, arguing that the script and its direction lacked imagination: 'Here is the same dreary old workmanlike proficiency that follows all the rules and stays firmly in a rut, a rut so deep that Messrs. Relph and Dearden seem unable to peer out over the edge' (*Films and Filming*, June 1955). For *The Manchester Guardian*, on the other hand, 'the anthropomorphic qualities of the motor-gunboat help rather than hinder a most exciting and well acted story' (23 April 1955). The *Evening Standard* appreciated the 'masculine Ealing' theme of the film: 'Like all who go to war they find peace a frightening affair' (22 April 1955); whereas for other commentators 'the direction, though workmanlike, lacks character' and the 'story, with its background of post-war shortages and servicemen's difficulties in coming to terms with civilian life, already looks a little dated' (*Monthly Film Bulletin*, June 1955). Against this grain, but true to form, *Kine Weekly* extolled the film as a 'thrilling, intriguing and salutary melodrama', pronouncing it 'an excellent booking' with 'first-class direction, detail, staging and outstanding camera work' (21 April 1955).

The film has a certain elegiac quality in its apparent lament for the passing of wartime; in particular for the loss of 'do-or-die' male comradeship and the simple clarity and unity of service, pride and moral purpose, juxtaposed against the apparently fragmented and more problematic insecurities of peacetime. As Cook has argued: 'our engagement with the film is governed by a complex narrative tension between what one might call a "realistic" level and a "metaphoric" level' (1986: 363); and indeed pivotal to the film is the metaphor of the ship (and her embodiment of the memory of Helen), and the struggle for her destiny in the uncharted, post-war waters, that develops between Randall/Birdie and Hoskins/Fordyce. In these terms, Michael Relph, when interviewed about the film many years after its release, maintained that the film had articulated a critique of British post-war society:

> The ship, in a sense, represented what people had done with the country they had inherited after the war. It was a sort of allegory, and it's probably better than one thought at the time. (McFarlane 1997: 482)

Cook's analysis leads him to suggest that the film expresses a striking critique of 'nostalgia and the drives which fuel it' (1986: 362); and it may be that it does emphasise the impossibility of recapturing or returning to the past.

However, the values of the past are held up as worth fighting for, as the problems of the present seem to derive precisely from the ways in which Hoskins and Fordyce – and to a degree Randall – turn their backs on them, allowing moral anarchy and corruption to take over.[20] In this sense, therefore, the critical target of the film seems more obviously to concern the *abandonment* of the virtues of wartime ethics and solidarity than it does any nostalgia for a mythical wartime past. Francis has recently argued that a significant number of films and novels in the late 1940s and 1950s signalled a deep masculine ambivalence about the return to family and domestic responsibilities; and that films such as *The Ship that Died of Shame*, provided elements in a broader 'masculine imaginary', which allowed

> men to constantly travel back and forward across the frontier of domesticity, if only in the realm of the imagination, attracted to the responsibilities (and pleasures) of marriage and fatherhood, but also equally enchanted by fantasies of the energetic life and homosocial camaraderie of the adventure hero. (2007: 181)

This theme of masculine negotiation between fantasy and adjustment was to be revisited and explored, albeit through different generic prisms, in two other Dearden and Relph films post-Ealing, as the 1950s gave way to the early 1960s.

THE LEAGUE OF GENTLEMEN (1960)

> The theme might seem meat for every deferential working-man's chuckling admiration of the rascally Toff, who combines illogically but powerfully, traditional authority with a bluff, bureaucracy-baiting, colourful right-wing anarchism. But it's subverted by the film's ironies. These officers and gentlemen, unprepossessing as Simon Raven's fictional characters, are a pressgang of moneygrubbing or dishonest scoundrels, largely caddish, seedy and mean. (Ramond Durgnat 1970: 35)

> No actor could have been other than excited by this brilliantly written story of an ex-army officer who collects a group of his former war-time comrades to plan and carry out a daring bank robbery. Certainly, this made a welcome change from the crusading atmosphere of *The Four Just Men*. (Jack Hawkins 1973: 137) [21]

In his biography, Jack Hawkins recalled that the script for *The League of Gentlemen* was the catalyst for the establishment of Allied Film Makers; a bold, post-Ealing venture, smaller than Bryanston, but also formed to co-operate in the production, finance and distribution of British films. Sydney Box had been the architect of the idea, but he was forced to withdraw on health grounds, and as a result AFM emerged as a partnership between Dearden, Relph, Richard Attenborough, Bryan Forbes, Jack Hawkins and Guy Green.[22] From the novel by John Boland,[23] the screenplay for the film was written by Bryan Forbes, under commission for the influential American producer Carl Foreman,[24] who had reportedly approached Cary Grant and then David Niven to cast them in the lead role of Hyde. Both had apparently turned the part down. Foreman was subsequently occupied with other projects at the time, and Forbes records that it was his agent's partner who alerted him to the fact that Dearden had acquired the script from Foreman, without knowing that he had written it.[25] The shooting scripts for the film are dated early November 1959 and it was released early in April, the following year.[26]

The film begins with a classic visual hook, as Hyde (Jack Hawkins),[27] immaculately attired in an evening suit, emerges in the early morning from a manhole, somewhere in the streets of London. To the jaunty, regimental tune which orchestrates key moments throughout the film,[28] he then calmly drives away in a Rolls Royce. Quite what he is up to is the enigma which starts the film, a crime thriller with comic twists, often referred to as a 'caper'.[29] The film concerns a daring bank robbery by a group of ex-army officers brought together by Colonel Hyde, the mastermind of the operation, and initially the film follows Hyde as he brings the League together. This sequence of the narrative is the first of three: once the League is assembled, the next segment deals with their preparation for the robbery; and the climax involves the robbery and its aftermath. Much of the pleasure of the film is derived from the build-up as the League members are introduced, organised and set on course for the crime and its resolution.

The first meeting of the League is engineered by Hyde, as he posts seven envelopes, each containing a lunch invitation, a paperback thriller, *The Golden Fleece*,[30] and half of a £5 note. In true Dearden and Relph 'compendium' style, the film follows the delivery of the envelopes into the apparently random lives of the characters he has sent them to. This device allows for a compressed sketch of each character and their circumstances before they are brought together, and an interesting range of male character types emerges: all flawed, living in less than ideal circumstances, all with some kind of guilty military past. They are also, in one way or another, all trapped in their current situations, and Hyde's promise of money and action offers an escape.

The parade of 'gentleman' begins with the introduction of ex-Major Peter Race, in a characteristically raffish and camp performance by Nigel Patrick,[31] a happy-go-lucky playboy, waking after yet another night of drinking and spectacularly unsuccessful roulette playing. The curious invitation, with its promise of money, coincides conveniently with his current lack of funds and

Colonel Hyde emerges in *The League of Gentlemen* (1960) (Courtesy of Steve Chibnall Archive)

an apartment, and the end of his romance with Peggy (Melissa Stribling). It is therefore perfectly timed to appeal to his Micawberism. The second envelope arrives at the address of ex-Major Rupert Rutland-Smith (Terence Alexander), the infatuated husband of Elizabeth (Nanette Newman),[32] his unfaithful and domineering wife. Despite the fact that he had 'a bloody good war', his current situation seems unfulfilled in every sense and male sexuality is the theme developed as the film introduces more recipients of Hyde's envelopes. Former Captain Mycroft (Roger Livesey) is encountered in the guise of a clergyman, but revealed as a seedy conman on the run, carrying a case of pornographic books. Ex-Captain Porthill (Bryan Forbes) appears as a dissolute gigolo and philanderer, making a living as a nightclub pianist, preying on older, wealthy women. Ex-Captain Stevens (Keiron Moore) works in a gymnasium, his outward, muscular 'normality' hiding his homosexuality, which has been compromised by a blackmailer.[33] Ex-Lieutenant Lexy (Richard Attenborough) appears less obviously officer material; working in his backstreet workshop, repairing radios and, more lucratively, fixing one-armed bandits for the spivvish Wylie (Patrick Wymark). Finally, ex-Captain Weaver (Norman Bird), outwardly mild-mannered, he appears trapped in a loveless suburban setting, somewhere between his nagging wife, her elderly, live-in father and the television set. Like all the others, he opens the envelope and reads its strange contents, and the film shifts to the first meeting of the League of Gentlemen, as in response to Hyde's invitation, they converge on a private dining-room at the Café Royal.[34]

Hyde initially orchestrates the occasion with geniality, after the meal handing round the matching halves of their £5 notes. In response to Race's question he also introduces himself as J. G. N. Hyde,[35] confirming that he outranks them all at the table. Although few of them have read the book he sent, he knows that they would all be interested in making 'easy money', revealing a more sinister side when he insists: 'Oh come now, you're all crooks aren't you – of one kind or another?'. to prove his point, he reveals them all as 'dishonourable gentlemen', each with his own guilty secret. Mycroft, the conman and trickster, was cashiered for gross indecency in a public place. Lexy was kicked out of the Royal Corps of Signals for selling information to the Russians in Berlin. Porthill lost his commission after shooting EOKA suspects in Cyprus. Race resigned his, just before his involvement in a lucrative black market racket was exposed. Stevens is revealed as a one-time Fascist, whose homosexuality was responsible for his downfall: 'The Sunday papers had a field day – there's nothing the British public likes better than catching the odd men out.' Weaver's army career came to an abrupt end when his drunkenness led to the death of four men in his Bomb Disposal squad. Finally, Hyde reveals Rutland-Smith's dishonour concerning his debts and mess bills, and as if to answer their/our unvoiced question, he proceeds to confirm that he has no criminal past, and that he served in the army as a real officer and gentleman for 25 years. However, this response also allows his bitterness to show; he was 'rewarded by being made redundant', and the film depicts this as his prime motivation in instigating the robbery – a means of striking back at a blinkered, insensitive and inept system.[36] He closes the meeting by indicating that with the use of their respective military training and expertise, he intends to rob a bank, which will net them £100,000 each and with this, he departs.

The crafty Race, however, follows him to his rambling, rundown Gothic mansion, where Hyde lives an enforced, Spartan, bachelor existence, the result of an embittered separation from his wife. He outlines his plan to Race, derived from the novel sent to the League members, a spectacular robbery involving 'a full-scale military operation', and Race quickly confesses himself 'sold' on the job and, at Hyde's invitation, moves in.[37] A second meeting of the League is called, held under the guise of an amateur drama group rehearsing *Journey's End*.[38] At this meeting, all six remaining members of the League agree to participate in the robbery on the basis of equal shares. While the promise of the money is influential for each of them, it is supplemented by the prospect of recapturing 'the old days'; the camaraderie, self-respect and unity of purpose associated with military service. Hill has argued in this context that this fascination is a telling and recurrent theme in Dearden and Relph's work: 'it is the all-male group which proves most positive and compelling and for which they all gladly abandon their domestic pasts' (1986: 93).

The middle segment of the film sees them assemble, 'on parade', at Hyde's house and re-entering a world governed by military discipline, duty rotas, room-sharing and fatigues. What emerges is a cross between a male public school and a barrack room culture, with their performance of mundane domestic duties matched by the schoolroom atmosphere of Hyde's lecture on the details of the forthcoming robbery. An initial target, to relieve an army depot of the arms and equipment needed for the bank raid, is carried out with precision and success, with members of the League – to some comic effect – running rings around the modern, peacetime army, using the IRA as a cover for the mission. Supplied with guns, ammunition, gas-masks and explosives, their next requirement is transport, and under Race's direction they steal and then disguise a number of vehicles, including a large furniture removal lorry. Full-scale preparation for the robbery, using models and film, gives a preview of events to come in Hyde's master plan. Each member of the League is given his own specialist areas of responsibility, and such is Hyde's meticulous grasp of detail, that Lexy remarks ironically, 'He'll end up with a knighthood'. There is only one small, unsettling moment during this smooth process, when a young constable appears at the warehouse where the vehicles are being readied; but this encounter is diffused by Hyde's affable intervention and seems of little consequence. As the day of the robbery approaches, Hyde instils confidence, mocking Churchill: 'This, gentleman, will be our finest hour', insisting that nothing has been left to chance. This segment of the film ends on the night before the heist, with nerves reminiscent of those experienced prior to operations in the war.

The final sequence of the film begins with an extended, striking series of shots which use no dialogue, but combine location footage, sound and music to follow the League as they drive into Central London and approach the bank.[39] Like a well-oiled machine, they take up their allotted positions and await the arrival of the security van carrying the money. When it does, Hyde is momentarily caught off-guard by a bouncing ball which he returns to a young boy playing on the pavement. What he does not see however – but the viewer does – is that the boy is also collecting car number plates. As the security van, having unloaded its money, departs, the robbery swings into action, with dense smoke, explosions and gas-masks; members of the League enter the bank and remove the money at gun point. It is loaded into the small car and driven away by Lexy, who, under the cover of the dense smoke and traffic chaos that they have created, turns into an adjacent street and drives up a ramp and into the back of the waiting removal lorry.[40] With its hidden contents, the lorry, accompanied by the League make their escape, completing, it would seem, the perfect crime.

This triumphant turn of events sees the League assemble for the last time at Hyde's mansion. In high spirits, an impromptu celebration breaks out as they prepare to leave, each with a suitcase containing their share of the money. First Weaver and Stevens, followed by Rutland-Smith, make their farewells and depart.[41] As the party escalates, to the increasingly manic tune of 'Soldiers of the Queen', events are suddenly interrupted by a loud knocking on the door. This heralds the arrival of an old army colleague of Hyde's, Brigadier 'Bunny' Warren (Robert Coote), a blimpish bore who scents a party. These final scenes become almost farcical as his bumptious arrival causes them to perform as if in an officers' mess. Porthill, Mycroft and Lexy take their leave; and Hyde, Race and the increasingly tipsy Bunny are left to hear the sudden ringing of the telephone. It is Police Superintendent Wheatlock (Ronald Leigh-Hunt), who indicates that the house is surrounded and that they should give themselves up. Hyde, stiff upper-lipped to the last, orders Race to leave; this he does, with the parting shot that Hyde should 'give them their money's worth at the trial and then flog your memoirs to the Sunday papers – there's always an angle'. Left alone with Bunny, Hyde returns to the phone to find out who betrayed them. The Superintendent confirms that there was no traitor, they have been caught out by pure chance: a combination of the

young boy collecting car numbers and the routine police work of the young
constable who visited the garage. The 'traitor' turns out to be Hyde's own
number plate. Realising that the game is up, Hyde escorts a befuddled 'Bunny'
out into the security cordon which awaits them. The film ends on a comic
note, with Hyde and his luckless companion joining the rest of the League,
all handcuffed in the back of a waiting Black Maria. 'Going on somewhere
are we Norman?' asks Bunny, as the van drives off to take them to face their
inevitable justice and retribution.

   The film was a major and significant box-office success for AFM and Rank
and it premièred at the Odeon, Marble Arch to some critical acclaim. It cost
£192,000 and by mid-1971 its profit was over £250,000.[42] 'I enjoyed every
felonious moment. It is a beautifully bloodless thriller', wrote C. A. Lejeune
(*Observer*, 10 April 1960), while for *Time and Tide*: 'Surprisingly, the film
is fun. It achieves excitement without violence; it is splendidly acted and
directed from an adroit and very human screen-play by Bryan Forbes' (16
April 1960). F. Majdalany found it to be 'So devilishly well worked out and
directed (by Basil Dearden) that I would need a lot of convincing that it is not
the best comedy-thriller to come out in the past decade' (*Daily Mail*, 8 April
1960). Many reviewers connected the film to the fortunes of AFM. Dilys
Powell, for instance:

> Another new group: one welcomes, one applauds *The League of
> Gentlemen*, the first production of Allied Film Makers . . . The names
> may not be new, but their conjunction makes itself felt in a liveliness of
> approach . . . a bit slow in getting going, but full of ingenious and enjoy-
> able excitement once the real business gets going'. (*The Sunday Times*,
> 10 April 1960)

For *The Guardian*: 'The first result of their association [AFM] is almost
without reserve a delight – a tribute, first of all to the screen-writing talent
of Mr Forbes' (9 April 1960); and Jympson Harman identified the film as: 'A
highly welcome and encouraging example of co-operative film-making . . .
It is a remarkably fine entertainment, yet I reckon it cost about £100,000
less than it might have done – this is the way to put British films on the map'
(*Evening News*, 7 April 1960). Even the *Monthly Film Bulletin*, despite finding
fault with the script and performances, admitted that:

> The handling of these scenes and the extensive location shooting suggest
> that, for Basil Dearden, the film's interest (and challenge) was mainly a
> technical one. In any case, it is his sharpest, most alive film for several
> years with rather less of his customary, mechanical shock-cutting. (May
> 1960)

And *Kine Weekly* found little to hold back on:

> The finest adventure thriller unveiled for many a day. Great stuff, it'll intrigue and grip all ranks and both sexes . . . Taut up-to-the-minute tale, fine acting by Jack Hawkins and hand-picked stars, expert direction, apt light relief, polished technical presentation, breathless penultimate suspense, excellent British general booking. (7 April 1960)[43]

Whether because, or in spite, of these critical accolades, at the 1960 San Sebastian Film Festival all eight members of the League were awarded the Zulueta Best Actor Award. Forbes' screenplay was also BAFTA-nominated. For many it appeared that this was almost Dearden and Relph's 'finest hour'. A typically perceptive Alexander Walker noticed how the film blended the traditions of comedy with the winds of change that were sweeping the country:

> It was a more wry, disenchanted kind of comedy than Ealing would have made, though it was visibly an off-shoot of that same tradition. It maintained Ealing's unflagging belief that the amateurs could outwit the experts, the irregulars could defeat the authorities; and the aggressive band of shady customers, all keeping up a pretence of respectability under Supremo Jack Hawkins, appeared in retrospect to be mirroring Britain's buoyant, acquisitive society in the 1960s. Prime Minister Harold Macmillan had boasted 'Most of our people have never had it so good' as election bait as early as 1957: but in 1959 'You've never had it so good' was suddenly *the* catchphrase of the year. *The League of Gentlemen*, with its target of quick capital gains, was the ideal comedy for a boom-time economy. (1974: 103–4)

The film did indeed kick-start the fortunes of AFM in very positive terms, although the venture was only to survive for five subsequent films. An immanent, tongue-in-cheek satire on the 'officer class' and the state of contemporary social life, it nonetheless draws on a sense that for Hyde and his colleagues, life at war was preferable to life in the peace. The film plays with the imagined, nostalgic masculine communities of the war and also articulates a sense of the disillusionment with and antipathy towards the post-war present. In its conventional ending, following the successful crime (a number of reviewers commented on its welcome lack of violence), the film at the time could do no other than spell out the moral message 'crime does not pay', although it manages to do this in a way that leaves overwhelming sympathies with the League as they are driven away to face the music.[44]

MAN IN THE MOON (1960)

A jolly, earnest, hardworking, class-unconscious, middle-class eager-beaver (Kenneth More) is put in the space-race against another 'league of gentlemen', a set of ex-public-school trainee astronauts, who constitute a First XI of steamingly intense Empire builders. They are absolutely confident that their lofty social status justifies their use of any and every dirty trick against our vulgar little upstart. (Raymond Durgnat 1970: 35)

It was bound to come along sooner or later – we mean a farce about these fearless astronauts and the business of getting them into condition to be blasted into space . . . With appropriately wacky illogic, it comes from Britain, which (as you may know) is comfortably withdrawn from the space race and so is in a position to kid it with wild and corny jokes. (Bosley Crowther, *New York Times*, 13 June 1961)

Well before the première of *The League of Gentlemen*, Dearden, Relph and Bryan Forbes had begun work on the second film for AFM. Intended as a comedy-romance, which rather daringly engaged with the 'space race',[45] the film starred Kenneth More, who since the early 1950s and his successes in *Genevieve* (1953) and *Doctor in the House* (1954) had been keen to move into more comic roles. The screenplay for *Man in the Moon* was developed by Forbes and Relph, and the shooting scripts are dated late March 1960.[46] The film was made at Pinewood under the aegis of Excalibur Films for AFM/Rank. Its première, attended by the Queen and the Duke of Edinburgh, took place some seven months later.[47]

The man of action in the film – unlike those discussed earlier in this chapter – is unencumbered by any baggage from the war, and rather than looking backwards, the film engages with the future. William Blood (Kenneth More) is an unlikely hero, first encountered in an incongruous setting; as the camera pans over a rural landscape we find him fast asleep in bed in the middle of a field.[48] As he wakes in this pastoral setting, his appearance startles a shapely young woman (Shirley Anne Field),[49] also looking out of place in feather boa and evening dress, as she teeters across the field and hurries away up the road.[50] These surreal opening events are partially resolved, when two, white-coated doctors from The Common Cold Research Centre arrive to examine William. It appears that he is a human guinea pig, part of one of their experiments; and in spite of his outdoor sleeping arrangements, they bemoan the fact that his health remains robust and normal. William puts this down to the fact that he refuses to worry about anything, and they return to the Centre, passing the young woman on the road. The Centre is part of a large scientific and bureaucratic complex, NARSTI (National Atomic Research Station and Technological Institute), comically emblazoned on the sign in front of the buildings. William arrives as another experiment – the British Summer Simulation – is in full swing; with howling gales, pouring rain and England apparently 87 for 6 in the cricket test. In a room full of sneezing and coughing people, he meets his friend Herbert (Norman Bird), before he is called to the Superintendent's Office. Here, Dr Hollis (Newton Blick) informs him that he is no longer required because he is just too healthy. This interchange is witnessed by Davidson (Michael Hordern) a boffin – with a cold – from Space Research, who cottons on to the fact that William seems to be immune to everything. He follows him to the car park, where William confides that the secret of his immunity lies in the fact that he has never let himself get anywhere near marriage; and with this he departs, somewhat eccentrically, in a small convertible bubble car. Davidson reports his discovery to his superiors Professor Stephens (John Phillips) and Dr Wilmot (John Glyn-Jones), at Space Research, and they agree – after much badinage about dogs, monkeys and politics – that William is the ideal candidate to be their 'pathfinder', for the first manned space flight to the Moon, in one month's time. Davidson is thus despatched to find William and bring him back.

Unaware of this, William has stopped at the local pub to meet Herbert, and as he arranges by phone to attend a sea-sickness trial in Portsmouth, he encounters the 'very fetching' young woman who caught his eye when he woke that morning. This does not prevent him, however, from expounding his misogynist philosophy to Herbert; and as they leave, Davidson arrives in hot pursuit, to offer him a job which is 'out of this world'. William, however, is not taken by this proposition and continues on his way. The comic sequence which follows involves a car crash, another meeting with Polly, the young woman, and a racy Jaguar driver (Jeremy Lloyd), and finally sees William and Polly walking to the local railway station. It transpires that she is an exotic dancer – a stripper – and notwithstanding, their romance seems set. At the station, however, Davidson finally catches up with William, and as a result, he misses the train, which departs with Polly on board. A sudden sneezing fit hints that there are signs that his immunity – in reaction to her feminine charms – is weakening, but he agrees to Davidson's generous offer and returns with him to the Space Centre.

Professor Stephens enquires about William and how he is settling into the 'team', the group of crack 'astronauts to be', trained at considerable public expense and led by Leo (Charles Gray), who are unaware that William is now in pole position for the first Moon shot. In a series of gym tests, William seems initially a complete failure, just an 'ordinary chap'. But as the tests escalate, first with extremes of temperature, then in a centrifuge, and finally sudden deceleration on the rocket sledge, the apparently impervious William wins out – in spite of Leo's crooked attempts to undermine him.[51] At this stage, however, he remains unaware of the announcement of a £100,000 prize (donated apparently by Billy Butlin) which adds increased zest to the competition to be the first man on the Moon. In an effort to diffuse the conflict between William and the 'supermen', Stephens has Leo brainwashed, and he 'soaks over night' in an isolation tank, emerging as William's best friend, totally suggestible to anything, including TV adverts.[52] On their subsequent night out at the pub, Leo confesses that he failed to deliver a letter to William from Polly; a letter declaring her love for him and proposing a meeting. William makes light of this, but on his way home with the tipsy Leo, they encounter Polly, who although saved from the river by Leo, is carried away by William; and they end in the bed in the field, where it all began – ousting the unfortunate Herbert, as Polly does an impromptu strip in the moonlight. On the following morning, talking wedding dresses and 'a little house', Polly departs by train. William undergoes anti-gravity tests on a plane, with slap-stick chaos involving a fire extinguisher, and as a result, he resolves to leave the space programme once and for all to get married. However, at the station, he reads in a newspaper of the £100,000 bounty for the first man to reach the Moon and this is enough to change his mind. After telephoning Polly, he returns with Davidson to complete the preparations for his space flight.

The final section of the film is compressed; William flies to the Woomera rocket range in Australia, dons his space-suit and enters the UK 1 Rocket. Dearden builds a tense sequence for the count-down, with the performers directed to play the scene with due ceremony and solemnity – the more effective to sharpen the satire; and everything appears to go according to plan as he is blasted into outer space, out of contact for 72 hours during the flight to the Moon. When transmission is re-established, all appears normal and William responds to Stephen's tremulous enquiries about what it is like on the Moon. It feels 'bloody hot' replies William, and he then leaves the space rocket to walk out onto the Moon's surface, and he does find himself to be in a kind of lunar landscape. While the boffins began to celebrate, however, William makes some strange discoveries on the 'Mare Imbrium'. Frightened by an alien sound, he falls headlong and comes to rest in front of an empty Heinz Baked Beans can, then spots a kangaroo, and then an old prospector (Noel Purcell), – his Geiger-counter was responsible for the noise that scared him. Realising that he is in fact on earth and not far from the launch site, he commandeers the startled prospector's dilapidated old truck and drives back to Woomera, crashing through the gates in an attempt to prevent UK 2 from being launched, with Leo and the team on board. This he narrowly achieves, arriving to the great consternation of all the assembled boffins in the control

An early 'leap for mankind': *Man in the Moon* (1960) (Courtesy of Steve Chibnall Archive)

room, announcing, 'I'm sorry chaps, it's back to the old drawing board!' After this, the final scenes segue back to the tranquil meadows with which the film began. In perfect rural bliss, William and Polly lie together in their open-air bed; but now accompanied by three small cots, each containing a baby. William and Polly are participating in the scientists' latest experiments into family planning, and the film ends on this comic note.

The film received mixed reviews, with many realising that there was more than a hint of the old Ealing comic tradition in the film, but generally finding that the mix of satire and farce had not worked. The critic of *The Times*, for instance, felt that the film was a 'near miss', and continued:

> If only the script-writers of *Man in the Moon* . . . could get their copy back and spend a day or two revising it! For *Man in the Moon* is so very nearly that rare thing, a good British film comedy with ideas and a cast that can put them across. Too often our film humour is a matter of routine with the same old faces turning up over and over again in the same old parts, but *Man in the Moon*, directed by Mr Basil Dearden, at least makes an effort to get out of the rut. It bumps, it lurches, it stalls in the process – and here the revising comes in – but throughout its length it refuses to be anonymous and strives after individuality. (7 November 1960)

Such a charitable view was not shared by all critics, however. Isabel Quigley, for instance, writing in *The Spectator*, found the film depressing in

> its mixture of whimsy and ineptness embodying, in an embarrass-ingly characteristic way, just what makes so many of our films in the wrong sense local, dated, home-cooked, unexportable, untranslated etc., etc. . . . If it weren't so characteristic, so dismally like so much else in British comedy, it wouldn't be worth a line; but its quite remarkable unfunniness, and above all the way it huffs and puffs to get its jokes, visual or spoken, seems symptomatic of something. Lack of fantasy, of fun, or invention? The old Ealing vein was worked out long ago, and nothing has since replaced it so we go on getting a washed-out rehashed Ealing, brisk as a week old lettuce. (11 November 1960)

Other reviews applauded the target of the film's satire, Majdalany, for example, suggesting that:

> Science has been ripe for satirical plucking for a long time. It has fallen to a former Ealing production team . . . to drive a blue streak through the solemnities of rocketry, the cult of science fiction, and the humourless chi-chi of scientists generally. The result . . . can most conveniently be

described as the best Ealing comedy since Ealing went out of business some years ago. (*Daily Mail*, 1 November 1960)

Some found the satire to be ultimately misplaced, Eric Shorter, for example, commented positively on the 'committed mood' of the script and its direction, welcoming the 'commitment against bureaucracy in general and science in particular', but

> Considering they are proposing to send a man so far, these dithering, obtuse boffins look a sorry lot. Doubtless their grotesque blend of fanaticism, callousness, and fitful somnolence is amusing in its way and will find easy favour as a popular misconception. (*The Daily Telegraph*, 5 November 1960)

The *Monthly Film Bulletin* felt that the script was 'an unattractive mixture of macabre savagery (in its brainwashing and training sequences) and tepid satire on bureaucracy, medicine and science', compounded by a 'general lack of directorial guidance' (December 1960). Whereas 'Any exhibitor who turns down "Man in the Moon" deserves a rocket!' was the verdict of *Kine Weekly* (3 November 1960).

Man in the Moon was part of a cycle of satirical films of the time that poked fun at British institutions, evident in a number of productions by the Boulting brothers and the popular series of *Carry On* comedies. In this spirit, Durgnat partnered the film with *League of Gentlemen*, 'both of which, refreshingly scathing, debunk the authorities, the team spirit and the gentlemen mystique' (1966: 32). More pointedly, the target of the satire in *Man in the Moon* was the technocracy of the scientists, presented here as venal, manipulative and self-serving. 'I love spending public money – so much more satisfying than spending one's own', expounds one boffin, who is so absorbed in the minutiae of rocket science he can barely attend to crucial policy matters raised by his senior colleagues. Geraghty locates the central conflict in the film between an elite and the 'ordinary chap'. As she observes: 'Blood, who carries ordinariness to extremes, uses it as a weapon against this system of expertise', a representation essentially enforced by Kenneth More's star image of 'cheerful breeziness' (2000: 64). The character resolutely refuses to succumb to the machinations of the scientists: a frustrating paragon of health at the Common Cold Research Centre and virtually indestructible in face of extremes of heat, cold and gravity. Crucially, William is the perpetual outsider to the 'team', conspired against both by the trio of scientists and his ex-public school fellow astronauts, a situation made more intense by the vulgar offer of a prize for the first man on the Moon, which brings the barely submerged attitude of 'I'm alright Jack' into the bright lights of the marketplace. The artificiality of the

concept of 'team' is further laid bare in the brainwashing of Leo, who is suddenly charged with a very special affection for William, and seeming proof
that modern man is easy prey to the 'hidden persuaders'.[53]

Man in the Moon gently raises questions about the role of the 'Man of
Action' in the modern, technologically-driven world. Lacking the clear-cut
certainties of wartime, and now too far distanced for any simple play-acting
of the thrills and spills of combat, the modern man has to confront the emas-
culating trends of affluence and materialism – and their attendant pressure for
domestication; as well as the constraining and debilitating forces of modernity
and technology that seek to eradicate the individual for the malleable ideal of
the mass. The 'ordinary chap', sandwiched between these two extremes, has
little room for negotiation or manoeuvring. The national space programme,
motivated by nothing more than a vain desire to win the race to the Moon
– and a very handy £100,000 – is proved to be technically bankrupt; while
the forces for domesticity ultimately overcome William, who by the end of
the film has settled, in a fashion, to family life. In the final 'pregnant' image,
Blood, caught in wedlock and serving the technological society, manages to
subvert the latter, defiantly asserting his potency and manhood, and correspondingly wrecking the scientists' latest experiments into family planning.

These films of 'Men in Action' reflect a noticeable male restlessness and yearn-
ing that followed in the wake of wartime urgency and combat. Martin Francis
has recently argued that masculinity in the period was marked by a 'flight
from commitment', a response that registered in the 'imaginary' of adventure
narratives; and these four Dearden–Relph films conform to the suggested
male ambivalence about domesticity (Francis 2007).[54] At the time, sociology
was tentatively grappling with the 'burdens of masculinity' thrown up by
contemporary society: the 'directions masculine roles are changing' and 'how
men are handling these changes'; and these films reveal the dread of action
men 'dwindling into husbands', and tentatively expose the 'guilt–hate–fear
complex' typical of the dominant sex 'striving to stand firm on traditional male
prerogatives' (Hacker 1957). Recent work on post-war social reconstruction
has paid attention to the contemporary concerns about the family and growing
anxieties about moral and national decline. The Director of the Marriage
Guidance Council, London, believed that Britain had been 'stabbed awake' to
the realisation that one in four marriages were failing. He pointed to 'a landslide
in sexual behaviour' and 'a zooming marriage breakdown rate' as the consequences of the altering social and moral climate of the war (Mace 1948: 6). The
male rejection of domesticity was a further troubling index of this change.

In preparing to fight the 'Battle of the Family', The Marriage Guidance
Council also took note of 'a disintegration of family discipline, revealed by a

wave of juvenile delinquency'. Dearden and Relph enjoined this 'battle' using the obvious means available to them: the social problem film. The following chapter examines the 'Teenage Trilogy' of lawless youngsters, as well as notable productions that tackle the emergent social issues of race and sexuality, a group of films widely considered the most prominent achievements of the Dearden–Relph partnership.

NOTES

1. Fores' novels often figured themes to do with flying. His other published works include: *Flight Eastward* (1954), *The Forgotten Place* (1956), *No Mercy in the Sky* (1957), *The Secret Island* (1959) and many others. *The Springboard* was first published as a tie-in for the film in 1956 (Hodder & Stoughton); however, it bears very little resemblance to the film in terms of narrative and characterisation. It differs in numerous ways; for instance, it deals with 'several weeks' in the airport, whereas the film is compressed into about 24 hours; Gus is caught smuggling contraband gold; Nick is married with children, and the book focuses on a race across the Atlantic between rival airliners.

2. In 1948, he had made *Three Dawns to Sydney*, a documentary travelogue commissioned by BOAC which showcased their new passenger service to Australia. Relph untypically co-produced *Out of the Clouds* with Eric Williams, perhaps mentoring him for a future producer role at Ealing.

3. Dearden's script is heavily annotated throughout with dialogue adjustments, scene changes and his usual instructions for camerawork. Very detailed breakdowns are given on pasted-in addenda sheets for filming scenes where the planes land, take off or taxi to and from the airport on runways. It also includes detailed instructions for filming in fog, as in the scenes when Brent performs the talk-down landing when the airport is temporarily shut down, and when Bill and Leah go on their tour of London.

4. In several sequences, such as those on approach to Cairo and Rome, the *Final Shooting Script* instructs 'aerial unit or stock', but in many of the airborne shots, including those of planes flying L–R or R–L to denote direction, sequences were shot specially by the aerial unit.

5. Many reviews praised the documentary photography of the airport and planes. Cinematographer Paul Beeson was a specialist at Ealing in location work and had recently shot the African adventures *Where No Vultures Fly* (d. H. Watt, 1951) and *West of Zanzibar* (d. H. Watt, 1954).

6. Beatty had previously worked with Dearden and Relph in *The Gentle Gunman* (1952) and *The Square Ring* (1953), although this film did not allow him the straightforward action accorded to 'Kid Curtis' or 'Shinto'.

7. Lee was a regular performer with Dearden and Relph – he was to play a slightly less benign customs officer in *The Ship that Died of Shame* several months later and worked with them in some of their post-Ealing films, for example *The Secret*

Partner (1961) and *A Place to Go* (1963). There was also a substantial role for
Melissa Stribling, who became Basil's wife and would later appear in *The Four Just
Men* (one episode), *The League of Gentlemen*, *The Secret Partner* (1961), *Only When
I Larf* (1968) and *The Persuaders!* (one episode).

8. Correspondence with authors (19 February 2004).

9. In this postscript, Monsarrat confirms that the short story had been first published in *Lilliput* magazine in 1952, was subsequently published in *Saturday
Evening Post* and the *Sunday Chronicle*, and was widely syndicated in European
and Commonwealth countries. A radio version of the story, featuring Trevor
Howard as Hoskins — was broadcast on the BBC Light Programme (31 March
1954), reviewed in *The Times* (1 April 1954).

10. Whiting was an actor turned playwright, who was to write with some distinction
for television and film in the post-war period. His work included screenplays for
The Captain's Table (d. J. Lee, 1958) and *The Devils* (d. K. Russell, 1970).

11. In the short story, the conclusion has Randall reflecting on his experiences while
about to serve ten years in prison for his part in smuggling stolen gold.

12. Perry also objected to this: 'The film was an uneasy coupling of a routine thriller
story with the sentimental notion of the ship with a soul, a concept that might
appeal to a few nautical experts but seemed bewildering and absurd to the great
mass of landlubbers' (1981: 165).

13. Baker had small parts in *The Intruder* (d. G. Hamilton, 1953) and *The Dam
Busters* (d. M. Anderson, 1954), but this was his first significant, credited screen
role. With some stage experience, he had tested unsuccessfully for the part of
the narrator for Huston's *Moby Dick* (1956) (the role went to Richard Basehart)
but this test was seen by Dearden and Relph and led to his casting in the film
(Information Folder: TSTDOS, Ealing Studios, undated).

14. The shooting script indicates that the original idea for the beginning of the film
was to start – in typical circular fashion – with the 'death' of the ship as it finally
settles on the seabed. In the event, this device was not used and the film begins
with *1087* at speed during the war, and this shot is used in the final scenes.
Throughout the film, Dearden and Dines use a combination of location shooting at sea, wartime stock footage and, where necessary, models and the studio
tank. Location shooting took place at sea and around the harbours at Weymouth,
Portland, Poole and Gosport. The ship was acquired in Falmouth, an ex-Polish
Navy MTB (See Information Folder: TSTDOS, Ealing Studios, undated). The
film acknowledges support from the Admiralty.

15. The characterisation, romance and tragedy are very like the relationship played
out between Lockhart (Donald Sinden) and Julie (Virginia McKenna) in *The
Cruel Sea*.

16. This brief intrusion of the feminine is now ruthlessly replaced by an exclusive
emphasis on the masculine as the men displace their energies into comradeship,
conflict and action.

17. The musical score by William Alwyn is especially effective in counterpointing
these and subsequent scenes.

18. Attenborough vividly remembered filming these scenes in the Studio 'tank'. In the struggle on the deck and caught by (Dearden's) release of simulated 'waves', he was hospitalised as a result of cuts and concussion sustained when he was flung against the bridge. This delayed the filming of his final death scene by two weeks (Attenborough 2008).

19. Ramsden has provided an insightful account of the critics' reception of British war films in the 1950s and what he calls the 'gap between the guardians of the canon and the taste of the mass public' (1998: 40).

20. In this vein, McFarlane has suggested in his survey of films that dealt with themes of post-war adjustment: 'There is very often a cautionary tone in these films, usually directed against the notion of succumbing to spurious and sometimes criminal temptations, but sometimes also in the way of a critique of the times for not offering more stimulating opportunities to those returning from the war. Losing the peace, that is, is seen as the fault of those who have not learnt enough from the experience of the war' (1998: 97) See also O'Sullivan (1997).

21. *The Four Just Men* was an independent television production by former Ealing producer Sidney Cole, with contributions from Basil Dearden (direction) and Janet Green (scripts). It was based on the story by Edgar Wallace, filmed by Ealing in 1939. See Cole (1997).

22. See Walker (1974: 102–10, 246–8) and Forbes (1974: 291) for further detail. The formation of the company began in September 1959 and was formally announced early in November (*The Times*, 3 November 1959). The original deal was to make six to eight films for Rank release (*Films and Filming*, January and May 1960).

23. First published by T. V. Boardman & Co. (1958), with later tie-in editions; first (true to the original book) by Pan Books (1960) and later (amended and based on the film) by Tandem (1966). In the original novel, there are significant differences; the names are changed throughout and, for instance, the film ends with the Hyde (Hemlingson) character committing suicide at the top of the house with no 'Bunny' Warren character. During the bank robbery, Porthill severely injures a bystander in the bank who dies and after this, the gang come to blows and Porthill shoots one of them. It is a much darker, less wry 'caper', more akin to 'The Great Train Robbery' which would take place some three years later. Boland subsequently wrote two sequels, *The Gentlemen Reform* (1961) and *The Gentleman at Large* (1962), which continued with the characterisations developed in the film, but strangely, given its popularity, these were not considered for film adaptation.

24. *Films and Filming* (February 1959).

25. See Forbes (1974: 290–1), where he maintains that Dearden initially appeared unaware of his authorship, and later in his commentary accompanying the DVD release of the film (2007), where he indicates that Dearden had paid £15,000 for the rights to the script and that it was Dearden's idea to cast Jack Hawkins in the lead role. There are divergences in this account, when compared to that provided by Hawkins, who suggests that it was Foreman who first sent him the script, and

that he then showed the script to Dearden, and that the first act of AFM was to buy 'the rights of the film from Carl Foreman, who prudently retained a little of the action himself' (1973: 138). See also Walker (1974: 102). Hawkins had some years earlier indicated his intention to enter into independent production (*Kinematograph Weekly*, 9 February 1956).

26. Bryan Forbes, in the commentary accompanying the DVD release of the film (Network 7952549, 2007), remembers that the production was shot in about eight weeks, wherever possible utilising a 'shoot in the streets' policy – for budgetary reasons as much as cinematic style. In his biography, he was to note: 'I think we all sensed that we were making a good film. Far from being a dictator on the set, Basil almost went to the other extreme: never could actors have been treated with such respect, and the atmosphere was relaxed and carefree for most of the time' (1974: 293). The film had a grand première at the Odeon, Marble Arch with a photo feature in *Kine Weekly* (14 April 1960).

27. The film provided Hawkins with an ideal role which allowed him to play his established character type of quintessential, 'square-jawed' British officer and gentleman, but also to subvert and parody this in certain ways. His biography records that, sadly, this was the film on which he was working when his throat cancer was diagnosed and began to interrupt his performance (1973: 134–49). See also Forbes (1974: 293).

28. The music was provided by regular composer Philip Green.

29. Reviews of the film frequently labelled it a 'caper': 'a likeable caper' (*The Times*, 11 April 1960); 'a dashing spirited affair, a caper which puts British pictures on the upbeat' (*The People*, 10 April 1960). Many reviews drew parallels between the film and Hollywood's *Ocean's Eleven* (d. L. Milestone, 1960) and *The Seven Thieves* (d. H. Hathaway, 1960).

30. By John Seaton – a pen-name used by Bryan Forbes. At this early stage, the film deviates from the sequence set out in the original novel and shooting script, which has Hyde visiting The London Hospital where a close ex-military comrade has died, and this book is found among his belongings. At the subsequent funeral, it becomes apparent that this friend had worked for a bank for thirty years, and this is where Hyde obtains the idea and plan for the eventual robbery, and may explain what he was doing under the manhole cover in the opening scenes. However, these scenes were edited or dropped from the final cut. Revealingly, *The Times* was to suggest: 'The synopsis presented to the audience at the Press show suggests that a good deal of last-minute cutting, resulting in the uncertainties of the film's opening, removed Mr Hawkins's motives for crime' (11 April 1960).

31. Bryan Forbes, in his commentary accompanying the DVD version of the film (2007), claims that he had originally written the part of Race for Trevor Howard, who was at that time unavailable. In the event, Patrick's performance is one of the highlights of the film.

32. The actress wife of Bryan Forbes.

33. A clear pre-echo of *Victim* (1961).

34. Race is last to arrive, explaining that 'I took a wrong turning and not for the first time. Found myself in a room full of Trade Unionists cooking up their next wage claim – all Tories, of course – didn't take to me at all'. As McFarlane notes, this is a telling piece of dialogue, 'which sums up a good deal of the film's thematic and tonal irreverence' (1998: 104). Race also later voices his hope that the bank to be raided is not the National Provincial – 'they've been very good to me recently'. The National Provincial Bank was Rank's financiers and had guaranteed the AFM operation (Walker 1974: 102).
35. Race asks him what the J stands for, suggesting that it might be Jekyll.
36. In 1957, the Conservative government introduced major spending cuts in defence, reducing resources for conventional forces and putting greater reliance on the nuclear deterrent. As a result many service personnel found themselves without a future (Smith 1991; Ball 1995).
37. Hill has argued that these scenes between the two lead characters suggest a relationship which becomes 'almost explicitly homosexual' (1986: 93–4). The scenes, dialogue and Patrick's performance do succeed in creating an air of comic and camp ambiguity here – but it may be that Hill overstates the case. See O'Sullivan (1997: 192).
38. Oliver Reed interrupts briefly, suitably incongruous as a camp ballet dancer, intent on rehearsing *Babes in the Wood*.
39. Forbes notes that these sequences were shot on Sunday mornings to minimise traffic and pedestrians (DVD commentary, 2007). Arthur Ibbetson was the lighting cameraman on the film.
40. A similar device was used later, albeit at speed on an autostrada, in *The Italian Job* (d. P. Collinson, 1969).
41. As they depart and thank Hyde for involving them in the robbery, it is clear that the members of the League have not just gained in financial terms; they have also regained self-respect, dignity and the confidence to face the future.
42. In his account Forbes notes that: 'We completed the film on schedule and for a cost of £174,000, which was amazing even for those halcyon days' (1974: 293–4).
43. The film attracted only a lukewarm review in *Films and Filming*, which felt let down by the predictable 'crime-must-pay' ending and generally overdrawn characterisation (May 1960).
44. This stands comparison with a different kind of 'League of Gentlemen', almost ten years later, left in a bus precariously balanced over the edge of a precipitous hillside in *The Italian Job* (d. P. Collinson, 1969).
45. The 'Space Race' was initiated in 1957 with the Soviet Union's launch of Sputnik. The film was made and released before President John Kennedy, in his celebrated speech to the US Congress, suggested that the United States should set as a goal: 'landing a man on the moon and returning him safely to earth' by the end of the decade (25 May 1961). Dearden and Relph had previously satirised the 'Space Age' in *Rockets Galore!* (1958).
46. They are credited for the script as an original piece of work. Other sources refer

to a novel by John Foley (unaccredited). Dearden was also involved in the development of the script, although he is unaccredited.

47. At the Odeon, Leicester Square on 31 October 1960, see *Kine Weekly* (3 November 1960). The trade press ran regular features on the film during its production. See *The Daily Cinema* (30 May 1960), *Kine Weekly* (2 June 1960).

48. Harry Waxman was the lighting cameraman, with Philip Green once again providing the musical score, ranging from futuristic sounds to light incidental background, as in these opening scenes.

49. More apparently picked her for this role (*The Daily Cinema*, 30 May 1960). In her biography, Field (1991) remembers working on the film with affection, during what was a hectic period in her film career (when she attended the première in Leicester Square, she was also in lights for *Beat Girl* and *Saturday Night Sunday Morning*). She has some interesting recollections of her working relationship with Dearden during this film's production.).

50. Durgnat was impressed by the 'fantasy-poetry' of this sequence, but felt the film slipped into a more predictable style (*Films and Filming*, January 1961).

51. The scenes were shot at the Royal Air Force Institute of Aviation Medicine and the Royal Aircraft Establishment, Farnborough.

52. Brainwashing was to be treated more seriously in Dearden and Relph's *The Mind Benders* (1963).

53. Durgnat greatly admired this sequence, finding in it some of the 'funniest queer jokes in British films since *The Captain's Table* (*Films and Filming*, January 1961).

54. Interestingly, his primary text of interrogation is the Ealing film *Scott of the Antarctic* (1948).

5

Dramas of Social Tension and Adjustment

The Blue Lamp (1950); *I Believe in You* (1952); *Violent Playground* (1958); *Sapphire* (1959) and *Victim* (1961)

Basil Dearden's work as a director constitutes a sustained body of films that are exemplary of the social problem film in the post-war era. At Ealing, Dearden worked on a wide range of topics – post-war recon-struction, generational conflict, juvenile delinquency, racial tension, and homosexuality – but his work is characterized by a consistent vision deriving in part from Ealing's emphasis on social issues and community. (Marcia Landy 1991: 462)

The post-war films of Dearden are less concerned with a literal recon-struction of wartime community than with the exploration of the con-ditions necessary to the construction of a new community or consensus appropriate to peacetime. To this extent, the concern of Dearden's films with social problems can be understood; for it is precisely such prob-lems (for example, youth and race) which threaten social stability and undermine the community or consensus of post-war Britain. The logic of the Dearden social problem picture is then towards an integration, or an assimilation, of troubling elements through an appeal to 'good sense' and reason. (John Hill 1986: 69–70)

Time, having exposed their ideological assumptions and prejudices, their fictions become less important than the realities of the attitudes they embody, turning them into cultural artefacts. (Robert Murphy 1992: 57)

The label that has most often been used to imply a unity in Dearden and Relph's work together is that of the 'social problem' film. As Durgnat has suggested: 'In many regards, most – maybe all – Dearden films are "social problem" films' (1997: 60); and Hill, Landy and others have tended to adopt such an inclusive approach to their cinema in these terms. Their work was often accused of 'snatching stories from the headlines', displaying a 'socio-logical concern or mission' and helping to establish 'a tradition of mixing entertainment with social awareness'.[1] This chapter adopts a more exclusive approach, identifying only five of their films, concentrated in the period 1950–61, which foreground pressing issues deemed contemporary social problems: law and order, youth delinquency, race and homosexuality. Contemporary critics clearly perceived coherence in the cinema of Dearden and Relph in this period. Bemoaning the scarcity of 'British pictures possessing any real social significance of important contemporary comment . . . despite our wartime legacy of documentary brilliance and the financial and artistic success of so many recent Hollywood productions in this genre', they pointed at this time to the 'Two men who have done more than most British producers to reverse this country's rapidly fading reputation in this field': 'Michael Relph and Basil Dearden, the alternating producer–director team responsible for such films as *Pool of London*, *I Believe in You* and *The Blue Lamp*' (*Films and Filming*, September 1957).

The post-war period witnessed a new emphasis within the social sciences on delinquency and deviance, marked by the appearance of *The British Journal of Delinquency* in 1950, coincident with Dearden and Relph's release of *The Blue Lamp*. Sociologists explored the root causes of juvenile delinquency and strug-gled with the perplexing determinisms of individual pathology, family-based criminality, environmental and social settings – encapsulated in John Barron Mays' famous concept of 'the delinquency producing neighbourhood'.[2] The new phenomenon of delinquency in girls also attracted speculation – referenced by Dearden and Relph in *I Believe in You*;[3] while race and sexual-ity were extensively debated in the later 1950s following respectively waves of immigration and the Wolfenden Committee Report (1957).[4] Numerous British films addressed troubling social issues bubbling up in the wake of the post-war settlement apparently contradicting the accommodations of the affluent society. Dearden and Relph, across five powerful dramas, became more associated with this production trend than any other filmmakers.[5]

THE BLUE LAMP (1950)

The Blue Lamp became a legend, so to speak, within its own lifetime, providing a welter of spin-offs for years to come in the cinema and, later, in television. The Documentary Police Movie. The first of its kind in England. It also altered, for all time, my professional life. Dearden pointed me in the right direction with his illuminating, over-simplified, approach to the camera. It was the first time I came near to giving a cinema performance in any kind of depth. (Dirk Bogarde 1979: 160)

The film's barely disguised didactic approach and narrative that leaves no space for moral ambiguities betray its origins in police public relations. Its strong ethic of Puritanism and self-sacrifice relate it firmly to the philosophy of Michael Balcon and Ealing's wartime morale boosters. (Steve Chibnall 1997: 141)

Although it became celebrated as one of the defining Ealing films of the 1950s,[6] the original idea for *The Blue Lamp* came from Sydney Box and Jan Read at Gainsborough Studios. Read had worked with Ted Willis to develop a play allegedly based on an actual incident: the murder of a London policeman in 1948;[7] and the idea was to tell the story from the police point of view. As Willis was later to recollect, he spent time in Metropolitan police stations, police cars and on the beat with policemen, researching their routines and developing an insight into the flavour and characteristics of their occupational and domestic milieu.[8] During this period, however, Rank rationalised their British production activities, closed Gainsborough and the play in development was passed to Ealing, where Balcon handed T. E. B. Clarke the responsibility of developing the full screen play.[9] In his autobiography, Clarke, who had served as a War Reserve Constable, recalled his first encounter with the play:

It was a behind-the-scenes story of the London police. Nowadays when police work is shown from the inside two or three times a week on television, it is strange to recall that in 1949 this was virtually an untapped seam of story material. . . . [A]s an ex-copper from the 'Met' force I was the obvious choice to take on the screenplay . . . my script of *The Blue Lamp* contained much that was not in the original play. (1974: 162–3)

The final shooting script for the film is dated May 1949,[10] with Alexander MacKendrick credited for additional dialogue on the script as well as second unit director (he was responsible for the thrilling car pursuit scenes on location). A number of commentators have remarked on how the film conforms to the classic narrative structure of order established, followed by order disrupted and order restored. The film begins with a dedication to the men and women of the Metropolitan Police and to their colleagues in the police service of Britain, and using a street killing as a metaphor for the wider crime wave, signalled by a series of newspaper headlines, the narrator pinpoints the vital importance of the police in protecting the public. Against a shot of the Old Bailey, the commentary continues by quoting Justice Finnemore, emphasising the crime wave which stemmed from insufficient numbers of uniformed police officers on the beat; and with a slow dissolve, the commentator then introduces the veteran constable, George Dixon (Jack Warner) and his young partner, fresh from training, Andy Mitchell (Jimmy Hanley).[11] In this move, the film and its shift from commentary to dialogue effectively anchors the two policemen in the wider context of the social problem of increasing crime and criminality, agents in the daily battle for law and order on the streets of Britain. Their stories are understood as emblematic of these more general institutional matters.

Charles Barr in his discussion of the film, has argued persuasively that the metaphor of the family is fundamental to the film, working on three levels; literally, young Mitchell becomes a member of Dixon's family, a surrogate for their son, Bert, a sailor lost in the war. He also joins – and this begins as they return to the station – a family of workmates: 'the close community of the police station in Paddington, characterised by convivial institutions – canteen, darts team, choir – and by bantering but loyal relationships within a hierarchy'. Finally, he suggests that the film, especially in its closing stages, draws on the idea of the nation as family – a collective bound together by shared values, standards of decency and codes of conduct, supporting the police against crime and criminality (1977: 83–4). In the introductory sequences, the film establishes Andy Mitchell in his new working environment and sketches the varied and good-natured bunch of policemen that he will work with and get to know. It also establishes his relationship with Dixon and his wife (Gladys Henson) as he moves in to lodge with them and share the everydayness of their domestic world. This settled unity of work and home is contrasted with that of the first case that Dixon and Mitchell are called out to, which concerns a 'domestic' and a missing girl, Diana Lewis (Peggy Evans).[12] As the film tracks her as she walks aimlessly through the crowds on Shaftesbury Avenue at night, the commentary intervenes to inform us that she is typical of many young people, the result of 'a home broken and demoralised by the war'. As the camera moves from her to encompass groups of young men she meets hanging around an amusement arcade, it continues: 'These restless and ill-adjusted youths have produced a type of delinquent which is partly responsible for the post–war increase in crime.' When 'Spud' Murphy (Patric Doonan) and Tom Riley (Dirk Bogarde)[13] come into shot, the commentary differentiates them as a class apart from 'regular criminals'; 'lacking the code, experience and self-discipline of the professional thief' and to index this, they are sent packing by Cranston (Michael Golden) the local underworld boss. Riley, Murphy and Diana, as Perry has noted, therefore embody 'the new outlaws – giving crime a bad name' (1981: 144), in the Ealing moral universe rejected by civil *and* criminal society; 'a post–war excrescence', as Barr (1977: 84) has it.

By this stage, the film has established the contending forces that will be brought into conflict as the narrative proceeds. It does this by oscillating between the everyday lives of Dixon and Mitchell at home, in the station and on the beat and the villainous anarchy of Riley and Murphy as they plan and carry out a robbery.[14] Initially, this involves robbing a jeweller, Mr Jordan (Norman Shelley), of the keys to his shop when he makes one of his apparently regular visits to the flat of his girlfriend Maisie (Dora Bryan), a friend of Diana's who has alerted Riley to this possibility. Young Mitchell arrives on the scene first, followed by Dixon, and although they discover that the keys are missing, the shop has already been raided, with Riley viciously coshing PC 'Taff' Hughes (Meredith Edwards, in standard Welsh, choir-leading form) as they make their getaway. The CID arrive in the person of Detective Inspector Cherry (Bernard Lee)[15] and his younger sergeant, Roberts (Robert Flemyng), and Dixon and Mitchell return to their respective beats.

Next day, Mitchell spots Diana with Riley on the street and escorts her back to the station. Here, she rejects the well-intentioned efforts of a woman police sergeant to return her home or to find her a place in a hostel, and she leaves, but not before her powder compact has been spotted by the sharp-eyed Roberts, who links it to the jeweller's robbery the night before. However, his subsequent enquiries at the snooker hall draw a blank. Riley, meanwhile, ensconced in his seedy flat with Diana, has procured a couple of revolvers and ammunition. After Murphy departs, leaving Riley alone with Diana, the revolver assumes phallic qualities, giving him a newfound power: 'You see, when you've got one of these in your hands people listen to you,' he says to her menacingly; as Hill has argued, his escalating threat of violence and his sexuality are fused in his possession of the gun in these and subsequent scenes (1986: 70).[16] In contrast, the only thing phallic at the Dixon household appears to be the state of the lovingly tended begonias which are admired when the now recovered Taff and another colleague from the station arrive to visit for tea. This meeting does, however, result in a minor narrative victory. Dixon's impending retirement from the service is postponed for five years when young Mitchell brings the issue out into the open. Neither George nor his wife can really contemplate a future outside of the police or the police-house which has been their home during his twenty years of service.[17]

Riley, Murphy and Diana meet in a cheap café and it becomes apparent that they are planning another robbery, this time at the cinema where Diana works as an usherette. Using their attendance at the Metropolitan Music Hall to create an alibi, Riley and Murphy leave the show during a performance by Tessie O'Shea (as herself), escaping by a back window to drive in a stolen car to the Coliseum Cinema in the Edgware Road, where they hold up the cashier. As Riley crams handfuls of banknotes into his pockets, they

With tragic restraint: *The Blue Lamp* (1950) (Courtesy of Steve Chibnall Archive)

are spotted by a couple of cinema-goers, who raise the alarm. Dixon arrives to confront Riley as he comes out of the foyer with his gun in his hand. In an iconic scene, under a poster advertising the film *Granny Get Your Gun* (d. G. Amy, 1939), Riley threatens Dixon, and in mounting panic shoots him twice before escaping with Murphy. Details of the crime and their getaway car are relayed to Scotland Yard and to a shocked Paddington police station. Riley and Murphy arrive back at the music hall and keep their rendezvous with their drinks and alibi at the bar. In the hospital, an anxious Mrs Dixon accompanied by Mitchell wait to see if Dixon will survive the operation to save his life, the surgeon informing Mitchell in an aside that Dixon has only a fifty-fifty chance. Routine police investigations at the scene of the crime, into the stolen car and interviews with witnesses follow the next day; while back on his beat, near a bomb site, Mitchell finds a little girl holding a revolver. He returns with the child and the gun[18] to the police station to learn that Dixon has just died, and is asked by Inspector Hammond (William Mervyn) to break the news to Mrs Dixon. He agrees, and they go to the house to find her preparing to leave for the hospital with a bunch of flowers from Dixon's garden. Barr has commented on the emotional power of the brief but moving scene which follows when Mitchell confirms her worst fears; noting that: 'It is observed and organised very precisely, finding a balance between "English" restraint and the unembarrassed expression of a grief that can't be contained', which, he argues, is emblematic of a core Ealing value dealing with 'decorum, decency, or choking private emotion'. The scene is shot in a 'classically restrained British style' and he is drawn to contrast this with the differing emotional appeal and style of Hollywood cinema (1977: 88–9).[19]

From this point, the film gains pace and urgency as the hunt for the killer intensifies. Riley, Murphy and Diana become increasingly isolated, and under the pressure, Dana becomes hysterical. In a ploy to save his own skin, Riley goes to the police and agrees to take part in an identity parade, but he is not picked out by witnesses. Released by the police, he is followed back to his bedsit and then to Murphy's place, where he finds Diana. He is on the verge of strangling her when the policeman tailing him intervenes. She identifies Riley as the killer, but when Murphy arrives, they overpower the policeman and escape in a fast car, nearly mowing Mitchell down as they do. What follows was to become a staple in the generic conventions of the police drama; the high-speed car chase, with police radio cars used to follow, contain and eventually cause Murphy to crash. Riley escapes the scene, however, running over rough ground and railway lines, doggedly pursued by Mitchell. However, Riley manages to evade him and enters the White City Stadium, thinking himself safe in the crowds attending the greyhound races. This is where the film reaches its final climax. The police arrive in force ('they're onto the bastard who shot George Dixon'); all the exits from the Stadium are locked down and word goes out – via the chain of tic-tac men around the track – to the criminal fraternity that the hunt for Riley the cop-killer is on. Riley has nowhere to hide and is soon spotted and cornered. As the police close in on him and with the crowd against him, he is finally disarmed and arrested by Mitchell, in a moment of due retribution. The films ends some days later with a circular return to the order and normality of its beginning; as Mitchell – like Dixon at the opening of the film – is seen on his beat, giving directions to a passer-by. In the final shot, the camera finally pans up to end where it started; on the police lamp of the title.

The release of the film attracted widespread publicity. As Chibnall has noted: 'for the modern viewer, *The Blue Lamp*'s moral certainties mark it as a period piece' (1997: 142),[20] but for many contemporary reviewers the film was received precisely as it was intended to be. 'A handsome and deserved homage to the force', itrumpeted the *Daily Graphic* (20 January 1950), 'a tribute to the London copper', agreed Jympson Harman (*Evening News* 19 January 1950), and *Kine Weekly* found it 'a worthy and eloquent tribute to our policemen' (12 January 1950). For Campbell Dixon, 'this is the story of the ordinary copper, brave, honest, tactful and tolerant, who is the rock on which our law and order rest' (*Daily Telegraph*, 23 January 1950). Critics were also engaged by the documentary realism of the film – especially the car chases and use of authentic street settings – and the fact that the film had been made with the co-operation of the Metropolitan Police carried a certain cachet. Donald Zec went so far as to suggest that: 'The public and everyone in Prisons and Borstal institutions throughout Britain should see the film . . . it justifies the pride and the confidence the nation has in its police force' (*Daily Mirror*, 18 January 1950); and Fred Redman, the crime reporter for the *Sunday Pictorial*, concurred: 'I guarantee that everyone who sees this film will look at the next policeman he meets with new respect' (15 January 1950). Most popular reviews of the film also compared it favourably to its American counterparts and commented positively on the main performances.[21]

However, some reviewers were less eulogistic in their appreciation, *The Spectator* complaining that 'the production encourages us in the belief that all policemen are courteous, incorruptible nannies but overplays its hand. The boys in blue are a trifle too typical to be real' (20 January 1950). *The Herald* appreciated the film as entertainment, but was uneasy about 'a two-faced film. Now it's entertainment, now it's propaganda. The quickness of the hand deceives the eye' (20 January 1950). For Frank Enley, writing in *Sight and Sound*, the success of the film was a mystery as it was 'a particularly specious brand of mediocrity which, to put it mildly, is having a fine run for its money'; and what seemed to infuriate some critics was what Enley went on to describe as the film's reliance on 'Huggetting' (April 1950).[22] The review in *Monthly Film Bulletin*, like Enley, was critical of the film's attempt

> to put all kinds of Real British Life on the screen, [which] results in the mixture of coyness, patronage and naïve theatricality which has vitiated British films for the last ten years, and which has been admirably defined by Richard Winnington as 'Huggettry'. (January 1950)

From such lofty heights, the performances of Warner, Hanley and Henson appeared 'wholly tabloid' and 'pre-fabricated', and while Dearden 'displays his usual fondness for melodramatic angles and the occasional shock-cut', technically the film 'is capable' but cannot compare with that achieved by Hollywood. In between the apparently opposed poles of the popular and the lofty, Dilys Powell steered her own interesting course, arguing that the style of the film was 'at least as distinctive, and as well worth study, as the celebrated "documentary" style of Hollywood's *The Naked City*'. Furthermore, she went on to make an interesting comment on its production context:

> The style proceeds here from the work of a team: producers, directors, writers, players, musicians, technicians; and it is no belittlement of the individual achievement of Basil Dearden as director and T. E. B. Clarke as script-writer to say that *The Blue Lamp* is a logical development of work which has gone before, that the team has learned to create in collaboration and that the film bears the stamp not simply of an author and a director but of a studio. (cited in Perry 1989: 87)

This is a characteristically shrewd observation that has a bearing on the work of Dearden and Relph together, both before and after *The Blue Lamp*. The film, as Barr has suggested, 'rests on a 'daydream' – of universal benevolence – and a structure that expresses it' (1977: 83). Even at the time of its release, this 'daydream' was becoming more difficult to sustain, part of the outlook of an older generation, increasingly beleaguered and out of touch with the times.

I BELIEVE IN YOU (1952)

> English do-gooders come movingly alive on the screen. (Raymond Durgnat 1970: 138)

It is generally known that the modern probation service grew out of the work of the Police Court Mission which sent its agents into the London Courts. These founder fathers were missionaries in the true sense of the word and they used the methods of missionaries – changing behaviour by changing feeling – through 'conversion'. Their methods were persuasion, exhortation and support. (George Newton 1956: 123)

Eighteen months and two films after *The Blue Lamp*, Dearden and Relph began work on *I Believe in You*, a project which sought to do for the probation service what their earlier film had done for the police.[23] The film was based on the surprisingly successful memoir *Court Circular* by Sewell Stokes, although the adaptation for the screen considerably revised the detail of the original book and the overall narrative and characters.[24] Relph, Dearden and Jack Whittingham worked together on the script, with additional scenes supplied by Nicholas Phipps. The working title for the project was *One Sinner* and Dearden and Relph's shooting scripts date from July 1951. They contain a detailed schedule for location and set filming which commenced early in September and was completed some eight weeks later.

The film opens in a magistrate's court where the central character and part-narrator, Henry Allardyce Phipps (Cecil Parker), in response to the call for the probation officer, stands and speaks in favour of a young man facing the bench. He is sentenced to one year's probation and this cues a dissolve and flashback as Phipps muses on the circumstances that led to his role in the court that day. 'About a year ago', he confides, having been made redundant after a career in the Colonial Office,[25] he could not settle to the life of a 'man of leisure' and resolved to 'do something'. The opportunity for this presents itself when a stolen car crashes outside his well-appointed gentleman's apartment, and while the police pursue the driver, the young woman passenger, Norma (Joan Collins), takes refuge with him. Refusing her offer 'to do anything for him', he does not give her up to the police but contacts her probation officer, 'Matty' (Miss Mathieson – Celia Johnson), who arrives to collect her. In this encounter, Phipps is suddenly taken by the prospect of a new, 'worthwhile' career in the probation service and this is confirmed when he attends the court to see Norma appear in the dock alongside Jordie Bennett (Laurence Harvey), the driver of the stolen car. He is sentenced to prison for six months, while Norma, partly as a result of Matty's intervention, is put on probation.

The patrician Phipps reports for work on his first day and enters a bewildering world between police station, cells and courts, full of seemingly eccentric characters and cases. Mr Dove (George Relph), the senior officer, guides him through this maze of 'unfortunate ladies' and young delinquents, one of whom, Braxton, who has been arrested for assaulting a police constable, becomes Phipps's first case. Braxton appears to have a habit of assaulting police officers and Phipps is called to the witness box to speak on his behalf. He undertakes to see if he can get Braxton's family to allow him to return home and on this proviso he is remanded. Phipps then encounters another young

Phipps encounters Norma in *I Believe in You* (1952) (Courtesy of Steve Chibnall Archive)

tearaway, Charlie Hooker (Harry Fowler), who has just been placed on probation for a year, and he is charged with taking him to the hostel. In these
early stages, Phipps appears as an incongruous figure of fun, his privileged
background, class, dress and worldview creating a gulf between him and the
cases he encounters.[26] Although unaccustomed to public transport, he visits
Braxton's home, discovers that Braxton had previously assaulted his father – a
police sergeant. His knowledge, restricted to the world of Knightsbridge and
St James's, has ill-equipped him for the places and cases he now has to deal
with. As he tramps around in the following months that follow, he confesses
that his feet 'took me to places I'd never heard of – never knew existed. Some
I don't believe ever did exist.' Furthermore, he encounters a perplexing resistance to his attempts to 'do good' for his clients: 'It seemed that a lot of them
didn't want to be helped, however much one tried – at least not by me.'

Although the film introduces a number of odd cases that the service has to
deal with – the drunken debutante and lonely old ladies – the film narrative
principally tracks the stories of Norma and Charlie Hooker and the attempts
of Matty and Phipps to help them remain on the 'straight and narrow' during
their probation. However, in a key scene, Matty takes Phipps to task for his
lack of sympathy and understanding in his approach to the clients they have
to deal with, 'for gazing down on them in a lordly way like a botanist at
beetles'. This salutary and chastening encounter begins a change in Phipps
and he gradually thaws, adopting a more caring and humanitarian approach,
taking time to try to understand the cases that he deals with.[27] In particular, he
visits Hooker's home and comes to appreciate his family circumstances – his
father killed in the war and subsequent animosity between Hooker and his
mother's new partner – and how they might account for Hooker's behaviour.
He even admits to Hooker after this visit that he cares. At one of their regular
probation meetings, Norma meets Hooker and they strike up a relationship,
which seems to have the potential to save them both. Matty, impressed by the
evident change in Phipps's approach, apologises to him for her earlier criticism
which he accepts was entirely warranted, and they go for a drink at his flat.
Here she recounts a little of her past; a well-to-do background, ambulance
driving in the war and mysteriously a change to probation work in 1943.
There is a veiled reference here perhaps to some personal tragedy or crisis,
signalled by her reluctance to continue, but the film leaves this unresolved at
this stage.

Armed with his new approach, Phipps continues his work, dealing with
Stevens, a young man who behaves like a little boy, and his protective
mother (Gladys Henson). He also learns of the real story behind the Hon.
Ursula (Ursula Howells), the drunken debutante who regularly visits Matty.
Her behaviour was triggered by the death of the pilot she fell in love with

during the war and in their discussion of her case, as the camera closes on a picture of a young naval officer in Matty's office, it becomes clear to Phipps that Matty too suffered a tragic wartime loss, which explains her dedication to the probation service in 1943. He also visits Miss Macklin (Katie Johnson), the lady who thinks her neighbours are trying to poison her or her cat. The relationship between Norma and Hooker is progressing well, he working and keen to move out of the probation hostel to be with her, and they announce that they want to get married. Phipps undertakes to see if he can change the condition of Hooker's probation, but when he approaches the magistrate, Mr Pyke (Godfrey Tearle), he refuses to rescind the order. Hooker responds to this news badly, as does Norma when he tells her that they can't get married as soon as they had planned.

The sudden and threatening reappearance of Jordie, following his release from prison, further complicates matters. He appears to offer Norma everything that Hooker cannot: money, excitement and thrills; and intent on sabotaging their relationship, Jordie takes her out to a club where they drink and dance.[28] Consumed by the music and the brooding sexuality of the encounter, she almost succumbs, but her loyalty to Hooker reasserts itself at the moment of Jordie's gloating triumph, and she flees the scene. When she meets Hooker the next day, however, he has already become involved in a plan to rob a lorry-load of spirits from his workplace; inspired by Jordie, who warns Hooker to keep away from Norma. When Norma admits that she saw Jordie the night before, Hooker decides to continue with the robbery; but she alerts Phipps and Matty to this, and Phipps sets off in an attempt to save Hooker. He arrives at the transport yard in time to confront Hooker, Jordie – armed with a revolver – and the rest of the gang; and his appearance, followed by the police, is enough to scupper the plan. As they hide under a lorry, Phipps tells Hooker that Norma loves him and that, perversely, they care about him; and with this, they are arrested by burly policemen.

The upshot of these dramatic events sees Phipps tendering his resignation to Mr Pyke, the magistrate, and then when he tells Matty of this decision, she tells him to go and tell Mr Dove. His farewell to Dove is however misconstrued, as he is ailing, worn-out by his lifetime of service and has finally been retired, and he entrusts Phipps with his files and his old, battered briefcase, in the hope that he will take them forward. In the spirit of this exchange, Phipps resolves to stay on, and after telling Matty of his decision, he goes down the corridor to the court, passing many of the people from the cases he has encountered on his way. On entering court, he hears that Hooker will be given another period of probation, but this time not requiring hostel residence, and Hooker is thus reconciled with Norma. In the final scenes of the film; as if in a *déjà vu*, Phipps stands in front of the court to speak for Johnson, more experienced than he was when he was first called upon to do this, and his mantra now contains the final lines 'I believe in him'.

The film received charitable reviews at the time of its release, with many applauding its mission to focus on the 'unsung', dedicated service provided by probation officers and their work, especially with young offenders. Joan Collins was singled out for particular praise in what was her first leading role: 'she can become a precious asset to British films, for she has fire and spirit in her acting and that odd combination of allure and mystery that spells eventual world stardom', wrote Ewart Hodgson (*News of the World*, 2 March 1952). Many reviewers commented on the absorbing nature of the story and the astute mixture of documentary and fiction: 'Here, pains have been taken not only with the background (which is of the beautifully photographed, authentic sort that has made Ealing famous), but with the well-spun plot and the homespun characters who spin it' (Paul Dehn, *Sunday Chronicle*, 9 March 1952). For *Kine Weekly*, the film was a 'box-office labour of love', which 'splendidly upholds the dignity and majesty of the law and is at once a heartening acknowledgement of a fine body of public workers . . . in short, a British film that all sections of the industry can be proud of' (6 March 1952). Only one or two reviewers deviated from this generally appreciative line and few were prepared to grasp the nettle of class. The critic in *The Daily Worker*, however (writing in mock cockney), took issue with the supposed 'life-like' depiction of the film: 'Trouble is, though, it ain't life, if you take my meaning. It's only the way life looks from a middle-class point of view, with all the working-class acting comical or pathetic and a lot of nice kind ladies and gentlemen sighing over them as if they was a lot of children or poor, benighted savages' (8 March 1952). For the *Monthly Film Bulletin*, the film was based on a popular but superficial approach:

> The ingredients combine sentiment, comedy and some artificial melo-drama in easily assimilated proportions, the manner is episodic, the technique has the smooth, journalistic proficiency that one expects from Basil Dearden – continually on the move, never penetrating far beneath the surface of a situation. (April 1952)

Subsequent discussions of the film have argued that it is entirely consonant with key aspects of Dearden and Relph's, and indeed Ealing's, vision of the post-war society. It represents, however, something of an advance on the absolute moral strictures of *The Blue Lamp*. As Hill has suggested, the film 'begins to flirt with environmentalism' as an explanation for youth delinquency (1986: 75), most obviously in its depiction of Hooker and the roots of his problems. Family background is therefore pinpointed as a crucial factor in attempts to understand why and how some young people behave as they do. However, the film also draws a firm line between the 'deserving' and 'undeserving' or 'redeemable' and 'unredeemable' youth. Hooker and Norma can be saved through support and understanding; but beyond the pale are types like Jordie and his gang, apparently born sociopaths with their guns and links with disruptive sexuality, music and dancing. Finally, although part of the film deals with the conversion of Phipps – notably when Matty criticises his approach and attitude to their clients – the perspective of the film remains profoundly improving and middle-class in outlook. Perry found this symptomatic of the 'patronising' view taken by many British films of the time (1980: 154); while Chibnall suggests that Phipps, 'as he moves from a state of arrogance to one of humility', 'could easily stand for Ealing's own socially isolated film-makers' (1997: 146).

VIOLENT PLAYGROUND (1958)

> To evoke the atmosphere of antagonism that many young people were feeling towards the police at that time, Kennaway spent some time in Liverpool, but as the script was being finalised during the autumn, reality came to the rescue of art. On 10 October in Terrazanno, Italy, two mad brothers, armed with guns and dynamite, burst into the local school and held to ransom ninety-two children and three teachers, threatening to kill them unless various unspecified demands were met. (Trevor Royle 1983: 128)

> In 1949, the Chief Constable of Liverpool, taking action against a growing wave of juvenile crime, instituted the Juvenile Liaison Officers Scheme. It is a known fact that when a child has once been before the magistrates and a record begun, he tends to commit further and more serious crime until there is a danger of his becoming a habitual criminal. It was to prevent this that the Juvenile Liaison Officers were appointed from the Detective Department of the City's Police divisions. (*Final Shooting Script*: Producers Note, 27 May 1957)[29]

Dearden and Relph returned to spotlight the social problem of youth crime and delinquency in their second film after they had embarked on work outside the Ealing fold. In 1957, having completed *The Smallest Show on Earth* and *Davy*, they began work on an original screenplay by James Kennaway, with the working title *Firefly*.[30] Kennaway may well have been influenced by the success of the earlier American film *Blackboard Jungle* (d. Brooks, 1955), and star Stanley Baker commented in an interview that he was attracted to a script that 'has the same kind of exciting quality as *Blackboard Jungle*' (*Films and Filming*, July 1957). Producer Michael Relph admitted that 'The story is like

Blackboard Jungle in texture', but continued: 'The difference is we are playing it on a wider canvas. We show the combined efforts of the schools, the police, the families and the church to solve the problem' (*Films and Filming*, September 1957). In typical Dearden style, the film was firmly set on an estate in Liverpool, with a strong documentary feel provided by extensive location shooting in and around the city. The film was made for Rank and work in the studio commenced at Pinewood in July (*Kinematograph Weekly*, 9 May 1957). Filming was completed before the end of 1957 and the film was selected for a Royal film première in early March 1958, held at the Odeon, Marble Arch, and attended by the Duke of Edinburgh in aid of the Trans-Antarctic Expedition (*The Times*, 29 January 1958). On general release, advertising and posters for *Violent Playground* screamed at audiences: 'EVERY CITY HAS ITS DANGEROUS YOUTH. Stark explosive drama – as the cameras lay bare the heart of a big city and probe the secrets of its violent playground!' (*Films and Filming*, April 1958).

The opening mode of address of the film strikes a substantially differ-ent register from their earlier efforts in *The Blue Lamp* and *I Believe in You*; as the raucous rock 'n' roll song 'Play Rough' ushers in shots of gangs of kids running wild among the tenements and slum clearances of inner-city Liverpool. These establishing shots introduce the police investigating another case of suspected arson, with Detective Sergeant Jack Truman (Stanley Baker) at the scene of a burnt-out warehouse, searching for clues. He is recalled to the station, however, to find himself 'volunteered' as a temporary Juvenile Liaison Officer: 'to prevent children from being locked up', as his superior tells him. From the outset, he seems ill-suited to his new role: 'I don't even like kids', he retorts, much to his chagrin and his former workmates' amusement. His first case brings him into contact with a petty shop theft, carried out by twins, Mary and Patrick; and in investigating their home circumstances, he first encounters the Murphy family: their elder sister Cathie (Anne Heywood),[31] a nurse, who – in the absence of their father and mother – looks after them, and Johnny (David McCallum) their brother, the leader of a gang of youths who hang around the tenements where they live, causing trouble. When Truman takes the twins back to the Scotland Road School, he meets the kindly head-master, 'Heaven' Evans (Clifford Evans), who appears unable to see anything but good in the children in his charge and who ticks off a young teacher for being too boring. When he meets Cathie, she rejects his apparent concern for the twins by calling him a 'bluebottle' intent on sticking his nose in where it's not wanted, and this nettles him further. His subsequent attempts to enlist the help of the Catholic priest, Father Laidlaw (Peter Cushing), in finding out more about the family are also met with a cold suspicion. In spite of this, Truman accompanies Cathie back to the flat where he offers to take the twins to a youth club, and on this visit he meets Johnny, who is edgy and hostile. When he leaves he has to run the gauntlet of the gang on the stairway, but Johnny lets him leave without incident.

The film continues to document Truman's efforts to help the twins and Cathie; he takes them to a youth club and to a local athletics event, and here he sees Johnny, who is persuaded by the headmaster to run in one of the races, revealing himself as a once promising athlete. His persistence appears to be worthwhile as his relationship with the twins, Cathie and even Johnny seems to be working, and there is even a hint of romance with Cathie. 'Why do you hang about with these layabouts?' he asks Johnny, but then when he goes back to the flat with Johnny and the twins, he watches as they and the gang become consumed by rock 'n' roll, their frenzied dancing serving to emphasise the deep gulf between him and them. The detective in him, however, begins to link Johnny and his Chinese friend Alexander, who drives a laundry van, to the continuing arson incidents carried out by 'the firefly'. After another big blaze down by the docks, these suspicions develop, and Truman goes to find Johnny, interrupting him when he seems on the point of confession with the priest. It transpires that Johnny, when he was young, heroically saved one of the twins from a house fire, and that ever since then he has had a fascination with fire. In a world where he seems estranged from everything and everybody, nothing gives him a kick like the memory of the blaze. The priest relates this to Truman and he in turn tells the priest of the clue linking Johnny with the fires. He leaves, having resolved to turn Johnny in.

Johnny and the gang are meanwhile reading newspaper reports of the latest exploits of 'the firefly' and they go into the city centre in the van. Johnny, reacting to the taunts and laughter of the gang, tries to go into The Grand Hotel, but is thrown out by the commissionaire. Truman arrives in time to witness Johnny threatening the hotel and when he meets Cathie later at the station, in spite of her protective pleading, he argues that he must let the police know about Johnny. Cathie tries to prevent Johnny, but the gang intervene and he forces Alexander to drive him to the hotel, where he starts a blaze. Alerted by Truman's warnings, however, the police arrive and the action begins to accelerate wildly, as the panic-stricken Johnny escapes in the laundry van, fatally running down the luckless Alexander as he does so. A full-scale police hunt for Johnny now ensues as the van is abandoned in the Mersey Tunnel, but not before Johnny has been given a machine gun (with a touch of the dramatic, hidden, gangster-style in a violin case) by one of the gang. Abandoned, frightened and on his own, Johnny takes refuge for the night in the old school, but Cathie finds out that he is now armed and goes to tell Truman. Just before she arrives with this news, however, and in a telling interchange, Truman finds himself defending Johnny – and the aims of the

Juvenile Liaison Scheme – in the face of the forthright condemnation voiced
by one of his old colleagues:

> Everybody's potentially a good boy . . . you can make too many allow-
> ances . . . I've got respect for the law. I'm tired of the tough-guy fever,
> sick and tired; they're snakes . . . like lepers, only they don't warn you
> with a bell.

In response, Truman rather lamely asserts the importance of 'a lot of Mum and
a little bit of Dad' as *the* vital factors which make the difference in preventing
the growth of young men's delinquent and criminal careers.

On the following morning, the final sequences of the film deal with an
extended siege at the school, as Johnny takes hostage a class of young children,
including the twins, and becomes locked into a stand-off with the police.
When the news spreads, in front of a playground crowded with anxious
parents, he threatens to kill all of their children. The priest, who tries to intervene, is pushed from a ladder and injured. When Cathie arrives she is spat on
by a mother in the crowd. Truman has the crowds cleared and advises caution
and, on this advice, the police initially try to reason with Johnny. When this
fails and they attempt to force entry, Johnny in desperation shoots and accidentally wounds one of the young girls. The police allow Cathie to go in
alone to tend to the little girl, and her presence reassures and calms Johnny.
Under her influence, the children are all allowed, gradually and quietly, to
file out of the classroom. Johnny is finally brought out by the police, but is
not placed in an ambulance as Cathie had asked, but is handcuffed and driven
away in a black police van. When she rounds on Truman for this, he insists
on the need for limits to her compassion, arguing that it is important for the
community, the parents and children that Johnny's crimes should be publicly
acknowledged and recognised in this way. 'He's too old for a perambulator',
he rejoins, as she is comforted by the priest. The film ends on an enigmatic
note, spurning full romantic closure between Truman and Cathie. As he drops
her off and asks if he will see her again, she in turn calls him a 'curious, kindly
bluebottle' and asks what his father did. When he replies that his father and
the father before him were shepherds, she kisses the palm of his hand and the
last shot of Cathie tracks her as she walks determinedly towards the church.
Truman is left, holding hands with a little, black street boy from the opening
scenes of the film, and the camera pans back as they walk along the path where
the kids, full of boisterous energy, are swarming in front of the estate.

Contemporary reviews of the film praised the performances of Heywood
and McCallum (several referring to him as the 'British James Dean') and
tended to celebrate its perceived intention, but were generally somewhat
disappointed with the overall result. For Philip Oakes, writing in *The Evening*

Johnny, Cathie and Truman in *Violent Playground* (1958) (Courtesy of Steve Chibnall Archive)

Standard, the film 'Only just falls short of being first-rate . . . The effect is something like a morality play scored for rock'n'roll' (27 February 1958). *Kine Weekly* extolled the virtues of the 'superb screen reporting and drama' in what it found to be a

> Gripping, thought-provoking, sociological melodrama, unfolded on Liverpool's seamy side. The tale rings true and gets to the heart of its urgent and disturbing matter without stooping to cheap sentiment or sensationalism . . . obviously inspired by fact, does not preach yet clearly proves that the law must be upheld and that most delinquents are victims of environment. (9 January 1958)

By contrast, *The Times* argued:

> As the story progresses all attempts to discuss any genuine social problems are abandoned in favour of a melodramatic and improbable climax . . . Thus a film which sets out with such self-avowed high purpose degenerates into something that is basically dishonest, since the real issues are evaded. (3 March 1958)

In a similar vein, *The Daily Worker* insisted: 'It is NOT a serious study of juvenile delinquency. It is a gangster film of the "crazy mixed-up kid" variety, and all its psychology and reform business is simply thrown in as a gimmick' (1 March 1958). The *Monthly Film Bulletin* found nothing redeeming to say about the film:

> Unfortunately the film is at the mercy of its own complacency and settles for a superficial, glib approach and a general reliance on formula . . . everything is conformist and predictable . . . the screenplay is stiff and lifeless, relying on false banter and recrimination scenes. Johnny's cravings, his insecurity and aggression are hurriedly diagnosed in between jaded bursts of rock'n'roll. It is very sad that such a wonderful opportunity to make a true to life film on such an important theme has been allowed, once again, to slip away. (February 1958)

One can only wonder what the forty boys on probation, who were forced to attend a Notting Hill cinema to watch *Violent Playground* as 'a lesson on the futility of juvenile delinquency', made of the film (*Sunday Express*, 6 April 1958). Although it addresses the recognised social problem of youth gangs and crime, and reiterates the significance of environment and family socialisation, the rational, reformist message of the film is at best ambiguous, at worst confused. Clearly, the film supports the work of Juvenile Police Liaison and similar initiatives in catching 'them' young and trying to nurture them – for the twins, there is hope, but not for Johnny. The conversion of Truman, from hard-boiled, authoritarian cop to a more subtle, sympathetic agent (or Good Shepherd) of the law bears this out. But Johnny remains the troubling figure; apparently, the film seems to suggest, propelled by psychopathology, inured to the interventions of church or education, and therefore 'irrecoverable', beyond the discursive boundaries of the social problem film, receptive, it would appear, only to the beat of rock'n'roll. As Hill has neatly put it: 'As a result, the film is torn between voluntarism and determinism in its account of delinquent behaviour' (1986: 82). Chibnall, in his account, notes, however, that it is likely that the film was made for younger audiences than the two predecessors and in these terms, the figure of Johnny can be read as subversive: 'a potent icon of youthful dissent' (1997: 150).

SAPPHIRE (1959)

'Riot Film to be made in Notting Hill'.
The Rank Organisation announced last night that they will make a film on the Notting Hill colour riots . . . The film, to be called *Sapphire*, will be made in colour by Michael Relph and Basil Dearden, and local coloured men and women will be used in the crowd scenes and possibly for bigger parts. (*The Times*, 10 October 1958)[32]

'Film not to be shot at Notting Hill'.
The Rank Organisation will not be shooting any scenes in the Notting Hill area when they begin to make the film *Sapphire*, a story based on colour riots. Mr Michael Relph, the producer, said yesterday that it had never been the intention to shoot any of the scenes of violence in the Notting Hill area and there was no mention of Notting Hill Gate in the film. (*The Times*, 15 November 1958)

After an exchange of roles and another brief foray into comedy on *Rockets Galore!*, in late 1958 Dearden and Relph, in what was to become one of their most celebrated social problem films, began shooting *Sapphire*. The film was again made for Rank at Pinewood by their front company of the time, Artna Productions; and even before it had gone into production, the film had hit the headlines and courted controversy.[33] The script, an original screenplay by Janet Green (with additional dialogue supplied by Lukas Heller), used a crime 'whodunit' format to explore the issue of racial prejudice, as experienced by black people in contemporary metropolitan Britain.[34] This was a timely and brave initiative, given the backcloth of recurrent tension, conflict and associated press coverage that had resulted from the so-called 'Notting Hill Riots', and which had commanded widespread public and political attention from August 1958 onwards.[35] Dearden and Relph were to make their intentions

clear in a production feature in *Kine Weekly* towards the end of the shooting
schedule: 'We plan to show this prejudice as the stupid and illogical thing it is'
(25 December 1958).[36] The *Final Shooting Script* dates from October 1958 and
location shooting began on Hampstead Heath on 17 November. Filming, in
bright Eastman Color, was completed early in 1959 with the release following
in May.[37]

The film begins with a classic crime drama enigma: children discover
a young woman's body just off a path in a deserted part of the Heath. In
place of Holmes and Watson, *Sapphire* begins with the arrival of Detective
Superintendent Hazard (Nigel Patrick) and Detective Inspector Learoyd
(Michael Craig) as they investigate the scene of the crime.[38] The woman
is young and strikingly beautiful and the pathologist confirms that she died
sometime on the previous evening from a series of fatal stab wounds to the
heart. The only clue to her identity is a blood-stained handkerchief, mono-
grammed 'S'. This sign is also found on the shocking-red petticoat, revealed
when the two policemen examine her clothing back at the station and Hazard
deduces that the victim may have been a student. In counterpoint, the film
cuts to David Harris (Paul Massie), an architecture student, who has just won a
scholarship to study in Rome, as he waits outside the Royal College of Music,
looking for his girlfriend Sapphire, and as if by magic, Learoyd arrives to ask
for his help in identifying the body. As word goes out among the students
who knew Sapphire that she was the 'murdered girl on Hampstead Heath'
David positively identifies the body and in his grief, confesses to Hazard that
they were engaged to be married. In the subsequent interview with the two
policemen, he appears to be the prime suspect, unable to provide a convincing
alibi and apparently hiding something.

While awaiting the arrival of Sapphire's brother, Hazard and Learoyd go
to her lodgings to search for further clues, and in a locked drawer they find
them: a collection of gaily coloured, sexy lingerie and a torn-off photograph
of Sapphire, dancing in similar exotic dress. Thus, Sapphire's hidden, 'other
side' is hinted at and then confirmed, when her brother, Dr Robbins (Earl
Cameron), arrives at the police station, to meet Hazard; Hazard is momentarily taken aback to encounter a big, black man[39] (with a sudden swirl of jazz
to underscore his reaction). After this meeting, Hazard indicates to Learoyd
that he thinks that it was race hatred that killed Sapphire; and Learoyd in turn
confirms that the autopsy indicates that Sapphire was pregnant. When Hazard
says he suspects that David was the father, there is a hint in Learoyd's response
of 'might have been anyone' of ingrained, racist assumptions at work, and the
reaction shot of Hazard's face underlines this and his own different position.

In subsequent sequences, the film introduces David's family and sketches
his social circumstances, as his sister, Mildred (Yvonne Mitchell) goes to

tell their father, Mr Harris (Bernard Miles), at his work as a signwriter, of Sapphire's death and that the police suspect David. Harris immediately returns home to find Hazard and Learoyd interviewing his son and searching his room. In the terraced, typically 'respectable' working-class home, Hazard ascertains that David's alibi, that he was returning from Cambridge at the time of the murder, is corroborated by the family; and furthermore that they knew that Sapphire was pregnant. She had apparently informed them of this on the day of her murder. The response to his parting question: 'Did you know that she was coloured?', however, reveals a note of tension, as the father reluctantly admits: 'We knew. That's sufficient.' After they leave, the two policemen interview the local constable whom David claimed to have met as he was returning from Cambridge. He acknowledges that he did see David, but also gives Hazard more food for thought in his description of the family; their 'respectable' drive for upward mobility and, in particular, in his surprise concerning the revelation of Sapphire's ethnicity and his characterisation of Mr Harris as 'very bigoted' and 'very ambitious for his son'. The significance of David's scholarship and Mildred's ambitions for her own children, in spite of her own failed relationship, are not lost on Hazard as he goes back to the scene of the crime, where he encounters Dr Robbins. He has learned that his murdered sister was pregnant and in the face of Hazard's assurances to the contrary, he confronts the detective with a scepticism born out of his experience concerning the outcome of his investigations. As an index of this, when he visits Sapphire's lodgings in the next scene, the film, by way of the landlady's response, gives clear evidence of the 'colour bar' and the typical racial prejudice experienced by blacks in London at the time.

The next day, amidst everyday scenes of breakfast domesticity, the tensions in the Harris family come to a head as the family blame David for becoming 'involved with a coloured girl'. His response, that he didn't know until they all found out that she was pregnant the previous weekend, meets with an acidic rejoinder from Mildred, who insists that 'that's what she banked on'. She then outlines how they all discovered that Sapphire was mixed-race. In response to Mr Harris's offer to meet her brother and to assure him that David would 'stand by' the pregnant girl, Sapphire apparently laughed and said, 'He'll be a shock to you; he's as black as a pot'. As this deeply prejudiced side of the family is revealed, Hazard follows the clue of Sapphire's colourful underwear – the red chiffon under the tweed skirt – or, 'the black under the white' as Learoyd puts it; and his incipient racism is exposed again when they interview the doctor who confirmed Sapphire's pregnancy. Their investigations confirm that Sapphire did indeed have a 'hidden life' before she began to pass herself off as white.

In the course of their inquiries with another bigoted landlady and some past friends and associates of Sapphire Hazard begins to piece together a picture of the girl and her life and he also encounters, in a variety of guises, racial prejudice. David Harris is spotted on the Heath, near where the body was found, apparently searching for something. When he leaves, he is followed and after he disposes of an object, the police retrieve a small carved piece of wood, a seemingly meaningless clue, but as a result he remains the key suspect in the case. As the mounting pressure on the Harris family results in recriminations, Hazard's investigations lead him to the International Club, where he meets a multiracial group of Sapphire's former friends, whom she disowned when she began to pass for white. However, when he leaves, a young black woman gives him a lead; Sapphire had an association with a black man called Johnnie, her dancing partner at a club called 'Tulips', and without further ado, Hazard and Learoyd visit the club. In one of the defining sequences in the film, they descend into the crowded basement bar, full of black people, dancing to wild, 'hot' jazz. In this 'inverted' environment, it is Hazard and Learoyd who are suddenly out of place; in a world of black culture and rhythm, a world where in response to their questions, the urbane manager 'Mr Tulip' puts it, even a 'lily-skin' like Sapphire's could not resist the beat of the bongo: 'No matter how fair the skin, they can't hide that swing' (this is apparently verified when the camera captures the tapping feet of a seemingly white, blonde-haired girl at the bar). Having apparently learned nothing from this visit to the 'underworld', Hazard and Learoyd leave, but their questions have flushed Johnnie Fiddle (Harry Baird) out of the club and they move to arrest him as in panic he bolts.

In the sequence of frenzied flight that follows, the film builds a sense of the double rejection faced by the black fugitive, as Johnnie flees through the backstreets and his appeals for help are rejected first by 'respectable' black householders and then by white racist bigots in a café. He is set upon and beaten up by a gang of Teds, and although a white shopkeeper's wife does help him, he runs into the arms of the police.[40] In the subsequent scenes, he is harshly interrogated by Hazard and Learoyd, shouted at and manhandled, as they try to discover his whereabouts at the time of Sapphire's death.[41] In parallel with this, David Harris undergoes his own, more subtle inquisition, as his mother, aware that her son is not telling the truth, tries unsuccessfully to establish where he was on the fateful Saturday night. Hazard and Learoyd, having failed in their attempts to break the terrified Johnnie, go to search his lodgings and in the squalid attic room, they find the full photograph revealing Johnnie and Sapphire dancing. This search also turns up a blood-stained shirt and flick-knife, and for the prejudiced Learoyd, this is enough to condemn Johnnie. Hazard, however, remains unconvinced, troubled by the detail of how Johnnie could have transported the body across London to Hampstead

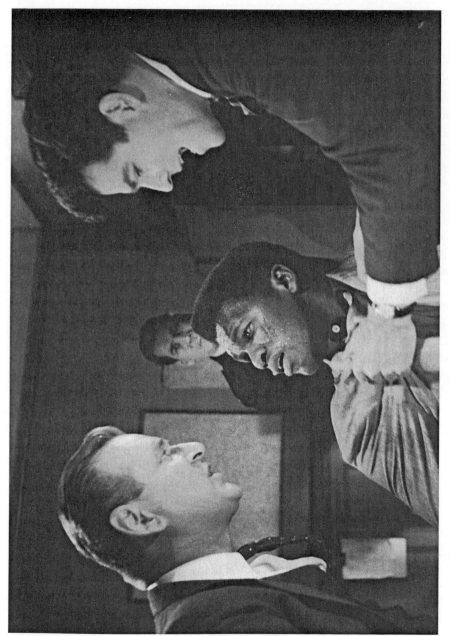

The interrogation of Johnnie Fiddle: *Sapphire* (1959) (Courtesy of Steve Chibnall Archive)

Heath. In response, Learoyd mockingly points to an old pram that they pass on their way out of the building. In their subsequent interchange as they return to the station, the film underlines Learoyd's position as a racist police-man: 'These spades are a load of trouble; I reckon we should send them back where they came from, we wouldn't have half this bother if they weren't here.' The urbane and infinitely reasonable Hazard, however, will have none of this and he articulates the central message of the film as he exposes his colleague's knee-jerk bigotry: 'Look Phil, given the right atmosphere, you can organise riots against anyone: Jews, Catholics, Negroes, Irish – even policemen with big feet.'

Developments with the case of David Harris now come to the fore, as the sales rep who gave him the lift back from Cambridge comes forward to corroborate his alibi; however, in his statement he confirms that he dropped David at six o'clock in the evening and not at eleven as David had maintained. As a result, Hazard puts pressure on David, quizzing him about his relation-ship with Sapphire, whether he knew of her background, how marriage to her would have jeopardised his scholarship and the significance of the piece of wood he found on the Heath. After this interview, Hazard's suspicions widen to include David's father and he questions the brittle Mildred and checks the father's workshop where he becomes interested in something hidden under a large dust-sheet. However, this line of investigation is temporarily suspended when the lab report on the blood from Johnnie's knife and shirt confirms it is the same blood group as Sapphire's. Police suspicion swings back to the hapless Johnnie, who finally, under repeated questioning, claims that the blood resulted from a fight he had with one Horace 'Big-Cigar', on the Saturday night in question. Learoyd is despatched to interview Horace and his black associates and he discovers that in fact Johnnie's version of the events is corroborated by their accounts – although they had given Johnnie the impression that he had killed Horace. With Johnnie now apparently in the clear, Hazard searches Mr Harris's workshop and removes a pram, big enough to carry twins. He is now convinced that one of the Harris family – or all of them – must have been responsible for the death of Sapphire and he decides on a novel way to get at the truth. When he and Learoyd go to interview the family, he invites Sapphire's brother, Dr Robbins, to attend. Mr Harris and Mildred are adamant that they don't want him in the house, but his presence provides the catalyst which enables Hazard to probe the family and their real feelings for David's intended marriage to Sapphire. In the tense final scenes, it is Mildred whose revulsion at the sight of Dr Robbins black hand holding one of her children's dolls finally cracks and betrays her hatred of black people in general and of Sapphire in particular,[42] for ruining her brother's career and her father's dreams and for taunting her about her own unfulfilled sexuality. In this bitter outburst, it becomes apparent that she stabbed Sapphire to death and then transported the body to the Heath using the old pram.[43] The film ends on this note, with David, in the face of his father's admission that 'we all had hate in our hearts', reiterating to Dr Robbins that he did love Sapphire, and Hazard after a final conciliatory handshake with Robbins, ruefully admitting to Learoyd: 'We didn't solve anything Phil; we just picked up the pieces.'

Critical reaction to the film was concerned primarily to assess the success with which whodunit and social problem had been merged, and the consequent effectivity of the film's message of racial tolerance (Tarr 1985: 54); for Dai Vaughan, writing in *Films and Filming*, it was a successful cross-fertilisation, with the 'mystery of who-done-it becoming the mystery of human responses' (June 1959).

In its depiction of race relations, prejudice and racism at the heart of an outwardly 'respectable' white family, *Sapphire* clearly touched a controversial nerve and when it was released it attracted extensive coverage, with many contemporary critics praising it not only as a good crime thriller, but also appreciating its 'eye-opening' mission to expose racist bigotry. As *Time & Tide* put it: 'a rarity. It combines a *roman policier* with a serious study of the colour problem' (16 May 1959). Also typical of this approach was *The Sunday Express*, which recommended the film as 'one of the most enthralling and intelligent whodunits I have seen for a long time . . . it is a picture of a London few people know, a searingly earnest attempt to take a look at a smouldering part of the world we live in and which, most of the time, we try to ignore'. As the reviewer concluded: 'If only it would produce films as good as *Sapphire* – films about our own problems, our people, the British film industry would be able to lift up its head as high as it ever did – and make money' (10 May 1959).

In spite of some misgivings concerning possible 'commercial calculation' behind the choice of theme, Richard Mallett writing in *Punch* agreed:

> 'Brilliant' is the first word I am inclined to use of *Sapphire*: it gave me almost continuous pleasure, and I can find nothing about it to disapprove . . . finely calculated to make even the unthinking bonehead take a second look at his emotional prejudices, it comes off superbly well. Everybody concerned with it deserves praise. (20 May 1959)

The Guardian detected that the 'Spirit of Ealing persists in "Sapphire" in the old Ealing style, with a real topical and new problem of post-war Britain, the problem of the colour bar' (8 May 1959); while Majdalany in *The Daily Mail* expressed a degree of surprise that the controversial film had 'slipped through the crushing net of Wardour Street middlemen to bring humour to a touchy topic' (8 May 1959). C. A. Lejeune argued: 'the film takes the colour problem very seriously, and if it arrives at no hard conclusion, at least it has fair arguments to advance on both sides' (*Observer*, 10 May 1959). For Dilys Powell:

> It is the achievement of *Sapphire*, while telling an exciting story, to take a steady look at a division comparatively new in English society: the antagonism between white and coloured . . . *Sapphire* gets nearer than any film I can think of to a state of what I will call acceptance. It doesn't patronise; it doesn't congratulate itself on being liberal; and it doesn't toady either. (*The Sunday Times*, 10 May 1959)

Like many critics, Paul Dehn praised by Janet Green's script as well as Dearden's direction, which he felt had resulted in 'The best British whodunit I can remember and I am sorry to hear that the Rank Organisation plans to make no more of its polished, professional, sort' (*News Chronicle*, 9 May 1959).

A number of critical accounts of the film, however, dissented from this general tone of approval and applause. David Robinson, writing in *The Financial Times*, while admitting the film was 'disturbing', went on to argue that it was exploitative, flawed and self-defeating: 'One does not feel that the film-makers were impelled to make a serious contribution to a social problem; simply that they saw a chance to cash in on a currently fashionable and respectably sensational controversy'. Furthermore, 'the portrayal of negroes in the film seems more likely to prejudice race relations' (11 May 1959). In a similar vein, William Whitebait, writing in *The New Statesman*, labelled *Sapphire* an 'above average thriller', but found that 'this film doesn't help us make up our minds about anything, especially about race prejudice which is dragged into an orthodox whodunit. Notting Hill, we may feel, deserves serious handling or none' (16 May 1959). And this theme of inadequate answers to decent questions was continued in Isabel Quigley's review in *The Spectator*:

> *Sapphire* asks all the large questions without beginning to answer them in any but the most superficial way. Mr Dearden is a tactful, dispassionate and un-indignant director. He has tried to give us sociology in the framework of a thriller, but the framework is too light and brittle, too neat and compact for a subject that involves some of our deepest feelings – racial prejudice. (15 May 1959)

The Times also complained that 'Thriller and Social Study' made for 'An Awkward Film Mixture' (8 May 1959).[44] Predictably, *The Monthly Film Bulletin* could find little positive to say about the film: 'Unfortunately, this film does not hold good on any level, and is flatly written and directed into the bargain.' Bemoaning its unconvincing nature, the reviewer continued to find fault with the 'studio-bound', 'mechanical acting' symptomatic of 'the lack of imagination which dogs the whole film'; concluding that 'The film is undoubtedly meant in earnest; its failure, consequently, seems twice as sad, though there are doubtless many who will be impressed by the politeness of its "liberal" gesture' (June 1959). In spite of these notices, however, *Sapphire* was recognised as the Best British Film of 1959 at the British Academy awards.

Durgnat, in his (re)assessment of the film almost forty years after its release, suggests that in common with *Victim*, Sapphire, when viewed now, 'may seem timid or deplorably reactionary' (1997: 63), and in its well-intentioned, liberal appeal for reasoned tolerance, and its construction of a world of black and white 'types', it has the anachronistic appearance of both, for the knowing – and unforgiving – modern viewer. Given the nature of the central theme, it is not surprising that the film has attracted a degree of subsequent academic and critical scrutiny, most of which has tended to find it wanting in terms of its point of view (the white, male, middle-class, liberal Hazard) and in its associated ideological misrecognition of the institutionalised nature of racial prejudice and oppression (it's not just a matter of individual attitudes). As a result, it is argued that the film fundamentally confuses 'culture' and 'nature' in its depiction/reproduction of myths of black, 'essential' difference – music, rhythm, and sexuality. As Hill has argued:

> The flaw of the film, however, is that its ascription of natural qualities is not natural at all, but the projection of its own culture's values, values which form part of the problem and not a solution to it. (1986: 89)[45]

Furthermore, and in these terms, the enigma of Sapphire's identity 'fuses the notion of blackness with female desire and sexuality' (Landy 1991: 477); and hence, as Tarr has it: 'the murder mystery constitutes a further red herring to keep us from spotting that the film is about women's sexuality' (1985: 54). Young also provides an insightful analysis, sensitive both to historical moment and in particular to the issue of Sapphire's 'passing' as white – 'not necessarily to be perceived solely as a desire not to be black: it is as much to do with the desire to have access to the privilege invested in whiteness by white people' (1996: 96). Writing at the time of the film's release, Dai Vaughan was a little perplexed by the emphasis on 'passing for white'; 'Is it true', he mused, 'that in London student circles a girl would have to "pass for white" in order to cultivate the society of white people?' For a later, more culturally experienced generation, such sentiments would seem naïve. However, Vaughan's perceptive review reads as a model expression of liberal sentiment of the time. The appearance of *Sapphire* heralds a 'time to rejoice', an indication that 'the cinema *itself* shows the influence of that spirit of social awareness which is reinvigorating the other arts'. He was impressed by the multilayered nature of racial prejudice as it was encountered in the investigation, believing 'the character of this prejudice – breeding upon itself, resting ultimately on nothing – is skilfully exposed': 'Through innumerable details and off-hand conversation we are made to understand how these small, un-violent, every-day things can build up to acts of gross brutality. If we do not reject racialism we accept it *whole*'. Vaughan was recognising the film's transcendence of a mere sensationalist treatment of the Notting Hill Riots, believing it carried 'complete conviction': 'No glib solutions are offered. And "solutions" to the colour problem could hardly be other than glib. What is needed is education in human values. And to this end *Sapphire* is a worthy contribution' (*Films and Filming*, June 1959).

VICTIM (1961)

'Victim' is a film that needs very careful handling. (*Kinematograph Weekly*, 25 January 1962)

I am really rather nervous of this script: Messrs Relph and Dearden are not sensational film-makers, but a lot of the material here is in itself pretty sensational; and the public may be getting a bit tired of exaggerated plain speaking on this subject. (*BBFC Reader's Report*, 29 June 1960)

It is extraordinary, in this over-permissive age, to believe that this modest film could ever have been considered courageous, daring or dangerous to make. It was, in its time, all three. (Dirk Bogarde 1979: 241)

Victim was, as Robert Murphy has it, 'the true successor to *Sapphire*' (1992: 40). The film was released in early September 1961, and the final shooting scripts, with the working title 'Boy Barrett', are dated late January of that year, but were not finalised until March.[46] However, the film began its relationship with the British Board of Film Censors much earlier, in May 1960, when Relph sent a synopsis for comment to its chairman, John Trevelyan. This ini-tiated a lengthy, detailed and revealing historical dialogue between the film-makers and censors before the film was finally passed, with an 'X' certificate in June 1961.[47] It was to be the third and final film Dearden and Relph would make for the AFM venture and the original script was another collaboration with Janet Green, this time working with her husband, John McCormick. Like *Sapphire*, the film focused on a topical and controversial theme, recur-rently present in the newspapers throughout the 1950s,[48] and it also employed the same kind of crime-whodunit formula to reveal and explore its distinctive, 'hidden' social problem agenda: male homosexuality, persecution, blackmail and the law.[49] However, unlike *Sapphire*, the film's narrative is not quite as centrally motivated by a police detective investigation, but concerns the story of a successful young barrister, Melville Farr (Dirk Bogarde), on the verge of becoming a QC.[50]

The film begins with a series of stark, atmospheric shots as the camera pans over the scaffolding and cranes of an imposing building site in London, orchestrated with jazz-tinged, atonal music.[51] As two plainclothes policemen arrive, 'Boy' Barrett (Peter McEnery), high on the scaffold, spots them and rapidly leaves the site and heads for a phone-box where he telephones his lodgings, speaks to Eddy Stone (Donald Churchill) and arranges to meet him to collect a parcel. As Eddy leaves, the police officers from the building site arrive, but he evades them and makes for the agreed rendezvous in a pub. Before he arrives, Barrett uses the phone again, to call Mr Melville Farr's chambers, and once he gets through to the barrister, deep in discussion of a case, he meets with a sharp rebuff and a threat that if he rings again, Farr will call the police. But as Farr puts the phone down and his eyes momentarily meet those of the woman in the photograph on his desk, an uneasy sense of tension sets in – all is not quite what it seems.

When Barrett meets Eddy in the pub, the enigma tightens; he seems frightened and hunted and in spite of his friend's reassurances, he quickly leaves with the bag containing the parcel. His edginess has, however, not gone unnoticed by one or two of the regulars in the bar. The film tracks Barrett as he tries to contact Farr, but each time his calls are refused. He visits a second-hand book-shop, run by Harold Doe (Norman Bird), who also refuses to help, cryptically referring to their 'secrets' and to 'horrid imaginings'. In parallel, Farr is seen at his club, at work and in his wealthy home in Chiswick, with his wife, Laura (Sylvia Syms) – revealed as the woman in the photograph on his desk – and they appear to be an ideally matched, loving couple.[52] After other fruitless attempts to enlist help, Barrett gets a lift out of the city and when he reaches the suburbs, he encounters an old friend, Frank, with his wife, Sylvie. She reacts hostilely, refusing Frank's offer of a bed for the night for Barrett, telling him to 'stick with your own sort'. However, as the sympathetic Frank walks with Barrett to the coast road, the latter explains that he is on the run because he has stolen some money. As they part, Frank tries to persuade Barrett to stay to face the police, but he will have none of it and with Frank's parting shot of 'well it used to be witches – at least they don't burn you', he leaves. After one more unsuccessful attempt to contact Farr, Barrett is spotted by the police in a transport café and arrested, but not before, in desperation, he has opened the parcel he collected earlier and torn up what appears to be a scrapbook, flushing it into the toilet. He is returned to the police station and in the subsequent interview with Detective Inspector Harris (John Barrie) and Sergeant Bridie (John Cairney), the puzzle of Barrett's predicament and his recent behaviour becomes clear. They establish that he has been embezzling a considerable amount of money from his job as wages clerk at the building site. Furthermore, although Barrett will not admit it, they realise that the boy is being blackmailed – 'more victim than criminal' as Harris puts it – and when they examine the contents of the retrieved scrap-book it becomes apparent why.

On the following day, just as he learns that his application to become a QC has met with success, Farr receives a phone call asking him to stop at the police station on his way home. When he arrives, he is quizzed about his relationship with Barrett, admits that he knew him and that he had for a time given him occasional lifts home, but denies any knowledge of blackmail. The scrap-book is revealed to contain a series of cuttings depicting Farr's career and professional prowess in the legal world. Harris asks if Farr knew that Barrett was a homosexual, so confirming for even the most naïve viewer the significance of the many implicit clues thus far in the film.[53] Farr admits that he 'had formed that impression', but distances himself from any real knowledge of Barrett and his circumstances.[54] However, as he leaves, he learns that Barrett has committed suicide by hanging himself in custody and his shock is underlined by a track in to a close-up of his face accompanied by a dramatic flourish of music. As he leaves, Farr passes Eddy Stone, who has been called in to identify Barrett's body and the police question him about the case but learn nothing. The subsequent interchange between the two policemen reproduces the device employed in *Sapphire*, with Bridie revealing his naïve but bigoted heterosexual 'Puritanism', which the more liberal, worldly-wise Harris is quick to point out was also 'against the law at one time'.[55]

Farr meanwhile has returned home and Laura is quick to sense that in spite of the news about his career promotion, he seems preoccupied and worried. On the following day, as he goes to his chambers, Farr is stopped by Eddy, who gives him a photograph, posted to Barrett's address. In their subsequent interchange, Farr realises that Barrett was in fact trying to prevent such images of their relationship becoming public – trying to protect him, not, as he thought, blackmail him. In spite of Eddy's warning about a likely scandal, he enlists his help and resolves in his remorse to bring the blackmailer down. As Barrett's death becomes known, the film returns to the pub where he met Eddy and traces a network of possible suspects. Meanwhile in his bookshop, Harold Doe is shown to be devastated by the news. The mysterious, blind 'P.H.' and his companion Mickey are seen posting what appear to be blackmail letters. In the pub, the two-faced barman, while purporting friendship and bonhomie, is revealed as another version of the popular voice against homosexuality in his aggrieved rant:

> Sorry for 'em? Not me. It's always excuses. Every newspaper you pick up, it's always excuses. Environment, too much love as kids, too little

love as kids, they can't help it, it's part of nature – Well to my mind it's the weak, rotten part of nature. If they ever make it legal they may as well licence every other perversion.[56]

The film follows Eddy as he leaves the bar and encounters another regular, Henry the hairdresser (Charles Lloyd Pack), who, rumour has it, has just sold his thriving shop. Alerted by Eddy, Farr goes to the premises and tries to find out if Henry is also a blackmail victim, but Henry denies any knowledge: 'nature played me a dirty trick' he admits and indicates to Farr that he is leaving to start a new life in Canada. At this point, the film gives the first real sight of the mysterious blackmailer, referred to throughout as 'the sandy youth' (Derren Nesbitt), as he smashes up Henry's shop, causing the old man to collapse and die. Sandy is then seen reporting by phone to his mysterious blackmailing mastermind and this device is used as the film develops from this point to amplify the enigma of the real blackmailer's identity. Farr meanwhile makes another attempt to contact someone who is being blackmailed, a well-known stage actor, Tony Calloway (Denis Price), but meets with waspish evasion. When he returns home, Laura, who has read of Barrett's suicide in the paper, confronts her husband and gradually gets the truth from him. In a pivotal scene in the film, she refers to an earlier incident in Farr's life – his involvement with a youth called Stainer – and asks him if, in this instance, he was again 'the other man'. Farr admits he was and that he stopped seeing Barrett 'because I wanted him'. Powerfully performed by Bogarde, this admission, as Medhurst has perceptively argued, acknowledges a

> desire that British cinema fought so long to suppress . . . In a heterosexual context the directness of these words, their deeper resonances, would be striking enough; as the unleashing of homosexual desire it borders on the revolutionary. (1996: 128)

Laura concludes that there is no more room in his life for her. Farr is then telephoned by one of his wealthy clients, Lord Fullbrook, who asks to meet him at the mews studio of a mutual acquaintance, Peter Mandrake. When Farr arrives, he finds Calloway in attendance as well, and the three reveal themselves as homosexuals who are being blackmailed, and in the interests of avoiding scandal, they attempt to dissuade him from his mission to unmask the blackmailer. When Farr demurs, his own homosexuality is used as a lever against him, in spite of his claims that: 'I may share your instincts, but I've always resisted them.' When Mandrake suggests that it was precisely this self-denial that caused the suicide of Stainer (revealed as a student friend of Farr's at university) – and by implication Barrett – Farr punches him to the ground.[57] In spite of this, and his deteriorating relationship with Laura, Farr follows

'Because I wanted him': *Victim* (1961) (Courtesy of Steve Chibnall Archive)

further leads provided by Eddy. He meets Phip (Nigel Stock) where he works in an upmarket car showroom and through him tries to set up a deal with Sandy, who again discusses Farr on the phone with the faceless blackmailer. To warn Farr off, he is given a taste of what may be to come, when 'FARR IS QUEER' is crudely daubed on his garage doors and discovered by Laura and her priggish, bigoted brother. At this stage it appears likely that Laura will leave Farr.

Farr remains in contact with the police, who are conducting their own investigations into the blackmail. They arrest 'PH' and Mickey, who turn out to be red herrings – not blackmailers at all, but running a begging letter racket. Farr, following instructions from the blackmailers, goes to Doe's bookshop, where he encounters Miss Benham (Margaret Diamond), the spinsterish, middle-aged woman who helps in the shop. Unobserved, Farr exchanges his envelope of money for the negatives and Phip's letters. As he leaves, he sees Doe, who rounds on him, accusing him not only of the death of Barrett, but also for breaking up the relationship he had with 'Boy'. After Farr has gone, the watching police who have been watching the shop follow Miss Benham as she leaves with the money in her bag. She leads them to Sandy's flat, where he is revealed as the photographer, responsible for the pictures used to blackmail Barrett, Farr and many others. When the police and Farr arrive it appears that Phip had been pressuried into giving Sandy and Miss Benham the names of likely victims. Miss Benham is revealed as the prime blackmailer, bitter and vicious, with an almost psychotic hatred of homosexuals. At one point in these closing scenes, Sandy refers to her as 'a sort of cross between an avenging angel and a peeping Tom', and her almost hysterical reply 'They disgust me! When I found out about Mr Doe and the boy I felt physically ill. They're everywhere – everywhere you turn. The police do nothing – someone's got to make them pay for their filthy blasphemy' places her in a strikingly similar structural position to Mildred in *Sapphire*.[58] As the police take the pair away, they both do their best to threaten Farr with the publicity he can expect in court, Sandy, for example, suggesting the likely headline: '"Eminent lawyer's astonishing private life". A real ball for the National Press.' But Farr confirms that he will testify and reassures Harris, who also foresees that the pair will do their utmost in court to blacken Farr's reputation and career, echoing Wolfenden in his closing words that 'somebody once called this law against homosexuals "the blackmailer's charter"'. In its final scenes, the film moves to resolve the one remaining loose end of the narrative, as Farr returns home and is initially taken aback to find Laura there waiting for him. He tells her what has happened and that he is going to court to 'show the fault in the existing law', in her words: 'deliberately doing this to plead a case for a minority, knowing it will destroy you utterly'. He does not want her to share his impending public humiliation: 'I shall be called filthy names, my friends will lower their eyes, my enemies will say they always guessed', and asks her to leave him until the trial is over. However, he tells her that he loves her and that he will need her then. Apparently reconciled by this she leaves. Left alone, Farr crosses to the fire and in a final moment of fatalistic acceptance and calm, takes the photograph – which the viewer has never seen – from his pocket and drops it onto the flames and watches as it burns.

The critical consensus has been summarised 'as regarding *Victim* as a well-intentioned piece of special-pleading, successful in making its social point, but in the process of doing so becoming schematised and propagandist and there-fore aesthetically unsatisfactory' (Medhurst 1996: 124). The film attracted widespread publicity, most of which placed the film in the context of the *Wolfenden Report* and found its message and performance, especially Bogarde's, brave and worthwhile. Julian Holland, writing in *The Evening News*, saluted the bravura 'heavyweight' performance of Bogarde in a film that 'makes one want to stand up and cheer' (31 August 1961).[59] For Paul Dehn, however, it was Janet Green who deserved the plaudits, for her 'humane, observant and often very moving plea for tolerance towards the homosexual . . . Only a moron could listen unmoved' (*The Daily Mail*, 1 September 1961); and this was echoed in the *Monthly Film Bulletin* by 'PJD', who reluctantly confessed: 'Janet Green has dressed up her new subject, male inversion, in a cleverly designed Crime Club dust-jacket. Surprisingly, the device – though again schematic – works rather well' (September 1961).

The Guardian suggested that the film was 'an exceptionally good and rather brave sermon' (2 September 1961), and Nina Hibbin agreed: 'The film, in fact, constitutes a forthright attack on the harshness of British law in rela-tion to homosexual behaviour . . . a sobering picture of the way homosexual inclinations make a permanent nightmare of private lives' (*Daily Worker*, 2 September 1961). *The Times* concurred: '*Victim* may not say a great deal about this difficult problem, but what it does say is reasoned and just; and it does invite a compassionate consideration of this particular form of human bondage' (30 August 1961). Dilys Powell also singled the film out for significant comment:

> It is a thriller (and a good one) with characters which could not have been shown and on a subject which would have excited horror or ribaldry a few years ago. To treat the theme as a thriller may not be particularly bold, but to treat it at all was brave. (*The Sunday Times*, 3 September 1961)

While *Kine Weekly*, with its customary eye on box-office appeal argued: 'It should intrigue and hold both men and women . . . a plea for the revision of the law appertaining to the sexually and emotionally abnormal' (27 July 1961).

For other reviewers, the film warranted direct comment on Dearden and Relph's work. The *Monthly Film Bulletin*, against the grain of its established critical tenor with regard to Dearden, admitted that the film had 'something of his old slickness, pace and economy; it has the drive and staying-power of the better Pinewood product – still superficial, but less shock-punctuated than most, (September 1961). For Thomas Wiseman, 'one must admire the sheer acrobatic skill displayed by the producer, Michael Relph, and the director, Basil Dearden, in walking the tightrope between holier-than-thou hypocrisy and dirtier-than-them offensiveness' (*Daily Telegraph*, 1 September 1961). For the reviewer in *Time & Tide*:

> *Victim* discusses its subject (the blackmailing of homosexuals) with far more realism than I had dared hope . . . Relph and Dearden did not intend this as pure entertainment. Naturalness has sometimes been sacrificed to their desire to put across the humane point of view, even if this means turning some of the characters into mouthpieces and speechmakers instead of people talking in more or less everyday terms . . . If they had been just a little bit braver and had kept the faint note of apology out of their voices, they would have served their purpose better. (14 September 1961)

William Whitebait, writing in the *New Statesman* in a review entitled 'Silken Miseries', suggested:

> A British thriller about homosexuality? It sounds unlikely . . . Inverts must be whitewashed, or else the prejudice of the audiences might tell against them . . . So few English films have had the courage to come out plainly for anything that *Victim* deserves at least commendation. The pity is that while it may make us think, we can scarcely help thinking also of the film's own shortcomings. (8 September 1961)

One critic who demurred from this generally appreciative evaluation of the film was Derek Hill, writing in *The Financial Times*, who felt 'The dénouement is quite startlingly silly, and the male actors . . . all seem convinced that their appearance as homosexuals deserves some kind of humanitarian medal' (1 September 1961).[60] While the reviewer at *Films and Filming*, generally appreciative, felt the handling of the controversial theme too simplistic: 'It is easy to understand the urge to hit hard, so that even the Primrose League lady in the back row of the stalls can be in no doubt about the opinions being expressed; but it takes more than clear exposition of an argument to persuade people to accept it' (September 1961).

In subsequent academic accounts, the film has come to be regarded as an important 'landmark',[61] the first British post-war film to make explicit representation of masculine homosexuality; even though, with hindsight, as one recent writer has put it: '*Victim* tackled homosexuality in a fashion at once corny and compelling' (Howes 2006: 64).[62] Some fifteen years after its release, within the changing contexts which accompanied the rise of the Gay Liberation Movement, the film began to receive serious critical scrutiny which sought to evaluate this landmark status. Richard Dyer's carefully attuned analysis of the film set the pattern for subsequent commentaries. In this nuanced and probing analysis, Dyer suggests that *Victim* should be understood as a 'hegemonic project', promoting a particular view of its subject matter and crucially attempting to paper over the cracks and contradictions within the dominant ideology of the time. He identifies a number of key and unresolved contradictions in the film: the construction of the police and the law as impartial, the avoidance of any meaningful address to matters of social class, and the uneasy issues concerning the film's depiction of the 'nature' of homosexuality – as epitomised for instance, in Farr and Laura's childless relationship. He suggests that 'its overt message (that the law on homosexuality should be liberalized) and one of its covert messages (that homosexuality is a sickness) are both aspects of the dominant ideology concerning homosexuality in 1961' (1993: 86). On this basis, he outlines a range of imagined gay readings of the film, concluding with the suggestion that its principal social significance resides in the ways in which it encouraged gays to adopt 'less harshly self-oppressive' ways of thinking of themselves than had historically been the case.[63]

In an analysis which built on Dyer's work, Medhurst (as noted above) hails the film precisely for the moments when its plea for liberal tolerance is unable to contain actual homosexual desire – most obviously in Farr's 'confession' to Laura, and the 'indictment of repression', which he sees following from this. In these terms, and in spite of its overall ideological formation, he celebrates the 'moments of radicalism' which can be snatched from the film by gay spectators (1996: 131). Hill has added to these accounts, noting in his discussion not only the consonance between the film and the parameters established by Wolfenden, but also suggesting that it articulated a contemporary anxiety or paranoia about sexual identity: 'a kind of worry about heterosexuality itself, that lurking behind normal heterosexuality there may indeed be a repressed homosexuality not so very far behind' (1996: 93).

For these and other writers, *Victim* deserves its subsequent status as a cinematic 'landmark' in its attempt to articulate a position regarding law reform and homosexuality. It is also perhaps the summit of Dearden and Relph's achievements in the context of the 'social problem film' and they never returned to work again in this format.[64] Even the most cursory comparison of the unbending moral messages and associated settings and characters which inhabit the worlds of *The Blue Lamp* or *I Believe in You*, with the more fluid ambiguities at stake in *Sapphire* and *Victim*, reveals significant shifts and mutations related not only to the changing worlds of cinema but also beyond this, in the transforming nature of British society itself. It is possible to argue that British cinema (and television) did and does continue to make social problem films, but they have been made in a style and register unfamiliar to the pioneering – and at the time adventurous – post-war work of Dearden and Relph.[65] From this point on, although their inclinations would continue occasionally to engage with melodramas focused on ethical dilemmas – embodied, for instance, in *Life for Ruth*, *The Mind Benders* or *A Place to Go*, the 'sociological' mission in their work and the associated drive to use film to educate and ask questions of audiences as well as entertain them, had reached a 'natural' if not inevitable historical end.

NOTES

1. See *Screen International* (3 February 1979: 17), a report on the National Film Theatre's British Cinema Series tribute to Dearden and Relph.
2. On Barron Mays' pioneering work on delinquency in Liverpool – hugely influential on *Violent Playground* – see Mays (1952, 1954, 1959, 1963).
3. The work of the Epps, published in 1951 and 1954, was exemplary, and the field is summarised in Cowie et al. (1968).
4. For an interesting contemporary view of the West London riots, see Malcolm (1958), and for a later overview of the 'race' issue in this period, see Waters (1997). For influential examinations into male homosexuality in the period, see the studies by Westwood (1953, 1960), the latter carrying a foreword by John Wolfenden.
5. The Wolfenden Committee reported on two problematics of sexuality troubling British society, homosexuality and prostitution, with Dearden and Relph only addressing the former in *Victim*. A handful of films tackled the matter of prostitution, and Melanie Williams (2006) examines *The Flesh is Weak* (d. D. Chaffey, 1957) and *Passport to Shame* (d. A. Rakoff, 1959).
6. Winning the Best British Film award for 1951.
7. In February 1948, PC Nat Edgar was shot by a twenty-two-year old army deserter named Donald Thomas. The film appears to be based on this incident and on the case of Alec de Antiquis a father of six children, shot dead in Charlotte Street attempting to stop three armed robbers escaping from a jewellery shop raid in April 1947.
8. Willis had written *Good Time Girl* (d. MacDonald, 1948) for Gainsborough – with Sydney and Muriel Box. For his account of the research he undertook for *The Blue Lamp*, its subsequent development for a stage play and then the long-running series *Dixon of Dock Green* for BBC television (1955–76), see Willis (1991).

9. Barr notes that Balcon had been keen to make a film about the police and their work as early as 1939, an idea snubbed by the Metropolitan Police at the time (1977: 189). Harper and Porter also note that the script was passed to Clarke 'much to Willis's chagrin' and that Clarke 'fundamentally altered its structures of feeling' (2003: 60). Chibnall has suggested that the decision to replace Willis with Clarke may have been based on political expediency – Willis was a former editor of the Young Communist League's newspaper – and the film would rely heavily on co-operation from Scotland Yard and the Metropolitan Police (1997: 138–9).

10. With the script submitted to the BBFC in April 1949. It was passed without cuts with an 'A' certificate in November of that year. See Chibnall (1997: 140) and Aldgate (1992: 68–9).

11. Balcon discusses the casting of Warner in this role, indicating that his earlier performance in *The Captive Heart* (1946) had been influential in the decision (1969: 175–6). In this film Warner's old soldier had played a similar fatherly role to Hanley's 'young' un'.

12. The film edits out a number of the scenes dealing with Lewis's home and his violent treatment of his wife, so he is seen only as he is arrested and taken away. See *Final Shooting Script* (11–13).

13. Bogarde was at this time on contract to Rank and had worked with Dearden before the war as 'his rather inept Assistant Stage Manager at the "Q" Theatre'. Dearden sent for him and offered him the part of 'the snivelling little killer. Neurotic, conceited, gets the rope in the end'. Bogarde remembers his work with Dearden on this and other films with affection and some significance (1979: 159–60).

14. The contrast between these two worlds is heightened in terms of cinematic style as Dearden and lighting cameraman Gordon Dines use a much darker, *film noir* approach for the scenes showing Riley, especially those in his bedsit with Diana.

15. In an interesting reversal in this film, Lee's character does not chain-smoke but incessantly sucks sweets in his attempt to give up smoking. He does resort to smoking at the conclusion of the film, however.

16. The *Final Shooting Script* indicates at this stage: 'Tom sits down in order to examine one of the guns. The weight and the feel of it in his hand give him an unhealthy excitement' (43). Medhurst suggests of Bogarde's performance in these and subsequent scenes: 'It is hard not to see his real crime as eroticism rather than murder' (1986: 348). See also Chibnall (1997: 143–4).

17. The screen relationship of Warner and Henson had developed through *The Captive Heart* and *Train of Events* (1949).

18. The ownership of the gun is never revealed in the film, although the girl does eventually lead the police to where she found it. It may have been Murphy's, but Riley has his own gun in the final scenes of the film.

19. More contentiously, he suggests that the scene manages to avoid the 'frozen theatricality', stereotypes and the 'petrified technique' which he associates with aspects of Dearden's post-Ealing work.

20. Interestingly, not only did the film become the basis for the long running TV series featuring a George Dixon brought back to life, it was also later used by the TV playwright Arthur Ellis for *The Black and Blue Lamp* (1988), which critically examined changing public perceptions of the police in Britain from the 1950s to the late 1980s. See Rolinson (2004).

21. *The Naked City* (d. J. Dassin, 1948), made in Britain by Twentieth Century Fox, was most often cited in comparison. John McCarten, reviewing the film in the *New Yorker*, admitted that his 'long exposure to Hollywood interpretations of the manoeuvres of the FBI and the local cops has left me too numbed to appreciate the sort of stationhouse under examination here' and found the first half of the film to be 'a cinematic miracle – a study of policemen without the intrusion of any violence' (20 January 1951). Chibnall in his later assessment compares the film with *Detective Story* (d. Wyler, 1951), *City Across the River* (d. Shane, 1949) and *Gun Crazy* (d. Lewis, 1950) (1997: 144–5).

22. After the quartet of films about the ups and downs of a working-class family called the Huggetts, directed by Ken Annakin and featuring Jack Warner and Kathleen Harrison (1947–49).

23. The intervening films were *Cage of Gold* and *Pool of London*, both of which had employed Whittingham as scriptwriter. Chibnall notes that the film is 'another recruitment poster, but a subtler and less strident one than *The Blue Lamp* (1997: 145).

24. *Court Circular: Experiences of a London Probation Officer*, first published by Michael Joseph in 1950, with a revised Pan 'tie-in' edition published in 1955. Francis Martin Sewell Stokes (1902–79) was a versatile English novelist, biographer, playwright, broadcaster and screenwriter. The novel recounts his experiences from 1941 to 1945, when having failed to get wartime service as a War Reserve Policeman, he joined the Probation Office attached to the Bow Street magistrates court in London. With his brother, he wrote the play *Oscar Wilde* on which the subsequent film (d. Ratoff, 1959) was based. He later acted as screenplay adviser on *The Loneliness of the Long Distance Runner* (d. Richardson, 1962) and *Tom Jones* (d. Richardson, 1963).

25. 'The Colonial Office, finding itself short of colonies had made a lot of cuts – I was one of them.' Unlike other Dearden and Relph films, however, on this occasion redundancy does not lead to crime, but to public service.

26. In fact, to the modern viewer, the combination of Cecil Parker and Celia Johnson (even though she takes him to task for his pomposity and dress), in particular in the manner of their speaking, seems to imply a cut-glass, upper-class approach to probation work. One reviewer, praising Celia Johnson's performance, was moved to remark that 'she could play Desdemona in tweeds' (*Daily Mail*, 7 March 1952).

27. This is signalled when to Mr Dove's approval, Phipps looks through the album of pictures of old Mrs Crockett in her youth.

28. In these and other scenes throughout the film, as Durgnat has suggested, 'The sullen, electric presence of young Joan Collins dominates the whole film precisely

because her grace, vigour and insolent *savoir-vivre* validate her character's subversive attitudes as the result not of being "misled", as the script imagines, but of a culture, of truths and experiences, from which the film is insulated' (1970: 138). These scenes are shot in a shadowy, noirish manner in contrast with much of the film.

29. A version of this statement appeared in *Films and Filming* as part of the publicity for the film which had been selected as 'Film of the Month', and the following additional copy was appended: 'These officers deal with children under 17 years of age who have committed a minor offence, who admit that offence, and who have never come to the notice of the Police before. Over 92 per cent of children handled in this way have not committed a second crime' (January 1958).

30. Royle, in his biography of Kennaway, indicates that during the summer of 1956, as a result of his earlier success with his novel *Tunes of Glory*, the author was commissioned to write an original script for Relph, who was then still at Ealing. This was Kennaway's introduction to writing for the screen (1983: 127). He would later work with Dearden and Relph on *The Mind Benders* (1963). It was reported in the film press that Dearden and Relph wanted to make a film in the Industrial North and assigned the young novelist Kennaway to work on it: 'He spent a week living in the dirt and doss-houses of Liverpool and learned about the city's juvenile liaison scheme which is run by a special branch of the police force' (*Films and Filming*, September 1957).

31. This was the first major role for Heywood, a former professional beauty queen who had modelled under the name of Violet Pretty. Critics were largely unimpressed by 'just a pretty girl trying out an Irish accent' (*Films and Filming*, March 1958).

32. On the following day, under the headline 'Tactless to film in Notting Hill', *The Times* reported the comments of G. H. Elvin, secretary of the industry trade union: 'His Union would object to anything likely to make the recent trouble start all over again' (11 October 1958: 3).

33. Complaints about *Sapphire* were forwarded from The Council of the Citizens of East London and the Mayor of Kensington, both seeking abandonment of the production (Aldgate 1995: 130).

34. Dearden and Relph had obliquely featured this theme in their earlier *Pool of London* (1951), but it forms a much more substantial theme in the narrative and setting of *Sapphire*. At the time, Janet Green had a modest reputation as a writer of crime fiction and drama, having penned the plays *Murder Mistaken* and *Matilda Shouted Fire* (*The Times*, 5 November 1952 and 2 March 1962).

35. Reports of clashes, and so-called 'race riots', between black and white people started in late May 1958 in Notting Hill and also outside London in Nottingham. In London, these reached a peak in the first week of September with over 140 arrests (*The Times*, 4 September 1958) and calls for a curfew in the Notting Hill area in an attempt to reduce the tension and nightly outbreaks of fighting. So serious was the situation that the Home Secretary, R. A. Butler, held crisis talks with the Prime Minister, local MPs and the Commissioner of the Metropolitan

Police (*The Times*, 4 September 1958). Although it was not fully acknowledged at the time, the series of violent attacks were instigated by gangs of young white men, including Teddy Boys who did not live in the Notting Hill area, often in response to the racist 'Keep Britain White' campaigns of local Fascists (including Oswald Mosley). These events sparked a series of long-running debates over racial prejudice, immigration and the social conditions of immigrant communities in Britain.

36. Earlier in the year, Relph was reported in the *Daily Express*: 'We always wanted to make a film about the growing colour problem in London. And during the riots we spent a lot of time around the Notting Hill trouble spots, Now Janet Green is writing a script and we begin filming next month' (10 September 1958).

37. Harry Waxman was the Director of Photography, with Philip Green providing the musical score performed by Johnny Dankworth and his orchestra. As part of the pre-release publicity (reminiscent of the *Frieda* campaign), for two weeks before the release date billboards and advertisements carried the question 'Who is Sapphire?'

38. As Tarr has argued in her study of the film: '*Sapphire* is firmly marked by the point of view of the white middle-class males (the police protagonists) who order the film's investigation both narratively and visually' (1985: 56–7). Len Mosley headlined his review of the film as a 'Psychological Strip-tease' (*Daily Express*, 8 May 1959).

39. In a recent interview, Cameron remembers that he was heavily made up for this part: 'They were trying to get my skin as dark as possible to get the contrast' (Guha and Brunsdon 2009 forthcoming).

40. The completed film sequence here is a much edited version of that outlined in the script, which included a scene with one of the girls from the club as a street-walker promising to help Johnnie as he leaves, and also more extended action involving the Teds when they attack the shop premises through which he has been allowed to escape (*Final Shooting Script*: 58, a, b, c, d.). The result was a compromise reached with the censors who had questioned 'the desirability of showing the escaping negro being beaten up by "Teddy Boys", and requested 'less emphasis' on the sequence (Aldgate, 1995: 131).

41. This troubling scene was also softened at the request of the censors, through the expedient of reducing the volume on the soundtrack (Aldgate 1995: 131).

42. In a recent discussion of actress Yvonne Mitchell and British cinema in the 1950s, Williams has argued that her distinctive star persona of 'suffering' 'sits uncomfortably with the "hegemonic project" of the social problem film genre' (2002: 38).

43. The pram, of course, contains a wooden doll with one of its legs missing; the piece of evidence David picked up on the Heath. Although David is apparently reconciled with his father at this point – as Mr Harris indicates that he knew that David thought it was he who had murdered Sapphire – the full extent of the family's knowledge of and involvement in Mildred's crime is not fully resolved. Did Mr Harris, for instance, help with the transportation of the body?

44. Later in the year, however, *The Times* reported on the positive praise for the film when it was released in America (5 November 1959).
45. See also Hill (1985).
46. Production began immediately after they had completed *The Secret Partner*, released in January 1961. Dearden's shooting script is copiously annotated with many amendments to dialogue as well as his customary notes for camera position and blocking. Many of the pages are revised replacement 'pinks' dated mid-February to mid-March 1961.
47. Robertson provides an important and insightful account of the issues at stake in this process of cautious negotiation and interchange, including the suggestion that the film's ending was rewritten by Bogarde himself (1989: 119–26). See also Trevelyan (1973: 119/183) and the detailed account given in Aldgate (1995: 133–6). The full correspondence concerning the film is available at the BBFC archive. Under pressure from recent Continental releases and the general discussion following Wolfenden, the film press in 1958 had speculated:

> The British Censor may shortly be asked to make an important decision – whether or not to approve the showing in Britain of films making honest drama of homosexuality, a subject which the British Board of Film Censors has always regarded as taboo . . . Whether the recent publication of the Wolfenden Committee's report will influence the British Board of Film Censors remains to be seen. (*Films and Filming*, May 1958)

48. Post-war tabloid papers and their equivalents (for instance, *The Sunday Pictorial*) regularly contributed to the spiralling moral panics concerning male homosexuality with lurid exposé stories (see Pearce 1973: 284–301). From the early 1950s onwards, the broadsheets reacted by adopting a more qualified, liberal stance in favour of decriminalisation, in line with The Wolfenden Committee (established 1954, Report 1957). Relph was later to recall: 'Homosexuality was something we accepted completely and it seemed to us absolutely preposterous that the law was the way it was. So when we were thinking of a social problem we could deal with after *Sapphire*, this seemed a natural one because the *Wolfenden Report* had just been published and it was very much in the news, and topical' (quoted in Bourne 1996: 158). The scriptwriters were undoubtedly aware of this climate of opinion and press reportage and may also have drawn on trials such as that in 1954 involving Montagu, Wildeblood and Pitt-Rivers (see Wildeblood 1955), and books such as *The Heart in Exile*, first published in 1953, a novel of London's homosexual 'underground' written by Rodney Garland (the pseudonym of Adam de Hedegus) and published in paperback in the year of the film's release. See Houlbrook and Waters (2006) for relevant discussion.
49. Durgnat argues that the detective story formula is used by Dearden and Relph to 'lure us on a Cook's tour round homosexual London' (1970: 196).
50. In his subsequent autobiography, and in a television interview that followed the film's release (reproduced on *Victim* Network DVD 7952428, see also *The Daily Mail*, 19 August 1961), Bogarde clearly indicates that given the nature of his established and developing star image, the role was a risky one for him at

the time, but one he was later to regard as a key moment in his career: 'I had achieved what I had longed to do for so long, to be in a film which disturbed, educated, and illuminated as well as merely giving entertainment' (1979: 242). Dearden, who had coincidentally bought and moved into Bogarde's old house (Beel House, Amersham) at that time, approached Bogarde during the 1960 Christmas break with the outline script and offered him the part of Farr. At this casting stage, there is a suggestion that Michael Redgrave was approached first for the role, but in a subsequent interview, Michael Relph was to confirm: 'Dirk was always our first choice. He was perfect for *Victim*. It was very courageous of him to play the gay barrister. Until then his career had been built on being an attractive heterosexual matinee idol' (quoted in Bourne 1996: 158–9). According to these sources, casting the role of Farr's wife was also problematic, but Sylvia Syms, after unspecified others had turned it down, accepted it 'readily and with warm comprehension' (Bogarde 1979: 241). It was reported at the time that Bogarde's character was made 'only a potential homosexual' on the insistence of Rank: 'The studios are afraid that their top contract star for fifteen years would lose his female following if he played an honest queer' (*Films and Filming*, April 1961). Star Bogarde and producer Relph both fired off letters to the periodical putting the matter straight: that Rank had no influence over AFM and that the part had been written before Bogarde was cast, and no changes were demanded by either star or studio (*Films and Filming*, May 1961).

51. Musical composition was again by Philip Green; while lighting cameraman Otto Heller and art director Alex Vetchinsky provided the monochrome atmosphere and realism.

52. Murphy notes in his account that the relationship appears as 'one of those repressed middle-class marriages which haunt British cinema', but that it is marked by a 'disturbing reversal' in that it is not the woman's but the man's unfulfilled desires which constitute the narrative enigma (1992: 41).

53. The 'H' word is not used until almost a third of the way into the film (25 minutes into the 96-minute running time). As Hill notes: 'much of the film is concerned with delaying the identification of homosexuality or surprising us with revelations of homosexuality in characters of whom we didn't expect it' (1986: 92).

54. As further clues for the viewer at this point, Harris, with impeccable politeness, also asks Farr if he knew that 'as many as ninety per cent of all blackmail cases have a homosexual origin'; and as Farr turns to leave, spells out his – and the film's view – that: 'there's no doubt that a law which sends homosexuals to prison offers unlimited opportunities for blackmail'.

55. Thus echoing the juxtaposed positions of Hazard and Learoyd vis-à-vis race and racism; although in *Victim* the film presents a version of the opposition between the 'popular' prejudiced and the 'reasonable' discourses characteristic of press coverage and public attitudes towards male homosexuality and Wolfenden recommendations.

56. This dialogue appears on a pink replacement page (43) in the *Final Shooting Script* dated 10 February 1961 and may have been included in response to BBFC

commentary concerning the need to ensure 'balance' in terms of the film's cover-age of perspectives regarding homosexuality and the law.

57. Medhurst also provides an insightful analysis of this scene, suggesting that in it: 'The film becomes an indictment of repression, an attack on the refusal to acknowledge the desire that Farr/Bogarde has in the previous scene finally affirmed' (1984: 33).

58. Kemp interestingly argues that the film codes the blackmailers as gay: 'a chunky leather-boy with pictures of naked Greek athletes on the walls of his room and an embittered middle-aged spinster whose hysterical aversion to gays invites us to read her as a lesbian in denial' (2005: 10).

59. Many reviewers saw the film as a courageous and accomplished *tour de force* for Bogarde and singled out his performance for special praise and recognition. For Leonard Mosley, writing in *The Daily Express*, who earlier in the year had anticipated the film as 'the most controversial ever made by a British studio – would Lord Rank really dare?' (8 July 1961), 'Bogarde wins "Forbidden Theme" Gamble' (30 August 1961); and Alexander Walker saw the film as an 'acting triumph for Bogarde' (*Evening Standard*, 31 August 1961).

60. When the film was released in America the Motion Picture Association withheld the Production Code Seal 'because sex aberration can only be suggested, not actually spelled out' (*Variety*, 20 December 1961). *Time* started its review of the film with the question 'A Plea for Perversion?', and ended with the homophobic crescendo: 'Everybody in the picture who disapproves of homosexuals proves to be an ass, a dolt or sadist. Nowhere does the film suggest that homosexuality is a serious (but often curable) neurosis that attacks the biological basis of life itself. "I can't help the way I am" says one of the sodomites in this movie. "Nature played me a dirty trick". And the scriptwriters, whose psychiatric information is clearly coeval with the statute they dispute, accept this sick-silly self-delusion as a medical fact' (23 February 1962).

61. This status is confirmed by a number of writers in the essays collected in Griffiths (2006).

62. Following the partial decriminalisation of male homosexuality in 1967, some film critics began to hope that 'at last homosexuality is going to be given genuine adult treatment in the cinema', and sarcastically looked back on the '*Victim* era', 'in which the good guy had been a homo once, was sorry about it, and hoped he never would be again' (*Films and Filming*, November 1967).

63. For evidence of the affirmation that *Victim* provided for gay viewers in the early 1960s, see the remarkable 'Victim Letters' collected in Bourne (1996).

64. There was brief mention in the film press that, following *Victim*, Dearden and Relph had acquired the film rights to Simon Raven's *Feathers of Death*, 'one of the best novels with a homosexual theme' (*Films and Filming*, April 1962).

65. At this time, Michael Relph laid out his conception of a responsible producer and the 'idea of freedom' as it applied to the making of films in *Films and Filming* (September 1961).

6

Ethical Dilemmas

Frieda (1947); *The Gentle Gunman* (1952); *Life for Ruth* (1962); *The Mind Benders* (1963)

> I should like to see a detailed breakdown of the different kinds of difficult moral situations in which human beings, living as they do in societies, find themselves, because in my opinion too much attention has been paid in contemporary ethical writing to the easy, rule-guided, moral situation . . . Such an analysis will require sympathetic treatment of real moral problems considered in detail, and it will require a proper analysis of the concepts of choice and decision – active moral concepts, rather than the passive, spectatorlike, concepts of good and right. Secondly, I would like to see a proper discussion of the arguments that go to resolve moral dilemmas . . . This will entail saying what constitutes a good and a bad moral reason for making a moral decision, and so will bring the moral philosopher out from his corner, where I think he has been too long, and back into the familiar but forgotten Socratic position of trying to answer the ever-present but ever-changing question: how should a man live? (E. J. Lemmon 1962: 158)

Often regarded as social problem films, the four films discussed in this chapter are distinctive variants, separated out by virtue of their attention to individual characters confronting acute ethical decisions and embodying dilemmas rather than problems shared across society. They represent a series of substantial emotional melodramas concerning nationalism and post-war identity; the politics of terrorism; the limits to religious belief; and the ethics of modern psychology. They offer further insights into Dearden and Relph's multifaceted fascination with the complexities of their contemporary social existence, in their exploration of the moral balances and contradictions involved in national revenge or forgiveness after a period of 'total war'; the limits to political extremism; and the place of personal belief, moral values and social responsibility within an era of scientific and technological advancement. Richards believes that these films demonstrate Dearden and Relph's deep liberal convictions and their hatred of prejudice, intolerance and violence, and in differing ways and contexts, each of these four films seeks to test and mark out the limits to tolerance (1997: 26–7). As such, they stand partly in contrast to the social problem films in that while they acknowledge the obstinacy of the 'problems' at their heart, they remain distanced from the easy solutions of the liberal sensibility and its faith in legal reform or appeal to the traditional values of fair play.

FRIEDA (1947)

> They already have to their credit that memorable production '*The Captive Heart*'. With a few more films of the same intelligence and production calibre as 'Frieda' they will be entitled to take their place alongside such Hollywood maestros as Alfred Hitchcock, William ('*Best Years Of Our Lives*') Wyler, King Vidor, Fritz Lang, John Ford and the rest of the experts out there who are wondering these days how much greater a menace the British film-making industry can overcome. (Ewart Hodgson, *News of the World*, 8 July 1947)

> As is the case in more than one Dearden 'social problem' film, the problem turns out to be a single woman. (Charlotte Brunsdon and Rachel Moseley, 1997: 136)

Frieda was the play that inaugurated Ronald Millar's career. It was first staged at the Westminster Theatre early in May 1946, and a television version was broadcast by the BBC in July featuring some of the stage players.[1] With the war barely over and the devastation that had resulted from the conflict still very much in daily evidence, the very idea of thinking about Germans and Germany in terms other than the hated enemy was to court controversy. Relph was responsible for the stage design of the play and he drew Balcon's attention to the cinematic possibilities it contained. Attracted by the way that *Frieda* fitted into Ealing's developing social agenda under his steward-ship; Balcon promptly bought the film rights and assigned Dearden to direct. As Millar later noted, he was contracted to write the screenplay, but as this was his first attempt at writing for the screen, he was paired with the more experienced Ealing scenario editor Angus McPhail (1993: 125–6). In this, as Ramsden has suggested, 'Millar thus contributed storyline and essential elements of plot and character, but the collective involvement of Relph, Balcon, McPhail and Dearden made this a classic case of Ealing teamwork' (2006:

312). In another significant sense, and as Durgnat has observed, this was the first film in which Dearden and Relph's 'moralising bent comes up against a topic which at the time was still controversial' (1966: 28).

Production was not delayed; the shooting script for the film is dated August 1946, and indicates that filming commenced in September, with three weeks devoted to location filming (in Woodstock, Oxfordshire) and ten weeks given over to studio work at Ealing. Filming was completed by January 1947 and the film opened in London at the Odeon, Leicester Square, early in July.[2]

At the casting stage, a rather revealing problem – given the theme of the film – was encountered. Flora Robson had been approached to play the forceful and apparently implacable Nell, the politician with an intellectual hatred of Germans; the key decision then was who might play the German girl, Frieda (in counterpoint to Nell). Millar remembered: 'the war was still an open wound and even if a German actress were to be granted a work permit, which was highly unlikely even by a Socialist government, we had seen no German artists on film since before the war' (1993: 125). Ealing tested 'several admirable English actresses with carefully coached German accents' but found this solution unsatisfactory.[3] Balcon, Dearden and Relph flew to Sweden to test Mai Zetterling (who spoke little English at that time), and she was quickly contracted.[4] In translating the original three-act play from stage to screen, Millar and McPhail developed the stage version in a number of ways, 'while Dearden and Relph darkened the piece in their design and direction' (Ramsden 2006: 313).[5]

The film opens in war-torn Cracow, in no-man's land in March 1945. In a shattered church, with the carnage of war raging, a priest conducts a hurried marriage ceremony. The young couple escape to the west by train and the film introduces Robert Dawson (David Farrar) an escaped RAF officer prisoner of war, and his new 'bride', Frieda Mansfeld (Mai Zetterling), a young German nurse who has assisted in Robert's escape and for whom this marriage represents her own way out of the war. Robert tries to reassure her that she has 'nothing to be frightened of in England', and the film cuts to a number of images of his home in Denfield, an 'ordinary town' full of 'ordinary everyday people'.[6] Frieda, however, remains apprehensive. With the camera moving into a big close-up, she questions, 'Can they like me – a German?' Prior to their arrival at Denfield station, the film shows a montage of local newspaper headlines announcing the return of Robert with his German bride, hinting at the differences of opinion which await them.

Their arrival at Robert's home (to the modern eye, almost as if he is accompanied by a Martian) does not altogether dispel Frieda's anxieties; and while outwardly Robert's mother (Barbara Everest) and the old housekeeper Edith (Gladys Henson) seem welcoming, there is a cool reserve in the response of Robert's Aunt Nell (Flora Robson). Several references to the war underline the tension that Frieda experiences. These develop as she insists on separate bedrooms, as the Protestant marriage ceremony did not encompass her Catholic faith. Judy (Glynis Johns) is introduced as Robert's sister-in-law, who tells him that Alan, also in the RAF, has been killed, shot down over Germany. Frieda also reveals her loss, when, with Robert's mother, she unpacks a picture of her parents, killed in an air-raid in Germany, earlier in the war.

Two interwoven strands of narrative develop this initial phase of the film and the introduction of Frieda into the household and community. The first features Nell, standing for Labour as parliamentary candidate in the local by-election. Gossip in the community and the election committee suggests that Nell's trenchantly anti-German views will be compromised by Frieda – 'the German girl' – and this turns out to be the case. However, when challenged on the hustings, Nell distances herself from Frieda, affirming her belief in the collective responsibility of the German nation, and the guilt of all Germans, including Frieda, in the monstrous crimes of war.[7] As she says to Frieda afterwards: 'war isn't a football match Frieda, when it's over you don't shake hands and wish your enemy luck in years to come'; although she also suggests that when the war is over, time will heal things.[8] Second, when Robert returns to take up his old job as schoolmaster, his relationship with Frieda leads to some of the pupils boycotting his class and this involves his young cousin Tony (Ray Jackson), who lives in the family home and attends the class, as the butt of schoolboy jibes and a fight. In the face of this Robert resigns his post.

After her public denouncement of the Germans and Frieda, Nell is elected to parliament. Judy, who has been Frieda's friend, leaves with Nell to work as her secretary, as it becomes clear that she cannot live in the house with Robert, who reminds her so much of Alan. In fact, old Mrs Dawson at this point confesses to Judy that Frieda is not what she wanted for Robert and how she had hoped that in time, Robert and Judy might have married. In response to these developments, Frieda asks Robert to postpone any plans for the wedding and to wait and see.

With Nell and Judy no longer at home, the film now portrays Robert and Frieda helping on the local farm, 'making the best of things' with healthy hard work – in images that would grace any Austro-German *Heimat* film; and in a letter to Judy, Mrs Dawson describes how Frieda is becoming a valued part of the household and accepted gradually into the community. This organic 'healing' process of outdoor labour and time passing is interrupted, however, by one of the most powerful sequences in the film. This follows Robert and Frieda on an innocent visit to the local cinema. Here, as they are about to leave, juxtaposed against the end of the romantic feature, they are unexpectedly confronted by newsreel images which graphically document: 'Horror in our Time' scenes from the liberation of the Belsen concentration camp, 'atrocious deeds committed in the name of Germany'. The static close-ups of Frieda's shocked face, intercut with the stark newsreel images as the commentary reaches its climax and gives way to a hymn of remembrance, acts as a sudden jolt to conscience and narrative. And the scenes which immediately follow, on the steps, as they leave the cinema, shot in shadowy, heavily *noir* style, when Frieda admits to knowing of such places ('I knew, we all knew . . . Some of us were inside them'),[9] reinforces the power of this sequence. In a moment, all the work and progress made in their past months is undone by this salutary encounter. They return home, and Robert, as if in a perverse attempt to make amends, proposes immediate marriage, only to be turned down again by the agonised Frieda. She thanks him tenderly for asking, and promises to try to put the events of the evening behind them.

The first peacetime Christmas sees Nell and Judy returning to Denfield for the Christmas Eve celebrations. Amidst the general celebrations, Mrs Dawson confirms to Nell that 'Frieda is one of us now'. Judy appears to have accepted that Alan is dead and that Robert can be no substitute, and she dances with a soldier (Barry Letts), recently returned from the war and badly scarred. His father confides to Nell that his injuries resulted from his treatment in a concentration camp. Seven months after their arrival in Denfield, Frieda and Robert appear to be 'over the worst', accepted and to all outward appearances genuinely in love. Robert is about to return to his old job at the prep school. Frieda looks forward to the New Year, and on the bridge over the river on their way home, Robert again asks her to marry him, on the forthcoming New Year's Day. Hesitantly, she accepts, and the household is thrown into a whirl of preparations. Judy in a selfless gesture offers Frieda her wedding dress. Time, it would appear, has healed all.

However, as Ramsden suggests, 'The second half of the film challenges the comforting idea that time is all that is needed to bring enchantment' (2006: 314). As carol singers leave the Dawson house, they make way for the sudden arrival of Richard (Albert Lieven), Frieda's brother. He arrives in a Polish uniform and in heavily accented English explains that he was able to move from the Afrika Corps to the Polish Army because of his birthplace. Frieda is overjoyed to see him, as she had thought him dead. In one clever scene shortly after this, Robert enters the shot at the top of the stairs, intervening between Frieda and Ricky.[10] On New Year's Eve, at the rehearsal for the Catholic wedding service, Judy asks Nell if she despises everyone for accepting Frieda. Nell replies in the contrary, intimating that 'it's our strength and our weakness', but she confirms that she wishes that the wedding was not taking place. During this rehearsal, Ricky gives Frieda his wedding present, a swastika on a chain, which she accepts with a look of frozen horror on her face, reminiscent of the scene in the cinema. As Nell, Judy and the priest travel back to Denfield, he quizzes Nell on her views – 'You believe that the good German doesn't exist?' She responds that all Germans are the same and that there is an evil kind of 'essence of Germanism . . . inborn, in the blood'. In the other car, adding to Frieda's disquiet, Ricky mocks the anti-invasion road-blocks they pass: 'They wouldn't have stopped our tanks for long'. When they are alone Ricky congratulates Frieda – 'You have succeeded where Germany failed, you have conquered the English people'. In response, she asks why he gave her the swastika, reminding him that Hitler is dead. In a powerful inter-change which juxtaposes close-ups of their faces, she distances herself from 'his' Germany and from him. His insistence 'that all Germans are one' echoes Nell's earlier comment, but Frieda also realises that he remains fundamentally committed to the Nazi cause and to war: 'You want it again', she accuses. Frieda pleads with him to stay in England to learn the ways of peace, and that she wants children who will grow up not to die in war and, in a final act of rejection, she returns the swastika.

Having exposed Ricky for what he really is, the narrative of the film quickly moves to resolve the problem he now represents – the 'bad' German[11] – and this happens in the crowded bar of the local inn, where Robert meets him. By chance, they also see Jim Merrick, the scarred soldier, who identifies Ricky as the guard from the Brandenburg concentration camp who five years ago caused his torture and disfigurement. Robert is at first reluctant to accept this and in the increasingly hostile bar asks for time alone with Ricky to get at the truth. In the billiards room, he refuses to let Ricky escape, and as he does so, Ricky's swastika is revealed. Robert's first concern is for Frieda and whether she knows of her brother's real nature. Ricky replies that she does, and that as Germans they are joined 'as one' by 'loyalty, faith and blood'; and he taunts Robert, claiming that this blood-line will be present in their children. A violent and energetically choreographed fight ensues as Ricky attempts to escape again, but he is overpowered by Robert, who in a final act rips the swastika from the unconscious Ricky's neck.[12]

These events act as the catalyst for the climax of the film. Robert returns to confront Frieda, whom Judy has been trying to comfort. Without a word, he drops Ricky's swastika in Frieda's lap and turns on his heel in an act of rejection. He admits to Nell that she was right, and that he now accepts 'her gospel'. Frieda witnesses this and although Judy, as a voice of conscience and reason, speaks out against Nell, a distraught Frieda walks past Nell and out of the house. Nell, as if in an act of separation, draws the curtains after she has gone. As in a number of other moments in the film, John Greenwood's musical score melodramatically highlights the mounting drama. Unable to

Dearden directs as Ricky and Robert fight it out, in *Frieda* (1947) (Courtesy of Steve Chibnall Archive)

reconcile herself, Nell comes to her senses and alerts Robert. Frieda meanwhile has gone through the snow to the bridge, where she accepted his offer of marriage. Apparently deaf to the shouts of Robert, who has pursued her, she throws herself from the bridge and into the icy waters below. As she sinks below the surface she hears voices: Robert wishing she were dead; Ricky's stentorian Nazi voice insisting that 'All Germans are one'; and Nell's accusing 'you're a German and that's all that counts', overlaid with the priest's voice intoning 'till death do you part'.

Robert, however, arrives in time to rescue her and carries her back to the house where she is revived.[13] The self-recriminations of the family begin, led by Mrs Dawson who feels responsible for not facing up to Frieda's predicament since she arrived, and even Edith is now able to see the truth – that all Germans are not bad. In relief, they praise Nell for warning Robert of Frieda's suicidal intentions. But Nell confesses that she in fact let Frieda go, as it seemed the 'one sure way out for all of us'. She accepts now that she was wrong, and it is left to Nell to voice the great truth of the film in her final lines: 'No matter who they are, no matter what they have done, you can't treat human beings as less than human without becoming less than human yourself.'[14] And it is on this note that the film ends, with Frieda embracing Robert in a final and presumably permanent act of loving union.[15]

In spite of its melodramatic and heightened *noir* overtones, as Lovell has argued, '*Frieda*, then, is almost a public service film' (1984: 31). Her insightful analysis locates the film – and the issues at stake in it – in the political context of the time concerning the attitude that the British should adopt towards a defeated Germany. Foremost among these were those uncompromising views that insisted on the collective guilt and responsibility of all Germans, known as Vansittartism,[16] the position which Nell represents, and comes finally to reject in the film. These views might have been widely adopted during the war, but the central dilemma that the film frames, concerns their viability as a *modus vivendi* for peacetime and the future.[17]

In these terms, the film was widely praised for its timeliness in dealing with its 'unspoken' subject and in provoking thought and argument. Indeed, *Kine Weekly* felt that 'some may consider it a bit early to talk about shaking our enemies by the hand' (26 June 1947). In a review that found the direction 'almost brilliant', the *Sunday Despatch* commented: 'Strong meat this story, bravely tackled with convincing results' (6 July 1947); and in direct response to the pre-release publicity for instance, the *Evening Standard* argued:

> *Frieda* asks the question whether *you* would accept Germany into the family of nations. Those who would say 'No' should see this film, and even those who disagree with its conclusions are bound to admit that

it is a serious effort to deal with a contemporary problem. For once the cinema is not behaving like an ostrich. (4 July 1947)

The *News of the World* critic was more effusive:

> It's a love story woven into such an important theme, and so well written and screened, that long before the end I lost three critical hats throwing them in the air as a gesture of gratitude and admiration to those two young Englishmen responsible for the picture, Relph and Dearden. (6 July 1947)

A review of the film's limited American release was highly supportive of this 'uncommonly interesting drama', praising it as

> thoughtful, provocative fare which treats a complex problem with candour, compassion and remarkable clarity. And, as a serious character study, it is expertly wrought, understated drama and a tribute to its producers who have not shied away from a topical, trenchant and adult theme. (*New York Times*, 15 August 1947)

Other reviews were more measured, arguing that the film's solution 'seems to confuse rather than clarify', as in the case of *The Manchester Guardian*, which took the film to task for its inability to provide a general answer to the problem it poses. Instead the film only offered an

> answer so far as it need be given to individual British people when dealing with individual Germans. That answer is the obvious one – or at least the answer which is obviously dictated by Christianity. Indeed, the only fault of this worthy film is that it is all a little slow and a little obvious. (5 July 1947)

In these terms, as Ramsden was much later to note: 'most critics concluded that the film had got it about right, but came to that conclusion mainly by clambering onto the fence alongside it' (2006: 316).[18]

On the surface, the film attempts to demobilise wartime notions of national identity and resolve the dilemma of anti-German feeling, arguing instead for tolerance and an enlightened public opinion. This was congruent with certain political initiatives emerging at the time of the Cold War; Churchill, for instance, in the year before the film was released, had called for a 'kind of United States of Europe'.[19] But, as Barr has argued: 'in *Frieda*, all kinds of conflict seem to be seething just below the rational surface, particularly in Robert himself' (1977: 75).[20] Landy echoes this, arguing that:

> While Nazism appears to be the external threat to the sense of community, the real enemy is Robert, whose actions are the source of conflict.

The film not only explodes the notion of an integrated community, it also locates the source of discontent in the protagonist's inability to confront his actions and his desires. The challenge of Dearden's film lies in its exposure of underlying sexual and class conflict, which is no way mitigated by the film's resolution. (1991: 464)

However, for other commentators the film's dilemma and Robert's power have to be recognised as primarily located within, and indeed 'fettered' by, a nexus of contending femininities. As Murphy has suggested:

She [Frieda] is nevertheless part of a network of women – Judy, Nell, Bob's mother, even Edith the housekeeper – who dominate the film. Barr's misconception of Robert as a sadist is understandable: to see this big, energetic man moving uncomfortably in the delicate female world creates an undercurrent of tension which is only finally dissipated in the brutal fight between Robert and Ricky, and Frieda's dramatic suicide bid. (2000: 186)

Frieda has thus attracted many competing interpretations, in which genre and style have been found to make for an 'unstable' ideological text. Melodrama has been pinpointed for the way that it undercuts the dominant realism of patriarchy operative at Ealing, where 'The excesses, coincidences and over-dramatic elements . . . could be read as evidence of the trouble that women created in the text' (Geraghty 2000: 79). Accordingly, recent feminist criticism has sought to shift the nature of the 'problem' in *Frieda* from that of Germany onto that of femininity, especially in the 'unfeminine' ambitions of Nell, who seeks to participate in the masculine world of politics (Brunsdon and Mosely 1997; Kirkham and Thumim 1997).[21] As suggested above, an alternative criticism has pinpointed Robert as the problematic centre of the film, the source of the conflicts in the drama; while a *noir* aesthetic hints at a suppressed world below the surface of peaceful Denfield and the Dawson family. In fact, expressionism is limited to a couple of scenes and destabilisa-tion is the result of Relph's sets and décor, especially the fabric of the Dawson family home.[22] Dearden and Relph would extend their stylistic experimenta-tions in *noir* and mise-en-scène in their forthcoming melodramas *Saraband for Dead Lovers* (1948) and *Cage of Gold* (1950), and further reveal their ability to undermine the certainties of patriarchal realism at Ealing.

THE GENTLE GUNMAN (1952)

It is the custom of mankind to divide the habitable globe into little sec-tions which are known as countries. Those who are born in any such territory are called its natives and have an inordinate love of their piece of the earth.

This love, harmless enough in many ways, is sometimes allowed to foster a hatred of others, and to become the justification of violence, terrorism and mass-murder.

It is for this reason that it can be said of man that he is the only animal in the entire realm of nature who hunts in packs against his kind. It is this quality of unreasoning patriotism which may lead him to annihilate himself. (*Final Shooting Script*, 1952)[23]

Ticklish British booking. (*Kinematograph Weekly*, 9 October 1952)

If their work on *Frieda* was an attempt to confront the ethical issues concerning Anglo-German relations in the immediate aftermath of the war, *The Gentle Gunman* sought to focus on matters somewhat closer to home, and to deal with 'the Irish question'. In this, the film followed on the heels of a number of earlier attempts to dramatise this agenda.[24] The theme concerns the extent to which violence can be justified as a means to achieving an ideal, in this case Irish national independence. The film was based on the play written by Roger MacDougall, who also adapted it for the screen.[25] According to Barton, the film

> plays on the classical 'hawk and dove' dichotomy that underlies so many Troubles narratives. This configuration pits the man of violence against the man of peace (the gender usage is not accidental since women played quite a different role in these dramas) – thus in *The Gentle Gunman*, brother is set against brother as one, Terence (John Mills), renounces his membership of the IRA in favour of peace, whilst the other, Matt (Dirk Bogarde), embraces violence. The audience's sympathies are directed towards Terence. (2004: 160)

A full unit was despatched to Dublin for location shooting in County Wicklow, and the *Campaign Folder* noted: 'Many of these Irish scenes were filmed on the romantically named Featherbed Mountain, not far from Dublin, where workmen had the difficult task of erecting buildings on the soft bog. A special scaffolding foundation had to be laid before the complete cottage and petrol station could be built' (Ealing Studios, n.d.). An announcement in *Kine Weekly* referred to the new production as 'basically a gangster story, but with an underlying serious content' (13 March 1952).

As Hill has noted (1987: 160), the film was loosely based on the IRA's English campaign of 1939; although it opens with a superimposed caption 'Northern Ireland 1941'and the voices of two old men, one Irish and one English, raised and bickering as they play chess. However, their argument is not about the game, but about another contested territory – Northern Ireland itself – and the rights and wrongs of Irish Nationalism. The camera pulls back from the chessboard to frame the two protagonists: the old Irish doctor, Brannigan (Joseph Tomelty) and his visiting 'friend', the irascible, blimpish and tweedy Englishman, Truethorn (Gilbert Harding).[26] As they glower at each other in these establishing shots, there is much to Hill's observation that 'The analogy of the game is both implicit and explicit' (1987: 161), serving as it does as a metaphor for their personal animosity and for the wider contest between the Irish and the English, as the film unfolds.

By means of a dissolve, the film shifts back to another location: London in the Blitz, a few months earlier, where another kind of game is being played out, by a pair of IRA men, Tim Connolly (Liam Redmond) and Patsy McGuire (Jack McGowran), who are constructing a suitcase bomb in their rented lodgings. They are disturbed by the arrival of Matt Sullivan (Dirk Bogarde) looking for his older brother Terry, only to be told that he is not *with us* any more, and is now assumed to be a traitor.[27] Matt reacts angrily to this and volunteers to substitute for Terry by planting the bomb in a nearby Tube station. During an air-raid, with Connolly's parroting of the official line, 'This is a gesture of protest – there must be no unnecessary loss of life', he nervously goes out into the streets carrying the suitcase and descends into the Tube station.[28] Here he is spotted by his brother Terry (John Mills) as he takes the bomb down to a platform full of civilians sheltering from the raid.[29] He arms and leaves the bomb well away from the possibility of any harm. However, as he waits to escape on the incoming train, some children cluster around the ticking suitcase and an ARP warden and none other than the figure of Truethorn, appear on the scene to investigate. With the thump of German bombs landing overhead, the case is suddenly snatched from the warden by Terry who throws it into the tunnel, where it explodes harmlessly. Matt and Terry escape the scene separately, but talk briefly in adjacent phone booths in the main station, though not before Matt has been identified as a suspect by the police. Unknowingly, he leads them back to the lodgings where the police arrest McGuire and Connolly. Matt now firmly believes that Terry is a traitor, despite his attempts to convince him about his renunciation of violence. 'If you value your life, don't ever set foot in Ireland again' is Matt's warning as they part company.

The film shifts location and style, from *noir* almost to travelogue, with accompanying music, as Matt returns to the Republic at an isolated border post. In a rural location, not far from the border, the film introduces Shinto (Robert Beatty) and the young lad Johnny (James Kenney) in the hills above the isolated roadside garage and cottage where Johnny lives with his mother, Molly (Barbara Mullen), and sister, Maureen (Elizabeth Sellars), Terry's erstwhile girlfriend. Shinto is represented as the hardened leader of the IRA gang, demanding unquestioning loyalty to the cause and violent overthrow of British rule. Molly hates his influence over Johnny and blames him for the loss of her husband some years earlier and she has arranged for Johnny to go to work in the docks in Belfast. However, Johnny is clearly already under the sway of Shinto, who unknown to Molly gives Johnny his father's revolver. In a heavily symbolic contrast, as Johnny leaves for Belfast by the roadside cross, Molly gives him his father's rosary and tries to make him promise that he will not return.

News of the arrest of McGuire and Connolly reaches the garage before Matt, and when he arrives, driven by Flynn (Eddie Byrne), he confirms that Terry has turned traitor. Maureen at first is disbelieving, thinking this a ploy to usurp her love for Terry, while Shinto sneers that Matt has 'come back to retrieve the family honour'. That evening, Maureen and Matt go to the cinema and it seems that she is transferring her love for Terry to Matt, whom she now regards as her hero. In a nearby bar, Shinto learns that McGuire and Connolly have been sentenced to ten years' imprisonment and that they are to be returned to Belfast to serve their term in the Crumlin Road Jail. He immediately plans their escape, but needs to know the details of their arrival. Matt is despatched to Belfast to contact young Johnny and to use his access to the docks to get this information. Molly, who is unaware of these developments, asks Matt to leave Johnny 'in peace'. As Matt is armed with a revolver, Maureen kisses him farewell, in a scene which Hill interprets as follows:

> In contrast to her mother's traditional 'feminine' role of calling a halt to violence, Maureen employs her sexuality as a stimulus to further violent endeavour. She is initially involved with Terence but once he has abandoned the IRA she quickly withdraws her affections. She then proceeds to turn her attentions to his brother once he has proved his commitment to violence. Set within this context, the use of the gun now assumes unmistakeable phallic connotations: Matt takes aim with his revolver and Maureen looks on in delight and admiration. (1987: 163)[30]

The next sequence shifts to the Belfast docks, where Matt meets Johnny and instructs him to get into the docks office to find the details concerning the incoming prisoners. Johnny agrees to do this and to meet Matt outside the dock gates that evening. Unexpectedly, the action cuts to a small fishing village on the coast, where in the dusk, Terry comes ashore from a small boat. He has, as he explains to the old fisherman who greets him, 'some unfinished business with my young brother'. At the garage, meanwhile, Shinto, Flynn and Maureen wait anxiously for news from Belfast. When a lorry pulls in, Maureen goes to serve the driver, but the lorry pulls away to reveal Terry standing in the road. He follows her into the garage where she regards him with contempt, and asks him, 'What does it feel like to be a traitor?' Shinto joins them and the tension between them escalates. Terry purports to be looking for Matt, but Shinto and Maureen deny that he has been anywhere near the garage, claiming that he is in London. Maureen also tells Terry that she is now in love with Matt.

With Shinto keeping a wary eye on Terry, the action cuts back to the docks, where in pouring rain, Matt waits in a car for Johnny. Inside the heavily guarded dockyard, Johnny breaks into the office and locates the details of the ship that will carry the two prisoners. As he comes out through the gates, however, he is stopped by the sentries and in panic makes a run for the car. Silhouetted in the headlights, with his arms outstretched in the form of a cross (see Hill 1987: 160), he is shot in the back. He is helped into the car by a passing prostitute (Eithne Dunne) and Matt drives off at high speed. Back at the garage, the lack of contact from Matt is causing concern, and Shinto and Maureen continue to accuse Terry of failing the cause, an accusation he rejects. When Molly joins them, she realises that Matt has gone to Belfast to involve Johnny in danger. She accuses Shinto of being responsible for the death of her husband, in spite of Maureen's rejoinder that 'It was the English killed our father'. When Shinto argues that 'He died for Ireland', Molly replies, 'Better he had lived for her like he did before you came along'. Terry joins with her in this attack on Shinto and what he represents, insisting that he will not let him make a gunman out of Matt. When the phone does ring, it is Terry who grabs Shinto's gun and answers. Matt is surprised but relieved to hear his brother's voice – 'Terry – you're back with us?' Terry evades this question by confirming that he is 'back', in Ireland, and Matt explains his and Johnny's circumstances. Listening to the phone call, Molly realises that Johnny is badly wounded. Holding Shinto and Flynn at bay, Terry makes his escape on an old motorcycle and rides to meet Matt and the barely conscious Johnny on a deserted mountainside near the border. Johnny is so badly wounded that he cannot walk and he has not told Matt about the ferry arrangements for the prisoners. When Terry arrives on his own, although relieved, Matt quickly becomes suspicious and pulls his gun on Terry. In a defining scene in the film, his brother persuades him to put away his gun and to help to get Johnny to a doctor:

> 'Put away your gun, Matt – it'll get you nowhere . . . Matt, it was me that taught you the game – and that kind of gives me the right to take your education a bit further. And I'm telling you – there are other ways of getting what you want than at the point of a gun.'

They agree to take Johnny to old Dr Brannigan's house and as the camera frames that location, the voices of Brannigan and Truethorn can be heard,

Brothers and arms: *The Gentle Gunman* (1952) (Courtesy of Steve Chibnall Archive)

vigorously and volubly arguing the rights and wrongs of the Irish cause over the chessboard, as they were in the opening scenes of the film. Their bickering is stopped by the brother's arrival with the now unconscious Johnny. While they tend to him, Matt and Terry carry on their own version of the argument, with Terry insisting that English people are the same as the Irish: 'It's not *against* people like that we should be working. It's *with* them! It's peace we want and a job, and security, and a decent life. And we'll not get them by shouting "ourselves alone" at the top of our voices.' He is interrupted by Brannigan, who confirms that Johnny will die without immediate hospital treatment. At first, Matt will not allow an ambulance to be called and he argues with Brannigan and Truethorn, who in their different ways try to dissuade him. Finally, he relents and as Johnny leaves, he tells the brothers the name of the prisoners' boat and its arrival time in Belfast. Shinto and Flynn arrive and disarm Terry and when Matt relays these details, they allow the ambulance to leave. With Shinto's gun covering Terry and Matt in one car and Flynn's covering Brannigan and Truethorn in another they race back to the garage, where Molly is distraught about the fate of Johnny. In a scene of direct confrontation between the two women in the film, she accuses Maureen of a fatal heartlessness: 'I think it's death that you're in love with.'

When they arrive, Brannigan and Truethorn are locked in a shed and Terry imprisoned in another room. Maureen greets Matt as a hero and he leaves with Shinto and Flynn to drive to Belfast to carry out the raid to free the prisoners. Terry pleads with Maureen to release him, but she remains unmoved, indicating that she will let him out only if he returns to the cause. At this point, Molly intervenes, accusing Maureen with an impassioned speech:

> Blood. That's all ye want. That's all you all want. You're like Ireland herself that keeps crying out always for blood and more blood. Wouldn't you think you'd be sick of it all? Wouldn't you think the whole wide earth would be vomiting blood from all the bright-eyed young fellas that went out in their day? You'd think the earth would be thick with blood. When will we all get sense!

And she pushes Maureen aside and releases Terry, who immediately drives off to the fishing village in the North, where disguised as a fisherman, he boards the *Ulster Queen*, the ferry transporting the two prisoners, before it docks. On board, he gets the prisoners out of their cabin, and they all jump from the ferry to be picked up by his old friend, the fisherman.

Unaware of these developments, in Belfast, Shinto, Matt and other members of the gang prepare for their armed raid on the van waiting for the prisoners. As they take up their positions, Terry arrives to rescue Matt and explains that Connolly and McGuire are already free. Shinto is suspicious and disarms Terry, refusing to believe him, even when he produces the handcuffs he has removed from the prisoners. Using them to secure Terry in the car, Shinto orders the raid to go ahead, and the peaceful dockside street, with children and people going about their normal business, is shattered in the attack on the van. As it appears, Matt pulls the pin from the grenade Shinto has given him, but when a group of children come playing down the street, he replaces the pin and tries to protect them. Shinto throws his grenade and the street erupts into a gunfight with the guards, and two members of the gang are shot dead. With the police arriving, Shinto, Matt and Flynn flee the scene with Terry still handcuffed in the car. As they speed back to the garage, Terry taunts Shinto with his failure; that he will 'go down in history as the man who lost two of the boys failing to open an empty van', responsible for 'adding three more martyrs to the roll of Ireland's glory'. With this reference to Johnny, the film cuts to Molly at his bedside in the hospital. Here, having heard of the abortive raid at the docks, she is joined by detectives who want to interrogate her son. Molly won't allow this and she tells the detective that Shinto was the ringleader. Witnessing this, Johnny in a final act, levers himself up and strikes Molly across the face.

The *finale* is played out at the garage, where Maureen confirms to Shinto that Connolly and McGuire have not returned as Terry had promised. Terry is given a summary IRA trial, found guilty and condemned to death. In spite of his protestations, he is led out to be shot, as Molly arrives back with the news of Johnny's death. An agonised Matt tries to save his brother, but Terry is taken out onto the desolate wind-blown moor behind the garage. However, as Flynn takes aim to carry out the execution, the sound of raucous, drunken singing is heard coming down the road, heralding the arrival of Connolly and McGuire. Having spent some time in the local bar, their arrival just in the nick of time, saves Terry. The subsequent celebrations are short-lived, however, as the police arrive to arrest Shinto, and, in an almost Keystone Cops-like sequence, the gang pile into their cars and make off in a gun-firing chase. As the dust settles after their departure, Terry asks Matt if he's coming. Matt pauses for a moment by Maureen, but then joins his brother and they stride off down the road together past the cross. Intercut with this ending, the film closes as it began, with the sound of Brannigan and Truethorn and their apparent eternal bickering over Ireland. Still confined, they drink a toast which acts as a semi-comic coda to the film. Truethorn's toast is: 'To England where the situation may be serious, but is never hopeless'; to which Brannigan responds: 'To Ireland where the situation is always hopeless, but never serious'.

Contemporary reviews were often drawn to remark on Harding's debut or Mills' performance, but tended in general to find the film 'not very good or convincing' (*Daily Mirror*, 24 October 1952); it was a film that 'treads on provocative ground, but soon loses its nerve' (*Kinematograph Weekly*, 9 October 1952). For *Time & Tide*, it 'has the outline of a thriller, but the spirit of a class-room debate on a set topic' (1 November 1952). *The New Statesman* followed this with: 'It tries to infuse urgency into IRA activities during the war, to instil a moral of non-violence; but the decencies of Ealing don't make for either conviction or sound thriller' (1 November 1952). For Milton Shulman, writing in the *Evening Standard*, the film was

> Torn between its desire to say something and the unrelenting demands of the box-office, *The Gentle Gunman* has become an orthodox, above average thriller frightened of its own conscience. The story has crowded out the message and the words get in the way of the suspense. (23 October 1952)

Harris Deans, the critic for the *Sunday Despatch*, felt that the film 'Will bore the un-politically minded and infuriate partisans on either side by the ham-handed way it washes this dirty linen' (26 October 1952). Whereas, *The Daily Worker* was infuriated:

> The film is a plea to oppressed peoples everywhere to stop fighting their oppressors and become collaborators. If a policeman is standing on your neck and you don't struggle, it suggests that's peace. If you bite his ankle, that's gangsterism and much to be deplored. With this basic confusion of thought, the film was bound to be stagey and contrived. (26 October 1952)

When reviewed in *The Irish Press*, Liam McGabhann complained that the filmmakers had seized on this specific campaign as 'a chance to paint the Irish anti-partition picture all black' (9 February 1953, cited in Hill 1987: 18).

The rhetorical flourish of the film's ending, which has the eternally bickering Brannigan and Truethorn at last agreeing on a comic inversion of their respective national traits, is not the only thing which makes the film easy to dismiss as a trite and simplistic travesty – a political melodrama, without the politics.[31] Almost sixty years of hindsight, not only of Anglo-Irish relations, but of the global development and understanding of 'terrorism', gives a privileged and much less innocent vantage point to the modern viewer perhaps denied filmmakers of the time.[32] There is no doubt that the film elides absolutely any meaningful historical context or political motivation to the Irish cause and its agents. Shinto and Flynn are portrayed simply as 'men of violence' – no better than mindless (and incompetent) gangsters, echoing Landy's comment on the film: 'If the Irish are not presented as childlike, they are portrayed as fanatical, mad or violent' (1991: 117). And this appears as almost a genetic quality when opposed to the highly generalised humanist message which holds the film together, seemingly unaware of the history of oppression referred to by Brannigan in one of his early argumentative asides with Truethorn. Durgnat suggests that in common with *Shake Hands with the Devil* (d. M. Anderson, 1959) and *A Terrible Beauty* (d. T. Garnett, 1960), 'Eire's attainment of independence is presented exclusively in terms of the Irish struggling against their own tendency to violence' (1970: 108). Hill concurs with this critical assessment of the shortcomings of the film and develops this by considering the film's depiction of masculinity and sexuality. As he suggests, although Terry represents a kind of decontextualised 'pacifism', contradictorily, he remains masculine, 'tougher' than the tough guys. Contrasting the film with Carol Reed's earlier *Odd Man Out*, he suggests: 'Violence and sexual satisfaction are not opposed but interlinked' (1987: 163); and in this sense he suggests that the film's denial of a romantic ending and the rejection of violence by the two brothers work hand in hand with their rejection of Maureen, and this he equates with a form of sexual repression, even 'castration':

> For in turning their backs on violence, so are they also rejecting the eroticism and excitement that goes with it. The 'decent', but anodyne, virtues, which the film has previously encouraged, offer, in this respect, a less than compelling compensation. The 'emptiness' of the men's decision would seem to be confirmed by the imagery which follows. The road along which they depart is seen to be bare and deserted. It is leading them away from the only community which they know and leads to an unidentified destination . . . The film's inability to supply an adequate conclusion to the problems which it has let loose is confirmed by the ending overall. (ibid.: 164)

The counter to this lies presumably in the recognition that the road leads over the horizon to the brothers' 'new life', reunited; who knows to where, but precisely away from the enforced regime of the unbearable, unethical choices forced by the environment of Fagan's garage, a life, furthermore, which allows for the possibility of true romantic and sexual fulfilment, and one not dependent upon endangering the lives of innocents or themselves. And in such a world, Maureen – as Molly demonstrates – is not the sole or exclusive model or destiny of femininity, romantic love or resolution.

LIFE FOR RUTH (1962)

> In an age which wants the pleasures, but not the responsibilities, of freedom, can't we respect his willingness to bear the responsibility of his daughter's destiny, rather than leave her to 'them'? Nonetheless, he should have been more resigned before God's will. And, although the

film criticizes the complacency of the humanitarian, liberal consensus, it does so by pleading for a double paternalism (God's, and fathers'). (Raymond Durgnat 1970: 159)

A finely crafted and undeservedly neglected film, which, like so much Dearden–Relph work, particularly from the post-Ealing days, has had scant critical notice. It offers not only an absorbing entertainment, but also an honest attempt to consider a serious ethical issue. (Brian McFarlane 1997: 203)

The final shooting scripts of *Life for Ruth* are dated December 1961, and it was the film that Dearden and Relph embarked on after their experience on the jazzy adaptation *All Night Long* (1962). It was to be their last effort for the brave AFM venture, following on the success of *Victim* (1961). The film was scripted by Janet Green and her husband, John McCormick, and it was in production for Rank at Pinewood very early in 1962, in the salubrious company of *Carry on Cruising* (d. G. Thomas, 1962) and *Play it Cool* (d. M. Winner, 1962) (*Kinematograph Weekly*, 25 January 1962).

The film opens with a series of atmospheric shots of the sea – waves breaking against the cold, inhospitable north-east coast – before the camera pans across roofs to a lighthouse and then into a small town, introducing a family in their everyday, domestic surroundings. Much of the film was shot on location in Durham, Sunderland and on the coast at Seaham, County Durham. Lighting cameraman Otto Heller adopts a harsh, high-contrast style with deep black shadows reflecting the starkness of the drama and the impenetrability of the ethical issues it confronts. John Harris (Michael Craig) departs for work at the local pit, bidding farewell to his wife, Pat (Janet Munro), taking in the car their young daughter, Ruth (Lynn Taylor), and Teddy, her friend from next-door. He drops the children at his father's house on the cliffs above the sea, where they will play on the beach. Later, they are joined by Pat, and after work, John returns to pick them all up, greeting his father (Malcolm Keen) in sight of the lighthouse. The everyday normality of this opening is shattered, however, when the children go out in a small rowing boat to retrieve a ball they have been playing with. In the strong tide they get into difficulties and are driven towards the rocks. Alerted by Pat, Harris, with great bravery, swims from the cliffs rescuing first Teddy and then returning to save Ruth, who has been badly injured.[33] The action then shifts to the waiting room in the nearby hospital, where an anxious Harris and Pat await news; they learn that Teddy has recovered enough to be sent home, but that Ruth is gravely ill. Dr Brown (Patrick McGoohan) indicates that a blood transfusion will save her but he is overwhelmed when her father refuses to allow the transfusion on the grounds that it is against his religion, against God's law, quoting from the Old Testament: 'Whatsoever man eateth any manner of blood, I will set my face against that soul.'[34] For Harris, allowing Ruth the transfusion might save her life on earth, but it would deny her any possibility of eternal life and salvation. He remains adamant, even when Brown enlists the support of his more persuasive senior colleague, Harvard (Michael Aldridge).

In these scenes the film pits the white-coated men of medicine, with their Hippocratic duty to save life, against the fundamental Christian beliefs of Harris. Caught in the dilemma is Ruth's mother, Pat, in torment, but apparently supporting her husband's decision. Having signed a declaration of responsibility, John and Pat return home, leaving the doctor and nurses contemplating whether to go ahead with the transfusion. Harvard is clear, however, that without parental consent this would be an illegal act, although it is clear that he – and the film at this stage – sympathise with Brown's frustration, expressed in his impassioned outburst:

> 'We're doctors aren't we? We're supposed to take any decisions we think are right for a patient, aren't we? But when it comes to an operation or a blood transfusion to save a child's life – do we make decisions then? Do we do what we know is right? No! Because we need the consent of some crank or half-wit who happens to be the kid's father.'

Later that night, despite her husband's assurance that Ruth will be all right, Pat runs to the hospital to beg Dr Brown to give the blood transfusion. At dawn the following morning, however, when she returns home, it is clear that her efforts have been in vain and she confirms to her shocked husband that Ruth has died.

Later that day at the hospital, Dr Brown, against the advice of the Senior Consultant, insists that a post-mortem be held to prove that Ruth died from loss of blood, claiming that the true circumstances of the case should be made public. In his view, Harris's action in refusing the procedure is tantamount to murder. And as the facts of the death of Ruth gradually become known, Harris encounters rejection and hostility. This begins when his father-in-law (John Barrie) hits him across the face as a 'psalm-singing bastard'. On the cliffs, by the lighthouse, he confesses his doubts and turmoil to his own father, who affirms his decision and faith. Returning home he is met by Pat, who in her grief accuses Harris of failing to save Ruth first, and then confesses that she had returned to the hospital and asked for the transfusion. She realises now that her faith is not that of her husband and as a result she no longer belongs with him, so she leaves the house.

Frustrated by the outcome of the inquest – 'accidental death caused by immersion in the sea' – Brown goes to the police to demand further action, but is informed by the Detective Superintendent that no criminal case can be forthcoming. At Ruth's funeral the following day Harris is barracked by onlookers. They have read of the case in the local paper, *The Citizen*, edited by the campaigning but circulation-minded Clyde (Leslie Sands), who stops Brown after the funeral and arranges for him to meet with a solicitor, to receive advice. The solicitor, Hart-Jacobs (Paul Rogers), indicates that a case of manslaughter might be a possibility, but he refuses to take the case on himself (The thing smacks of persecution to me)[35] and he refers them to colleague, Mapleton (Basil Dignam), who agrees to act in the case. In a melodramatic aside, Pat visits her old Church of England vicar to seek his advice with regard to Ruth's death. He is unable to resolve her dilemma other than to tell her that the truth – 'the supreme law' – must lie in her heart. At the hospital, Brown indicates that he will take a private action against Harris for manslaughter. His colleagues counsel caution, initially in terms of his own future career, the worldly-wise senior consultant insisting that: 'Doctors should stick to doctoring and leave law to the lawyers. Would you like a high court judge to take out your appendix?'

As a result of Brown's action, Harris is arrested under the Prevention of Cruelty to Children Act, although the arresting officers have little sympathy for the case. When Pat hears of his arrest, she rushes to the police station to see her husband; Harris however, refuses to see anyone. As she leaves, Pat is approached by Hart-Jacobs, the solicitor who refused to prosecute, who asks if he can defend her husband, on the grounds that in his opinion Harris is innocent. Pat consents, but first goes to see Brown to try to dissuade him from continuing with the prosecution. Despite her pleading and arguments that he has his own 'blindness' and that 'there is something beyond science', he remains unmoved, hell-bent on preventing any recurrence of a child's death in Ruth's circumstances.

At the preliminary hearing, Pat has to run the gauntlet of reporters in order to get into the court. Initially, Harris refuses to be represented by Hart-Jacobs, insisting on his manifest innocence, but his father's counsel that it is their whole faith that will be on trial finally convinces him. After the brief hearing, both he and Pat encounter a hostile crowd. As a result, Hart-Jacobs arranges for police protection of their home, but this does not prevent the intrusion of a camera-carrying reporter (Brian Wilde), seeking a photograph of Ruth, an act that appals them both. His parting shot – that Harris and Pat are headlines in all the national papers and that the story is going to get bigger – only adds to their shock and insecurity.[36] This state of siege, however, sees them temporarily reunited.

As McFarlane suggests, 'the dialectical centre of the film is the court case' (1997a: 208) and this is depicted with due ceremony and procedure. In front of all shades of opinion represented in the onlookers and press, Brown appears

On trial: *Life for Ruth* (1962) (Courtesy of Steve Chibnall Archive)

first to outline his case and to repeat the events that led up to Ruth's death. His medical opinion is supported by a tearful ward sister and by the declaration of responsibility signed by Harris. The fact that Pat later returned to the hospital to ask for the transfusion, but to no avail, is also made public. After an adjournment the jury returns, and Kent (Michael Bryant), who has been retained to defend Harris, decides to put his client before the court. Prior to this he confides to Hart-Jacobs that he feels that Harris, in terms of his action, is 'guilty as hell', but in terms of his motivation, 'as innocent, as Heaven itself'. In his opening address, Kent does not dispute that Harris caused the death of his daughter, but insists that his client is on trial for the heresy of setting aside medical science in favour of religious belief, and that in law a man may worship what he chooses. Harris is then called to the stand and falteringly at first, in response to Kent's questions, he outlines the logic of his religious faith and how he came to refuse the transfusion. The prosecution counter this by emphasising that Ruth was too young to understand Harris's beliefs and imply that he had relied on a miracle to save her. However, in response Kent does enough to draw out Harris's integrity and his deep love for Ruth and how he acted to give her eternal life in Heaven. This closes the defence case and as the jury adjourn to consider their verdict, even the hard-bitten editor Clyde is moved by Harris's sincerity and conviction: 'I'm not sure if crucifying Harris is the right answer', he remarks. Brown too senses that Harris is close to breaking point after his ordeal in the court. When the verdict of 'not guilty' is announced – to noisy dissent in the gallery – Brown's concern appears correct, as Harris cries out in an agonised voice that he is guilty and that like Abraham he had hoped for a miracle to save his child. On the point of collapse, he is led from the court. In an especially powerful sequence, Brown follows Harris from the court and just prevents his attempted suicide as he steps out in front of a bus. The interchange which follows between the two, intercut in shadowy close-ups of their faces, sees Brown emerge more genuinely humanitarian and less zealous than he has appeared so far in the narrative, and he manages to convince Harris that his own death will not resolve his problems. Pat arrives to ask Harris to return home, but he walks off, insisting that 'Ruth would always stand between us'. Pat and Brown realise that Harris has to return on his own, and this sets the scene for the final climax of the film which returns to the cliff top, high above the beach where Ruth's accident took place. Here, above the waves, caught in the flashing beacon of the lighthouse, Harris grapples with his conscience and faith and whether he can live with himself. After some time, children's voices break through the sound of the waves and the dramatic musical score, courtesy of William Alwyn, and the final sequence of the film sees Harris walking away from the cliff, passing the children playing, on and up the street; suggesting a return to home and the possibility of a life after Ruth. In this ending, the film has an element of the conversion drama about it, as Landy (1991: 249) argues is characteristic of many tragic melodramas. Harris, while in no way rejecting his beliefs, has become less of a 'blind believer' and his tragic experience has altered him for good: his life will never be the same. Dr Brown remains committed to his humanist agnosticism and the importance of medical science, but he too has learned from this case.

'This is strong stuff, and the film about it has been made by Basil Dearden and Michael Relph, who are expert carvers of red cinematic meat', wrote Leonard Mosley (*News of the World*, 2 September 1962); and many reviews followed this generally positive line, even, if they were also less than happy with the final outcome. The film was seen as 'typical' Dearden and Relph fare, with Craig, Munro and McGoohan adjudged to have acquitted themselves well. For Alan Dent, 'Those who do stay away from *Life for Ruth* will miss one of Basil Dearden's most sensitive productions, and some very sincere and searing performances' (*Sunday Telegraph*, 2 September 1962). 'They don't make them much better than this', wrote Felix Barker, 'they have made a film which deals with a real human quandary without false sentiment. They have handled conflict of science and medicine, public prejudice and private conscience – and made it fascinating' (*Evening News*, 30 August 1962); and in a similar vein, Edward Eildon noted that he had seen 'A film which could have been dogmatic and emotional, or both, but which in fact is astringent, realistic, and still moving' (*Time & Tide,* 13 September 1962). Addressing exhibitors, *Kine Weekly* concurred: 'Powerful, provocative and heart searing problem play . . . The acting and direction are impeccable and its typically English Northern town backgrounds cannot be faulted. Outstanding British offbeat melodrama, carrying obvious popular and feminine appeal' (5 July 1962).

Against this there were those who found the film offensive. For an uncompromising Alan Lovell, for instance, writing in *The Observer*: 'The way that Relph and Dearden have turned all this into a conventional "entertainment" reveals an appalling vulgarity and insensitivity' (2 September 1962). Other critics took issue with aspects of the film, Patrick Gibbs, for instance, taking it to task for its vagueness concerning the identity of the religious sect involved: 'Are they Shakers, Seventh Day Adventists, Plymouth Brethren, Jehovah's Witnesses? It remains tantalisingly unspecified' (*Daily Telegraph*, 1 September 1962). The *Monthly Film Bulletin* on the other hand, congratulated Dearden and Relph on their customary 'knack' of combining the commercial with the controversial, but found that 'the weakness is that of most British problem pictures . . . the film is completely uncommitted. Meticulously it gives free speech to every shade of opinion on the subject, while taking sides with none'

(August 1962). In a similar vein, Derek Prowse, writing in *The Sunday Times*, admitted: 'I just wish that finally one was not left with such a nagging resentment at being led up a series of garden paths' (2 September 1962).

This was typical of the 'damned if you do, and damned if you don't' criticism that dogged Dearden and Relph continually in their work on problem pictures. *Life for Ruth* is, in fact, admirably open-ended and intentionally provides space for a thoughtful audience to work through the complex ethical issues at stake. The drama introduces and carefully delineates a number of individuals and couples who are affected by and respond to the consequences of Harris's religious conviction: neighbours who are grateful that Harris saved their son, but appalled at his decision to refuse his daughter a transfusion; hospital administrators who are caught between the contradictions of the law and their professional responsibilities; an Anglican vicar who is unable to steer Pat through the conflicting dogmas of Christianity; and the newspaper editor whose conscience is pricked by his haste to get at the circulation-grabbing story. This was recognised in the film's promotion, where one advertising image had the faces of Dr Brown, Pat and Harris inset within large question marks, alongside the statement: 'Each in some way must share the guilt . . .'. The overall lack of resolution to the film, which only hints that Harris will retain his faith and return to married life with Pat, also reinforces the sense of openness of the drama and the ultimate irresolvability of the ethical dilemmas introduced.[37]

Alexander Walker, who reviewed the film at the time in the *Evening Standard* as 'a dramatic conundrum picture . . . a neat puzzle that had me in a flat moral spin' (30 August 1962), was however later to record that the film was far from a box-office success, arguing that it was one of the final 'financial blows' that led to the demise of the AFM initiative.[38] Subsequent critical accounts of the film are few and far between. Durgnat felt that Dearden and Relph had backslid into their 'besetting sin': 'moral complacency,' and sensed a touch of sensationalism: 'It may strike Jehovah's Witnesses as daringly controversial, but for the rest of us is merely depressing' (1966: 32); while Murphy provides a short, thoughtful assessment, noting the intensity of Craig and Munro's performances and the admirable work of Heller in creating the bleak, shadowy interiors (1992: 42–3). As he suggests, the theme of the film, 'religious bigotry', was by no means such a controversial or clear-cut issue as race or homosexuality had been in the earlier success of *Sapphire* and *Victim*. For McFarlane, in his subsequent revisionist account of the film, 'Its "moment" was in some ways not propitious to its receiving the attention it warranted' (1997a: 203). In his detailed and shrewd discussion of the film's contexts, he argues that the film – and Dearden and Relph's characteristic cinematic signature – was by now deeply at odds with the British 'New Wave' of the time, not necessarily in its concern for the lives of ordinary working-class people

in northern locations, but in 'its adoption of a powerful melodramatic framework and narrational mode' (ibid.: 205).[39] In the light of his discussion of
the refractive influence of these contexts, his subsequent re-evaluation of the
film succeeds in both provoking and promoting a more open analysis available to modern viewers. In his review for *Films and Filming*, Roger Manvell
was correct in his assumption that 'there will be opponents of this film on
the grounds that it is too precise in its characterisation and too obvious in its
emotional stress'; however, he acknowledged the sincerity of the producers,
adding: 'it succeeds through sheer, sustained conviction in writing, direction
and acting' (August 1962).[40]

THE MIND BENDERS (1963)

> Can 'brainwashing' force a man to surrender any belief or loyalty he may
> have? Can the 'brainwasher' make his victim believe in any absurdity?
> Can he force the victim to carry out any act, however atrocious? If not,
> how often, with whom, and in what respects has 'brainwashing' been
> variously successful or unsuccessful? (Albert Biderman 1962: 551)

Having dealt a year earlier with the immovability of apparently perverse, personal religious faith clashing with medical science in *Life for Ruth*, Dearden
and Relph's next project explored the extent to which science itself could
transform or 'bend' personal belief, 'truth' and personality, and confronted the
ethical dilemmas involved.[41] In this their work swung rapidly between what
Durgnat has characterised as a 'non-conformist-conformist attitude to the
scientist' (1970: 160). The script for the film was by James Kennaway, who
had written *Violent Playground* (1958) and whose reputation had been recently
enhanced by the success of his novel and film script for *Tunes of Glory* (d. R.
Neame, 1960).[42] The screenplay had, however, undergone a 'long gestation',
having begun life at the end of Ealing, with the working titles *The Visiting
Scientist* and *If This Be Treason*. However, as Kennaway's biographer notes:

> It had been shelved because its subject, that of brainwashing, had been
> thought too far advanced for its time. Its fortunes revived in 1961 when
> Basil Dearden persuaded Dirk Bogarde to play the role of Longman,
> the Oxford scientist who takes part in experiments involving sensory
> deprivation. (Royle 1983: 160) [43]

The serious nature of *The Mind Benders* was very much in the vogue of the
new, realistic style of the spy thriller being introduced at this time in the writing
of Len Deighton (*The Ipcress File*, 1962) and John le Carré (*The Spy Who Came
in From the Cold*, 1963); and adaptations of their novels were filmed to great

success in the1960s. The theme of brainwashing had also recently featured in the controversial *The Manchurian Candidate* (d. J. Frankenheimer, 1962), from the best-selling novel by Richard Condon, and mind manipulation, particularly in the United States, was a significant feature of Cold War thinking within the military, psychological and political science communities.[44]

The shooting scripts for the film date from July 1962, with Dearden's script heavily annotated throughout with copious revisions and amendments, many of which were overtaken by subsequent alterations during filming and editing.[45] As Aldgate (1997) has documented, the film was subject to a detailed and lengthy process of pre-release negotiations with the British Board of Film Censors, less concerned with the subject of brainwashing but more focused on the graphic revelation of intimate details in the film. In spite of attempts to modify these, the film was eventually released with an 'X' certificate.[46] The film was made at Pinewood Studios by Relph and Dearden Productions for Novus Films and distributed by Anglo-Amalgamated Films and premièred early in March 1963 at the Warner Theatre, Leicester Square (*Kinematograph Weekly*, 7 March 1963).

The narrative begins in London, in the hallowed surroundings of that bastion of scientific discovery The Royal Institution, with a sequence which introduces Professor Sharpey (Harold Goldblatt), an eminent physiologist, in a trance-like state, examining his briefcase full of banknotes.[47] When he leaves, to meet his junior colleague Tate (Michael Bryant),[48] for the train for Oxford, he is followed by the anonymous Hall (John Clements). When he subsequently throws himself from the speeding train and the case of money is found by his dead body, the opening enigma of the film is set in play.[49]

The spires and colleges of Oxford anchor the principal location of the film, as Hall arrives at the Department of Biology to quiz its Head, Calder (Geoffrey Keen), about Sharpey and his work. Hall is revealed as a Military Intelligence officer, who believes that Sharpey has sold vital research secrets to foreign agents and interviews Tate who confirms that Sharpey, with his colleague Dr Longman (Dirk Bogarde), was conducting research into the effects of isolation. Tate shows Hall a strange documentary film, shot in the Arctic, of an eminent French scientist, frighteningly disoriented by prolonged experimental exposure to extreme low temperature. In Sharpey's commentary on the film, however, it becomes clear that Longman had realised that this state of utter confusion and breakdown was not induced by the freezing temperature, but had resulted from isolation and sensory deprivation. The commentary ends by indicating that this realisation had taken them into a 'new and frightening world', dealing with 'the physics of the soul'.

Hall questions Tate about the experiments subsequently undertaken by Sharpey and Longman, but Tate remains defensive and evasive. Hall wants to speak with the mysterious Longman, who has not been seen in the university for weeks. Tate cycles through Oxford to Longman's home, a large rambling house, where Tate was once a lodger. In this sequence, the film introduces Longman's rather eccentric family, his young children and beautiful wife, Oonagh (Mary Ure), and Longman himself, played with great insouciance by Bogarde. Longman appears to have retreated to this family haven from his unspecified work in the laboratory. Tate breaks the shocking news of Sharpey's death and outlines Hall's suspicions concerning his possible treason. When Tate returns to the lab, he finds Hall investigating a room containing a large tank of water and he explains the principal of the isolation tank; that the subject is suspended in a diving suit in blood temperature water, unable to see, hear or exercise any of the other senses, deprived of sensation and entirely isolated for lengthy periods of time. Initially, Hall is sceptical: 'You wouldn't think it would be so difficult to take a warm bath in a dark room"; but Tate's response – 'Two men have tried it – one's dead and the other ran away' – gives a chilling hint of things to come. Cutting to Longman – the one who 'ran away' – the film shows him deeply disturbed by the prospect of returning to the lab and this panic is sensed by Oonagh that night as they make love. When Hall arrives on his doorstep the following morning, Longman is hostile, emphasising the power of isolation and the consequences it may have had for Sharpey; how the tank can dissolve personality until it becomes 'a sort of soul-less, mindless, will-less thing – not even a man at all – a kind of sea anemone'; and in these terms he defends Sharpey against Hall's allegations. The devious Hall, however, demands proof, and in response to this challenge, Longman agrees once again to submit himself to the horror of the tank in order to prove its power and so exonerate his old colleague and mentor.

As a result, and after due preparation, Longman goes into the isolation tank, 'strictly Frankenstein country', and the film then reveals his fate as he is observed by Hall who records four distinct stages: childish irritation, melancholy, panic and finally, after six hours, hallucination.[50] With Longman still underwater after eight hours, Hall excitedly recognises the power – and the potential – of the tank:

> 'It's fantastic! It would take months of solitary confinement to reduce a man to this state. Even if he were kept awake with lights and all the rest of it . . . This is an experiment on the fringes of brainwashing-indoctrination. No wonder they were after Sharpey! We could persuade Longman into anything now . . . I mean, change his most fundamental beliefs.'

In order to put this to the test, Hall enlists the reluctant Tate, to help him 'bend' Longman's mind: to alter one of his firmest beliefs. Initially, they can't

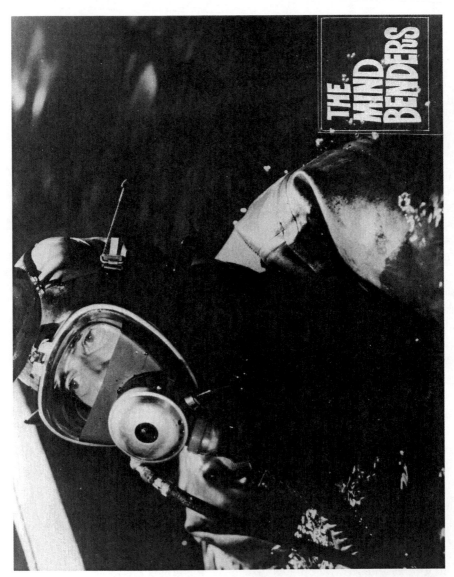

Into the tank: *The Mind Benders* (1963) (Courtesy of Steve Chibnall Archive)

decide what is fundamental in Longman's outlook, but Hall quickly picks up on the suggestion that Longman is devoted to his wife and decides to try to break this. When the totally disoriented Longman is eventually taken from the tank, Hall and Tate employ techniques of interrogation and the threat of a return to the tank to suggest to him that his wife is unbalanced, 'almost a tart'; and that he has never really loved her. Longman collapses at this point, coming to on a stretcher outside the lab, where his confused mental state is signified by a swirling mass of starlings flying overhead. However, he appears to make a rapid recovery and, refusing further assistance, returns to the lab, where his only abnormality seems to be his sense of time (he's 'lost' twelve hours). Furthermore, he purports to know what Hall and Tate have been trying to do to him and declares it a failed experiment; and as if to prove this, when Oonagh arrives, he greets her with a loving embrace, behaviour that seems to convince Hall and Tate. However, in later scenes, when Oonagh and he are alone and she tells him of her pregnancy, Longman's cool response begins to hint at a changed man.

A classic dissolve and cut to scenes of autumn leaves and bonfire preparations indicates the passage of time, as several months later, the film catches up with Tate, cycling to the Longman house to invite them to a fireworks party on his barge. The family have been away, touring Europe, to allow Longman rest after his experience in the tank. Tate is disconcerted by the change he sees in Longman, especially in his attitude to his heavily pregnant wife, who appears strained and worn down. Longman agrees to go to the party, but Tate leaves with serious misgivings.

With the wild party in full swing, Hall – alerted by Tate – arrives to observe a drunken Longman flirting with Annabelle (Wendy Craig). He joins Tate and Oonagh on the barge and she confirms that Longman has been acting out of character since he was 'twisted' in the tank, six months earlier. As evidence of this, she haltingly relates an incident on their travels in Amsterdam when Longman rented one of the prostitutes 'shop-windows' and displayed her in it. This convinces Hall that the 'experiment' did not fail and they follow Longman to the lab in an attempt to de-programme him by playing the tape of the original events. A deranged Longman with the naïve Annabelle are cornered at the scene of the original interrogation and, as the tape is played, the full implications of what happened register on the faces of Oonagh and the others. Hall explains to the disturbed Longman that he has been indoctrinated, but although shaken, he is resistant and leaves with Annabelle as Tate, and then Hall, attempt to apologise to Oonagh. Hall also tries to justify their actions to Tate, who by now is in deep self-recrimination.

Back at the barge, Annabelle leaves Longman on the towpath, where he is joined by Oonagh. He remains cold and indifferent to her, but as she slips and falls on the bank and goes into labour the 'old' Longman is suddenly reborn, and he carries Oonagh onto the barge where, with some trepidation, he delivers the baby, and the intensity of the birth confirms his restoration to his former, real self. As Durgnat interprets the scene: 'his spell in rubber, water, darkness and isolation (a hideous impersonal womb) is lifted by the most intimate physical contact with his wife's flesh (delivering their child from her womb)' (1966: 32–3). In a final interchange alone with Hall, Longman confesses that he has 'come through' and that they now know that Sharpey was innocent – 'Z for Zombie, not T for Traitor' – and the film ends on this note of uneasy reconciliation between them.

'There are power maniacs in the world who are prepared to exploit science unscrupulously by seeking to bend men's minds to their own evil wills' wrote an alarmed Vincent Firth in *ABC Film Review* (March 1963: 14). 'Dearden and Relph have, as usual, contrived to snatch a plot out of the headlines' was the verdict of the *Monthly Film Bulletin* (March 1963) in a review that went on to argue that the fascinating potential of the subject matter had been reduced to a simple tale of Jekyll and Hyde. 'Dearden's direction shows a dogged, if laboured, determination to prove equal to the vulgarity of the film's concep-tion', it moaned; and this was not the only review to take the film to task for its apparent disregard for the ethics of Hall and Tate's unscrupulous col-laboration in the brainwashing. 'The film that gets its values wrong', echoed *The Times* in its condemnation (1 March, 1963); and even the normally mild-mannered *Kine Weekly* felt that the film went 'slightly off the rails' in this respect, although concluding that 'its box-office potential, heightened by feminine appeal and star values, is unquestionable' (31 January 1963).[51]

In his biography of Kennaway, Royle notes that:

> The novel received goodish reviews, but the film was savaged by the critics, not because the script creaked, but because no one would believe that brainwashing experiments involving sensory deprivation could be made in a civilised country. The critics' ignorance angered Kennaway. (1983: 160)[52]

Michael Relph was also angered by the critical reception, and was 'injudi-cious enough' to write to *Films and Filming*, which had printed 'so inadequate an assessment of the film' (April 1963). The original review had featured in the March issue, written by the assistant editor, Robin Bean. In his com-ments, Bean criticised the work of Dearden and Relph as lacking the 'vital basis of human relationships': 'stated fact replaces subtlety; dramatic contriv-ance is preferred to sensitive feeling'. Specifically: '*The Mind Benders* is another example of British film-makers playing it safe, where interesting themes are used merely as a background to stories developed on a conventional pattern'.

In particular, Relph was concerned to counter the 'disturbing comment on our recent films as being lacking in the development of character and human relationships':

> The review suggests that the story has been told entirely in terms of a spy thriller and I think that this gives quite a false impression. It starts as such, certainly, but this merely provides a strong motive for the young scientist, Longman, to jeopardise in a dangerous experiment the thing he holds most dear – his love for his wife. It is this love – this human relationship – and how it ultimately conquers all that science can do to destroy it that forms the essential part of the film.

The producer, in turn, criticised Bean for not commenting on the acting or direction of the film. Relph gave special praise for the performances, believing Bogarde demonstrated a 'wider range and greater maturity' than in anything he had previously done; that Dearden, 'in addition to his customary technical adroitness, shows an unexpected subtlety and sensitivity'; and he praised the writing of Kennaway as 'some of the best and most characterful that has been heard in a British film about literate people'.[53]

In the first serious attempt to understand and explain the cinema of Dearden and Relph, Raymond Durgnat argued that their films could be grouped into '(a) explorations of society, and (b) moral affirmations', recognising that the two strands often interweave. While a useful initial exercise in bringing a critical focus to the work of the filmmakers, Durgnat's suggestions are too crude and it is not possible to reduce the complexity of their social vision or moralising to simply that of 'the English upper-middle-class "establishmentarian" ethos' (1966: 27).[54] The ethical dilemmas at the heart of the four films examined in this chapter cannot be easily explained away, and, with the possible exception of *The Gentle Gunman*, they are constructed in an admirably open-ended fashion, with audiences being credited with intelligence and some freedom to weigh up the issues and make up their own minds. Significantly, authority figures in these films – often in contrast to their counterparts in the social problem films – are not always to be trusted. Aunt Nell, the parliamentarian and voice of the public in *Frieda*, perpetuates the hatred of wartime; the Military Intelligence officer in *The Mind Benders*, in service of the nation, is ruthlessly destructive of the individual; and the Third Estate in *Life for Ruth* selfishly pursues circulation at the cost of individual conscience. In laying bare these dilemmas confronted by modern society, Dearden and Relph provide few easy answers. In this sense the films offer a welcome counter-balance to the social problem films with their generally reassuring visions of policing and liberal tolerance. Taken together, this cinema of 'ethical dilemmas' and 'social problems' (and the conflicting critical views it has attracted) embodied the contradictory impulses of the times; reflecting the intransigence of the emergent problems of power, compulsion and freedom, and registering the complexity of responses to the apparently incoherent and threatening new forces thrown up by that modernising society.

NOTES

1. *The Times* reviewed the play finding it to be 'theatrically effective . . . The piece should thrive on its good acting and "strong" situations' (3 May 1946).
2. The film's release was given a novel publicity campaign by Monja Danichewsky, head of the Ealing Press Department. In selected newspapers prior to release, 'Would you take Frieda into your home?' was the enigmatic question used to arouse public curiosity. According to Millar, who had just returned from Hollywood working on *So Evil My Love* (1948), this was highly effective (1993: 142). *Kine Weekly* adapted this question to 'Would you take Frieda into your cinema?' (24 July 1947).
3. Frieda had been played on the stage by Valerie White.
4. See Millar (1993: 125–6) and Balcon (1969: 170), with the latter recording that they had seen Zetterling in *Frenzy* (d. A. Sjoberg, 1944), in London at that time. Ramsden notes that Zetterling's 'blond plaits and strong cheekbones fitted British preconceptions of what a German woman ought to look like' (2006: 313). See also Brunsdon and Moseley (1997: 129–36).
5. Relph designed the film, utilising for the first time a system of set-up sketches that would be even more extensively used in the pre-planning of *Saraband for Dead Lovers* (1948). This approach, together with Dearden's direction and Gordon Dines work as the lighting cameraman, gives the film some very dark, *noir* elements throughout; epitomised in the sequence when Robert and Frieda leave the cinema. Murphy classes the film as a British *film noir* (2007: 107).
6. Denfield, the Denbury of the play, is constructed as emblematic of 'the typical English community'; (Barr 1977: 74; Lovell 1984: 31). The name change must have been a late amendment as the shooting scripts refers to Denbury through-out. These early scenes also contain an important evocative flashback to Alan (Robert's brother) and Judy's marriage.
7. 'The German Problem' had proved a thorny issue for Labour throughout the war, but socialist supporters of 'Vansittartism' like Clement Attlee, Ernest Bevin and Hugh Dalton occupied senior positions in the party. See Tombs (1996).
8. The figure of Nell encompasses the classic moral dilemma that is tested by the drama; as a representative politician she has a *duty* to her conscience and constitu-ents, while as a member of the Dawson household, she has an *obligation* to her family. For a discussion of these ethical distinctions, see Lemmon (1962).
9. This is an ambiguous reference which could be taken to mean 'inside', as guards – as transpires with Ricky – or, to those German Jews and others who were also 'inside', but as victims.
10. This is a similar dividing device to the shot used in *Cage of Gold*, when at a key

moment in the narrative Farrar is positioned between Jean Simmons and James Donald.

11. On the theme of the 'Good/Bad German', see Falcon (1995) and MacKenzie (2003).

12. Ricky is never seen again, although the film suggests that he is handed to the police to face trial for his war crimes.

13. In these scenes, as Landy (1991: 464) and Brunsdon and Moseley (1997: 132) have argued, the film makes use of a horror iconography.

14. In these terms, Millar in his autobiography argued that the film was wholly true to the theme of the play (1993: 141).

15. The insertion of this 'happy ending' was one of the major changes that Millar and McPhail implemented in the script. In the original play, Frieda returns to Germany to extirpate her own – and her nation's – culpability and guilt, and to contribute to regeneration. Some critics remarked that in these terms, the film's ending was less than satisfactory (e.g. *The Daily Worker*). For Ramsden it is an ending 'that beggars belief' (2006: 313).

16. After Lord Vansittart, Chief Diplomatic Adviser to the British government, who in 1940 made a series of broadcasts called 'The Black Record', published in 1941. In these, he emphasised the innate brutality of the German race. As Lovell notes: 'paradoxically, a model which gave a reverse mirror-image to that offered by Hitler of an "Aryan" super-race' (1984: 31).

17. For a contemporary discussion of Vansittartism and other writing on the 'German Problem', see Lach (1945), who concludes that 'while the Allied nations were quite definitely on the defensive in the present war, the studies produced tended to be of the Vansittart type; as the Allies gradually assumed the military initiative and had military successes, an increase could be observed in the number of more lenient studies' (243), although the revelation of the Final Solution in 1945 probably hardened public opinion once more.

18. *Frieda* appeared in several 'Best Film of the Year' lists, including the *Daily Mail* and the *Daily Express*. It featured in the *Motion Picture Herald's* – annual list of 'Box-Office Champions', while Mai Zetterling was named in the *Kinematograph Weekly's* 'Annual Film Survey' as a 'most promising newcomer' (Noble 1950: 157–63).

19. See the contemporary discussion of attitudes towards Germany in Hermens (1945–46).

20. Furthermore, Barr argues:

> Though Frieda was a financial success, it seems to close many doors for Ealing . . . there is a suppression of a dark world: a reluctance not only to look levelly at Nazism and what it represents, but to go beyond the bland exterior of the hero and his community and actually investigate the passions and their conflicts. It makes us ask seriously what kind of adult hero, or heroine, Ealing can encompass, and whether there is any dynamic in this community that can reach outwards and forwards. (1977: 76)

21. It should be conceded that the film, in Nell, Judy and Frieda (labouring at the farm), has several examples of modern career and working women.

22. See Ede (1997: 253) and discussion in Chapter 1.
23. This statement was to have followed the opening credits of the film, setting out its message in advance. In the event, it was not used.
24. For instance *Captain Boycott* (d. F. Launder, 1947), but more obviously *Odd Man Out* (d. C. Reed, 1947), which as Hill (1987: 160) has noted, articulated a similar, 'very British' reaction to Irish nationalism and political violence.
25. MacDougall was a writer and director of documentaries and plays. He had first worked with Dearden when they co-scripted *This Man is News* (d. D. MacDonald 1938). Later, he worked with Dearden and Relph on the script of their first film together, *The Bells Go Down* (1943). He worked at Ealing intermittently between 1939 and 1953 and is best known for his play and subsequent script for *The Man in the White Suit* (d. A. Mackendrick 1951). He was the cousin of Alexander Mackendrick, and Richards dubs him 'one of the keepers of the Ealing ethical conscience' (1997: 26).
26. Harding was an interesting if possibly controversial casting choice. At this time, his career had moved from work in radio to gain notoriety in the very popular early 1950s BBC television show *What's My Line*, where he became 'Britain's rudest man'. Medhurst, in his sensitive analysis, notes that 'his potential as a box-office draw proved an irresistible temptation' for filmmakers of the time; further commenting that: 'With the exception of *The Gentle Gunman*, a deeply confused drama about the IRA that uses Harding, in scenes outside the main narrative, as a symbol of stubborn Englishness, it's notable that the films he appeared in are all comedies' (1991: 69). Dearden reportedly found him to be a 'well-disciplined' member of the cast, who 'obeyed instructions' (*Campaign Folder*, Ealing Studios, n.d.).
27. Dirk Bogarde's film career was in its ascendancy. He had worked with Dearden and Relph to some acclaim in *The Blue Lamp* (1950) and would later work with them in *Victim* (1961) and *The Mind Benders* (1963). He first encountered Dearden at the 'Q' Theatre before the war and he appeared as a film extra in *Come On, George!* (d. A. Kimmins, 1938), on which Dearden acted as assistant director.
28. London Transport collaborated in converting the Aldwych section of Holborn station for these location scenes, including sign changes, a second hand fitted to the clock, and the import of Ealing telephone booths (See Campaign Folder, Ealing Studios, n.d.). The shooting script notes that the Tube platform aimed to capture the look of a Henry Moore drawing (the 'Shelter Sketches').
29. John Mills' film career was also in ascendancy at this time and he had just finished his contract with Rank. He had recently completed the suspense melodrama *Mr Denning Drives North* (d. A. Kimmins, 1951) and was about to start work (with Elizabeth Sellars) on the haunting British *noir The Long Memory* (d. R. Hamer, 1952). These films and *The Gentle Gunman* he recorded as 'rent and tax jobs', 'honest pieces of work and nothing to be ashamed of', although he wryly noted of *The Gentle Gunman*: 'if a re-make was considered now the title would unfortunately need changing' (1980: 321). He had first worked with Dearden in *The Black Sheep of Whitehall* (d. Dearden/Hay, 1941).

30. The shooting script doesn't fully concur with this analysis. The commentary at this point indicates the following: 'She [Maureen] stands expectantly, giving herself to him for the first time. The surge of physical desire sweeps away the possibility of analysis. They kiss. But it is Matt who breaks the kiss. He has a grim, purposeful determination in his manner as he moves away' (35–6).

31. Barr commented that the film is 'an abandonment of the political issues as such in favour of a generalised humanism' (1977: 147), and suggested that it is 'The film which marks the transition in Dearden's work from open to closed, live to dead: a stiff stage adaptation, with Bogarde and Mills cast unconvincingly as Irish brothers and a platitudinously worked–out anti–violence, all–men–are–brothers, message' (Ibid.: 191). Durgnat was taken by the film's lack of topicality: 'one supposes that R–D were trying to persuade boys who thought it tough to use coshes that the really tough boys (who used guns) preferred being gentle' (1966: 30).

32. See for relevant discussion McIlroy (1998), which gives a very brief mention of the film, and Schlesinger, Murdock and Elliott (1983).

33. While some of these scenes were shot on location, the action in the water was filmed in the 'lot tank' at Pinewood (*Final Shooting Script*: 11–12).

34. This appears to be based on Leviticus 17: 10.

35. The film suggests that Hart-Jacobs is Jewish and that Clyde is a Catholic.

36. The press are not given 'a good press' in the film, which tends to emphasise its sensation–seeking, scandal–mongering qualities at the expense of any responsible public interest role. In a later scene with Hart-Jacobs, Harris refuses to raise money for his defence by selling his story to the papers on the basis that 'if they buy my name, they'll print anything and I can't stop them'.

37. Of course, viewers did adopt specific moral positions in relation to the drama. Roger Manvell was influenced by the stance of Dr Brown, admitting that 'I now realise that, as the law stands, children could be prevented from receiving the treatment they need through the prejudice of their parents' (*Films and Filming*, August 1962).

38. He suggests that the film cost £126,800 to make and by mid-1971 had only grossed £53,788 world-wide. With an Eady levy of only £18,626, it did not cover its production costs and fell a long way short of profitability for AFM. Rank's profit margin was, however, guaranteed (1974: 248).

39. He goes on to suggest that the film is a much more *structured* piece in these terms, when compared for instance with *A Taste of Honey* (d. T. Richardson, 1961) or *Saturday Night and Sunday Morning* (d. K. Reisz, 1960).

40. In its 'Best of the Season' round-up, *Films and Filming* awarded *Life for Ruth* a 'highly recommended' rating (October 1962).

41. In their final film together, the psychological thriller *The Man Who Haunted Himself* (1970), Dearden and Relph would again visit the possibility of multiple personalities.

42. For a period in the late 1950s, Dearden and Relph had planned to head the production of *Tunes of Glory*.

43. The novel was simultaneously released in paperback by Pan Books as a film tie-in.

44. See, for example, Badsey (1998) and Scheflin (1978).
45. *Kine Weekly* recorded that it was in production from mid-July through to September at Pinewood. The signing of Wendy Craig completed casting (23 August 1962); location shooting in Oxford is recorded as late as November (29 November 1962).
46. Aldgate provides an insightful account of this process suggesting: 'To the last, the censors exerted their influence to ensure that the degree of harrowing intimate detail invested in the film was well and truly constrained.' Furthermore, as he maintains, it was precisely these details that Kennaway's script sought to depict and explore (1997: 220).
47. An opening statement, wishing to establish scientific validity, records that the story was suggested by experiments on 'The Reduction of Sensation' recently carried out at the University of Indiana and other universities in the United States.
48. *Kine Weekly* carried a feature on location shooting for these scenes at Windsor station (30 August 1962). Bryant had first come to Dearden and Relph's attention in *Life for Ruth*.
49. This is a similar opening to *The Ipcress File* (novel 1962; film 1965), which also deals with the brainwashing of top scientists.
50. Dearden's shooting script indicates that the sequences in the pool using underwater equipment were shot using facilities at Siebe Gorman, a London-based company which had pioneered underwater diving and marine salvage equipment from the early 1900s. Their tank, set up for underwater filming, was hired for recording the scenes of Longman shot from below the surface of the water.
51. In this, *Kine Weekly* was rather isolated on this occasion as reviews in general dismissed the film: 'a tepid mess of sentiment' (*Time*, 10 May 1963); 'a pretty shabby and sordid example of the genre' (*Daily Express*, 28 February 1963); 'a rather simplistic and silly film' (*Observer*, 3 March 1963).
52. Later developments, following from the 1979 US Freedom of Information Act, revealed that Britain had been co-operating with the CIA since the early 1950s in experiments similar to those depicted in the film. In 1978, Britain was also criticised in the European courts for allowing the army to employ such methods in Northern Ireland.
53. In a later feature on Dirk Bogarde ('A great actor who has never appeared in a great film'), *Films and Filming* further dismissed *The Mind Benders* as 'a fine theme trivialised' (November 1963). Bogarde himself later recalled the film as a 'thumping failure', which at the time 'depressed me deeply' (1979: 221).
54. Implicit in his criticism is the desire to acknowledge the honesty of conviction in the filmmakers; as Durgnat concedes, 'when their films irritate, it is on the strength of their genuine presence' (1966: 33).

7

The International Years

Woman of Straw (1964), Masquerade (1965), Khartoum (1966), Only When I Larf (1968), The Assassination Bureau (1969) and The Persuaders! (TV, 1971–72)

> British production was down in the first six months of this year compared with the corresponding period in 1963. This will surprise no one. After all, 1964 started off as one of the darkest periods in the history of the industry. What will come as a surprise to many is that the decline is not greater. (*Kinematograph Weekly*, 25 June 1964)

In the second half of the 1960s, Dearden and Relph worked together on a series of big-budget films aimed at the world market and made for Hollywood companies operating in Britain. They were all in colour, extensively used exotic foreign locations and featured international stars. With the single exception of the imperial epic *Khartoum*, none of the films has attracted critical attention. Alexander Walker's weighty treatment of the cinema in Britain in the 1960s, *Hollywood England*, has nothing at all to say about Dearden and Relph after their black-and-white social dramas of the early 1960s; Robert Murphy's more scholarly examination, *Sixties British Cinema*, acknowledges the existence of the films, but shows no particular interest in them beyond their 'glossy cosmopolitanism' (1992: 43); while the official post-war history of United Artists (UA) by Tino Balio (1987) ignores the three films Dearden and Relph made for the company between 1964 and 1966, despite a careful examination of UA's production policy in Europe in the period. Most tellingly, apart from a brief discussion of *Only When I Larf* as part of an examination of Dearden and the 'English comic tradition' by Paul Wells, the anthology of writings brought together in *Liberal Directions: Basil Dearden and Postwar British Film Culture* has nothing at all to say about the films of this later period.

All of the major Hollywood companies had a history of financing production in Britain. In the 1950s, the American studios took advantage of lower filmmaking costs and the subsidies derived from the Eady levy to finance local productions. Film critic Dilys Powell observed that by 1956 a third of the films made in Britain had some form of American involvement (cited in Oakley 1964: 215). The films ranged from colourful spectacles like *Captain Horatio Hornblower R.N.* (Warner Bros., 1951) and *The Bridge on the River Kwai* (Columbia, 1957), to lower-key black-and-white dramas like *Sons and Lovers* (Fox, 1960) and *The L-Shaped Room* (Columbia, 1961), and included genre films such as the popular Miss Marple mysteries starring Margaret Rutherford (MGM, 1961–64).

The overseas market became increasingly important to Hollywood producers who were finding it more and more difficult to break even at home. It has been calculated by Tino Balio that, by 1960, foreign sales accounted for 40 per cent of Hollywood's total income and UA proved to be the best-equipped and most aggressive company in this aspect of the business. With no studio of its own, UA had flexibility to deal with independent producers wherever they were based, and proved an attractive partner to creative talents who did not relish being shackled to the expensive production facilities of the other majors and were left free to arrange production to suit the requirements of the film. By 1972, UA had captured more than a quarter of the overseas theatrical market (Balio 1987: 222). The company opened a production office in London in 1961 under the control of George H. (Bud) Ornstein, and a piece of good fortune brought producers Cubby Broccoli and Harry Saltzman to Ornstein in his first year of operations. These two North American producers had been active in the British film industry for a number of years – Broccoli at Warwick Films and Saltzman at Woodfall – and a deal was signed to produce the inaugural James Bond film. The modestly budgeted *Dr No* was released in 1962 to profitable, if unspectacular, success; but the increasingly extravagant and popular *From Russia With Love* (1963), *Goldfinger* (1964) and *Thunderball* (1965) launched the most successful series in motion picture history (Walker 1974: 178–98; Balio 1987: 253–74). Ornstein was also fortunate to conclude a deal with John Osborne and Tony Richardson's Woodfall production company, to finance its adaptation of Henry Fielding's *Tom Jones* in 1962. The spectacular success of that release in 1963, coupled with the fortunes being made by the Bond films and the first Beatles' film, *A Hard Days Night* (1964),[1] raised UA to an unassailable position as the leading American company producing in Britain.

The other leading Hollywood film companies were bound to be tempted by such conspicuous success and by the mid-1960s the impact of the American companies on the British film industry was transformative. As Robert Murphy has remarked:

The energy and panache of the Beatles and Bond films, the success of British pop music, and the development of the myth of Swinging London made British society suddenly exciting, charismatic and fashionable. After decades in which Britain had followed American trends, it seemed that the process had been reversed. London was seen as the centre of a youth-oriented cultural revolution which young Americans found fascinating and appealing. By the mid-60s all the majors and two mini-majors – Filmways and Avco-Embassy – had set up British production subsidiaries.

Official figures supplied by the National Film Finance Corporation revealed that 75 per cent of production finance for British films came from American sources by 1966; only a year later it reached a staggering 90 per cent (Murphy 1992: 257–8). While attention has understandably been directed at the films most reflective of the exuberant youth scene centred on London, such as *The Knack* (UA, 1965) and *Blow-Up* (MGM, 1966), many productions, ranging from *A Countess From Hong Kong* (Universal, 1966) to *Where Eagles Dare* (MGM, 1969), were conservative and cautious, and remained firmly tied to the traditional family audience. As experienced and accomplished filmmakers, Dearden and Relph were attractive prospects and consequently signed production agreements with American companies, first of all with UA and subsequently with Paramount; however, their ages and temperament did not lead them to the cultural and stylistic novelties of the Swinging London films, but rather to the solidly crafted and glossy international features that were also part of the production scene of the latter half the 1960s. This partly explains the lack of critical attention for their cinema in the period, as it appears old-fashioned and respectable in comparison to the energy and experimentation that was taking place around it. The modest commercial success of the films also reduced their visibility and profile.

WOMAN OF STRAW (1964)

More people will probably leave their television sets to see *West Side Story*, *55 Days in Peking*, *The Longest Day* or *South Pacific*, than for a good British film costing a fraction as much and without spectacle, colour or international star names. A modest return to the producer may be sufficient to support this type of production, but exhibitors would obviously rather play blockbusters if they are available – and, with only two circuits to fill – enough are now available. (Michael Relph, *Films and Filming*, June 1964)

Writing in *Films and Filming* in June 1964, Michael Relph deplored the 'Machiavellian' character of the two main cinema circuits, believing that Rank and ABC had decided that 'no further subsidy of British production shall be part of their policy' (12). Catching the prevailing wind of change blowing in from the west, Dearden and Relph signed an attractive production deal with Ornstein at UA early in 1963, shortly before *A Place to Go* (1963) began shooting.[2] The contract stipulated that the team would make three big-budget pictures costing around $2 million each;[3] the programme would commence with *Woman of Straw* starring Gina Lollobrigida, from the novel *La Femme de Paille* by Catherine Arley, published in France in 1957. Later in the summer it was announced that Sean Connery and Sir Ralph Richardson would join the Italian starlet in what was clearly intended as a top-draw production. This would be Connery's first chance to break out from the typecasting likely to arise from the Bond roles.[4] Shooting commenced at Pinewood early in August 1963 and wrapped late in October; while the unit spent a period on location in Majorca during September.[5] There have been suggestions that it was a difficult shoot, with the demanding and temperamental actress clashing with both Dearden and Connery (Sellers 1990: 61–2).

At the time, Dearden and Relph were arguing the need for more lavish British films and that some way must be found of financing bigger British pictures. The deal with UA was clearly one way forward. Interviewed by *Kinematograph Weekly*, Relph asserted that '*Woman of Straw* is the antithesis of the near-documentaries. With its production values it has an affinity with the films made in the '30s. It's what the public wants.' As Relph saw it, 'The choice of subject is the keystone of any big-budget picture':

> There's a basic difference in your choice of story because you know you're going to have an international star cast. You start with big stars in mind. You couldn't make this type of picture on a 'British' budget. It would be lacking in its main elements – stars, locations, elaborate settings. (7 November 1963)

There was a clear meeting of minds on *Woman of Straw*, with Dearden and Relph bringing Ornstein the type of production he felt he could sell on the international market. Throughout the decade the three filmmakers would continue to collaborate on the assumption that 'stars, locations and elaborate settings' were the basis for a commercial cinema based in Britain, one financed from America, drawing largely on British talent, and with a genuine prospect in the world market.

Woman of Straw was granted a prestigious world première at the Odeon, Leicester Square, on 30 April 1964, and put into general release in June when it would have maximum opportunity in the popular summer holiday period. It attracted good reviews in the trade press, which was receptive to the obvious box-office potential of big star names, grand settings and colour.

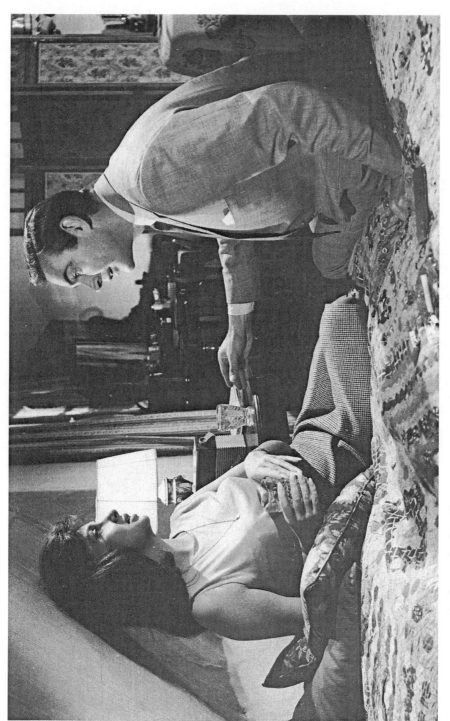

Anthony pleads with Maria in *Woman of Straw* (1964) (Courtesy of Steve Chibnall Archive)

Here the production values were foregrounded and praise heaped on the 'lush atmosphere of extreme riches' that 'envelops the whole film and gives it a glossy appeal'. The film was also appreciated for its 'dramatic values', with the reviewer at *Kine Weekly* reporting that 'The way in which the tension is built up and the final villainy concealed make this a first-class thriller, and it is very well acted by all' (30 April 1964). The critics attached to the film journals and the serious newspapers were far less impressed. They tended to dismiss the film as a vacuous exercise, 'slow to get under way and unexcitingly but capably made with a luxury budget to compensate for the absence of low-cost ingenuity'.[6] While conceding that *Woman of Straw* was pleasing on the eye, the script was dismissed as artificial, the playing only adequate and the mood insufficiently developed. It was considered inferior to such recent 'exotic but truth-observing thrillers' as the French *Plein Soleil* (d. R. Clement, 1963); and that Dearden lacked the necessary artistry and 'flamboyant sense of dramatic symbolism to bring it to life' (*Films and Filming*, June 1964).[7] According to *Monthly Film Bulletin*, what the film needed was

> a towering Wellesian view of a lift climbing slowly past arches and chandeliers, a more shattering use of the visual imagery of polished cars such as Losey can make, a touch of Hitchcock to sharpen suspense and turn the howl of a dog into something inhuman instead of noises off. Any film of such glamorous pretensions cannot fail to evoke memories of what *can* be done with similar material. (emphasis in original)

As for the film's failure, 'the reason lies, as so often in British films, in a reluctant approach to the theme' (31, 360/371, 1964). It was common to remark how much better Hitchcock would have done with this material; he at least, through sheer cinema, would have overcome the deficiencies in the script; whereas 'Mr Basil Deardon [*sic*], the director on this occasion, stumbles grimly into every one' (*The Times*, 30 April 1964). Ray Durgnat found the main story 'merely competent', but discerned the life of the film in the 'vignettes of the browbeaten skipper and suspicious butler', sequences of 'needle-sharp penetration': the qualities of spite, fear and other craven emotions brewing under a friendly or correct façade 'an emotional range which R-D always handle very well indeed' (1966: 32).

The story concerns the recruitment of a nurse (Maria, played by Lollobrigida) in a plot to inherit the fortune of an ageing and invalided millionaire, Charles Richmond (Richardson). She is guided by the nephew Anthony Richmond (Connery), who acts as the old man's secretary, and is bitter that he is provided for only £20,000 in his uncle's will. Anthony also bears a hatred for his uncle who had ruined his father and subsequently married his mother. He therefore schemes to have the old man marry Maria with the view to a much larger settlement when she inherits the considerable estate upon Charles's death. In the outcome, the naïve Maria is duped by Anthony who has plotted all along to murder Charles, place the blame on the nurse and inherit the whole fortune. Maria is convicted of the murder, but, with the help of a loyal servant, a wily policeman traps Anthony into making a last-minute confession, and the killer is conveniently killed crashing down a stone stairway while trying to flee.

In a very general sense the contemporary critical views were fair: Dearden turned in a sumptuous production with attractive star performances, but his approach lacked the kind of depth and signature auteurism preferred at the *MFB*. The film's substantial achievements could be described as 'architectural' and resided in the ostentatious production designs of Ken Adams and the elegant colour cinematography of trusted colleague Otto Heller. These were at their best in the scenes set in the cavernous interiors of Foxhurst, Charles Richmond's estate, where the grasping characters are dwarfed by the palatial surroundings which constantly reflect the weight of their material desires. The camera weaves elegant patterns around the scheming principals and resplendent mise-en-scène; however, it is not well served by regular editor, John D. Guthridge, who unnecessarily disrupts the intricate movements and reframings with conventional reaction shots. Many critics were right in attributing the central problem of the drama to the script by Robert Muller and Stanley Mann, which failed to find convincing motivations for the characters enacting a rather implausible melodrama.[8] Moreover, the deviations from the source novel demanded by popular cinema made the film more predictable and unsatisfying, with the revelation of the real murderer hastily and unconvincingly contrived in the final moments and despatched in a moment of forced ironic retribution. In the original, the drama is played much more grimly, with the accused nurse entirely ensnared within the trap laid by the murderer, and, reduced to hopelessness, taking her own life in the dismal surroundings of her police cell. The novel is permeated with a sense of evil that is suggestively linked back to the moral desolation of the war. The film dispenses entirely with any sense of historical determination and opts for the more restricted horizons of a chamber piece. It additionally softens and conventionalises the characters, especially the nurse and the secretary: one made more naïve and thus less culpable; the other explained away in oedipal terms rather than the figure of despicable evil that stalks through the book. The film also serves up the 'happy' ending expected of popular cinema and therefore abandons even the modest moral complexities of the novel.

Joseph Losey or Alfred Hitchcock might arguably have made more of the material, while the latter in particular would have had an affinity for the Pygmalion-like drama of the novel and its moral probing of guilt and

retribution. However, it should be borne in mind that immediately following his work with Dearden and Relph, Sean Connery went on to work with
the 'Master of Suspense' on *Marnie* (1964), a film bearing some similarity to
Woman of Straw, but which turned out to be a critical failure and began what
many felt to be the long decline of the celebrated filmmaker. Furthermore,
when Losey joined forces with the kind of budgets offered by UA in the late
1960s, his characteristically ornate approach to *Secret Ceremony* and *Boom* (both
1968) proved disastrous at the box office. Ornstein preferred to invest UA's
substantial budget outlays in a more conventional approach, and retained faith
in the less risky commercial potential of Dearden and Relph and the tradition
of the well-made film.

MASQUERADE (1965)

> The basic assumption governing the pattern of expectations we bring
> to the reading of thrillers can thus be defined as the belief that precisely
> because it is hermetic and self-referential, the spy novel – like the world
> of play – preserves its value by *not* being serious. (Marc Silverstein, cited
> in *Twentieth-Century Literary Criticism 50*, 1993; emphasis in original)

Early in September 1964, Michael Relph flew to New York to meet with
UA executives to discuss promotion plans for *Woman of Straw*, due to open
in key American cities later in the month. *Kine Weekly* reported chairman Arnold Picker as saying: 'We at UA are particularly delighted with
"Woman of Straw", and have a very high expectation for the picture on the
American market' (3 September 1964).[9] Relph also took the opportunity to
make arrangements for the launching of *Shabby Tiger*, the latest production
of the Dearden–Relph team for UA release. This was an adaptation of the
novel *Castle Minerva* (1955) by thriller writer Victor Canning and renamed
Masquerade shortly before its general release in April 1965. Production had
commenced late in May 1964 with three weeks' location in Spain, before a
return to Pinewood for seven weeks in the studio.[10] The film became the official British entry at the San Sebastian Film Festival held in June the following
year (*Kinematograph Weekly*'s, 20 May and 3 June 1965).

Dearden and Relph had been associated with the project for a decade, it
having been announced as far back as the autumn of 1955, at the time the
partnership was shooting *Who Done It?*, that the team would adapt the book
for Ealing (*To-Day's Cinema*, 10 October 1955; *Kinematograph Weekly*, 15
December 1955). It is not surprising that they were attracted to an exciting
adventure yarn that had at its centre an ageing Second World War hero, now
involved with the secret service, but disenchanted and feeling inadequately

rewarded for his sacrifices and long service. It has clear points of similarity with *The Ship That Died of Shame* in its reunion of wartime comrades for a dangerous mission; and in the moral polarity between its two protagonists: one who is prepared to abandon the values of loyalty and duty for material gain; the other more inclined to maintain the certainties and standards of comradeship and humanism. If Dearden and Relph had made the film in the mid-1950s, it would have been played like the novel as a straight action drama with right winning out at the conclusion. However, by the end of the 1950s, and as clearly exemplified in *The League of Gentlemen*, Dearden and Relph had already modified this linear approach to their characteristic theme of masculine adjustment to that of ironic comedy. Therefore, the post-Suez realities of emasculated British diplomacy and its reduced world standing similarly reconfigure *Castle Minerva* into the gently parodic *Masquerade*, which pokes fun at Britain's imperial decline and its outdated officer stereotypes.

The effect is reinforced through the casting of Jack Hawkins as the embittered senior intelligence officer Colonel Drexel, who hatches a complicated plot of kidnapping and ransoming a Middle Eastern boy-prince, while ostensibly serving the interests of his diplomatic masters and the powerful Anglo-Median Oil Company. Partially reprising his role of Colonel Hyde from *The League of Gentlemen*, Hawkins turns in another jaded and resentful officer-type seeking monetary reward for all the years of danger, hardship and service that he has devoted to his country. Recruited into the adventure on the promise of £500 is the unwitting Frazer, a wartime comrade who now lives a life of shady deals, and whom Drexel is prepared to sacrifice as the scapegoat to a mission intentionally gone wrong. The part was originally intended for Rex Harrison, but when he dropped out he was replaced by Cliff Robertson, who had recently come to prominence in Franklin J. Shaffner's *The Best Man* (1964), and young scriptwriter William Goldman was brought in to recast the role to suit the American lead (Goldman 1985: 170).[11]

The main themes of the film, the nostalgia for the war with its moral certainties and the subsequent replacement of the active service officer by the 'passionless and practical' bureaucrat, are summarised in an exchange between Drexel and Frazer early in the drama and before the play of cross and double-cross has commenced:

> *Drexel*: David, do you ever miss the war? Oh, I do! Everything was so much simpler then.
> *Frazer*: Just the good guys and the bad guys eh!
> *Drexel*: That's what I miss about the war David. I can't spot the bad guys anymore. That's why we were good soldiers; all the bad guys were visible then. We haven't done so well since have we? Funny, I'm one

of the least successful men I know. Even my marriages didn't work out and I want a bit of peace. Sometimes I think I should settle for a cottage in the country.

At this point, Drexel nods off after the exertions of kidnapping the prince, as age inexorably creeps up on the man of action.

Drexel's plan is to have the unsuspecting Frazer blamed for the kidnapping, pay him from the ransom money and let him disappear in South America. In the event, the American is surprised to find that he has 'scruples' and resists the traitorous intelligence office and his gang of circus performers. The moral and physical confrontation between the antagonists is played out in the film's best scene. Frazer has been held in the deserted Castle Minerva, and while in the act of breaking out discovers that Drexel is behind the disappearance of the prince and intends to put the blame on him. The two meet in the dilapidated chapel of the castle, the scene bathed in a blood-red light, and the dense religious iconography heightens the unfolding moral conflict. Initially, Drexel wins Frazer over with the promise of £50,000; however, the Christian icons, crowding into the frame, impress themselves upon Frazer's conscience and the two men are forced to fight it out. Drexel informs the younger man that he too once had scruples, but 'they had to go':

> Now you knew me during the war; well, I was a good soldier, a good man I think. But since then you don't know the sort of jobs they've put me to. What's a patriot David? I think I'm one. But I've had to kill men – patriots like me – simply because they were on the other side. Sometimes I don't think I know what's right or wrong anymore. I had to lose my scruples; and what did they give me instead: A pat on the back, a word of praise in a secret report, a dinner at the club. I want more than that – materially I mean.

In the ensuing fight, Frazer subdues the older man, but is quickly reclaimed into the power of the circus troupe that is being paid by Drexel to help realise his plan.

The two former comrades confront each other again at the film's climax. Drexel is attempting to get the prince to the final rendezvous to collect the ransom money and Frazer has trapped them on a flimsy rope bridge. Inevitably, the bridge collapses under the strain and Drexel and his captive are left dangling precariously high over a gorge. In the original novel, Drexel rediscovers his integrity at this moment of peril, sacrifices himself to save the boy and, refusing Frazer's proffered hand, allows himself to fall to his death in the ravine below. The film rejects this altruistic act of redemption to allow for a more cynical conclusion. Instead, Frazer saves the senior man and is repaid

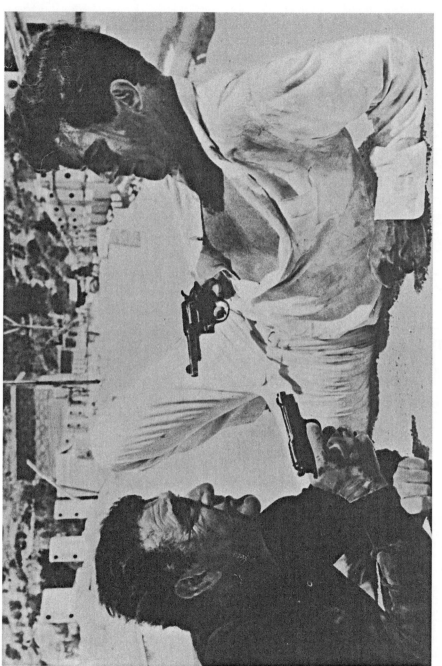

Drexel and Frazer in the final stand-off in *Masquerade* (1965) (Courtesy of Steve Chibnall Archive)

by a further act of treachery from Drexel who refuses to abandon his lucrative plan, leaving the two men locked in a 'Mexican stand-off' – aiming their pistols at each other and wondering who has the nerve to shoot first. They are prevented from killing each other by the arrival of the Spanish police and Benson (Charles Grey), a British diplomat, who descends imperiously from a helicopter onto the field of combat. Back in London, Drexel and Frazer are congratulated by an ingenuous Chief of British Intelligence (John Le Mesurier) for an 'entirely successful mission'. Drexel is rewarded with a lucrative position with the Anglo-Median Oil Company; while Frazer has to make do with the offer of dinner at the Chief's club (a knowing look from Drexel) and £11 9s. 2d. – the balance left from the £500 after the deduction of back taxes.

Masquerade was one of a spate of parodic espionage films that appeared in the mid-1960s and was accordingly accused of 'jumping on the Bondwaggon' (*Daily Mail*, 14 April 1965);[12] it duly incorporated the generic trappings of a catchy theme song, exotic locations and trendy, self-referential nods to James Bond.[13] For the reviewer at *Monthly Film Bulletin*, this was all very obvious and added up to little more than a 'sluggish thriller' wrapped up in a 'laborious overlay of modish cynicism'. Struggling to find any merit in the film, it eventually concedes that the 'Spanish locations are attractive'. In what had become orthodoxy at the periodical, the failings were laid squarely at the feet of the director, where Dearden wasn't considered to be the 'lightest or most inventive of directors':

> He films very much as the plot comes. Most of the thrills, such as they are, come from foolproof standbys like the last-minute rescue from the crumbling suspension bridge, or Frazer's escape along a perilously high and narrow ledge; the one really striking scene, when Frazer is abducted in a circus, by four clowns in full view of the audience, is painfully mishandled so as to rob it of all its potential effect. (32: 372/383, 1965)[14]

In complete contrast, *The Times* reviewer felt that 'Mr Basil Dearden has directed with right tongue-in-cheek verve, and carries off the suspense set-pieces as though they had never been done before'. A sentiment echoed at the *Saturday Review*, where it was acknowledged that 'There is nothing in *Masquerade* that has not been done dozens of times before . . . But what makes it work is the director's wink, his tacit admission that he knows it's nonsense, but isn't it lots of fun' (8 May 1965). There was also praise at *The Times* for Relph and Goldman, who had 'ingeniously' worked over a rather 'ordinary, stiff-upper-lip novel' (15 April 1965); and at the *Sunday Times*, which felt Robertson had exactly and agreeably found the 'unheroic bearing of the hero' (18 April 1965). The trade press was also receptive to the commercial formula of the film and informed its readership of cinema exhibitors that *Masquerade* had 'most of the qualities for big success'. It was felt that Dearden had handled the blend of humour and excitement expertly, and kept firm control of an intricate plot, thus warding off any danger of confusion, and added: 'the penultimate climax when Frazer rescues Drexel and Jamil from the dangling remains of a footbridge over a ravine will have audiences on the edges of their seats' (*Kinematograph Weekly*, 1 April 1965).

The general assessment was that *Masquerade* offered a pleasurable blend of action and light comedy, and had a few worthwhile satirical comments to make regarding espionage narratives and the concomitant fictions of Britain's world standing. Viewed from the vantage point of today, and despite its trendy elements, the film has a distinctly old-fashioned feel about it. This was partly the result of casting well-known character actors like Bill Fraser and John Le Mesurier, who had appeared in numerous service comedies of the 1950s and who reprised archetypes that had served them well in such films as *Carlton-Browne of the FO* (1958), and partly the outcome of Dearden and Relph's investment in material that had its origins in the post-war decade and hence resisted to an extent the degree of modernity that came effortlessly, for example, to the *Flint* films starring James Coburn.

KHARTOUM (1966)

The origins of this imperial epic lie with the independent American producer Julian Blaustein, who contracted to make the film with United Artists in the autumn of 1963 and was no doubt looking to emulate the commercial and critical success of *Lawrence of Arabia* (1962). *Khartoum*, an immense production, was three years in preparation. Originally, the intention had been to shoot the film in the Sudan, only a short distance from Khartoum, with a budget of around $4 million and shooting to commence in February 1965. Burt Lancaster would play the central role of General Gordon; Laurence Olivier was announced to play the Mahdi; Lewis Gilbert was signed to direct; and Freddie Young would photograph the film in Ultra Panavision.[15] However, civil unrest in the Sudan meant a postponement and drastic revisions to the production plans. Despite some set construction in the Sudan, the production, now proposed at $5–6 million, was relocated to Egypt (*Variety*, 18 November 1964). The main role of Gordon was eventually accepted by Charlton Heston early in 1965, and Ralph Richardson and Richard Johnson were confirmed in the cast in July as Prime Minister Gladstone and Colonel Stewart respectively (*Kinematograph Weekly*'s, 29 April and 29 July 1965).[16] The assignment of a director was a similarly protracted business. Heston pushed for Carol Reed, with whom he had developed a rapport making *The Agony and the Ecstasy*

(1965); but the British filmmaker declined, feeling unable to take on another large-scale production. Bernhard Wicki, Ken Hughes, Guy Green and Guy Hamilton were also considered. In March, possibly at the urging of United Artists, Heston screened *Sapphire* and a second undisclosed film by Dearden to assess his suitability for directing *Khartoum*, but was left undecided, finding them good, but stronger on plot than on character (Heston 1978: 218–23). In the absence of an alternative candidate, the assignment finally went to Dearden, but Heston could never rid himself of his doubts about the British director, noting, ungrammatically: 'He impresses me about as his films do: seriously but not overwhelmingly' (1978: 224).[17] The responsibility for cinematography finally went to Ted Scaife who had worked with Dearden three years earlier on *All Night Long*.

There were five weeks of shooting at Pinewood, beginning early in August, followed by extensive location work in Egypt involving two full units, then a short return to the studio to complete the scenes involving Laurence Olivier, who had been unavailable until later in December.[18] *Khartoum* was granted a Royal Charity première in the presence of Princess Margaret at the Casino Cinerama Theatre, London, where it opened to 'smash business', despite the uncommonly warm weather (*Kinematograph Weekly*'s, 31 March and 16 June 1966).

The film gathered good reviews and was widely appreciated as an intelligent epic, lovingly crafted, handsomely mounted and sensitively acted. The edifice on which all this was built was Robert Ardrey's script, which attracted much praise from the critics for its literate quality and authenticity.[19] Heston had instantly recognised its exceptional nature and reckoned it to be one of the best he had ever read (1995: 385). *The Times* was impressed that *Khartoum* managed the rare task of marrying spectacle with intelligence, offering an 'absorbing' screenplay,

> [W]hich really tries to make sense of Gordon, Gladstone, and the whole messy business of Khartoum, and does so by making all the participants what they were, articulate, complex characters whose unpredictable interaction brought about an almost inevitable disaster. (9 June 1966)

There was also praise for the direction of Basil Dearden, the reviewer at *Kine Weekly* believing he had revealed 'hidden heights' (16 June 1966); while the 'astonished' reviewer at the *Sun* 'did not know he had it in him' (18 June 1966). The contemporary account of the making of *Khartoum*, recorded in Heston's journals, relates a generally efficient production and a commendable performance by the crew in often difficult circumstances.[20] Although Dearden is rarely mentioned by name, the director must take some credit for this aspect of the work. After its release in the United States, Heston was pleased

DIRECT FROM ITS RESERVED SEAT PRESENTATION
Continuous Performances! Popular Prices!

CHARLTON HESTON
as GORDON

LAURENCE OLIVIER
as THE MAHDI

RICHARD JOHNSON
RALPH RICHARDSON

THEY SAY THE NILE STILL RUNS RED FROM THE BATTLE FOR KHARTOUM!

A JULIAN BLAUSTEIN
PRODUCTION

"Khartoum"

Produced by	Written by	Directed by	Filmed in
JULIAN BLAUSTEIN	ROBERT ARDREY	BASIL DEARDEN	ULTRA PANAVISION

ORIGINAL MOTION PICTURE SCORE AVAILABLE ON UNITED ARTISTS' RECORDS.
FERRANTE & TEICHER SINGLE OF MAIN THEME AVAILABLE ON UA RECORDS.

TECHNICOLOR Released thru **UNITED ARTISTS**

T H E A T R E

with the film's positive critical reception and the emergent view that it was his best film and performance to date. He concluded that 'Khartoum seemed to me to be a very, very good film' (1978: 252). The actor was less generous in his assessment of Dearden when he came to write his autobiography. Acknowledging that 'We had a superb script, a very high-powered cast, and a dedicated and intelligent producer', Heston dismissed any contribution by the director, believing Dearden had only managed a 'routine job on the shoot', 'contributing little to the performances' (Heston 1995: 367).[21]

This is disingenuous. Heston had put much primacy on the script and was effusive in his praise of the acting, clearly relishing the opportunity to play opposite Olivier and Richardson. It is quite evident that Dearden also held the script in high regard and in his approach honoured the integrity of the unusually literate screenplay and trusted the experienced and talented actors to make the most of the exceptional opportunity. This was an achievement recognised by some of the more thoughtful critics, who noted that 'Between them the director and his scriptwriter have achieved a rare blend of verbal and visual drama' (*Daily Mail*, 8 June 1966); and there was general praise for the calculatedly detached approach of the director, which had resulted in an 'uncommonly cool epic'. While this style had not been appreciated in *Woman of Straw*, it was welcomed in *Khartoum* as serving the drama in a 'straightforward but interesting way', and wisely allowing unfettered space for the superb dialogue and clashes of powerful personalities. Gordon Gow at *Films and Filming* was particularly sensitive to Dearden's finesse in handling the complex characterisations and appreciated the intimate balance between direction, script and acting in the film when, commenting on the wit in the early scenes involving the Liberal prime minister, he judged that 'the political mess is savoured discreetly by director Basil Dearden, writer Robert Ardrey, and Ralph Richardson, whose articulate irritation as Gladstone quite steals the show'. Gow appreciated the sensitivity of the director and further underlined the achievement of Dearden, stating that

> The dialogue passages are inclined to be very ordinary to look at; but then the dialogue is so good, so one doesn't mind too much. On the other hand, Dearden's application of traditional technique to the scene of Gordon's famous death on the steps is wholly cinematic, the key shot intercut with quick close views of faces in the crowd. (August 1966)[22]

The delicate tripartite relationship of screenplay, direction and performance was further acknowledged at *The Times*, which generously offered praise 'all round':

> To Robert Ardrey, who wrote the script as an original historical drama rather than a reach-me-down adaptation . . . To Basil Dearden, the

principal director, for handling the bitter comedy of Westminster politics with such cool finesse. And to nearly all of the large and distinguished cast, led by Charlton Heston, an underestimated actor . . . who excels himself as the mysterious, contradictory Gordon. (9 June 1966)[23]

Dearden's reverential approach to *Khartoum* can be demonstrated through reference to some key scenes in the film. A good example is the long exchange between Gladstone, his ministers and military advisers, which comes early in the story. A Turco-Egyptian army commanded by General Hicks has been wiped out in the desert by the forces of the Mahdi and the British leaders are meeting to consider a response. Dearden commences the scene with a close-shot of a held newspaper; he tracks back to reveal a perplexed Gladstone who wants an explanation of the calamity.[24] The new framing has the prime minister seated among his standing Cabinet colleagues, and Dearden uses the widescreen image for studied group compositions, with a dominant, static Gladstone sparring with his anxious and shifting ministers. General Wolseley (Nigel Green) ushers in Colonel Stewart who has just returned from North Africa with fresh intelligence.[25] He is seated opposite the prime minister and Dearden reverts to closer one and two-shot framings with reverse cutting to cover their discussion. Only slowly, as Stewart reveals the true immensity of the situation and boldly stands up to the 'Grand Old Man', does the director allow the camera forward to a true close-up. However, the device is used sparingly and the scene reverts to the characteristic pattern of wider framings and group compositions, and captures the undulating movement of the dialogue around the participants without fragmenting the scene unnecessarily through excessive cutting. The approach intelligently allows the players to register their reactions to the evolving drama, notably those not presently participating in the dialogue, but positioned in the frame so as to mark an emotional response to a point.

The climax of the scene demonstrates these principles perfectly. Gladstone is searching for a way out of the mess with honour intact, and using a wide frame, Dearden has him seated in the centre of the image looking around his assembled advisers for suggestions. After an uncomfortable pause, Granville, the Foreign Secretary (Michael Hordern), slides into the near frame with his back to the camera and in a whisper proposes sending General Gordon.[26] The audience is able to register the reaction of all those present except Stewart (with his back to the camera) who is the only character with nothing to gain from the appointment. The reactions are punctuated with some brief closer-shots, before the scheming Granville slowly traverses the scene, countering objections and impressing his colleagues with this purely political solution to the problem. Stewart objects to such a risky venture which will in all probability fail; to which Granville disingenuously comments, 'What a pity'. As Stewart angrily turns on the Foreign Secretary, Dearden sandwiches him in a diagonal composition that has the military man pressed between the combined forces of Granville (foreground) and Gladstone (background). The latter rises to come alongside the officer to defuse his outburst, and, praising him for his invaluable intelligence, ushers him out of the room. The politicians have found their scapegoat and the audience have been subtly treated to the machinations of an elite, who effortlessly sacrifice moral responsibility to political expediency.

The following shorter scene is also of considerable interest as Heston makes specific reference to it as an example of a well-played scene.[27] It involves a clandestine – and wholly invented – meeting between Gladstone and Gordon prior to the latter's embarkation for Egypt and takes place at a small country railway station. It is a private meeting; therefore Dearden has to approach the scene differently, without the possibility of taking account of the reactions of subsidiary characters. Gordon enters the cramped office and the two men contemplate each other in silence. As the military man is now the dramatic focus, Dearden, in an inversion of the previous scene, has him seated in the centre of the room while the prime minister nervously paces up and down as he attempts to persuade him to accept the dangerous mission. Once again, the director is sparing in his use of closer-shots, preferring to organise the wide frame to emphasise the distance between the two powerful men, and has the camera follow the anxious movements of Gladstone around a confident, calm and static Gordon. Some conventional reverse-field shots are employed, but these are seldom more intimate than mid-shots and the camera maintains a respectful distance. As the scene reaches towards its climax, Gladstone seats himself opposite the general and declares frankly that he mistrusts him as a mystic and an insubordinate officer. Dearden captures this adversarial confrontation side on in a two-shot, pushing the characters to the outer edges of the wide frame and using the composition to symbolise the unbridgeable gap between the antagonists. Heston had questioned, early in the production, the director's limited use of close-ups, believing that this would compromise the actor's performance and reduce the effectiveness of the drama (Heston 1978: 232). It is apparent that his view was not as considered as Dearden's regarding the most effective approach to filming the unusually literate script and protecting its quality and integrity. Heston's response was quite conventional and selfishly put the individual actor before the scene, while Dearden took the more novel and thoughtful course and approached the drama in terms of scenes and collective performance as was inherently laid out in the screenplay.[28]

Critical regard has remained consistently high for *Khartoum*, especially in terms of its intelligent script and the quality of performances. Surprisingly, it is widely claimed that the film attained a commendable degree of historical accuracy, when in fact it has numerous inventions and fabrications typical of cinema's treatment of the past.[29] The reviewer at *Kine Weekly* revealed a keener appreciation of the historical film as a popular vehicle when he wrote: 'What relation the story bears to real history is of no consequence so long as a film tells such a rousing tale as this one' (16 June 1966). The *Daily Telegraph* (10 June 1966) and the *New Statesman* (17 June 1966) were critical of the film's historical inaccuracies; while Sir Ronald Wingate, whose father succeeded Gordon as Governor of the Sudan, wrote a piece in the *Daily Telegraph* in support of the film (11 June 1966). In the fullest examination of the film's historical recreation, Herman finds the right balance, concluding that 'within the limitations that the medium and its consumers impose on the "simple facts," *Khartoum* represents a subtle and sophisticated rendition' (1979: 9).[30]

ONLY WHEN I LARF (1968)

You've probably heard the story of the English explorers who were attacked by African natives. This tall English chap is struck by a spear and then another, until there are so many spears in him that he looks like a pin cushion. Another member of the expedition looks at him and says, 'My goodness, Roger, you are terribly, terribly cut about, you poor feller. Does it hurt?' and the fellow with the spears in him says, 'No, by jove, Sydney. Only when I laugh'.

George Ornstein left United Artists in 1964 to try his hand at independent production. Initially, he teamed up with Brian Epstein, the manager of the Beatles; but that proved abortive and he went on to work with Broccoli and Saltzman on the James Bond films *Thunderball* and *You Only Live Twice* (1967). He later rejoined the studio system when he was appointed head of production in Britain for Paramount in November 1966, where he hoped to work the miracle a second time (Walker 1974: 270, 393; Murphy 1992: 262).[31] He was fortunate that a film already in production, *Alfie* (1966), was a great success; and he added *Romeo and Juliet* (1968) and *If . . . .* (1968) to the company's list of commercial achievements. Ornstein, wanting filmmakers he could rely on during this early period of consolidation, concluded another deal with Dearden and Relph to contribute productions for distribution by Paramount; and in September 1967, two films were announced, both to be directed by Dearden: *Only When I Larf* would be produced by Len Deighton and Brian Duffy; and *The Assassination Bureau* would be produced by Michael Relph (*Kinematograph Weekly*, 30 September 1967). The arrangement and these two films conformed perfectly to the previous ethos established between Ornstein, Dearden and Relph: the productions would be generously budgeted and fore-ground the pleasures granted by stars, exotic locations and elaborate settings.

Author Len Deighton had formed Beecord Productions in 1967 with his photographer partner Brian Duffy. His popular spy novel *Funeral in Berlin* had been filmed by Paramount in 1966 and Ornstein could have some optimism in the production arrangement, which planned to adapt Deighton's forthcom-ing comedy-thriller *Only When I Larf*. There was a close liaison between the preparation of the book and film. The novel had attracted the highest advance of the year, with Sphere paying £27,500 for the paperback rights; while the script and shooting were completed before the publication of the novel in April 1968 (*The Times*, 23 December 1967 and 13 April 1968). The launch of the film was preceded by what was described as 'one of the biggest "tie-in" book promotions ever mounted' (*The Times*, 20 June 1968).[32] It was probably Ornstein who recommended the experienced and reliable Dearden as director. Shooting had commenced in London in October 1967, with scenes taken at the Natural History Museum, Westminster Hall and the Orangery in Holland Park; there were additional location trips to New York and Beirut.[33]

Only When I Larf, starring Richard Attenborough, David Hemmings and Alexandra Stewart, was released in June 1968 to generally fair reviews, but seemingly disappointing box office. The story concerned three big-time con artists and the *ménage à trois* they formed, and was part of a modest cycle of films about confidence tricksters such as *One Born Every Minute* (1967) and *Dead Heat on a Merry-Go-Round* (1967). The trade press retained its support for the cinema of colour, excitement and glamour adopted by Ornstein in his work with the two British filmmakers. 'Behind-the-scenes mechanics of high-class confidence trickery and sumptuous settings in New York and the Lebanon play an intriguing part in this very entertaining film' opined *Kine Weekly*, which went on to praise the 'well-written script' and 'first-class acting' (18 May 1968). John Russell Taylor at *The Times* found the film a quite 'jolly' meditation on the 'ethics of the con game'; adding approval for director Basil Dearden who had 'kept the story moving brightly along'. Unfortunately, though, the film couldn't sustain it momentum and

> The last of their tricks, played out in the Lebanon, is too silly to take, even with a sizeable pinch of salt, and the slight romantic complications involving the third partner (Alexandra Stewart) remain uninteresting, since she is so underwritten as a character. (20 June 1968)[34]

Michael Armstrong also thought the film ultimately insubstantial and nothing more than 'amusing, fairly entertaining, easy to watch and equally as easy to forget – which is a pity, as it might have been more' (in *Films and Filming*,

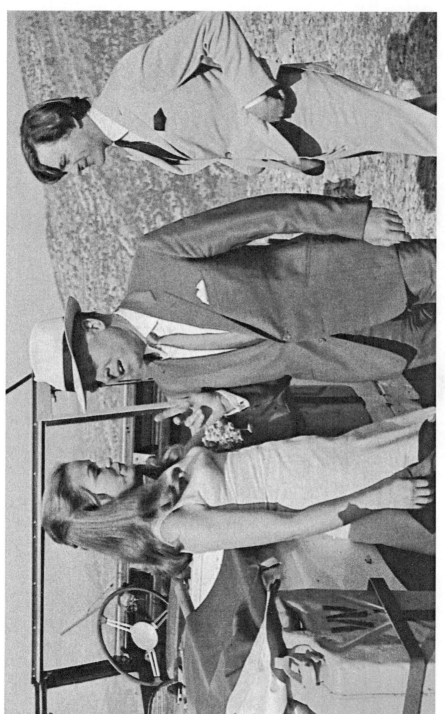

Liz, Silas and Bob in *Only When I Larf* (1968) (Courtesy of Steve Chibnall Archive)

October 1968). The most consistent praise was for Attenborough who played Silas, the senior member of the trio; a 'virtuoso performance', according to *Monthly Film Bulletin*. However, the film itself failed to rise above the 'technically adept' or offer much more than 'tourist-type local colour' (35: 408/419, 1968). The *Spectator* felt that the film was 'Blandly directed by Basil Dearden', 'all effortless stuff, as pleasant and as instantly forgettable as crèpes de volaille' (28 June 1968).

   The story contains elements typical of Deighton, which he had so successfully brought to bear in his espionage novels: detailed attention to the particulars of tradecraft; the endemic practice of deceit, deception and betrayal; the class battle waged between a youthful proletarian and more senior representative of the Old Boy network; and the drama's more general symbolic commentary on the morality of the times.[35] The drama offered Dearden yet another ageing protagonist whose character and outlook had been formed in the war and who, in an echo of *The League of Gentlemen*, brought military-type precision to the operations he planned and executed to defraud unsuspecting innocents. The eighteen-minute pre-credit sequence, detailing an elaborate 'sting', is a superb example of his skill in narrative organisation: it was commended at the *Daily Telegraph* as 'An amusing opening sequence and briskly directed by Basil Dearden' (21 June 1968). The sequence consists of three elements. The first and third, in which the characters busily prepare the scene for the operation of swindling two unsuspecting businessmen in a bogus property deal and then hurriedly depart with their ill-gotten gains, are very brisk, with the average shot-length deliberately held short, reflecting the urgency of the action and the nervous tension affecting the principals. Dearden approaches these scenes *verité*-style, positioning the camera close to the actors, often with objects in the near-ground partly obscuring the action, with numerous hand-held shots taken in real locations. This is an effective cinematic realisation of Deighton's well-known obsession for accurate detail in the construction of an authentic-seeming milieu. Ron Grainer's jaunty score is orchestrated with a pronounced snare drum for this sequence, hinting at the military-like approach to the exercise. The middle section, wherein the dupes are gently persuaded to hand over their money, is handled by Dearden in a calmer and more conventional manner. The scene is set in a generously proportioned executive's office, and although the coverage is a typical arrangement of scene dissection, the camera constantly dollies and reframes to keep pace with the animated movements of the confidence tricksters around their static targets, who are softened up by the disorienting whirlwind of action and unexpected developments taking place around them. Despite the potential restrictions presented by a single space, Dearden keeps the action and momentum irresistibly moving forward and the tension never slackens.[36]

Unfortunately, the script rarely gives the director such an opportunity again, and as many critics recognised, the story degenerated from this exciting and promising introduction into a series of increasingly far-fetched swindles peopled by cartoon Africans and Arabs. The main problem, as in the novel, was that credible – and potentially fascinating – action was sacrificed for a simplistic physical comedy requiring very broad playing and unsophisticated caricatures. Critics had been encouraged by the pseudo-philosophising of the leader Silas, who justified confidence tricksters in Darwinian terms as an 'essential part of the life-cycle of the capitalist system', which might have been developed as part of a sustained critique. There was also reason for hope in the serial clashes between Silas and his proletarian underling Bob (Hemmings), who wants to break away from his perpetual roles of chauffeur, servant or other menial hireling. However, these typical preoccupations of Deighton are never fully developed as social satire and Dearden is therefore required to do no more than efficiently record the breezy action and accelerating zaniness.

While the drama suffers due to its simplicity, Deighton does strike an accurate note in terms of the social dynamics of the confidence tricksters and their interactions. As one sociological study had observed, 'An important element in an analysis of fraud (particularly in the confidence game situation) centers around the fact that the con game is, in a very real sense, *a game*' (Schur 1957: 298; emphasis in original). Furthermore, the social interaction of the swindle is a moment of empowerment for the tricksters, a point recognised by Alexander Klein, who wrote: 'Above all, every deception, every imposture is an assumption of power. The person deceived is reduced in stature, symbolically nullified, while the imposter is temporarily powerful, even greater than if he were the real thing' (quoted in ibid.: 299). The principals in *Only When I Larf* perfectly observe both these facets: they joyously relish the role-playing aspect of the scheme, and, indeed, this dimension spills over into their normal lives, where Silas and Bob in particular are continually inventing dramas and participating in play; moreover, the characters equally delight in the domination of their victims. There is perhaps something deeper in this latter oppression of their victims where the drama has the emasculated parties represented by greedy American businessmen and power-hungry colonial dictators having the tables turned on them by a scion of the British establishment; and privileged sons of the establishment being outwitted and fleeced by a member of the new classless society thrown up by the cultural revolution of the1960s.[37]

Many of the films of Swinging London – *The Knack*, *Georgy Girl* (1966), *Blow-Up* – have characters that participate in pantomime and make-believe, and, in part, reflect the contemporary youthful rejection of their parents' world and a preference for play. In contrast, the aspect of play in *Only When I Larf* is less counter-cultural and more anti-social, reflecting what sociologist

C. Wright Mills has called 'structural immorality', a condition linked to increased affluence and condoned by 'fading personal integrity' (1956: 343–4). The emphasis on salesmanship and the easy acceptance of risk-taking structure the world of both the capitalist and the confidence trickster, a point made by criminologist George Taft, who observed that, for the criminal,

> success is based somewhat increasingly upon financial gain similar to that of the banker or speculator . . . Whatever the economists may say, speculative gains look more like luck than hard work, and more nearly approximate the something-for-nothing philosophy of the pickpocket. (quoted in Schur 1957: 302)

In a highly auteurist reading of *Only When I Larf*, Paul Wells sees Dearden constructing an effective critique of the 'amoral governing principle of modern culture', with the trio of principal characters acting as 'ciphers for discourses of selfishness, greed and irresponsibility' (1997: 54). This is an unduly generous assessment and overvalues Dearden's governing role to the detriment of Deighton. Unfortunately, this socially critical dimension, commented on by several critics at the time, comes through only weakly in a drama that is given over to increasingly silly disguises and broad mimicry.[38]

THE ASSASSINATION BUREAU (1969)

> It's a trademark not thought very much of in some circles today, but the firm of R[elph] and D[earden] may well have the last laugh. With American money beginning to drain away from the British film industry, principally because so many fingers have been burnt backing trendy beginners, the old reliables stand in a better position than most to get hold of what remains. (Derek Malcolm, *The Guardian*, 19 March 1969)

It had been announced in the spring of 1966 that Dearden and Relph would be making *The Assassination Bureau* for United Artists and that the two filmmakers had flown to New York for discussions with Burt Lancaster about a leading role in the comedy adventure film. They also visited San Francisco to hunt locations, and production was planned to commence in the summer, with further locations in France, Germany and Italy (*Kinematograph Weekly*, 10 March 1966). Relph had written the script with a suave English lead in mind and he was not pleased to have pressure put on him by UA to cast Lancaster. However, none of the extensive revisions to recast the role met with the American star's approval and Lancaster withdrew. Instead, Relph managed to interest Rex Harrison in the part, but at the time the English actor was apparently unacceptable to UA and the studio gradually went cool on the idea (Relph 1990). The project was later resurrected for Ornstein at Paramount, with an international cast headed by Oliver Reed, Diana Rigg, Telly Savalas, Curt Jurgens and Philippe Noiret (*Kinematograph Weekly*, 17 February 1968). The film was granted a trade show in March 1969 and went into general release in April where it attracted some good notices. John Russell Taylor at *The Times* enjoyed the comedy and punningly tagged it a 'Killingly funny film' (20 March 1969). There was general praise for Reed (at last showing a talent for comedy) and Rigg (in her feature film debut), the admirable elegance of the production and the witty script by Relph. Taylor continued: 'The background calls for style in the playing and the way the film is made'. He was gratified that 'For once, the call is answered' (ibid.). *Films and Filming* praised the 'extremely good screenplay' and predicted that the tongue-in-cheek adventure 'will have the Saturday night audience cheering in their seats' (May 1969). *The Guardian* found the film 'elegant, quite witty, engaging' and considered it 'skilfully directed by Basil Dearden' and 'charmingly written and smartly designed' by Michael Relph (21 March 1969). Alexander Walker at the *Evening Standard* believed 'A crueller, cooler tone' was required; while the hostile reviewer at the *Daily Express* 'didn't like the beginning or the middle, but I loved the end – simply because it meant the ordeal was over'. Moreover, it was felt that the jokes had been 'squeezed dry of mirth by Basil Dearden's laborious direction' (18 March 1969). As usual, *Monthly Film Bulletin* found little of merit in a Dearden film, other than some attractive sets and an engaging performance from Oliver Reed. It felt that Dearden made 'very heavy weather of this latter-day Ealing comedy', that 'the whole thing seems to move at a snail's pace through endless, not very inventive murder attempts' and that the entire exercise was 'ponderous' (36: 420/431, 1969). In the event, the film was nominated for a Golden Globe as Best English-Language Foreign Film of the year.

The novella, *The Assassination Bureau, Ltd.*, had been published in 1963, completed by the mystery writer Robert L. Fish from an unfinished manuscript and notes compiled by Jack London in 1910. Appearing shortly after the assassination of President Kennedy the book with its secret organisation that accepts commissions to murder people drew some controversy. Michael Relph's adaptation was a very loose rendering of the original story, sacrificing much of the book's philosophical leanings, with its repetitive discussions of morality and ethics, and playing up the adventure yarn.[39] The action was also switched from America to England and the continent, befitting a European-based production. The basic outline story is retained: a secret organisation, the Assassination Bureau, accepts commissions for murder. It is an ethical institution and will only assassinate individuals who, after careful research, it decides deserve to die. A member of the public, appalled by this morality, turns the tables on the Bureau by proposing a commission to assassinate its chairman, Ivan Dragomiloff (Reed). Trapped within its own rigid logic, the commission is accepted and Dragomiloff elaborately proceeds to kill off each of the board members in pursuance of his own defence. This tale is given a more light-hearted treatment in the film and the opportunity is taken to present a pictur-esque romp around a tourist Europe as Dragomiloff locates and executes each of his victims in turn.

The *Assassination Bureau* was clearly influenced by Blake Edwards' *The Great Race*, released by Warner Bros. in 1965, and a model for a handful of comedy adventure yarns like *Those Magnificent Men in Their Flying Machines* (1965) and *Monte Carlo or Bust* (1969) set in the Edwardian period. For example, Relph introduced a feminist reporter into the plot, Sonya Winter (Rigg), a direct steal from *The Great Race* with its character of Maggie Du Bois (Natalie Wood). Overall, though, *The Assassination Bureau* is less cartoonish than the earlier film and lacks Edwards' obsession with slapstick humour; however, it similarly exhibits an interest in broad physical comedy, played within a meticulous and luxurious mise-en-scène, with an episodic narrative peopled with caricature villains.[40] Relph's script jettisons London's characteristic inter-est in radical and socialist politics for a formulaic master-villain, Lord Bostwick (Savalas), a renegade member of the Bureau, whose megalomania drives him into a plot to assassinate the gathered heads of Europe so that he can rule as an autocrat in their stead. Similarly, Winter's feminism is presented as little more than historical colour and her presence used to provide the conven-tional romantic sub-plot; although Rigg's penchant for comedy and physical action exactly catches the spirit of the film. The attempt to abandon the rather awkward moralising of the novella could only ever be partial and the script struggles to overcome the reprehensible ideals of Dragomiloff and his organi-sation and convert him into a standard action hero. This problem is largely masked by the overt stock villainy of Lord Bostwick and the shift in allegiance of Winter from antagonist to romantic partner. However, there is still a need to explicate this matter in the drama directly, but it is rendered unconvincing in a dialogue exchange between Dragomiloff and Lord Bostwick conducted high up in an airship as the villain prepares to drop a bomb on a congress of European leaders meeting to secure peace.

> *Dragomiloff:* Don't do it Charles. Indiscriminate destruction will engulf you too.
> *Bostwick:* One death or a million, where's the difference?
> *Dragomiloff:* We're surgeons, not butchers. We only kill to destroy evil.
> *Bostwick:* Hypocrite. You kill for money.
> *Dragomiloff:* Only those who deserve to die. We must judge before we kill.
> *Bostwick:* Judge, young fool. You're not an assassin, you're a critic.[41]

Such an argument hardly redeems Dragomiloff, who, despite the apostasy of Lord Bostwick, is revealed as little more than a proponent for the contemporary vogue of eugenics, with the additional inconvenience of physically acting on his impulses for Social Darwinism. Nor do the various references to the Great War, in the drama and the iconography, add up to a biting satirical comment on the senseless slaughter of the conflict. The parallels observed by Alberto Manguel in his reading of the Assassination Bureau in the original novella – 'London's Dragomiloff conceived a social machine to kill on request after payment of ready cash; we have set up economic machineries to make limitless amounts of cash, no matter what the cost in lives' – are simply expunged in the film to play up the adventure yarn and caper comedy aimed at a popular audience (Manguel 2008).[42]

There was widespread praise for Relph's design of *The Assassination Bureau*. John Russell Taylor at *The Times* was moved to write a special piece commending Relph's 'witty and elegant design' and acknowledged his crucial contribution to the film in his additional roles of producer and scriptwriter (22 March 1969). The rich use of colour and exquisite décor were marvellously captured by lighting cameraman Geoffrey Unsworth and ably served by the direction of Dearden, who kept 'the plot moving briskly forward while packing the corners of the film with pleasing half caught detail and avoiding all the excesses (comic speeded-up motion and the like) which so often these days disfigure the period romp' (*The Times*, 20 March 1969). The film only seems to have done modestly well at the box office but made no impact at all in the crucial American market.[43]

Even before the release of *The Assassination Bureau* there were clear signs that the Hollywood production companies were considering withdrawing from Britain. As Alexander Walker later explained of the general situation:

> For the truth is that just as their British-made films were, for the most part, being spectacularly unsuccessful in the United States, the American film companies, through their own profligacy, were running into serious economic difficulties that threatened to engulf them. In 1969–70 it really looked as if Hollywood would go corporately bust, so vast was the debt the 'majors' had piled up in the last year or two of the 1960s, when they had indulged in an orgy of over-production and over-spending. (1974: 441)

Unfortunately, none of the Dearden–Relph productions had fared well in the United States and, like many other British filmmakers, they found that American finance dried up towards the end of the decade. Paramount was the first Hollywood corporation to cease production in the UK (*Films and Filming*, February 1969). The company had been a perennial underachiever

Michael Relph's design for Cesare Spado's Palazzo (exterior) in *The Assassination Bureau* (1969) (Courtesy of Simon Relph)

throughout the 1960s and had recently been beset by colossal failures like *Is Paris Burning?* (1966) and *Half a Sixpence* (1968). Having been acquired by Gulf and Western in 1966, the time was ripe for a corporate shake-up and the pull-out of British production was followed by an overall reduction in corporate staff numbers, closing of branch offices and the selling off of real estate (Dick 2001: 109–25). There was mention of a further production for UA, *Megakill*, a futuristic thriller from a script by Relph, but clearly the writing was on the wall and the prospect of continuing American finance was slight (*The Guardian*, 19 March 1969). As producers, Dearden and Relph had enjoyed six years of generous American support on a profit-sharing basis, and had provided films that in the main had proved popular in Europe. However, the lack of commercial success in the United States was a deciding factor and the two filmmakers would in future have to look to the precarious resources within the British industry to support their productions.

THE PERSUADERS! (1971–72)

Hollywood's Tony Curtis in his first-ever television series . . . Roger Moore, in his first series since 'The Saint' . . . internationally famous guest stars . . . glittering settings on the Côte d'Azur and in other famous pleasure spots . . . glamorous girls by the hundred . . . and tingling adventure combined with exhilarating comedy. 'The Persuaders!' has everything . . . a series with all the sparkle of vintage champagne. (Publicity handout for *The Persuaders!*)

'One of the most significant television coups' was announced in the trade press in February 1970: for the first time, ITC's new production *The Friendly Persuaders* would feature two major stars, Roger Moore and Tony Curtis, in a single television package which had been made possible through pre-selling it to the powerful ABC Network in the United States (*Kinematograph Weekly*, 28 February 1970). It was further announced several weeks later that 'Many leading directors will take various episodes' of the expensive and prestigious series, which would be produced at Pinewood and on foreign locations (*Kinematograph Weekly*, 11 April 1970). Basil Dearden was offered the all-important pilot episode, 'Overture', and two further instalments, 'To the Death Baby' and 'Powerswitch'.[44] In all likelihood, Dearden came to the series at the instigation of Roger Moore with whom he had recently worked on *The Man Who Haunted Himself* (1970); Moore, as well as co-star, was a director of Tribune which was producing the show for ITC and consequently had a say in production decisions.[45] Robert Baker, who devised and produced the series, later referred to Basil Dearden as 'a really top director' and claimed that 'we gave the show everything we possibly could'.[46] The series began shooting on location early in May 1970; the unit returned to Britain in September to shoot interiors at Pinewood, the first TV show to take over completely the studio's £600,000 'L & M complex' designed for dual-purpose film and TV productions (*Kinematograph Weekly*, 11 April and 16 May 1970). *The Persuaders!*, as it was now named, was launched at the MIP TV Festival at Cannes in April of 1971 and first aired on British television between September 1971 and February 1972 (*Kinematograph Weekly*, 27 March 1971).

James Chapman has been insistent that there should be no auteurist claims for Dearden with regard to *The Persuaders!* (Chapman 2002: 263).[47] Correspondingly, Dearden's contribution to the series should be appreciated as that of a reliable and experienced professional, who was entrusted with the pilot episode of the most expensive television series in Britain thus far. However, it is also fair to credit the producers with sufficient awareness of Dearden's competencies and his recently proven ability to stage and manage productions in glamorous locations featuring internationally recognised performers. It was a simple case of a filmmaker working with sympathetic material and a proven relationship with one of the stars.

'Overture' conforms perfectly to the approach and ethos of the recent work Dearden had undertaken with American film companies; the attention to stars, locations and elaborate settings equally being the hallmark of *The Persuaders!* – albeit in the slightly more restrained context of television production. An early sequence is indicative of the approach: it has the two characters, Lord Brett Sinclair (Moore) and Danny Wilde (Curtis), arrive in Nice on the Côte d' Azur. In their expensive and desirable cars (an Aston Martin and a Ferrari) the protagonists engage in a thrilling race along the narrow cliffside road to glamorous Monte Carlo, eventually pulling up simultaneously at the exclusive Hôtel de Paris. Constant and defining use is made of the sun-drenched coast of southern France and its alluring resorts. As a 'buddy' adventure drama, narrative and visual focus are centred on the charismatic stars who play their roles in a light-hearted but consummately professional manner; indeed, much of the lasting admiration for the series lies in the endearing relationship between Sinclair and Wilde achieved through relaxed performances and expert ad-libbing from both leads. The subsequent episode of 'Powerswitch' also centred its adventure on the Côtes d' Azur; while 'To the Death Baby' utilised striking coastal and mountain scenery in Spain.[48] The series was very successful in Europe and many overseas territories, but failed to make any impact in the United States, where it was unsympathetically scheduled by the ABC network, which pitted it against the top-rated show *Mission Impossible*. Accordingly, a second series wasn't commissioned and *The Persuaders!* was left to be 'rediscovered' as a camp cult classic of 1970s British television (Hunt 1998; Sellers 2006).

Looking back on the period of seven years of international films for the world market, Michael Relph felt that the partnership had never really found its feet in what was essentially a very different kind of operation from their usual British productions (Relph 1990). This is perhaps an unduly harsh criticism on a set of films that were visually stylish and often found favour in Europe and other territories. It was an approach that attracted the consistent support of experienced production executive Bud Ornstein and reflected a genuine attempt to provide intelligent stories with popular attractive performers to an international audience. Admittedly, it was representative of a more traditional form of filmmaking, but as such proffered assurance against the modish and nominally experimental movies aimed at the increasingly important youth market which became such an important feature of cinema in the 1960s. The contrast between the films of Dearden and Relph and the New Hollywood are numerable and their old-fashioned air mitigated against a widespread acceptance in the crucial American market and seemingly led to a reluctance among critics to take them seriously.

NOTES

1. The fortuitous decision to produce a Beatles film had come about simply as a favour to the record division of UA, which wanted a soundtrack LP of the group to exploit in the American market (Balio 1987: 249).
2. An independent production placed for distribution with Bryanston, *A Place to Go* had to wait ten months for release on the ABPC circuit, demonstrating the precarious nature of the independents in the industry.
3. The remarkably generous budgets confirm the confidence UA had in Dearden and Relph. These were four times greater than the $500,000 budget of *A Hard Day's Night*, twice as much as was made available for the first Bond film, *Dr No*, and considerably more than the $1,250,000 provided for *Tom Jones*.
4. It has been suggested that Connery was also eager to work with his favourite actor, Ralph Richardson (Sellers 1990: 61).
5. Details taken from *Films and Filming* (January 1963) and *Kinematograph Weekly* (30 May, 13 June, 22 August and 24 October 1963).
6. Much later, even Michael Relph dismissed *Woman of Straw* as 'a lot of real old bollocks really' (Relph 1990).
7. The review in *Films and Filming* concedes that '*Woman of Straw* is quite entertaining', and in the fashion typical of treating Dearden – any praise should be offered as a back-handed compliment – concludes: 'though in too much of a negative way, is Dearden's best film in some time'.

8. Alexander Walker suggested that the story was as if 'Agatha Christie has been allowed to get at Lady Chatterley' (*Evening Standard*, 30 April 1964).

9. Picker's optimism was probably unfounded, and although *Woman of Straw* seems to have been a success in Europe, it proved less so in the United States.

10. Details taken from *Kinematograph Weekly* (30 April, 28 May, 25 June and 20 August).

11. The screenplay credit went to Relph and Goldman.

12. See, for example, *Charade* (1963), *Where the Spies Are* (1965), *The Liquidator* (1965), *The Silencers* (1966), *Arabesque* (1966) and *In Like Flint* (1967).

13. The music and photography are by regulars Philip Green and Otto Heller. In one scene, the prince dismisses Ian Fleming's novel *Goldfinger* as 'far-fetched'; this of course was UA's latest Bond production released in 1964.

14. All of these action set-pieces were in the original novel.

15. Details taken from the *Sunday Telegraph* (3 November 1963) and *Kinematograph Weekly* (3 October 1963, 30 April, 14 May, 25 June and 5 November 1964).

16. Heston claims that he was first approached in 1963 (1978: 218). In February 1964, Laurence Olivier was offered the role of Gordon, but later switched to that of the Mahdi (Olivier Papers, British Library).

17. Michael Relph was listed in publicity materials as working in a 'special production capacity with Dearden and Blaustein in the design and preparation of the picture'. His responsibilities included acting as Dearden's representative during the shooting of the action sequences by the second unit (Relph 1990).

18. Details taken from *Kinematograph Weekly* (10 June, 29 July, 12 August, 19 August, 11 November and 23 December 1965). The second unit, led by the veteran American Yakima Canutt, with photography in the care of Harry Waxman, handled the 'Hicks' Army', 'Cattle Raid' and 'Battle of the Camel Square' sequences. The main unit also covered some action sequences, being responsible for 'Gordon's Entry into Khartoum' and 'Battle for Berber and Felucca'. Both units worked on the 'Attack on Khartoum'. Details taken from material appended to the *Final Shooting Script*. The prologue and narration were directed by photographer, art collector and later documentary filmmaker Eliot Elisofon.

19. The screenplay was nominated for an Oscar, but lost out to the popular French film *A Man and a Woman* (1966).

20. There were some problems on the set with Egyptian locals, a union dispute in the UK which meant a period of work to rule and a consequent over-run on the schedule (*Sun* and *Daily Mail*, both 25 October 1965).

21. Richard Attenborough (2008) has made the interesting point that Dearden's careful preparation coupled with his natural self-effacement could make him appear to the 'unknowing' as slightly 'glib' and 'superficial', when in fact he had given the film 'the most tremendous and most meticulous care in relation to what he did'.

22. The hard-to-please *Monthly Film Bulletin* dissented from this common view, believing *Khartoum* a 'not particularly interesting history lesson', let down by its quality of 'restraint', and the acting 'disjointed' (33: 384/395, 1966).

23. The paper's only criticism, a view expressed in some other reviews, was of Olivier's interpretation of the Mahdi, which it dismissed as a 'formidable display of eye-rolling and lip-licking' complete with a 'weird Peter Sellers-oriental accent'. There was, of course, much made of the comparison between Olivier's portrayal of the Mahdi and his controversial interpretation of *Othello* in which he was then appearing at the National Theatre.

24. The politicians were under tremendous pressure at the time from the jingoistic press.

25. Ardrey's literary script describes the entrance and characters thus:

    Wolseley, adjutant-general of the army is in uniform. Stewart is handsome, rugged, a seasoned soldier in his late thirties, one of the empire generation of British officers who, despite the most stinking conditions of warfare, never quite lose their elegance and aristocratic impregnability. He's so darkly tanned that he makes all present look like fish dredged up from some North Sea deep. (*Final Shooting Script*: 9)

    An earlier pre-production screenplay from 1965, which has some significant differences from the *Final Shooting Script*, is deposited in the UCLA Film and Theatre Arts Library Archive, and is briefly discussed in Herman (1979).

26. Dearden captures Ardrey's intention here perfectly. The script comments on Granville's action thus: 'The Foreign Secretary is a showman. He has been prepared for this inevitable moment for some time. His whisper electrifies the group, including Gladstone' (*Final Shooting Script*: 13).

27. Heston later claimed that appearing opposite Richardson was a 'lesson in acting' (1995: 361).

28. It is instructive to compare the two scenes depicting the (fictitious) meetings of Gordon and the Mahdi. The first occasion plays like the previously described scene between Gladstone and Gordon with a non-intrusive camera, the characters separated across the distance of the wide frame, and constant movement and reframing as the antagonists warily shuffle about the set and take the measure of each other. For the second meeting, Ardrey's script aims to bring out the essential similarity between Gordon and the Mahdi – their mysticism, religious fervour and sense of sacrifice; and as the recognition of this fact dawns on the protagonists, it is only then that Dearden brings them into close proximity with much tighter framings. Such subtlety was seemingly beyond Heston, who, however, later described these two scenes as 'wonderfully balanced confrontations, duets for two voices', but remained ignorant of how well Ardrey and the performers were being served by the director.

29. Brian Taves, for example, believes *Khartoum* is a 'meticulously constructed re-creation . . . a strictly historical account', and a model of how an adventure film 'can utilize history' (1993: 96–8).

30. Historical research had been conducted over a three-year period by Mary Bruce. See *The Times* (7 June 1966).

31. He replaced Robert Evans who returned to head up production in the United States, eventually alongside Peter Bart. The pair gave the ailing Paramount some

of the seminal films of the New Hollywood: *The Godfather*, *Paper Moon*, *Serpico*, *Chinatown* and *Nashville* among others.

32. Sphere printed 500,000 copies of the paperback edition and had sold over half of these prior to the release of the film. A 'unique' in-store promotion had a five-minute compilation of clips from the film running in selected London bookshops.

33. Details taken from *Kinematograph Weekly*'s (30 September, 28 October and 25 November 1967).

34. Stewart, a Canadian actress and former model, was better known in the French cinema, having appeared in films by François Truffaut and Louis Malle.

35. Earlier in 1967, Deighton had perpetrated his own 'swindle' for publicity purposes connected with the launch of his latest spy novel, *An Expensive Place to Die*. He had 'faked' some 'top secret' papers – described as 'memorandums from the White House, the United States Defense Department, the American C.I.A., and Mr Harold Wilson' – and an unsuspecting dupe had apparently tried to sell these to the Russians (*The Times*, 28 April 1967).

36. The editor was Fergus McDonnell.

37. The casting of Attenborough and Hemmings intensifies such a reading, following their roles in such recent films as *Guns at Batasi* (1964) and *Blow-Up* (1966).

38. Equating confidence swindling as a *reductio ad absurdum* of capitalism goes back to the nineteenth century and was offered as a critique by some radicals, as in the wonderful tales of Grant Allen collected as *An African Millionaire* (1897).

39. The title credit ran: 'Original Story and Screenplay by Michael Relph. Based on an idea from "The Assassination Bureau, Ltd." by Jack London'. Additional dialogue was provided by Wolf Mankowitz.

40. Ron Grainer's score and the theme song *Life is a Precious Thing*, sung by a girl and boy choir, is very much in the Mancini-style perfected on *The Great Race*. Stylistic conventions from the silent cinema are also evident in both films, such as art title-cards and scratchy black-and-white film inserts.

41. This exchange is considerably enlarged from the few words Dragomiloff offers in the *Final Shooting Script*, where he simply shouts to Lord Bostwick who is occupied aiming the bomb, 'Don't do it Charles, Indiscriminate destruction will engulf you too . . . We must operate like surgeons – not butchers. Killing is a precise science' (155). The additional material, presumably added during shooting, acts to put the emphasis on Lord Bostwick's unspeakable evil and deflect attention from the problem of Dragomiloff's culpability.

42. Relph (1990) later maintained that the ceaseless revisions wrought on his original script eventually sapped the story of any life.

43. Relph (1990) maintains that the film suffered as the result of a power struggle between Robert Evans and Bud Ornstein, with the head of production in Hollywood, in a private vendetta, ensuring that *The Assassination Bureau* was quietly buried.

44. Other experienced film directors who worked on the series included Val Guest, Roy Ward Baker and Leslie Norman. The series comprised of twenty-four one-hour episodes.

45. The various and often contradictory recollections of the leading participants as to the origins and production of the series are gone over in Chapman (2002: 225–42) and Sellers (2006: 212–25).
46. The remarks are made in his commentary for 'Overture' on the *The Persuaders! Special Edition* DVD, Network Video 7952454.
47. Chapman's viewpoint is directed against Cook (1997).
48. On 'Powerswitch', Dearden worked once again with his actress wife, Melissa Stribling.

Appendix

The following unpublished essay is Michael Relph's brief recollection of his colleagues at Ealing Studios in the 1940s and 1950s. Ostensibly, it was written as a proposal or preface for a fuller study, to serve as a corrective to 'academic' studies that appeared in the 1970s and to the 'front office' view as presented in Michael Balcon's autobiography, published at the end of the 1960s. Idiosyncrasies of spelling and inconsistencies of capitalisation have been retained, and there has been no attempt to correct some factual errors. Although undated, the document was probably written in the early 1990s and now provides a glimpse into a hitherto unknown Ealing.

'INSIDE EALING'

BY

MICHAEL RELPH

Until now Michael Balcon's reign at Ealing Studios, which established a genre of British film making famous throughout the world, has been treated only from the point of view of the academic outsider. Charles Barr's *Ealing Studios* covers the films from a critics' viewpoint and give his ideas of the social significance of the Studio's output. However interesting and significant such theories may be, the films were usually embarked upon for quite different reasons which only an 'insider' can know about. Balcon, in his staid autobiography, gives only the front office version and he was often ignorant of the machinations of the film makers in persuading him to put the studio's resources behind a particular project. Always there was the pressure of a large permanent workforce that had to be paid and often a film was embarked upon for no better reason than that a team had come up with a script that was halfway makeable.

The most important factor about Ealing was that it gathered together, in permanent employment, a young creative team of film makers who cross-fertilised their ideas over a great many years. Together they devised ways of getting round Balcon's prejudices or became expert in producing ideas which catered for his restrictive preferences. The real power-house of Ealing Studios lay across the road in The Red Lion pub, where we forgathered. Although neither Balcon or any other member of the 'front office' ever set foot in it, to my knowledge, it was there that the most animated creative discussions took place – fuelled by alcohol, around which the lives of many of Ealing's film makers revolved.

They were a colourful bunch. Doyen of the Red Lion habitués was Robert Hamer, in some ways the most brilliant of us all. Holder of a Cambridge Honours degree in Mathematics, he also had a fine literary mind which showed itself to its full advantage only once, in my view, when he co-wrote and directed 'Kind Hearts and Coronets', which I produced. I never felt that he otherwise lived up to his promise. He had a nervous habit of addressing remarks towards his left shoulder as though everyone was an epigram but, more often than not, they were merely aphorisms. We all liked and respected him. Monja Danischewski – 'The White Russian with a Red Face' – as the title of his autobiography describes him – was the mercurial P.R. man who was largely responsible for creating Ealing's image. A renowned wit and friend of the most influential editors in Fleet Street, Balcon could not move without him. Charles Crichton – a brilliant comedy cutter whose intervention salvaged 'Whisky Galore' – was the director of 'Hue and Cry', 'The Lavender Hill Mob', and the 'Titfield Thunderbolt'. Many years later he was to direct the sensationally successful 'A Fish Called Wanda' and, despite his diffident, pipe-smoking manner, is an expert comedy director. Charles Frend was always Balcon's favourite. He and David Lean had been cutters at Gaumont British during Balcon's spell as Production Chief and Charles conformed to the gentlemanly pattern which he favoured. Charles' films had integrity although they inclined towards dullness and he always received the pick of the subjects such as 'The Cruel Sea' and 'Scott of the Antarctic'. A staunch beer drinking 'Man of Kent' he was everybody's favourite uncle until he went onto the studio floor – when he became a fiend in human shape! I always put this down to his basic insecurity as a director.

Basil Dearden had been inherited from the previous studio chief, Basil Dean, with whom he had worked in the theatre. Although the most professional director of the lot he was rather looked down upon for having been a theatrical A.S.M. instead of having gone to Oxbridge. There was a feeling that he was not quite 'one of us'. Neither was Sidney Cole, small and chunky, who was Supervising Editor and later a producer. A crusading trade unionist, he was very active in the A.C.T. and was later to become its President.

Angus McPhail was Scenario Editor and very much Balcon's man, having held the same job at Gaumont British (where I also started my career). A Cambridge M.A, Angus was fastidious to the point of eccentricity. Tall, thin and giraffe-like in appearance, he chain-smoked from one of the flat yellow boxes of 50 State Express which were posted to him monthly in bulk. All script conferences were held in his office and his influence was considerable. At the end of the day, a hired car would collect him and drive him to his elegant flat in Bayswater. The block – whose real name I forget – was always known as Hangover Towers and housed many of Ealing's film makers. There, Angus's fastidious austerity would be abandoned for two hours of uninhibited drinking before retiring, insensible, to bed. He was a true neurotic who could not face life outside his work. He ended up drinking himself to death alone in an Eastbourne Hotel but in those days he was cared for by Marjory Russell, a matronly lady who was Constance Spry's[1] second in command. She shared his flat (but not his bed), and cooked him cordon-bleu meals which he seldom ate.

Henry Cornelius, director of 'Passport to Pimlico', was a South African Jew whose ambitions were too akin to Balcon's own for him to be content for long to be one of 'Mr. Balcon's Young Gentleman'. He soon set up on his own and made the phenomenally successful 'Genevieve' before dying sadly young.

The 'Eminence Grise' of the studio was undoubtedly Alberto Cavalcanti, the Brazilian guru and documentarist who Balcon brought to Ealing from the Crown Film Unit. He and the abrasive Scot, Harry Watt – director of 'Target for Tonight' – were largely responsible for the switch to documentary realism after the fiasco of 'Ships With Wings', a ridiculously fictionalised story about the Ark Royal. Surprisingly when Cavalcanti came to direct himself – he was at first a producer – he chose such fanciful and quintessentially English subjects as 'Nicholas Nickleby' and 'Champagne Charlie', and planned his version of 'Wuzzerin Eets' – the way he pronounced 'Wuthering Heights.'

Watt's 'Overlanders' retained his documentary realism but 'West of Zanzibar' and 'Where no Vultures Fly' were marred by the naivety of their fictional elements. Naive or not, his films were consistently successful, except for the Roman musical 'Fiddlers Three', in which he abandoned his style completely. It was Cavalcanti, however, who was the big influence on Balcon. It was he one had to get on one's side if we hoped to get a project approved. This was surprising in that Cav, as we called him, remained obstinately foreign – his English was almost incomprehensible – and his homosexual bohemianism might have been expected to offend Balcon's straight laced principles.

Alexander McKendrick was someone whom I brought to Ealing as a writer and sketch artist. He became one of the studio's most successful directors. A relentless theorist, Sandy was an American who had never lost his didactic Scottish roots. He learned a lot of lessons on his first picture, 'Whisky Galore'. It was also Danischewski's first film as a producer and needed Charles Crichton's professional editing before it emerged as the classic that it is.

Leslie Norman – Barry's father[2] – was another cutter whom Balcon promoted to be a producer and later a director. This emphasis on ex-editors as directorial material revealed Balcon's mystification with this area of film making. He felt safe when entrusting projects to expert cutters and the fact that many of them were uneasy with actors and stilted in their use of the camera did not worry him. Most of them soon picked it up anyway. Les Norman was an old pro who I had worked with at Warner Brothers before the war and he brought a refreshingly down-to-earth Cockney humour and wisdom to the predominantly middle-class studio mix.

There were other producers or directors who attended the monthly round-table policy meetings. Soft, gentlemanly Michael Truman – again an ex-editor; John Croydon, who had been Studio Manager at Gaumont British; Basil Emmet who had been a famous Newsreel commentator; Dennis Van Thaal – now an important agent, and others.

I myself was the studio's Art Director when Cavalcanti suggested that I should become a producer, teaming me with Basil Dearden – presumably because Art was the element that he thought Basil lacked! Perhaps he was right. At any rate our talents complemented each other and we formed a partnership which long outlasted Ealing and almost everyone in it!

Although they did not attend the policy meetings – where Angus McPhail represented their interests – it was the writers who were perhaps the most important influence at Ealing. Two in particular – T. E. B. Clarke and William Rose – could be said to have produced the work that set the style of the studio. 'Tibby' Clarke, the author of famous comedies like 'Passport to Pimlico' and 'The Lavender Hill Mob', as well as dramas like my production 'The Blue Lamp' and my horse-racing epic 'The Rainbow Jacket', was a comic journalist writing a weekly page in the Evening News. This had always seemed unreadable to me because of the exceptionally unfunny drawings that illustrated it. Monja Danischewski, however, penetrated beyond these to Tibby's genuine comic genius and shrewdly persuaded Balcon to take him on. A solid and respectable suburbanite from Oxshott, Tibby had a streak of anarchy in him and understood those foibles of the British character with which the studio became associated.

The other key writer was American. William Rose – physically in the Scott Fitzgerald mould – had an undoubted touch of genius although in some ways

I thought him mentally unbalanced. I sat straight faced as he described to me how Princess Margaret had seduced him in a wood, and I remember him lining up six treble whiskies on a pub counter and drinking them one by one as I delivered some unpalatable criticisms of his script. After Ealing he wrote 'The Smallest Show on Earth' for Basil and me, 'Genevieve' for Cornelius, and went on to write 'It's a Mad, Mad, Mad, World', 'Guess who's Coming to Dinner' and 'The Russians are coming' in Hollywood, before retiring to live a hermit-like existence in Jersey until his death.

Roger McDougal wrote several key films, including 'The Man in the White Suit' and such famous writers as Nigel Balchin, John Whiting, Nicholas Montserrat, Graham Greene, Rumer Godden, Paul Gallico, Harry Kurnitz and many others wrote scripts for us.

Music was the province of another famous Ealing character. Ernest Irving, the aged musicologist, lived in Hogarthian squalor in the house next door to the studio. Every music session was under threat of Ernest's ill health.

His assistant Doc Mathieson – brother of Muir Mathieson, Korda's Director of Music – was always on stand-by, but at the last moment Ernest would rise from his bed, don his white suit, and proceed (at least once on a stretcher) to the recording studio where he would vigorously conduct the orchestra. The musicians seemed to give him a temporary new lease of life and he was universally liked and respected. His prestige attracted such famous composers as Vaughan-Williams, Alan Rawsthorn, William Alwyn, John Ireland, William Walton, Georges Auric and many others to score our pictures.

This is a general picture of the elements that combined to make the name of Ealing Studios famous. For fifteen years I was at the centre of all this, first of all as Art Director – Production Designer, I would now be called – and then as Producer under Michael Balcon, and usually as Basil Dearden's partner. There were women of course. Ealing films were not noted for their female content but some of the most beautiful actresses in Europe worked at the studios from time to time. The sixteen year old Joan Collins, Kay Kendall, Jean Simmons, Joan Greenwood, Valerie Hobson and many others. The great French actress Francoise Rosay was an Ealing regular and the young Simone Signoret came from France for one film. She was sensationally attractive and Michael Truman claimed to have had an affair with her. I always believed it to be a figment of his imagination and now we shall never know. It wasn't only the stars. I remember Lindsay Anderson and I competing for the favours of a pretty canteen waitress, and Basil Dearden married the most attractive girl in the cutting rooms. Everyone fancied her and Robert Hamer did not think that her marriage should stand in the way. Blind drunk, he crawled along the cornice of Hangover Towers – a hundred feet above Lancaster Gate – to Basil's flat, only to find his own wife, Joan, waiting for him.

They were uproarious times and our sessions in The Red Lion would carry on in The Crown at Lancaster Gate, the back bar of the Cafe Royal, and all over Soho. My wife was a beautiful young actress who was lodging with the Hamers. I thought that she needed to be rescued, although I am not sure that she wanted to be! Disaster was never far away. Joan Hamer fell down an area and broke her back, Robert killed himself with drink. Angus died a lonely death. Michael Truman committed suicide. Charles Frend never made another film after the friendly gates of Ealing closed, and a lifetime passed before Charles Crichton's great comeback. Sandy McKendrick directed one great American film 'The Sweet Smell of Success' then, plagued by ill health, retired to an academic post in California. For a time it seemed that Basil and I had survived in the outside world better than everybody – then Basil was killed in a car accident.

Now so many are dead and the era is almost over. It seems right that it should all be put on record. Not the official view – Balcon has done that – or the view of an outside academic like Charles Barr. The record that is missing is how it was for those of us who made the films. The story of 'Inside Ealing!'

MICHAEL RELPH

NOTES

1. Famous florist and author.
2. Leslie Norman's son Barry became a well-known film critic.

Filmography

The following abbreviations have been used:

ad	art direction	*ap*	associate producer	*d*	director
des	design	*ed*	editing	*mus*	music
p	producer	*pc*	production company	*ph*	photography
sc	script				

Basil Dearden (BD) started his film career as assistant director on *It's in the Air* (d. A. Kimmins, 1938), *Penny Paradise* (d. C. Reed, 1938), *Come On, George!* (d. A. Kimmins, 1939), and co-scripted *This Man is News* (d. D. MacDonald, 1938). He was associate producer and co-scriptwriter on *Let George Do It!* (d. M. Varnel, 1940) and *Spare a Copper* (d. J. P. Carstairs, 1940) and associate producer on *Turned Out Nice Again* (d. M. Varnel, 1941) and *The Ghost of St Michael's* (d. M. Varnel, 1941).

Michael Relph (MR) worked unaccredited as art director on numerous films produced at Gaumont-British and Warner Bros. (British) between 1932 and 1938. He then enjoyed a successful period as a designer for the West End stage, before joining Ealing as an art director in 1942. He occasionally returned to the stage in the 1940s.

The Black Sheep of Whitehall (1941). *pc*: Ealing. *d*: BD, Will Hay, *ap*: S. C. Balcon, *sc*: Angus MacPhail, John Dighton, *ph*: Gunther Krampf, Eric Cross, *ad*: Tom Morahan, *ed*: Ray Pitt, *mus*: Ernest Irving, *cast*: Will Hay, John Mills, Basil Sydney, Henry Hewitt, Felix Aylmer, Frank Cellier.

The Goose Steps Out (1942). *pc*: Ealing, *d*: BD, Will Hay, *ap*: S. C. Balcon, *sc*: Angus MacPhail, John Dighton, *ph*: Ernest Palmer, *ad*: Tom Morahan, *ed*: Ray Pitt, *mus*: Bretton Byrd, *cast*: Will Hay, Charles Hawtrey, Peter Croft, Barry Morse, Peter Ustinov.

The Bells Go Down (1943). *pc*: Ealing, *d*: BD, *ap*: S. C. Balcon, *sc*: Roger MacDougall, *ph*: Ernest Palmer, *ad*: MR, *ed*: Mary Habberfield, *mus*: Roy Douglas, *cast*: Tommy Trinder, James Mason, Philip Friend, Mervyn Johns, Billy Hartnell, Finlay Currie, Philippa Hiatt.

My Learned Friend (1943). *pc*: Ealing, *d*: BD, Will Hay, *ap*: S. C. Balcon, *sc*: Angus MacPhail, John Dighton, *ph*: Wilkie Cooper, *ad*: MR, *ed*: Charles Hasse, *mus*: Ernest Irving, *cast*: Will Hay, Claude Hulbert, Mervyn Johns.

The Halfway House (1944). *pc*: Ealing, *d*: BD, *ap*: Cavalcanti, *sc*: Angus MacPhail, Diana Morgan, *ph*: Wilkie Cooper, *ad*: MR, *ed*: Charles Hasse, *mus*: Lord Berners, *cast*: Mervyn Johns, Glynis Johns, Tom Walls, Françoise Rosay, Esmond Knight, Guy Middleton, Alfred Drayton, Valerie White, Richard Bird, Sally Ann Howes, Philippa Hiatt, Pat McGrath.

They Came to a City (1944). *pc*: Ealing, *d*: BD, *ap*: Sidney Cole, *sc*: BD, Sidney Cole, J. B. Priestley, *ph*: Stan Pavey, *ad*: MR, *ed*: Michael Truman, *mus*: Scriabin, *cast*: John Clements, Googie Withers, Mabel Terry-Lewis, Frances Rowe, Norman Shelley, Raymond Huntley, Renée Gadd, A. E. Matthews, Ada Reeve, Ralph Michael, Brenda Bruce, J. B. Priestley (himself).

Dead of Night (1945). *pc*: Ealing, *d*: Cavalcanti ('The Christmas Party', 'The Ventriloquist's Dummy'); Charles Crichton ('The Golfing Story'); BD ('Linking Story', 'The Hearse Driver'); Robert Hamer ('The Haunted Mirror'), *ap*: Sidney Cole, John Croydon, *sc*: John Baines, Angus MacPhail, *ph*: Stan Pavey, Douglas Slocombe, *ad*: MR, *ed*: Charles Hasse, *mus*: Georges Auric, *cast*: Mervyn Johns, Roland Culver, Mary Merrall, Googie Withers, Frederick Valk, Anthony Baird, Sally Ann Howes, Judy Kelly, Miles Malleson, Ralph Michael, Basil Radford, Naunton Wayne, Michael Redgrave, Hartley Power.

The Captive Heart (1946). *pc*: Ealing, *d*: BD, *ap* and *ad*: MR, *sc*: Angus MacPhail, Guy Morgan, *ph*: Douglas Slocombe, *ed*: Charles Hasse, *mus*: Alan Rawsthorne, *cast*: Michael Redgrave, Rachel Kempson, Mervyn Johns, Rachel Thomas, Jack Warner, Gladys Henson, Gordon Jackson, Margot

Fitzsimons, Derek Bond, Jane Barrett, Basil Radford, Guy Middleton, Jimmy Hanley, Ralph Michael, Jack Lambert, Karel Stepanek, Frederick Richter.

Frieda (1947). pc: Ealing, *d*: BD, *ap* and *des*: MR, *sc*: Angus MacPhail, Ronald Millar, *ph*: Gordon Dines, *ad*: Jim Morahan, *ed*: Les Norman, *mus*: John Greenwood, *cast*: David Farrar, Glynis Johns, Mai Zetterling, Flora Robson, Albert Lieven, Barbara Everest, Gladys Henson.

Saraband for Dead Lovers (1948). *pc*: Ealing, *d*: BD, *ap* and *des*: MR, *sc*: John Dighton, Alexander Mackendrick, *ph*: Douglas Slocombe, *ad*: Jim Morahan, William Kellner, *ed*: Michael Truman, *mus*: Alan Rawsthorne, *cast*: Stewart Granger, Joan Greenwood, Flora Robson, Françoise Rosay, Frederick Valk, Peter Bull, Anthony Quayle, Michael Gough.

Train of Events (1949). *pc*: Ealing, *d*: Sidney Cole ('The Engine Driver'); Charles Crichton ('The Composer'); BD ('The Prisoner of War', 'The Actor'), *ap*: MR, *sc*: BD, T. E. B. Clarke, Ronald Millar, Angus MacPhail, *ph*: Lionel Banes, Gordon Dines, *ad*: Malcolm Baker-Smith, Jim Morahan, *ed*: Bernard Gribble, *mus*: Leslie Bridgewater, *cast*: Jack Warner, Gladys Henson, Susan Shaw, Patric Doonan, Valerie Hobson, John Clements, Irina Baronova, John Gregson, Joan Dowling, Laurence Payne, Peter Finch, Mary Morris, Michael Hordern.

Kind Hearts and Coronets (1949). *pc*: Ealing, *d*: Robert Hamer, *ap*: MR, *sc*: Robert Hamer, John Dighton, *ph*: Douglas Slocombe, *ad*: William Kellner, *ed*: Peter Tanner, *mus*: Mozart, *cast*: Dennis Price, Valerie Hobson, Joan Greenwood, Alec Guinness.

The Blue Lamp (1950). *pc*: Ealing, *d*: BD, *ap*: MR, *sc*: T. E. B. Clarke, *ph*: Gordon Dines, *ad*: Jim Morahan, *ed*: Peter Tanner, *mus*: Ernest Irving, *cast*: Jack Warner, Jimmy Hanley, Dirk Bogarde, Robert Flemyng, Bernard Lee, Peggy Evans, Patric Doonan, Gladys Henson.

Cage of Gold (1950). *pc*: Ealing, *d*: BD, *ap* and *des*: MR, *sc*: Jack Whittingham, *ph*: Douglas Slocombe, *ad*: Jim Morahan, *ed*: Peter Tanner, *mus*: Georges Auric, *cast*: Jean Simmons, David Farrar, James Donald, Madeleine Lebeau, Herbert Lom, Bernard Lee, Gladys Henson, Harcourt Williams.

Pool of London (1951). *pc*: Ealing, *d*: BD, *ap*: MR, *sc*: Jack Whittingham, John Eldridge, *ph*: Gordon Dines, *ad*: Jim Morahan, *ed*: Peter Tanner, *mus*: John Addison, *cast*: Bonar Colleano, Susan Shaw, Renée Asherson, Earl Cameron, Moira Lister, Max Adrian.

I Believe in You (1952). *pc*: Ealing, *d* and *p*: BD, MR, *sc*: Jack Whittingham, MR, BD, *ph*: Gordon Dines, *ad*: Maurice Carter, *ed*: Peter Tanner, *mus*: Ernest Irving, *cast*: Cecil Parker, Celia Johnson, Harry Fowler, Joan Collins, George Relph, Godfrey Tearle, Laurence Harvey.

The Gentle Gunman (1952). *pc*: Ealing, *d*: BD, *p*: MR, *sc*: Roger MacDougall, *ph*: Gordon Dines, *ad*: Jim Morahan, *ed*: Peter Tanner, *mus*: John Greenwood, *cast*: John Mills, Dirk Bogarde, Robert Beatty, Elizabeth Sellars, Barbara Mullen, Joseph Tomelty, James Kenney, Gilbert Harding.

The Square Ring (1953). *pc*: Ealing, *d*: BD, *p*: MR, *sc*: Robert Westerby, *ph*: Otto Heller, *ad*: Jim Morahan, *ed*: Peter Bezencenet, *cast*: Jack Warner, Robert Beatty, Bill Owen, Maxwell Reed, George Rose, Bill Travers, Alfie Bass, Ronald Lewis, Sidney James, Joan Collins, Kay Kendall, Bernadette O'Farrell, Eddie Byrne.

The Rainbow Jacket (1954). *pc*: Ealing, *d*: BD, *p*: MR, *sc*: T. E. B. Clarke, *ph*: Otto Heller, *ad*: Tom Morahan, *ed*: Jack Harris, *mus*: William Alwyn, *cast*: Kay Walsh, Bill Owen, Edward Underdown, Fella Edmonds, Robert Morley, Charles Victor, Sidney James.

Out of the Clouds (1955). *pc*: Ealing, *d*: BD, *p*: MR, Eric Williams, *sc*: John Eldridge, MR, *ph*: Paul Beeson, *ad*: Jim Morahan, *ed*: Jack Harris, *mus*: Richard Addinsell, *cast*: Anthony Steel, Robert Beatty, David Knight, Margo Lorenz, James Robertson Justice, Eunice Gayson, Isabel Dean, Gordon Harker, Bernard Lee.

The Ship That Died of Shame (1955). *pc*: Ealing, *d*: BD, *p*: MR, *sc*: John Whiting, MR, BD, *ph*: Gordon Dines, *ad*: Bernard Robinson, *ed*: Peter Bezencenet, *mus*: William Alwyn, *cast*: Richard Attenborough, George Baker, Bill Owen, Virginia McKenna, Roland Culver, Bernard Lee.

Who Done It? (1956). *pc*: Ealing, *d*: BD, *p*: MR, *sc*: T.E.B. Clarke, *ph*: Otto Heller, *ad*: Jim Morahan, *ed*: Peter Tanner, *mus*: Philip Green, *cast*: Benny Hill, Belinda Lee, David Kossoff, Garry Marsh.

The Smallest Show on Earth (1957). *pc*: Relph–Dearden for British Lion, *d*: BD, *p*: MR, *sc*: William Rose, John Eldridge, *ph*: Douglas Slocombe, *ad*: Allan Harris, *ed*: Oswald Hafenrichter, *mus*: William Alwyn, *cast*: Virginia McKenna, Bill Travers, Margaret Rutherford, Peter Sellers, Bernard Miles, Francis de Wolff, Leslie Phillips.

Davy (1957). *pc*: Ealing, *d*: MR, *p*: BD, *sc*: William Rose, *ph*: Douglas Slocombe, *ad*: Alan Withy, *ed*: Peter Tanner, *mus*: Wagner, Puccini, Mozart, *cast*: Harry Secombe, Alexander Knox, Ron Randell, George Relph, Susan Shaw, Bill Owen, Peter Frampton.

Violent Playground (1958). *pc*: Rank, *d*: BD, *p*: MR, *sc*: James Kennaway, *ph*: Reginald Wyer, *ad*: Maurice Carter, *ed*: Arthur Stevens, *mus*: Philip Green, *cast*: Stanley Baker, Anne Heywood, David McCallum, Peter Cushing.

Rockets Galore! (1958). *pc*: Rank, *d*: MR, *p*: BD, *sc*: Monja Danischewsky, *ph*: Reginald Wyer, *ad*: Jack Maxsted, *ed*: John D. Guthridge, *mus*: Cedric Thorpe Davie, *cast*: Jeannie Carson, Donald Sinden, Roland Culver, Catherine Lacey, Noel Purcell, Duncan Macrae, Gordon Jackson.

Sapphire (1959). *pc*: Artna Films for Rank, *d*: BD, *p*: MR, *sc*: Janet Green, ph: Harry Waxman, *ad*: Carmen Dillon, *ed*: John D. Guthridge, *mus*: Philip Green, *cast*: Nigel Patrick, Yvonne Mitchell, Michael Craig, Paul Massie, Bernard Miles, Olga Lindo, Earl Cameron, Harry Baird.

Desert Mice (1959). *pc*: Artna, *d*: MR, *p*: BD, *sc*: David Climie, *ph*: Kenneth Hodges, *ad*: Peter Proud, *ed*: Reginald Beck, *mus*: Philip Green, *cast*: Alfred Marks, Patricia Bredin, Sidney James, Dora Bryan, Dick Bentley, Reginald Beckwith, Irene Handl.

The League of Gentlemen (1960). *pc*: Allied Film Makers, *d*: BD, *p*: MR, *sc*: Bryan Forbes, *ph*: Arthur Ibbetson, *ad*: Peter Proud, *ed*: John D. Guthridge, *mus*: Philip Green, *cast*: Jack Hawkins, Nigel Patrick, Roger Livesey, Richard Attenborough, Bryan Forbes, Kieron Moore, Terence Alexander, Norman Bird, Robert Coote, Melissa Stribling, Nanette Newman.

Man in the Moon (1960). *pc*: Allied Film Makers, *d*: BD, *p*: MR, *sc*: MR, Bryan Forbes, *ph*: Harry Waxman, *des*: Don Ashton, *ad*: Jack Maxsted, *ed*: John D. Guthridge, *mus*: Philip Green, *cast*: Kenneth More, Shirley Anne Field, Michael Hordern, Charles Gray, John Glyn-Jones, John Phillips, Norman Bird.

The Secret Partner (1961). *pc*: MGM, *d*: BD, *p*: MR, *sc*: David Pursall, Jack Seddon, *ph*: Harry Waxman, *des*: Elliot Scott, *ad*: Alan Withy, *ed*: Raymond Poulton, *mus*: Philip Green, *cast*: Stewart Granger, Haya Harareet, Bernard Lee, Hugh Burden, Lee Montague, Melissa Stribling, Conrad Phillips, John Lee, Norman Bird.

Victim (1961). *pc*: Allied Film Makers, *d*: BD, *p*: MR, *sc*: Janet Green, John McCormick, *ph*: Otto Heller, *ad*: Alex Vetchinsky, *ed*: John D. Guthridge, *mus*: Philip Green, *cast*: Dirk Bogarde, Sylvia Syms, Dennis Price, Anthony Nicholls, Peter Copley, Norman Bird, Peter McEnery, Donald Churchill, Derren Nesbitt, John Barrie, John Cairney, Margaret Diamond.

All Night Long (1962). *pc*: Rank, *d*: BD, *p* and *des*: MR, *sc*: Nel King, Peter Achilles *ph*: Ted Scaife, *ad*: Ray Simm, *ed*: John D. Guthridge, *mus*: Philip Green, *cast*: Patrick McGoohan, Marti Stevens, Betsy Blair, Keith Michell, Paul Harris, Richard Attenborough.

Life for Ruth (1962). *pc*: Allied Film Makers, *d*: BD, *p*: MR, *sc*: Janet Green, John McCormick, *ph*: Otto Heller, *ad*: Alex Vetchinsky, *ed*: John Guthridge, *mus*: William Alwyn, *cast*: Michael Craig, Patrick McGoohan, Janet Munro, Paul Rogers, Michael Bryant, Frank Finlay, Maureen Pryor.

The Mind Benders (1963). *pc*: Novus Films for Anglo Amalgamated, *d*: BD, *p*: MR, *sc*: James Kennaway, *ph*: Denys Coop, *ad*: James Morahan, *ed*: John D. Guthridge, *mus*: Georges Auric, *cast*: Dirk Bogarde, Mary Ure, John Clements, Michael Bryant, Wendy Craig.

A Place to Go (1963). *pc*: Bryanston, *d*: BD, *p*: MR *sc*: MR, *ph*: Reginald Wyer, *ad*: Bert Davey, *ed*: John Guthridge, *mus*: Charles Blackwell, *cast*: Rita Tushingham, Mike Sarne, Bernard Lee, Doris Hare, Barbara Ferris, John Slater, David Andrews, William Marlowe, Michael Wynne.

Woman of Straw (1964). *pc*: Novus Films for United Artists, *d*: BD, *p*: MR, *sc*: Robert Muller, Stanley Mann, *ph*: Otto Heller, *des*: Ken Adam, *ad*: Peter Murton, *ed*: John D. Guthridge, *mus*: Beethoven, Berlioz, Mozart, Rimsky-Korsakov, *cast*: Gina Lollobrigida, Sean Connery, Ralph Richardson, Alexander Knox, Johnny Sekka.

Masquerade (1965). *pc*: Novus Films for United Artists, *d*: BD, *p*: MR *sc*: MR, William Goldman, *ph*: Otto Heller, *des*: Don Ashton, *ad*: Jack Stevens, *ed*: John D. Guthridge, *mus*: Philip Green, *cast*: Cliff Robertson, Jack Hawkins, Marisa Mell, Christopher Witty, Bill Fraser, Michel Piccoli, John Le Mesurier.

Khartoum (1966). *pc*: Julian Blaustein Productions for United Artists, *d*: BD, *p*: Julian Blaustein, *sc*: Robert Ardrey, *ph*: Edward Scaife, *ad*: John Howell, *ed*: Fergus McDonell, *mus*: Frank Cordell, *cast*: Charlton Heston, Laurence Olivier, Richard Johnson, Ralph Richardson, Alexander Knox, Johnny Sekka, Nigel Green, Michael Hordern, Zia Mohyeddin, Hugh Williams.

Only When I Larf (1968). *pc*: Deighton/Duffy Productions for Paramount, *d*: BD, *p*: Len Deighton, Brian Duffy, *sc*: John Salmon, *ph*: Anthony Richmond, *ad*: John Blezard, *ed*: Fergus McDonell, *mus*: Ron Grainer, *cast*: David Hemmings, Richard Attenborough, Alexandra Stewart.

The Assassination Bureau (1969). *pc*: Paramount, *d*: BD, *p*: MR, *sc*: MR, *des*: MR, *ph*: Geoffrey Unsworth, *ad*: Roy Smith, Frank White, *ed*: Teddy Darvas, *mus*: Ron Grainer, *cast*: Oliver Reed, Diana Rigg, Telly Savalas, Curt Jurgens, Philippe Noiret, Warren Mitchell, Beryl Reid, Clive Revill.

The Man Who Haunted Himself (1970). *pc*: Associated British Productions, *d*: BD, *p*: MR, *sc*: BD, MR, *ph*: Tony Spratling, *ad*: Albert Witherick, *ed*: Teddy Darvas, *mus*: Michael J. Lewis, *cast*: Roger Moore, Hildegard Neil, Thorley Walters, Anton Rodgers, Olga Georges-Picot, Freddie Jones.

In addition, Dearden was uncredited supervisor on *The Green Man* (d. Robert Day, 1956), and in 1971 he directed 'Overture', the pilot episode of the television series, *The Persuaders!*, followed by two further episodes in 1971 and 1972: 'Powerswitch' and 'To the Death, Baby'.

Bibliography

Affron, Charles and Mirella Jona Affron (1995), *Sets in Motion. Art Direction and Film Narrative*, New Brunswick, NJ: Rutgers University Press.

Aitken, Ian (2000), *Alberto Cavalcanti: Realism, Surrealism and National Cinemas*, Trowbridge: Flick Books.

Aldgate, Anthony (1992), *Cinema and Society: Britain in the 1950s and 1960s*, Milton Keynes: Open University Press.

— (1995), *Censorship and the Permissive Society. British Cinema & Theatre 1955–1965*, Oxford: Clarendon Press.

— (1997), 'The Appliance of Science: *The Mind Benders*', in Burton, O'Sullivan and Wells, pp. 213–21.

Aldgate, Anthony and Jeffrey Richards (1986), *Britain Can Take It. The British Cinema in the Second World War*, Oxford: Basil Blackwell.

Allen, Steven W. (2006), 'Will Hay and the Cinema of Consensus', *Journal of British Cinema and Television* 3(2), pp. 244–65.

Armes, Roy (1978), *A Critical History of British Cinema*, London: Secker & Warburg.

'Attenborough, Interview with Richard', conducted with Tim O'Sullivan, June 2008.

Badsey, Stephen (1998), *The Manchurian Candidate*, Trowbridge: Flicks Books.

Balcon, Michael (1969), *Michael Balcon Presents . . . A Lifetime of Films*, London: Hutchinson.

— (1971), 'The British Film During the War', *Penguin Film Review*, London: Scolar Press.

Balio, Tino (1987), *United Artists. The Company That Changed the Film Industry*, Madison, WI: University of Wisconsin.

Ball, Simon J. (1995), 'Harold Macmillan and the Politics of Defence. The Market for Strategic Ideas', *Twentieth Century British History* 6(1), pp. 78–100.

Barr, Charles (1974a), '"Projecting Britain and the British Character": Ealing Studios. Part I', *Screen* 15(1), Spring, pp. 87–121.

— (1974b), '"Projecting Britain and the British Character": Ealing Studios. Part II', *Screen* 15(2), Summer, pp. 129–63.

— (1977), *Ealing Studios*, London and Newton Abbot: Cameron and Tayleur in association with David & Charles.

— (ed.) (1986), *All Our Yesterdays. 90 Years of British Cinema*, London: BFI Publishing.

— (1993), *Ealing Studios* (second edition), London: Studio Vista.

Barton, Ruth (2004) *Irish National Cinema*, London: Routledge.

Baxendale, John (2001), '"I Had Seen a Lot of Englands": J. B. Priestley, Englishness and the People', *History Workshop Journal* 51, pp. 87–111.

Bells Go Down. The Diary of a London A.F.S. Man, The (1942), London: Methuen.

Biderman, Albert D. (1962), 'The Image of "Brainwashing"', *The Public Opinion Quarterly* 26(4), pp. 547–63.

Bogarde, Dirk (1979), *Snakes and Ladders*, St Albans: Triad/Panther.

Bond, Derek (1990), *Steady, Old Man! Don't You Know There's a War On?*, London: Leo Cooper.

Bourne, Stephen (1996), *Brief Encounters. Lesbians and Gays in British Cinema 1930–1971*, London: Cassell.

— (2001), *Black in the British Frame. The Black Experience in British Film and Television*, London: Continuum.

Boyd-Bowman, Susan (1984), 'War and Comedy', in Hurd, pp. 39–42.

Brown, Geoff (1977), *Launder and Gilliat*, London: BFI.

— (ed.) (1981), *Der Produzent. Michael Balcon und der englische Film*, Berlin: Verlag Volker Spiess.

— (1984), 'A Knight and His Castle', in Fluegel, pp. 17–41.

Brunsdon, Charlotte and Rachel Moseley (1997), '"She's a Foreigner Who's Become a British Subject": *Frieda*', in Burton, O'Sullivan and Wells, pp. 129–36.

Burton, Alan (1997), 'Love in a Cold Climate: Critics, Filmmakers and the British Cinema of Quality — the Case of *The Captive Heart*', in Burton, O'Sullivan and Wells, pp. 116–28.

— (2009), 'Ealing Studio's Wartime "Mild Revolution": The Filming of J. B. Priestley's *They Came to a City* (1944)', *Anglistik: International Journal of English Studies*, 20(2), September.

Burton, Alan, Tim O'Sullivan and Paul Wells (eds.) (1997), *Liberal Directions. Basil Dearden and Postwar British Film Culture*, Trowbridge: Flicks Books.

Butler, Ivan (1967), *The Horror Film*, London: Zwemmer and Barnes.

Carr, R. E. and R. M. Hayes (1988), *Widescreen Movies. A History and Filmography of Wide Gauge Filmmaking*, Jefferson, NC: McFarland.

Chapman, James (1997), 'Films and Flea-puts: *The Smallest Show on Earth*', in Burton, O'Sullivan and Wells, pp. 194–202.

— (1998a), *The British at War. Cinema, State and Propaganda, 1939–1945*, London: I. B. Tauris.

— (1998b), 'Our Finest Hour Revisited: the Second World War in British Feature Films since 1945', *Journal of Popular British Cinema* 1, pp. 63–75.

— (1999), 'British Cinema and the "People's War"', in Hayes and Hill, pp. 33–61.

— (2002), *Saints and Avengers. British Adventure Series of the 1960s*, London: I. B. Tauris.

Chatten, Richard (1997), 'Basil Dearden: Filmography', in Burton, O'Sullivan and Wells, pp. 267–78.

Chibnall, Steve (1997), 'The Teenage Trilogy: *The Blue Lamp, I Believe in You* and *Violent Playground*', in Burton, O'Sullivan and Wells, pp. 137–53.

— (1999), 'Ordinary People: "New Wave' Realism and the British Crime Film 1959–1963', in Steve Chibnall and Robert Murphy (eds.), *British Crime Cinema*, London: Routledge, pp. 94–109.

Clarke, T. E. B. (1974), *This Is Where I Came In*, London: Michael Joseph.

'Cole, Interview with Sidney' (1997), in Burton, O'Sullivan and Wells, pp. 260–6.

Collins, B. Abby (1945), 'Spiritualism and the Law', *The Modern Law Review* 8(3), pp. 158–62.

Conrich, Ian (1997), '*The Man Who Haunted Himself*', in Burton, O'Sullivan and Wells, pp. 222–30.

Cook, Jim (1986), 'The Ship That Died of Shame', in Barr, pp. 362–7.

Cook, John (1997), '"Men Behaving Badly?': Basil Dearden and *The Persuaders!*', in Burton, O'Sullivan and Wells, pp. 231–40.

Cowie, John, Valerie Cowie and Eliot Slater (1968), *Delinquency in Girls*, London: Heinemann.

Curran, James and Vincent Porter (eds.) (1983), *British Cinema History*, London: Weidenfeld & Nicolson.

Danischewsky, Monja (ed.) (1947), *Michael Balcon's 25 Years in Films*, London: World Film Publications.

Dean, Basil (1973), *Mind's Eye. An Autobiography 1927–1972*, London: Hutchinson.

Dearden, Basil (1946), 'Ealing – in Germany', *The Cine–Technician* (January–February), pp. 3–7.

— (1948), 'Organised Inspiration', in *Saraband for Dead Lovers. The Film and Its Production at Ealing Studios*, London: Convoy Publications, pp. 65–71.

Dick, Bernard F. (2001), *Engulfed. The Death of Paramount Pictures and the Birth of Corporate Hollywood*, Lexington, KY: University Press of Kentucky.

Dill, Sir John (1944), 'The Psychological Approach to the Transition from War to Peace', *Proceedings of the Academy of Social Science* 21(1), pp. 111–20.

Dixon, Winston Wheeler (1997), 'The Halfway House', in Burton, O'Sullivan and Wells, pp. 108–15.

Durgnat, Raymond (1966), 'Dearden and Relph. Two on a Tandem', *Films and Filming* (July), 12(10), pp. 26–33.

— (1970), *A Mirror for England: British Movies from Austerity to Affluence*, London: Faber and Faber.

— (1997), 'Two 'Social Problem' Films: Sapphire and Victim', in Burton, O'Sullivan and Wells, pp. 59–88.

Dyer, Richard (1993), '*Victim*: Hegemonic Project', in Richard Dyer, *The Matter of Images: Essays on Representation*, London: Routledge.

Eames, John Douglas (1979), *The MGM Story*, New York: Crown Publishers.

Ede, Laurie (1997), 'Michael Relph as Art Director', in Burton, O'Sullivan and Wells, pp. 249–59.

— (1999), The Role of the Art Director in British Films, 1989–1951', PhD thesis, University of Portsmouth.

Ellis, John (1975), 'Made in Ealing', *Screen* 16(1), pp. 78–127.

Everson, William K. (1987), 'British Film Noir', *Films in Review* 38(5), pp. 285–9.

— (2003), 'William K. Everson and the British Cinema – Program Notes for the New School of Social Research', *Film History* 15, pp. 279–375.

Falcon, Richard (1995), 'Images of Germany and the Germans in British Film and Television Fictions', in Cedric Cullingford and Harald Husemann (eds), *Anglo-German Attitudes*, Aldershot: Avebury, pp. 67–90.

Field, Shirley Anne (1991), *A Time For Love*, London: Bantam Books.

Fire Over London. The Story of The London Fire Service 1940–41 (1941), London: London County Council, Hutchinson.

Fisher, Michael (1961), *Bethnal Green*, London: Cassell.

Fluegel, Jane (ed.) (1984), *Michael Balcon: The Pursuit of British Cinema*, New York: MOMA.

Forbes, Bryan (1974), *Notes for a Life*, London: Everest.

Fores, John (1956), *The Springboard*, London: Hodder & Stoughton.

Francis, Martin (2007), 'A Flight from Commitment? Domesticity, Adventure and the Masculine Imaginary in Britain after the Second World War', *Gender & History* 19(1), pp. 163–85.

Front Line 1940–1941 (1942), London: HMSO.

Gaskin, M. J. (2005), *Blitz. The Story of 29th December 1940*, London: Faber and Faber.

Geraghty, Christine (2000), *British Cinema in the Fifties. Gender, Genre and The 'New Look'*, London: Routledge.

Goldman, William (1985), *Adventures in the Screentrade*, London: Futura.

Granger, Stewart (1982), *Sparks Fly Upwards*, St Albans: Granada.

Griffiths, R. (ed.) (2006) *British Queer Cinema*, London: Routledge.

Grindon, Ledger (1996), 'Body and Soul: The Structure of Meaning in the Boxing Film Genre', *Cinema Journal* 35(4), pp. 54–69.

Guha, M. and C. Brunsdon (2009), '"The Colour of One's Skin": Earl Cameron', *Journal of British Cinema and Television* 6(1) (forthcoming).

Hacker, Helen Mayer (1957), 'The New Burdens of Masculinity', *Marriage and Family Living*, pp. 227–33.

Hadfield, J. A. (1967), *Dreams and Nightmares*, London: Penguin.

Hammond, Ion (n.d.), *This Year of Films. What the Critics Said and Other Features*, London: Dewynters.

Harper, Sue (1994), *Picturing the Past. The Rise and Fall of the British Costume Film*, London: BFI Publishing.

Harper, Sue and Vincent Porter (2003), *British Cinema of the 1950s. The Decline of Deference*, Oxford: Oxford University Press.

Harrington, John (1978), 'Alberto Cavalcanti on *Nicholas Nickleby*', *Literature/Film Quarterly* 6, pp. 48–56.

Harris, Jose (1992), 'War and Social History: Britain and the Home Front during the Second World War', in *Contemporary European History* 1(1), pp. 17–35.

Hasegawa, Junichi (1999), 'The Rise and Fall of Radical Reconstruction in 1940s Britain', *Twentieth Century British History* 10(2), pp. 137–61.

Hawkins, Jack (1973), *Anything for a Quiet Life*, London: Elm Tree.

Hayes, Nick and Jeff Hill (eds.) (1999), *'Millions Like Us'? British Culture in the Second World War*, Liverpool: Liverpool University Press.

Henthorne, Tom (2004), 'Priestley's War: Social Change and the British Novel, 1939–1949', *The Midwest Quarterly* 45, pp. 155–67.

Herman, Gerald (1979), 'For God and Country: *Khartoum* (1966) as History and as "Object Lesson" for Global Policemen', *Film and History* 9(1) (February), pp. 1–15.

Hermens, Ferdinand A. (1945–46), 'The Danger of Stereotypes in Viewing Germany', *The Public Opinion Quarterly* 9(4), pp. 418–27.

Heston, Charlton (1978), *The Actor's Life. Journals 1956–1976*, New York: E. P. Dutton.

— (1995), *In the Arena. An Autobiography*, New York: Simon & Shuster.

Hewison, Robert (1988), *Under Siege. Literary Life in London 1939–1945*, London: Methuen.

Higson, Andrew (1984), 'Five Films', in Hurd, pp. 22–6.

— (1997), 'Pool of London', in Burton, O'Sullivan and Wells, pp. 162–71.

Hill, John (1985), 'The British Social Problem Film: "Violent Playground" and "Sapphire"', *Screen* 26(1) (January/February), pp. 34–48.

— (1986), *Sex, Class and Realism. British Cinema 1956–1963*, London: BFI Publishing.

— (1987) Hill, John, Kevin Rockett and Luke Gibbons, *Cinema and Ireland*, London: Croom Helm.

Houlbrook, Matt and Chris Waters (2006), '*The Heart in Exile*: Detachment and Desire in 1950s London', *History Workshop Journal* 62, pp. 142–65.

Howard, Tony (2000), 'Shakespeare's Cinematic Offshoots', in Russell Jackson (ed.), *Shakespeare on Film*, Cambridge: Cambridge University Press, pp. 295–313.

Howes, Keith (2006) 'Are There Stars out Tonight?', in Robin Griffiths (ed.), *British Queer Cinema*, London: Routledge.

Hunt, Leon (1998), *British Low Culture. From Safari Suits to Sexploitation*, London: Routledge.

Hunt, Martin (2002), 'New Labour, New Criticism: A Contemporary Re-Assessment of Ealing and The Archers', *Quarterly Review of Film & Video* 19, pp. 261–9.

Hurd, Geoff (ed.) (1984), *National Fictions. World War Two in British Films and Television*, London: BFI Books.

Hutchings, Peter (1993), *Hammer and Beyond. The British Horror Film*, Manchester: Manchester University Press.

— (2000), 'Authorship and British Cinema. The Case of Roy Ward Baker', in Justine Ashby and Andrew Higson (eds.), *British Cinema, Past and Present*, London: Routledge, pp. 179–89.

— (2001a), 'The Histogram and the List. The Director in British Film Criticism', *Journal of Popular British Cinema* 4, pp. 30–9.

— (2001b), *Terence Fisher*, Manchester: Manchester University Press.

— (2004), 'Uncanny Landscapes in British Film and Television', *Visual Culture in Britain* 5(2), pp. 27–40.

In Search of Skyhooks, undated manuscript by Michael Relph.

Jones, Ernest (1951), *On the Nightmare*, London: Liveright.

Kee, Robert (1990), *A Crowd is Not Company*, London: Cardinal.

Kelly, Terence, Graham Norton and George Perry (1966), *A Competitive Cinema*, London: Institute of Economic Affairs.

Kemp, Philip (1991), *Lethal Innocence. The Cinema of Alexander Mackendrick*, London: Methuen.

— (1998), 'Paradise Postponed: Ealing, Rank and *They Came to a City*', *Cineaste* 23(4), pp. 45–7.

— (2005) 'I Wanted Him', *Sight and Sound* 15(8), p. 10.

Kirkham, Pat and Janet Thumim (1997), ' Men at Work: Dearden and Gender', in Burton, O'Sullivan and Wells, pp. 89–107.

Kydd, Sam (1973), *For You The War Is Over . . .*, London: Futura.

Lach, Donald F. (1945), 'What They Would do About Germany', *The Journal of Modern History* 17(3), pp. 227–43.

Landy, Marcia (1991), *British Genres. Cinema and Society, 1930–1960*, Princeton, NJ: Princeton University Press.

Lejeune, C. A. (1947), *Chestnuts in Her Lap 1936–1946*, London: Phoenix House.

Lemmon, E. J. (1962), 'Moral Dilemmas', *The Philosophical Review* 71(2), pp. 139–58.

Lovell, Terry (1984), 'Frieda', in Hurd, pp. 30–4.

Low, Rachael (1985), *Film Making in 1930s Britain*, London: Allen & Unwin.

Lunden, Walter A. (1949), 'Captivity Psychoses among Prisoners of War', *Journal of Criminal Law and Criminology* 39(6) (March–April), pp. 721–33.

Mace, David R. (1948), 'What Britain is Doing', *Marriage and Family Living*, 10(1), p. 6.

MacKenzie, S. P. (2003), 'Nazis into Germans', *Journal of Popular Film & Television*, Summer 31(2), pp. 83–93.

— (2004), *The Colditz Myth. British and Commonwealth Prisoners of War in Nazi Germany*, Oxford: Oxford University Press.

Malcolm, Jean (1958), 'Nightfall at Notting Hill: A Study in Black and White', *The Phylon Quarterly* 19(4), pp. 364–6.

Manguel, Alberto (2008), 'Engine of Destruction', *The Guardian* (12 April).

Mays, John Barron (1952), 'A Study of a Delinquent Community', *The British Journal of Delinquency* 3, pp. 15–19.

— (1954), *Growing up in the City. A Study of Juvenile Delinquency in an Urban Neighbourhood*, Liverpool: Liverpool University Press.

— (1959), *On the Threshold of Delinquency*, Liverpool: Liverpool University Press.

— (1963), 'Delinquency Areas – A Re-assessment', *British Journal of Criminology* 3(3), pp. 216–30.

McArthur, Colin (2003), *Whisky Galore! & The Maggie*, London: I. B. Tauris.

McFarlane, Brian (1997), *An Autobiography of British Cinema*, London: Methuen.

— (1997a), '*Life For Ruth*: Con/texts', in Burton, O'Sullivan and Wells, pp. 203–12.

— (1998), 'Losing the Peace: Some British Films of Postwar Adjustment', in T. Barta (ed.), *Screening the Past: Film and the Representation of History*, Westport, CT: Greenwood Press, pp. 93–107.

McIlroy, Brian (1998) *Shooting to Kill: Filmmaking and the 'Troubles' in Northern Ireland*, Trowbridge: Flicks Books.

Medhurst, Andy (1986), 'Dirk Bogarde', in Barr, pp. 346–54.

— (1991), 'Every Wart and Pustule: Gilbert Harding and Television Stardom', in John Corner (ed.) *Popular Television in Britain: Studies in Cultural History*, London: BFI, pp. 60–74.

— (1996), '*Victim*: Text as Context', in Andrew Higson (ed.), *Dissolving Views. Key Writings on British Cinema*, London: Cassell, pp. 117–32.

Millar, R. (1947), *Frieda: A New Play in Three Acts*, London: English Theatre Guild.

— (1993) *A View From the Wings*, London: Weidenfeld & Nicolson.

Miller, Laurence (1994), 'Evidence for a British Film Noir Cycle', in Wheeler Winston Dixon (ed.), *Re-Viewing British Cinema, 1900–1992. Essays and Interviews*, New York: SUNY, pp. 155–64.

Miller, Maud M. (ed.) (1948), *Winchester's Screen Encyclopedia*, London: Winchester Publications.

Mills, C. Wright (1956), *The Power Elite*, New York: Oxford University Press.

Mogey, J. M. (1955), 'Changes in Family Life Experienced by English Workers Moving from Slums to Housing Estates', *Marriage and Family Living* 17(2), pp. 123–8.

Monsarrat, Nicholas (1961), *The Ship that Died of Shame and other Stories*, London: Pan Books.

Moore, Roger (2008), *My Word Is My Bond: The Autobiography*, London: Michael O'Mara Books.

Morgan, Guy (1945), *Only Ghosts Can Live*, London: Crosby Lockwood.

Mortimer, Gavin (2005), *The Longest Night. Voices from the London Blitz*, London: Weidenfeld & Nicolson.

Murphy, Robert (1989), *Realism and Tinsel. Cinema and Society in Britain 1939–49*, London: Routledge.

— (1992), *Sixties British Cinema*, London: BFI Publishing

— (1997), 'Cage of Gold', in Burton, O'Sullivan and Wells, pp. 154–61.

— (2000), *British Cinema and the Second World War*, London: Continuum.

— (ed.) (2006), *Directors in British and Irish Cinema. A Reference Companion*, London: BFI Publishing.

— (2007), 'British Film Noir', in Andrew Spicer (ed.), *European Film Noir*, Manchester: Manchester University Press, pp. 84–111.

Newnham, John K. (1946), "Mr Balcon's Young Gentlemen'. The Work of Five Ealing Directors', *Film* (Autumn), pp. 39–43.

Newton, George (1956), 'Trends in Probation Training', *British Journal of Delinquency* 7(2) (October), pp. 123–35.

Nichol, John and Tony Rennell (2003), *The Last Escape. The Untold Story of Allied Prisoners of War in Germany 1944–45*, London: Penguin.

Nicholas, Siân (1995), 'Sly Demagogues and Wartime Radio: J. B. Priestley and the BBC', *Twentieth Century British History* 6(3), pp. 247–66.

Noble, Peter (1946), 'Some Films of 1946', *Film* (Autumn), pp. 9–12.

— (ed.) (1950), *British Film Yearbook 1949–50*, London: Skelton Robinson.

Oakley, Charles (1964), *Where We Came In. Seventy Years of the British Film Industry*, London: Allen & Unwin.

Oates, Joyce Carol (1987), *On Boxing*, London: Bloomsbury.

Ogden, Denis (1948), *The Peaceful Inn. A Play in Three Acts*, London: Rylee.

O'Sullivan, Tim, (1997), 'Not Quite Fit for Heroes: Cautionary Tales of Men at Work – *The Ship That Died of Shame* and *The League of Gentlemen*', in Burton, O'Sullivan and Wells, pp. 172–93.

Paroissien, David (1977), '*The Life and Adventures of Nicholas Nickleby*: Alberto Cavalcanti Interprets Dickens', *Hartford Studies in Literature* 9, pp. 17–28.

Pearce, Frank (1973), 'How to be Immoral and Ill, Pathetic and Dangerous, All at the Same Time: Mass Media and the Homosexual', in Stanley Cohen and Jock Young (eds.), *The Manufacture of News. Deviance Social Problems and the Mass Media*, London: Constable, pp. 284–301.

Perkins, Victor (1972), 'The British Cinema', in Ian Cameron (ed.), *Movie*, London: November Books.

Perry, George (1985), *Forever Ealing. A Celebration of the Great British Film Studio*, London: Pavilion Books.

Peterson, R.W. (1954), *The Square Ring: The Story of the Play and Film*, London: Arthur Baker.

Pirie, David (1973), *A Heritage of Horror. The English Gothic Cinema 1946–1972*, London: Gordon Fraser.

Porter, Vincent (1983), 'Creativity at Ealing and Hammer Films', in Curran and Porter, pp. 179–207.

— (1999), 'Review: *Liberal Directions: Basil Dearden and Postwar British Film Culture*', *Journal of Popular British Cinema* 2, pp. 157–9.

— (2001), 'The Hegemonic Turn: Film Comedies in 1950s Britain', *Journal of Popular British Cinema* 4, pp. 81–94.

Priestley, J. B. (1950), *The Plays of J. B. Priestley*, Volume III, London: Heinemann.

Ramsden, John (1998), 'Refocusing "The People's War": British War Films of the 1950s', *Journal of Contemporary History* 33(1), pp. 35–63.

— (2006), *Don't Mention the War: the British and the Germans since 1890*, London: Little, Brown.

Rattigan, Neil (1994), 'The Last Gasp of the Middle Class: British War Films of the 1950s', in Wheeler Winston Dixon (ed.), *Re-Viewing British Cinema, 1900–1992. Essays and Interviews*, New York: SUNY, pp. 143–53.

Relph, Michael (1948), 'Designing a Colour Film', in *Saraband for Dead Lovers. The Film and Its Production at Ealing Studios*, London: Convoy Publications, pp. 76–84.

— (1961), 'My Idea of Freedom', *Films and Filming* (September), pp. 24, 37.

'Relph, Interview with Michael' (1990), ACT/BECTU Archive.

'Relph, Interview with Michael' (1997), in Burton, O'Sullivan and Wells, pp. 241–8.

Richards, Jeffrey (1984), *The Age of the Dream Palace. Cinema and Society in Britain 1930–1939*, London: Routledge & Kegan Paul.

— (1986), 'Raise a Laugh. *Let George Do It*', in Aldgate and Richards, pp. 76–95.

— (1997), 'Basil Dearden at Ealing', in Burton, O'Sullivan and Wells, pp. 14–35.

Richards, Jeffrey and Dorothy Sheridan (eds.) (1987), *Mass-Observation at the Movies*, London: Routledge & Kegan Paul.

Richardson, M.L. (1941), *London's Burning*, London: Hale.

Robertson, James C. (1989), *The Hidden Cinema. British Film Censorship in Action, 1913–1975*, London: Routledge.

Rolf, David (1988), *Prisoners of the Reich. Germany's Captives 1939–1945*, London: Leo Cooper.

Rolinson, Dave (2003), "If They Want Culture, They Pay': Consumerism and Alienation in 1950s Comedies', in Ian Mackillop and Neil Sinyard (eds.), *British Cinema of the 1950s: a Celebration*, Manchester: Manchester University Press, pp. 87–97.

— (2004), 'Screenplay: The Black and Blue Lamp', posted at www.The_mausoleum_club.org.uk.

Rose, Sonya (2003), *Which People's War? National Identity and Citizenship in Britain 1939–45*, Oxford: Oxford University Press.

Royle, Trevor (1983), *James and Jim. A Biography of James Kennaway*, Edinburgh: Mainstream.

Scheflin, Alan W. (1978), *The Mind Manipulators*, New York: Paddington Press.

Schlesinger Philip, Graham Murdock and Philip Elliott (1983) *Televising Terrorism: Political Violence in Popular Culture*, London: Comedia.

Schur, Edwin M. (1957), 'Sociological Analysis of Confidence Swindling', *Journal of Criminal Law, Criminology and Police Science* 48, pp. 296–304.

Seaton, Ray and Roy Martin (1978), *Good Morning Boys. Will Hay, Master of Comedy*, London: Barrie & Jenkins

Sell, Colin (2006), 'The Ghost in the Machine: Wartime Adaptation in "The Halfway House"'. Unpublished paper presented at the *Ealing Revisited* conference, University of Hull.

Sellers, Robert (1990), *The Films of Sean Connery*, London: Vision Press.

— (2006), *Cult TV. The Golden Age of ITC*, London: Plexus Publishing.

Simpson, Helen (1935) *Saraband for Dead Lovers*, London: Heinemann.

Slocombe, Douglas (1948), 'Colour Through the Camera', in *Saraband for Dead Lovers. The Film and Its Production at Ealing Studios*, London: Convoy Publications, pp. 85–7.

'Slocombe, Interview with Douglas', conducted with Alan Burton, January 2007.

Smith, Adrian (1991), 'Command and Control in Postwar Britain. Defence Decision-making in the United Kingdom, 1945–1984', *Twentieth Century British History* 2(3), pp. 291–327.

Sperling, Otto E. (1950), 'The Interpretation of the Trauma as a Command', *The Psychoanalytic Quarterly* 19, pp. 352–70.

Spicer, Andrew (2001), *Typical Men. The Representation of Masculinity in Popular British Cinema*, London: I. B. Tauris.

Spotnitz, Hyman (1961/62), 'The Narcissistic Defense in Schizophrenia', *Psychoanalysis and the Psychoanalytic Review* 48(4), pp. 24–42.

Stanfield, Peter (2005), 'A Monarch for the Millions: Jewish Filmmakers, Social Commentary and the Postwar Cycle of Boxing Films', *Film Studies* 7, pp. 66–82.

Stead, Peter (1989), *Film and the Working Class. The Feature Film in British and American Society*, London: Routledge.

Stedman, H. W. (1943), *Battle of the Flames*, London: Jarrolds.

Sutton, David (2000), *A Chorus of Raspberries. British Film Comedy 1929–1939*, Exeter: University of Exeter Press.

Tarr, Carrie (1985), 'Sapphire, Darling and the Boundaries of Permitted Pleasure', *Screen* 26(1) (January/February), pp. 50–65.

Taves, Brian (1993), *The Romance of Adventure. The Genre of Historical Adventure Movies*, Jackson, MI: University Press of Mississippi.

Thomson, David (1980), *A Biographical Dictionary of the Cinema*, London: Secker & Warburg.

Tombs, Isabelle (1996), 'The Victory of Socialist "Vansittartism": Labour and the German Question, 1941–5', *Twentieth Century British History* 7(3), pp. 287–309.

Trevelyan, John (1973), *What the Censor Saw*, London: Michael Joseph.

Tynan, Kenneth (1955), 'Ealing's Way of Life', *Films and Filming* (December), p. 10.

Walker, Alexander (1974), *Hollywood, England: The British Film Industry in the Sixties*, London Michael Joseph.

Wallington, N. (2005), *Firemen at War. The Work of London's Fire-fighters in the Second World War*, London: Jeremy Mills.

Wassey, M. (1941), *Ordeal by Fire*, London: Secker & Warburg.

Waters, Chris (1997), "Dark Strangers' in Our Midst: Discourses of Race and Nation in Britain, 1947–1963', *Journal of British Studies* 36, pp. 207–38.

Wells, Paul (1997), 'Sociability, Sentimentality and Sensibility: Basil Dearden and the English Comic Tradition', in Burton, O'Sullivan and Wells, pp. 36–58.

Westwood, Gordon (1953), *Society and the Homosexual*, New York: E. P. Dutton.

— (1960), *A Minority. A Report on the Life of the Male Homosexual in Great Britain*, London: Longmans.

Wildeblood, Peter (1955), *Against the Law*, London: Weidenfeld and Nicolson.

Williams, Melanie (2202), '"Light on a Dark Lovely": Yvonne Mitchell and Stardom in British Cinema', *Quarterly Review of Film and Video* 19, pp. 31–41.

— (2006), '"Shop-soiled Women": Female Sexuality and the Figure of the Prostitute in 1950s British Cinema', *Journal of British Cinema and Television* 3(2), pp. 266–83.

Williams, Tony (2000), *Structures of Desire. British Cinema, 1939–1955*, New York: SUNY.

Willis, Ted (1991), *Evening All: Fifty Years over a Hot Typewriter*, London: Macmillan.

Winston, Brian (1999), *'Fires Were Started –'*, London: BFI Publishing.

Young, Lola (1996), *Fear of the Dark. 'Race', Gender and Sexuality in Cinema*, London: Routledge.

Young, Michael and Peter Willmott (1962), *Family and Kinship in East London*, Harmondsworth: Penguin.

Index